Office of Hope

Office of Hope
A History of the Public Employment Service
In Great Britain

David Price

psi

Policy Studies Institute

UNIVERSITY OF WESTMINSTER

PSI is a wholly owned subsidiary of the University of Westminster

© Policy Studies Institute, 2000

All rights reserved. No part of this publication may be reproduced, stored in a retrieval system or transmitted in any form or by any means, electronic or otherwise, without the prior permission of the copyright holder.

A CIP catalogue of this book is available from the British Library

ISBN 0 85374 771 7
Report number 828

Typeset by PCS Mapping & DTP, Newcastle upon Tyne
Cover design by Andrew Corbett
Printed in Great Britain by Athenaeum Press

The author and PSI are grateful to all the individuals who supplied the photos used in the plate section of this book, in particular:

- The British Newspaper Library, Colindale, for images from *The Daily Mirror* 12 February 1910; *Illustrated London News* 12 February 1910; and *The Graphic*, 12 February 1910.
- Museum of Labour History, Manchester, for images of Ernest Bevin; exteriors of early Labour Exchanges; earliest plan of a Labour Exchange (Office of Works); Middlesborough Labour Exchange; Oldham cotton workers; the 50th anniversary of the employment exchanges; Hemel Hempstead Employment Exchange; Shoreditch, Fountain Street Manchester, Ealing, Folkestone, and Finchley Jobcentres; and the artist's impression of a jobcentre.
- PA News Photo Library for the image of Winston Churchill.
- Hulton Getty Picture Library for the image of the Labour Supply Board.
- The Employment Service for images of modern jobcentres.
- Hodder & Stoughton for the photo of William Beveridge, from *Beveridge and His Plan*.

psi

Policy Studies Institute

100 Park Village East
London NW1 3SR
Tel: (44) (020) 7468 0468
Fax: (44) (020) 7388 0914
Email: pubs@psi.org.uk

For Judith

Contents

List of Abbreviations		*ix*
List of Tables		*xi*
Foreword by Sir Geoffrey Holland		*xiii*
Acknowledgements		*xvi*
1	Introduction	1
2	Origins to 1914	6
3	Time of Trial, 1914–18	30
4	The 'Ten Year Chaos', 1918–29	46
5	Office of Despair? 1929–39	72
6	Mobilising the Masses, 1939–45	86
7	Post-War Full Employment, 1945–60	105
8	The Stirring of Reform, 1960–70	124
9	Modernisation, 1970–74	146
10	The New Model Employment Service, 1974–79	169
11	The Challenge of Thatcherism, 1979–81	197
12	The Era of Peter Morrison, 1981–85	217
13	Lord Young's Revolution, 1985–87	236
14	Warfare and Welfare, 1987–90	258
15	The Employment Service as an Agency, 1990–93	276
16	The Jobseeker's Allowance, 1993–97	294
17	Reflections	309
Notes and References		*323*
Chronology of Main Events		*349*
Further Reading		*355*
Index		*359*

List of Abbreviations

ACAS	Advisory, Arbitration and Conciliation Service
AMA	Association of Metropolitan Authorities
AOML	Association of Officers of the Ministry of Labour
BA	Benefits Agency
CBI	Confederation of British Industry
CEP	Community Enterprise Programme
CP	Community Programme
CPSA	Civil and Public Services Association
CSD	Civil Service Department
CUB	Central Unemployed Body
DAC	Disability Advisory Committee
DEP	Department of Employment and Productivity
DE	Department of Employment
DfEE	Department for Education and Employment
DHSS	Department of Health and Social Security
DRO	Disablement Resettlement Officer
DSS	Department of Social Security
EAS	Enterprise Allowance Scheme
ED	Employment Department
EEG	Employment and Enterprise Group
ES	Employment Service
ESA	Employment Service Agency
ESD	Employment Service Division
FPS	Federation of Personnel Services
HQ	Headquarters
ILO	International Labour Organisation
JSA	Jobseeker's Allowance
LEC	Local Employment Committee
MbO	Management by Objectives
MLSA	Ministry of Labour Staff Association
MoSS	Ministry of Social Security
MP	Member of Parliament
MSC	Manpower Services Commission
NCVO	National Council of Voluntary Organisations
NUWM	National Unemployed Workers' Movement

PAC	Public Assistance Committee
PAR	Programme Analysis and Review
PER	Professional and Executive Recruitment
OECD	Organisation for Economic Cooperation and Development
PRO	Public Record Office
PSA	Property Services Agency
RMSD	Regional Manpower Services Director
SB	Supplementary Benefit
SBR	Stricter Benefit Regime
SCPS	Society of Civil and Public Servants
SCS	Society of Civil Servants
TEC	Training and Enterprise Council
TSA	Training Services Agency
TUC	Trades Union Congress
UAB	Unemployment Assistance Board
UB	Unemployment Benefit
UBO	Unemployment Benefit Office
UBS	Unemployment Benefit Service
UISC	Unemployment Insurance Statutory Commission
URO	Unemployment Review Officer
VDU	Visual Display Unit
YOP	Youth Opportunities Programme
YTS	Youth Training Scheme

List of Tables

2.1	Labour exchange statistics, 1911–14	26
2.2	Disallowance of claims to unemployment benefit, July 1913–July 1914	28
3.1	Number of staff engaged in employment exchange work, 1914–19	32
3.2	Business volumes of exchanges, 1913–18	45
4.1	Unemployment among the insured population, 1921–29	60
4.2	Vacancy and placing performance of the exchanges, 1919–29	67
4.3	Number of staff in the Ministry of Labour, 1919–29	69
5.1	Unemployment among the insured population, 1929–38	75
5.2	Vacancy and placing performance of the exchanges, 1929–38	81
5.3	Number of staff in the Ministry of Labour, 1929–38	82
7.1	Staffing of the Ministry of Labour, 1943–60	109
7.2	Demobilisation, 1945–48	111
7.3	UK unemployment, 1945–60	112
7.4	Placing performance of employment exchanges, 1946–60	117
7.5	Unemployment among ethnic minorities, 1953–58	122
8.1	Unemployment, 1960–70	125
8.2	Unemployed claimants receiving unemployment benefit and supplementary benefit, 1968	142
9.1	Placings and vacancies, 1969–74	166
10.1	Unemployment, 1974–79	184
10.2	Referrals for refusal of suitable employment, neglect to avail of suitable opportunities and restricted availability, 1968–78	189
10.3	Vacancy and placing performance, 1973/74 to 1978/79	193
11.1	Unemployment, 1979–85	200
12.1	Number of staff in Employment Service, 1979–85	234
12.2	Unemployment, vacancies and placings, 1977/78–1984/85	235
13.1	Restart pilots for those unemployed for 12 months or more, January–June 1986	244
13.2	Unemployment, vacancies and placings, 1984/85–1987/88	252
13.3	Unemployment and long-term unemployment, 1985–87	257
14.1	ES performance data, 1986/87–1990/91	264
14.2	Staffing in the Employment Service, 1987–91	265
14.3	UK claimant unemployment by duration, 1986–90	269
15.1	Regular attitude survey of ES employees,1988–98	285

15.2 Assaults on members of ES staff, 1989–98 288
15.3 UK claimant unemployment and staffing in ES, 1990–94 291
15.4 Range of opportunities for 1992–93 292

Foreword
Sir Geoffrey Holland
Vice Chancellor of the University of Exeter,
Former Permanent Secretary of the Department
of Employment and the Department for Education

When I joined the Ministry of Labour in September 1961, the induction training of young graduates fresh from university included an early visit to what was then called an Employment Exchange and then, within two years, extended periods of working in local Employment Exchanges – in my case in Wales and then Scotland.

There is no doubt that, at that time, governments and, perhaps, the public at large wanted to put unemployed people out of sight and out of mind. Thanks to full – indeed over-full – employment, a very large number of people had never been near an Employment Exchange and those who had wanted to forget the experience and never go back.

It was easy to see why. The Employment Exchanges were in back streets. They had separate entrances for men and women. Inside the Spartan rooms – usually very large because they had served during the 1930s depression – there were bare cubicles – into which those who called were summoned one by one. People went there to sign on and many of the staff on the other side of the counter had found themselves so employed because they were taken across, initially as casual workers, during the high unemployment of the 1930s.

To a young man fresh from one of the old universities, all this was rather frightening and deeply depressing. At the end of the day's work, the aim was to get away from the building as soon as possible. You did not want to be linked with it or what went on inside it or, worse still, with those whose circumstances compelled them to visit it.

Yet, at the same time, as a young man, I was acutely aware that there were many people in the Ministry who looked back with pride to the golden days of the Second World War when they and all staff of the Ministry had mobilised the nation. They had done so efficiently and brilliantly – whether that mobilisation was for service in the armed forces or in the home economy, where the light touch of regulation by the Ministry had been flexible enough to enable the nation to do what it had to do and when it had to do it. People spoke with pride of those days and remembered a task well done – and well recognised by the Ministers of the day.

Within five years of my joining the Ministry, the newly-arrived Permanent Secretary, Sir James Dunnett, caused eyebrows to be raised elsewhere – and in some parts of the Ministry – by convening and chairing a Working Party on the modernisation of the Employment Service. He appointed a new and purposeful fighter of an Under-Secretary, Robin Keith, to lead the charge, and I had the privilege of acting as secretary to that Working Party.

New ideas abounded. The Employment Service could be an instrument of active labour market policy contributing towards competitiveness in the economy, dealing with people at all levels of skill for all occupations, encouraging and supporting mobility between jobs and different parts of the country. Job changing was not to be something that we were ashamed of – it was something vital to the success of a modern economy. The Employment Exchange and the Employment Service could become the gateway to government services – new services, too, like the Occupational Guidance Service. The new technologies could revolutionise administration. Unemployment benefit did not have to be paid in cash. And, not least, the Employment Exchange could come out of the back streets on to the high street, a shop like any other which people could be pleased to enter and where they could find their own way around.

In those five short years, there was evident, in a nutshell, what David Price, in this history, describes as the struggle between three alternative models or ideal types of Employment Service: the labour market transparency model; the benefit control model; and the social welfare model. As the author rightly points out, at any given point in time, one or other of these three models has been dominant in the minds of those responsible for the direction of the Service.

And so the history of the Employment Service has ebbed and flowed. Beyond the day to day narrow political and other discussions about the role of the service lay, for me, something more important still. It enabled the Ministry of Labour and, subsequently, the Department of Employment to be the voice of the individual at work – the only voice, when you come to think of it, in the whole of Whitehall. Other Departments tend to come at their responsibilities top down. Not so the Department of Employment or the Employment Service. When I had the privilege of being Permanent Secretary of the Department, I knew that, at any time of day, on any day of the week, I could call any part of our country – any town, large or small – and get a first hand account of what was happening there and what individual men and women felt about the situation or needed. I also knew that, whatever the government wanted delivered, even if it were entirely novel and wanted in very short order, there were a thousand offices out there, with committed men and women in touch with the local community, employers, local organisations and individual employed or unemployed people, who could and would deliver the goods reliably. There are few Departments of Whitehall which can say that.

Foreword

Perhaps surprisingly, this book is the first full history of the Employment Service. It is not an official history, but it has been prepared with the full cooperation of the Department and the Employment Service itself. Not entirely coincidentally, it is being published at a date which closely coincides with the 90th anniversary of Churchill's original founding of the Employment Exchanges in February 1910. The author tells a fascinating tale. He deserves congratulations for proposing that such a history should be written, and our warm gratitude for all the research he has done and for telling the tale so well. I am sure that students of contemporary history, social policy and public administration will regard this history as definitive and that future generations of students will regard it as an essential source and reference.

But the book is not for the full-time or part-time student alone. It is for everyone who is fascinated by employment and unemployment, by changing attitudes to those who lose jobs or change jobs and by different theories and approaches to the modernisation and efficiency of government. For me, it is a worthy tribute to all those who, for the best part of a century, have worked in the Employment Service and, in so doing, have contributed in no small way to making the lives of millions of citizens a little better than they might otherwise have been.

Acknowledgements

I owe debts of gratitude to many people for help in the preparation of this book.

First, I am grateful to Sir Michael Bichard, Permanent Secretary of the Department for Education and Employment, for giving me access to the Department's files for the last 30 years and to Collin Crooks and his colleagues in Departmental Records for their help in making relevant files available. I have also had much help from Julia Reid and her colleagues in the DfEE Library at Moorfoot, Sheffield, and from the Public Record Office.

Secondly, I am grateful to Sheffield Business School, which is part of Sheffield Hallam University. The School gave me a Visiting Fellowship and set up a Support Group which has given me invaluable assistance in this project. The Group was chaired by Michael Hunt and included Royce Turner, Nick Clay and Charlotte Dent of the Business School, David Martin and David Phillips from the University of Sheffield and John Child and Leslie Longstone, who were in turn Head of Research in the Employment Service. Another great source of wisdom and encouragement has been Professor Rodney Lowe of the University of Bristol. Other historians and social policy specialists who have helped me include Professor Alan Deacon, Roger Davidson, Dan Finn, Professor Jose Harris, Professor Desmond King and Professor John Roach.

Thirdly, I am grateful to Nick Mansfield, Myna Trustram and Phil Dunn at the Museum of Labour History in Manchester for the title of this book (used by them in their 1998 exhibition about the Employment Service) and for most of the illustrations, which come from their archives.

Fourthly, I have been assisted by numerous former colleagues, who have been most generous with their time and insights, including Roderick Allison, Keith Baker, Sir Kenneth Barnes, Valerie Bayliss, Alan Brown, Sir John Cassels, John Cooper, Ken Cooper, John Davies, Roger Dawe, Tony Dechant, Bryan Emmett, Mike Emmott, Dan Finn, Mike Fogden, Richard Foster, Joan Fraser, Derek Grover, Sir Geoffrey Holland, Mike Horsman, Kate Jenkins, Bert Johnson, Ian Johnston, Malcolm Killcross, Jean King (formerly Collingridge), Leigh Lewis, Steve Loveman, Norman McGlynn, Graham Reid, Rhys Robinson, Norman Singleton, Ron Stephenson, Jeremy Surr, Rosemary Thew, Clive Tucker, Dudley Turner, John Turner, Sir John Walley, Greg Watkins, Bill Wells, Robin Wendt and Kevin White.

Office of Hope

Finally, I am grateful for permission to quote from certain documents, notably to the National Archives of Scotland and the Sauchie Estate for the use of John Hilton's 'Reflections on a Tour of Certain Employment Exchanges', from the Steel-Maitland papers; to the British Library of Political and Economic Science for the use of the Beveridge Papers; to Churchill College, Cambridge, for the use of the Bevin Papers; and to the Office for National Statistics for the use of material from *Labour Market Trends*.

The responsibility for the opinions expressed in this book and for any mistakes rests, of course, with me.

1

Introduction

It was in February 1910 that Winston Churchill, President of the Board of Trade, inaugurated a national network of labour exchanges and the public employment service in Britain was born. Philip Gibbs, a well known writer of the time, went to Camberwell in south London to see one of the new exchanges in action and commented:[1]

> *It is a branch office of the new Labour Exchange; but after spending some part of a morning there, it seemed to me that a better name for it would be Office of Hope.*

Gibbs described the clientele of the new office:

> *I had seen faces like this in the flickering lights of the lamps under Westminster Bridge at midnight, unshaven, hungry, cold-looking, dull-eyed faces... I had seen such faces in offices of the Boards of Guardians... Yes, here they were, the unemployed, the casuals, the men who were going down, down, down into the abyss of destitution...*
>
> *But as I studied them more particularly, I saw that not all of them were in this class. There were men here who held themselves more upright, not yet having acquired the slouch of hopelessness... There were younger men in cloth caps, and with scarves around their necks. Some of them were mere boys of eighteen and nineteen, white-faced, pinched-face, blue-lipped lads, who sucked the fag-ends of unlighted cigarettes...*
>
> *What they found was the long counter with several polite, patient clerks, who asked them what work they had been doing, what work they wanted, how old they were, and where they lived, and other questions of this kind... 'Give me a chance, guv'nor. I'm ready for anything that's goin'.' I heard these words several times, in a kind of pleading, confidential whisper, after the official questions had been answered. And nearly always the polite,*

> *patient clerks, having written down particulars on cards, handed another card to each of the applicants and said, 'Well, look in next week' or 'We'll let you know if anything turns up'.*

He described the men going out slowly 'with drooped heads':

> *It seemed that their last hope had flickered out. The happy miracle had not happened and they were still 'out of a job'.*

Gibbs concluded his article:

> *I have called the Labour Exchange the Office of Hope. There is another name for it. It is the Office of Despair.*

Gibbs' article reminds us that the public employment service is not engaged in dry-as-dust administration, but in work affecting the hopes and fears, the emotions and self-respect of millions of citizens. There is pathos to be found in the story of this service, involved as it is in unemployment – one of the great curses of the 20th century. Gibbs points to the link between unemployment and poverty, to the subtle differences between different groups of unemployed people and to the danger that hopes would be raised only to be swiftly dashed. All these issues have haunted the public employment service throughout its history. Moreover, its work became even more highly charged from 1912 onwards with its involvement in state financial provision for the unemployed. The role of the service was to raise deeply controversial political issues.

The aim of this book is to show how politicians and civil servants have developed and changed the role of the public employment service over the last 90 years, what influences led to the changes and what results flowed from them. It is necessarily 'a view from the bridge', written from the angle of those at the centre seeking to steer a nationwide service. This is partly to keep this book within a reasonable compass and partly to reflect my own involvement at the centre of the service for over 20 years.

'Labour exchanges' were defined in the 1909 Labour Exchange Act as:

> *any office or place used for the purpose of collecting and furnishing information, either by the keeping of registers or otherwise, respecting employers who desire to engage workpeople and workpeople who seek engagement or employment.*

This remains the core function of the public employment service. Its importance has been rated very highly by leading labour market experts of the 20th century, starting with William Beveridge, the architect of the new labour exchanges.

This book will demonstrate the unquestionable value of the service in wartime as an instrument of labour supply, enabling the state to harness the nation's population for war.

Introduction

The peacetime role of the employment service has proved much more debatable. At first sight, the role seems simple enough: that of acting as an information broker for participants in the labour market. The simplicity of the concept is illustrated in the fact that the original Labour Exchanges Act of 1909 was less than three pages in length. In practice, however, these institutions can be used for a wide variety of purposes and the state may have a variety of motivations for providing the necessary resources.

One analytical approach is to distinguish the economic and social roles of the service – a dichotomy popular in the Department of Employment in the 1960s and 1970s. My own approach is to suggest that three models, or 'ideal types' (to use Max Weber's terminology), have been struggling with each other since the inception of the service:

- the *labour market transparency* model
- the *benefit control* model; and
- the *social welfare* model.

At no point, of course, has the service been entirely dominated by one model to the exclusion of the others. There has always been a mixed approach, with consequential tensions and contradictions, and it is healthy that this should have been so. But, at any given point in time, one or other of the three models has been dominant in the minds of those responsible for the direction of the service.

The labour market transparency model was dominant in Beveridge's mind when he originally set up the service, even if the word 'transparency' belongs more to the 1970s than the Edwardian era. In his 1909 book, *Unemployment: A Problem of Industry*,[2] he points out that, whereas for most commodities buying and selling takes place in an organised market place, in the case of labour, 'the prevailing method is to hawk it from door to door'. He continues as follows:

> *What then are the objects of organising the labour market? What good purpose can be served by any or the most complete system of labour exchanges?*
> *...The spread of information is a matter that cries out for organised rather than individual action.*

Later, he sums up as follows:

> *The object of labour market organisation is the close, continuous and automatic adjustment of existing demand and supply over the largest possible area.*[3]

Beveridge (and many of his successors) argued that the greater the extent to which recruitment took place through the exchanges, the greater the economic benefit:

> *When all over the United Kingdom and for every trade in it there is a connected system of Labour Exchanges, so that no man thinks of applying anywhere else either for workpeople or employment and would not get either if he did, then the labour market for the United Kingdom can be said to be completely organised...*
>
> *The perfect organisation just described is ...the ideal and must be the aim. Every step towards it, everything done to concentrate the demand for labour at known connected centres, will be an advance towards the State's mastery of unemployment.*[4]

In part, the argument is about minimising frictional unemployment. But Beveridge's vision went beyond that. If the labour exchanges became focal points in the supply and demand of labour, this would make possible other forms of government intervention to make the labour market work better, such as decasualising labour, providing careers guidance for young people and identifying those who were 'unemployable'.

The second model is that of benefit control. Again, the rationale for this model can be found in Beveridge's 1909 book. It comes as the last of six 'special uses' of labour exchanges, but none the less he describes the concept as 'of fundamental importance':

> *This is the function of an efficient Labour Exchange in affording a direct test of unemployment. The central problem of the Poor Law is to relieve without relieving unnecessarily. The only principle on which it has hitherto attempted to secure this is the principle of deterrence – the making of relief so repellent that men might be presumed to have exhausted every other resource before they would accept it.*
>
> *...as the State itself undertakes the search for, ie the registration of, employment, it is on the way to get all and more than all the security it had before against unnecessary pauperism. It can with perfect safety help the unemployed more freely because it knows that so soon as work is to be had it will have notice thereof and be able to hand on the notice to those who are being relieved. The Labour Exchange thus opens the way to 'dispauperisation' more humane, less costly and more effective than that of the 'workhouse test' – the way of making the finding of work easy instead of merely making relief hard.*[5]

From the start, the labour exchanges were destined both to administer the new unemployment benefit when it was introduced in 1912 and also to apply work tests. Given the harshness of the Poor Law test that Beveridge and other reformers of the time were trying to get away from, the use of the labour exchanges to administer a work test can be seen as a major social advance. However, the use of the exchanges for benefit control purposes was to prove far more problematical than Beveridge realised in 1909.

Introduction

The third model is that of social welfare. From this point of view, the main purpose of the service should be to provide individual help and advice to people facing problems in the labour market. The British public employment service has never had 'social welfare' as its primary rationale, but social welfare has been dominant in some important programmes run by the service or linked with it. Outstanding examples are the disablement resettlement service, established as a result of the Disabled Persons (Employment) Act 1944, and the Careers Service, both of which need a separate history of their own and cannot be fully described in this volume. Both these services may be justified in part on grounds of labour market efficiency or benefit control, but their primary rationale is to help individuals.

An important part of the story told in this book will be the tension between these different conceptions of the service. The tension between the first two models was summed up as follows by Desmond King in his interesting book *Actively Seeking Work*:

> *The public employment system, designed to dissipate informational deficiencies, proved Janus-faced since it acquired, concurrently, responsibility for regulating labour.*[6]

Quite apart from these policy dilemmas, the public employment service is also interesting from the point of view of the development of public administration in Britain in the 20th century. Unlike most public bodies, it has always had to operate in a competitive market situation, and this may help to explain the pioneering role which it has played in the development of the public sector in Britain.

2

Origins to 1914

'If you are going to deal with unemployment, you must have the boy Beveridge.' (Sidney and Beatrice Webb to Winston Churchill, 1908)[1]

Introduction

On 11 December 1908, the 34-year-old Winston Churchill, President of the Board of Trade, put a paper entitled *Unemployment Insurance: Labour Exchanges* to his colleagues in Asquith's Cabinet. The paper set out the most radical plan for addressing the problem of unemployment that had ever been put to a British Cabinet. In the next four years, the plans were put into effect and much of the framework which was introduced then still exists to this day.

This chapter explains the background to Churchill's proposal for labour exchanges and the critical role which the young William Beveridge played as the principal architect of these new institutions. It goes on to look at the interrelationship between the labour exchanges, which were introduced in 1910, and unemployment insurance which was introduced in 1912–13, and the vigorous way in which the Board of Trade implemented these reforms.

Winston Churchill and the Asquith government

In 1908, Winston Churchill was a rising star in British politics. Entering Parliament in 1901 as a Unionist, he had crossed the floor of the House in 1904 to join the Liberals in protest against the Unionist drift towards tariff reform. He quickly became a leading figure in his new party. When in December 1905 a Liberal government was formed under Campbell Bannerman, he became a junior minister. In April 1908, when Asquith became Prime Minister, he became President of the Board of Trade.

At this stage in his career, Churchill was a leading advocate of social reform. As an imperialist, he could 'see little glory in an empire which can rule the waves but is unable to flush its own sewers.'² He spent time with Sidney and Beatrice Webb, two of the leading social reformers of the day. His attitude to them was equivocal. Explaining why he did not want to head the Local Government Board, he remarked: 'I refuse to be shut up in a soup kitchen with Mrs Beatrice Webb'.³ He was never a 'collectivist' like the Webbs, but at this time he drew heavily on their insights, like the idea of a 'minimum standard':

> *I do not want to impair the vigour of competition, but we can do much more to mitigate the consequences of failure. We want to draw a line below which we will not allow persons to live and labour yet above which they may compete with all the strength of their manhood.*⁴

For Churchill, the plan for labour exchanges and unemployment insurance was part of a wider radicalism. In December 1908, he wrote to Asquith:

> *The minister who will apply to this country the successful experiences of Germany in social organisation may or may not be supported at the polls but he will at least have left a memorial which time will not deface of his administration.*⁵

A further clue to his motivation is found in remarks to a *Daily Mail* reporter about unemployment insurance in August 1909:

> *The idea is to increase the stability of our institutions by giving the mass of industrial workers a direct interest in maintaining them...With a 'stake in the country' in the form of insurance against evil days, these workers will pay no attention to the vague promises of revolutionary socialism...it will help to remove the dangerous element of uncertainty from the existence of the industrial worker...*⁶

Fifty years later, Beveridge recalled another, more personal, reason that Churchill gave for 'getting on quickly with Labour Exchanges ... he had not himself many years to live; he expected to die young like his father, Randolph. But this was before he wed. Just after, he saw and settled with Clementine and gave up the idea of dying young'.⁷

Within the Asquith government, Churchill's closest ally in promoting this radical programme was Lloyd George, the Chancellor of the Exchequer. Indeed, the two politicians were known as the 'heavenly twins of social reform'. In August 1908, Lloyd George made his pilgrimage to Germany to study the German model of social insurance. It was Lloyd George who introduced the National Insurance Bill into Parliament, though Churchill's successor, Sydney Buxton, was responsible for unemployment insurance. Later, Lloyd George and Churchill made rival claims to be the originator of unemployment insurance.

In reality, both men were brilliant at seizing ideas that were current among expert opinion and moulding them to their own purposes.

The problem of unemployment

It was at the time of the major trade depression of the 1880s that unemployment came to be recognised as a major problem in its own right[8] and the words 'unemployed' and 'unemployment' first appeared in the *Oxford English Dictionary*. Unemployment was seen to be one of the worst consequences of trade depressions and a major cause of social distress and even of occasional riots. The problem of unemployment began to be investigated and analysed by experts such as Hubert Llewellyn Smith, Head of the Labour Department of the Board of Trade. Political interest in unemployment thereafter fluctuated with the level of unemployment. There were no comprehensive unemployment figures, but the figures maintained by trade unions showed the unemployment cycle reaching peak levels among their members of 9 per cent in 1886, 7 per cent in 1893–4, 6 per cent in 1904 and 8 per cent in 1908–9.[9] However, it was soon found that it was not just a problem that arose in times of depression. Whole industries such as agriculture might decline, forcing redundant workers to seek their fortune in the overcrowded cities. Moreover, in the cities, as social investigators such as Charles Booth discovered, there was a link between poverty and chronic casual unemployment. There was chronic under-employment in London's inner city economy.[10] There were sectors of the economy, like the London docks, which relied for their operation on a surplus of labour. As a result, casual workers suffered many weeks of unemployment in a year, interspersed with brief spells of work. These casual workers were one of the most significant groups living below Booth's definition of subsistence.

The official remedy for pauperism was the Poor Law Amendment Act of 1834, under which there was a network of Poor Law Guardians to administer workhouses and operate systems of relief. The overriding principle was that any public relief given to those who were destitute and able-bodied should be 'less eligible' (ie less attractive) than the conditions of the lowest class of independent labourer. This could mean requiring those seeking relief actually to move into the workhouse. Alternatively, they might continue in their homes but have to meet the 'outdoor labour test' of working long hours in the workhouse stoneyard. Practices varied, but there were pressures on the guardians from the Local Government Board and from volunteer vigilantes in the Charity Organisation Society (COS) to follow 'the principles of 1834' to the greatest possible extent. At the same time, social investigators found that the families of many 'independent labourers' lived below any reasonable subsistence level.

In reality, the Poor Law was not a major source of relief to the unemployed.[11] 'Respectable' unemployed workers shunned the workhouse, because of the stigma attached to it and because attendance at the workhouse prevented them from looking for work elsewhere. This left a major gap in social provision and, from the 1880s onwards, politicians and social reformers sought ways of filling this gap.

One widely canvassed option was to enlist the unemployed to carry out 'public works'. In 1886, Joseph Chamberlain as Chairman of the Local Government Board issued a circular to local authorities, urging them to schedule necessary public works for periods of depression and cooperate with the Poor Law Guardians to provide temporary work for the deserving poor. But this circular was almost a complete failure, mainly because of the difficulty of raising the necessary funds, particularly since the authorities with the most unemployment tended to be those which could least afford the expenditure.[12] In the 1890s and in the early years of the 20th century, there were continuing attempts to set up public works for the unemployed. These drew not only on local authority funds but also on charity, such as successive Mansion House appeals and the Queen's appeal in 1905. Other ideas for tackling unemployment included setting up farm colonies and encouraging unemployed people to emigrate. The largest and most ambitious programme was developed by General Booth of the Salvation Army, offering three stages: city colonies (with food and shelter in return for work), rural labour colonies and assisted emigration to the colonies.

Against the background of a serious trade depression in 1904–05, the crumbling Conservative government under Balfour took two steps in its last few months that had a profound influence on the subsequent course of events. First, they set up a Royal Commission on the Poor Law, with 20 members, including not only a solid phalanx of Poor Law administrators and defenders but also radical critics of the Poor Law, such as Beatrice Webb and George Lansbury. Secondly, as an interim step pending the Royal Commission's report, they introduced the Unemployed Workmen Act of 1905, which permitted contributions from the rates to the expenses of Distress Committees, farm colonies, labour exchanges and emigration. Distress Committees were set up in all towns with high unemployment. In London, a Central (Unemployed) Body (CUB) was set up to coordinate the Distress Committees in the London boroughs. CUB included George Lansbury, a staunch advocate of farm colonies, Nathaniel Cohen,[13] a pioneer of labour exchanges, and also the young William Beveridge. The Act came to be regarded as a failure, but it provided a valuable testing ground for new ideas for tackling unemployment.

Early labour exchanges in Great Britain

The development of labour exchanges in Britain had lagged behind their progress in Germany. From the 1880s onwards, public labour exchanges were established in the principal cities of the German Empire, so that by the early 20th century labour exchanges filled a 'prominent and growing place in the industrial organisation of Germany'.[14] They were also developing on a considerable scale in some other Continental countries. By contrast, their development in Britain had been piecemeal and small-scale. They included some union offices acting informally as labour bureaux.

While some of the features of a labour exchange can be found in Britain as early as the 17th century, the first properly constituted labour exchange was that set up by the Tory philanthropist, Nathaniel Cohen, in Egham in February 1885.[15] He was concerned about the position of former building workers in Egham following the completion of major projects. In one case, an Egham labourer tramped 40 miles in vain, only to find on his return that a job near home had been available all along. Cohen recalled seeing labour exchanges in Germany. He persuaded WH Gardiner, the local Registrar of Births, Marriages and Deaths, to maintain and advertise a register of men seeking work and to encourage employers to notify vacancies. The registry lasted till 1894, when Gardiner retired. In these 10 years, there were in all 2966 applicants, of whom 2334 (79 per cent) were found employment – an impressive record which owed much to Gardiner's skill and local knowledge.

Cohen's initiative aroused interest in *The Times* and elsewhere. A similar exchange was set up in Ipswich in October 1885, which lasted for several years. In 1886, some 25 registries were set up in country districts and several registries were set up in London, though few of these survived for long. In the next economic downturn in 1892–3, another wave of labour bureaux emerged, 31 of them set up by municipalities. In Sheffield, for instance, on 9 February 1893, an announcement invited persons out of work to sign a 'register of unemployed workpeople' which employers wishing to hire men were invited to inspect.[16] However, most of these bureaux served only to register men for relief works and came to an end with the winter. In evidence to a Royal Commission on Labour, several witnesses recommended a national system of exchanges, but this idea was not taken up in the Royal Commission's Report in 1894. The Salvation Army set up bureaux to help men at their city colonies to find jobs. But several of the municipal bureaux in London were suspended in 1901 because of doubts about the legality of support under the rates in London – a doubt which was set at rest by legislation in 1902. In 1905, an official inquiry discovered only 21 municipal and three non-municipal bureaux in existence, which had between them filled upwards of 16,000 vacancies in the previous year. They were mostly taken over by the new bodies set up under the Unemployed Workmen Act.

Thus the labour exchange movement in Britain in 1905 was a fragile plant. Most exchanges were short-lived. Coverage was very limited, with about half in London. Some were moribund. Most exchanges were identified with relief work or charity, which was fatal to their relationship with employers.[17] The Unemployed Workmen Act, by encouraging local authorities to support labour exchanges from the rates, led to some expansion but did not lead to a dramatic improvement. However, at this time the labour exchanges found a new and formidable advocate, who would argue that their value to society could be greatly enhanced by a businesslike approach within a national organisation.

William Beveridge

William Beveridge was central to the establishment of the public employment service in Britain. Of course, he was not alone. The political drive came from Churchill. Much of the original thinking and the vital administrative back-up came from Sir Hubert Llewellyn Smith, who by now was Permanent Secretary to the Board of Trade. But Beveridge's contribution was critical to the conception, design and implementation of this reform in a way that is rare among social reformers.

At the point in 1905 when he steps into our story, Beveridge was a rather intense young man of 26. In September 1903 he had moved from the intellectual forcing ground of Balliol to become Sub-Warden of Toynbee Hall in Whitechapel in the East End of London. He explained to his disappointed mother that he had rejected a career at the bar in favour of 'getting to know something about human society and working at some part of its machinery'.[18] This indeed would be the direction of his whole career. Although he now became a charitable volunteer, his motivation was very different from that of many who work for charities. As his biographer, Jose Harris, writes: 'His concern for reform was inspired less by philanthropic emotion than by a passion for efficiency and by an almost obsessive dislike of social and individual waste.'[19]

Beveridge's base for his new career was well chosen. In joining a settlement house, he was following a path trodden by many of the small band of politicians and civil servants who designed the social reform legislation of 1900–14.[20] Beveridge was at Toynbee Hall for the next two years and learned much from its influential founder and Warden, Canon Samuel Barnett. At this time, Barnett was heavily involved with the Mansion House fund for the relief of unemployment. So Beveridge, who 'at this stage knew virtually nothing about the unemployment problem',[21] was immediately drawn into the administration of this fund and into intensive work on unemployment, investigating schemes of assistance such as farm colonies and the characteristics of the unemployed people they were supposed to assist. He found, for instance, that most of those seeking relief were the chronically under-employed rather than regular workers displaced by the depression, for whom the Act had been designed. His reputation as an expert on unemployment grew, and in December 1905 he was co-opted on to the Central (Unemployed) Body (CUB). At the same time, he became a leader writer for the *Morning Post* and severed his connection with Toynbee Hall. His life was frenetic, experimenting with and analysing unemployment during the day and writing at the *Morning Post* at night.

He became chairman of CUB's Employment Exchange Committee. It was agreed to establish a metropolitan network of exchanges and Beveridge was heavily involved in setting them up. It was at this time that Beveridge became strongly committed to labour exchanges as a reform that would both improve the lot of the individual workman and improve industrial efficiency. In private, he 'never stopped talking about labour exchanges' and was a 'terrible bore to my friends'.[22]

During 1907, Beveridge expounded his vision of a national labour exchange system to John Burns, President of the Local Government Board, a former trade unionist who had advocated labour exchanges back in 1893.[23] Burns now was unpersuaded, suspecting that exchanges would be used to depress wages and break strikes.[24] Much more promising was Beveridge's conversion of Sidney and Beatrice Webb to the cause, leading to an invitation to Beveridge to present evidence on unemployment to the Royal Commission on the Poor Laws. Beveridge later said that the Webbs were 'the most important people in getting the labour exchanges going'.[25] With their encouragement, he investigated labour exchanges in the German Empire in September 1907. Beveridge found that there were over 4000 labour exchanges of various kinds in the German Empire, which filled over 1.25 million vacancies a year. He concluded that these exchanges were

> *still only at the beginning of their development...yet no-one can doubt that they have come to stay and to grow as the many services they may render come to be more fully recognised. They do not solve the unemployment problem. They simplify it enormously and are indispensable to a solution.*[26]

On his return, Beveridge submitted both written and oral evidence to the Royal Commission. His evidence was later embodied in his important book *Unemployment: A Problem of Industry*.[27] As this title indicates, his thesis was that unemployment was caused more by problems of industrial organisation than by the personal defects of those who were affected by it (which had been so much emphasised by Victorian commentators). He accepted that the unemployed might be physically and morally inferior to those in work but argued that this was a consequence, not a cause, of their irregular employment. He distinguished three types of unemployment:

- chronic under-employment in the casual labour market, caused by maintaining excessive reserves of labour;
- structural unemployment, caused by the decline of an industry or occupation; and
- unemployment caused by seasonal or cyclical fluctuations in demand.

In contrast to many previous commentators, Beveridge saw the first of these – the widespread 'overstocking' of the market for labour – as the most important. The solution lay not in temporary relief nor in labour colonies:

> *The cure and the only cure for under-employment is the organisation of the demand for, and the supply of, labour through labour exchanges...*

Beveridge's writings at this time showed that he recognised that decasualisation would require more than labour exchanges.[28] But the exchanges, through concentrating the pool of labour in one place, formed the 'indispensable permanent basis for nearly all other remedies whether of organisation or relief'. The exchanges would address the second problem – structural unemployment – since they would 'facilitate the passage to a new occupation of men permanently displaced from their old one by a change of industrial conditions'. As to seasonal unemployment, the exchanges could 'facilitate the use of subsidiary trades by seasonal workers'.

The problem of trade depressions was more difficult and it led Beveridge to propose contributory insurance against unemployment, which was already being provided by many trade unions. It was at this time that Beveridge became an advocate of social insurance. He was fascinated by the German model of contributory insurance against sickness, infirmity and old age and industrial accidents. He was deeply critical of the Liberal government's decision to introduce old age pensions on a non-contributory and means tested basis, since he saw means tests as a penalty on thrift. He noted that Germany had not introduced compulsory unemployment insurance, but he found that a major German report on the subject in 1906 had emphasised the mutual interdependence of labour exchanges and unemployment insurance:

> *German writers treat the labour bureaux in close connection with proposals for 'unemployment insurance' as the only satisfactory safeguard against malingering. In Strasburg before a man can get help from the Poor Law he must present a note from the superintendent of the labour exchange that no work can be found.*[29]

In his evidence to the Royal Commission, Beveridge recommended the 'gradual growth' of unemployment insurance, probably building on trade union systems, though 'your labour exchange could quite naturally and directly become the centre of an insurance system'.[30] He recognised that insurance would not work for the 'casual labour class'. But, as indicated in the Strasburg example quoted above, in the case of people seeking public assistance, he saw the exchanges as offering a 'direct test of unemployment'.[31]

While his evidence was compelling, there was one key area of ambiguity. On the one hand, he insisted that labour exchanges were to be business organisations; their future depended on:

> *their complete dissociation from the direct relief of distress and from any authority mainly concerned, or identified by public opinion, with such relief. They should become a piece of permanent industrial organisation under an authority of national scope (the Board of Trade)...*[32]

On the other hand, his recommendation that the exchanges should administer the tests upon which both insurance benefits and public assistance would depend meant that the exchanges would be involved in the relief of distress. As discussed in Chapter 1, the tension between these different functions of the labour exchanges was to have a profound impact on their subsequent history.

Beveridge's evidence was a remarkable *tour de force*. It combined mastery of the relevant data with a restless and highly practical searching for solutions. Not surprisingly, it had a strong influence on the Royal Commission, which from then on was united on the desirability of a national system of labour exchanges. Early in 1908, the Webbs began to interest Winston Churchill in the 'organisation of the labour market' and in March invited Beveridge to dine with Churchill. A few weeks later, Churchill became President of the Board of Trade, soon making clear his intention to take initiatives about unemployment. The Webbs told him:

> *if you are going to deal with unemployment, you must have the boy Beveridge.*[33]

Churchill took their advice and in July 1908 Beveridge joined the Board of Trade on a salary of £600 per year.

The Labour Exchanges Act 1909

Starting from July 1908, it took just over a year to get the Labour Exchanges Act onto the statute book. It may seem a long time to produce a very short piece of legislation, but along the way various important policy issues had to be resolved, including:

- which Department was to have the lead role;
- whether the new exchanges were to be managed directly by the Department or to be provided by other bodies under a grant-in-aid;
- whether the initiative would embrace compulsory unemployment insurance;
- whether the use of labour exchanges was to be compulsory or voluntary; and
- whether the trade unions and employers would support the new exchanges.

The first issue – the question of Departmental responsibility – had largely been resolved by the sequence of events in 1907–09.[34] The main alternatives to the Board of Trade were the Home Office (which was responsible for the Factories Acts) and the Local Government Board (whose responsibility for the Poor Law might extend to the new ideas of unemployment insurance now under consideration). There seems to have been no serious consideration of giving the work to the Home Office. As to the Local Government Board, John Burns, the President, was suspicious of labour exchanges on trade union grounds, while in other respects he was frozen into a position of extreme conservatism by his officials. By contrast, Churchill was keen to innovate. Moreover, if unemployment was a 'problem of industry', then the task of dealing with it belonged to the Board of Trade as the Department with already well established relationships with trade unions and employers' organisations. Finally, the Board of Trade also offered the venture the best chances of success. In 1908, it was one of the most dynamic and innovative departments of state. Its Permanent Secretary, Sir Hubert Llewellyn Smith, was, like Beveridge, a graduate of Balliol and Toynbee Hall. He had built up his Department's expertise in industrial and labour matters and was now at the height of his powers as a formulator of policy and a master in the 'technique of legislation'.[35] He was also an ideal mentor to the young Beveridge. Given the logic of the situation and the personalities involved, it is not surprising that a meeting of officials from the two Departments agreed in July 1908 that: 'the subject of labour exchanges ought to be considered as a question of Employment and not of Relief and consequently should be dealt with by the Board of Trade'.[36]

In one area, however – that of juvenile employment – departmental rivalries continued. Beveridge and others in the Board of Trade wanted the exchanges to help young people who were leaving school for the labour market and to discourage them from dead end jobs which would trap them in casual underemployment. Juvenile Advisory Committees, with educational representatives, were planned to secure the necessary guidance. But the Board of Education saw this as trespassing on their territory. A classic inter-departmental battle followed between Beveridge and JD Chambers, a Shakespearian scholar in the Board of Education. A junior participant later commented:

> *I never saw a prettier quarrel than that. Neither Beveridge nor Chambers was in those days particularly tactful and there was little pretence of politeness in our discussions. In the end, the Board of Education persuaded the Treasury to let them have a bill enabling local education authorities, if they wished, to start up choice of employment schemes of their own.*[37]

The Bill became the Education (Choice of Employment) Act 1910. In areas where the education authority chose to set up its own employment bureaux, the Board of Trade ceased dealing with juveniles.[38] Thus emerged a curious British dual approach to youth employment, which, despite reviews in 1921 and 1945 and some legislative modification along the way, was to survive until 1974.

The second key question to be resolved was the management of the labour exchanges. Would they be managed directly by central government like the Post Office or by grants to local authorities or other local bodies, like education? This was resolved quickly by Churchill himself. Against his own centralist instincts, Beveridge had cautiously recommended grants-in-aid, but Churchill without hesitation favoured 'a national scheme directly under the Board'. He was probably influenced by his wish to use the labour exchanges for a scheme of unemployment insurance, which would necessarily involve a national, rather than local, system of control.[39] Beveridge later saw this as a historic shift from localism to administrative centralisation.[40]

The third question – whether the initiative was to embrace compulsory unemployment insurance as well as labour exchanges – raised more difficult issues. Unemployment insurance was already a familiar concept in that many trade unions provided it for their members. In his evidence to the Royal Commission, Beveridge had opened up the question of state intervention to promote unemployment insurance. This could take one of two forms: state support for trade union insurance (known as the Ghent scheme) or a national system of compulsory unemployment insurance. Both the Majority and the Minority Reports of the Royal Commission, when they emerged in February 1909, leant towards the more cautious Ghent approach. This was supported by precedents abroad, whereas there was no example of a successful state-run unemployment insurance scheme. The one attempt to run such a scheme, in the canton of St Gall in Switzerland, had ended in failure (due, according to Beveridge, to the absence of three vital features: employer contributions, deductions from wage packets and a satisfactory work test).[41] The German Empire's 1906 review was 'hesitant about the possibility of defining insurable employment and testing whether it had occurred'.[42]

Despite the meagre supporting evidence, Ministers decided in the autumn of 1908 to proceed with state-run unemployment insurance – a decision which was, as Bentley Gilbert says, 'wildly experimental'.[43] It is not clear quite how the decision was taken. It must have been influenced by the high unemployment prevalent at the time. Moreover, there was an interventionist mood in the Board of Trade, with the combination of Churchill, Llewellyn Smith and Beveridge, and a 'doubt whether (the alternative Ghent model of granting of subsidies to trade union schemes) would do anything serious to prevent distress'.[44] Finally, there was the dominant personality of Lloyd George. His enthusiasm for German social insurance following his visit to Germany in August 1908 must have made him positive about unemployment insurance, even if the Germans did not have it.[45]

The idea of a combined package of labour exchanges and unemployment insurance survived a variety of discussions in the autumn of 1908, involving other Ministers and outside experts such as Sidney Webb and trade union leaders, culminating in Churchill's paper to Cabinet of 11 December.[46] This paper made no pretence to offer a complete solution to the unemployment problem. It did 'not enter into the social and educational aspect of prevention on the one hand nor into any form of relief, whether by a modernised Poor Law or State industries on the other'. (In fact, the Asquith Cabinet would never grasp the nettle of reforming the Poor Law.) The paper was designed to 'organise both the mobilities and stabilities of labour'. The paper used vivid language which may have owed more to Churchill than to Beveridge:

> The custom in many trades to resort to abrupt discharges of workpeople... smashes households like eggshells. The helplessness of the displaced worker, left to himself to find fresh employment upon chance or rumour, leads to aimless wanderings and loiterings often fatal to character.

Unemployment was 'primarily a question for the employers', but the employing class would welcome compulsory unemployment insurance, which would 'associate directly for the first time the practical interest of the employer and the unemployed workman'. Insurance would 'enable the workman to tide over a temporary depression without selling up his home or losing his status'. But when a particular trade or industry definitely contracted, the nationwide labour exchange network would enable the superfluous worker to 'survey the whole labour market...If anywhere in the British Islands, there is a job for him, he can be conveyed to it as fast as the trains will travel', with if necessary an advance of fares. It was a persuasive case which met with Cabinet support.

Shortly afterwards, however, Churchill and Lloyd George decided that it was impractical to introduce both labour exchanges *and* unemployment insurance by a single early piece of legislation. Unemployment insurance had to be deferred until Lloyd George had found a way to deal with infirmity insurance (since workers moved between sickness and unemployment). So the legislation for labour exchanges, which were relatively cheap, straightforward and uncontentious, went ahead in 1909, decoupled from that for national insurance.[47] In the event, there were further delays in the national insurance legislation because it was caught up in the constitutional crisis over Lloyd George's 1909 Budget.

The fourth issue – whether use of the labour exchanges was to be voluntary or compulsory – was resolved in favour of a voluntary approach. Beveridge's arguments for concentrating the supply of, and demand for, labour in labour exchanges (pages 3–4) could imply a case for compulsion. But Churchill seems consistently to have favoured voluntarism. Indeed, before recruiting Beveridge he checked with him whether voluntary exchanges could succeed. Beveridge replied that he felt certain that 'without compulsion exchanges could secure a sufficient volume of general work; whether they could touch the problem of casual employment was another question altogether'.[48] The issue cropped up again later in discussions with Sidney Webb, who drafted the Minority Report of the Royal Commission and advocated voluntary unemployment insurance, together with compulsory use of the exchanges for all engagements lasting less than one month.[49] This was the converse of what Ministers wanted. Churchill later justified his rejection of Webb's proposal on the grounds that an attempt to force through decasualisation without having a satisfactory way of dealing with the surplus of labour that would arise could cause the 'gravest possible disaster'.[50] Thus, Churchill's Cabinet paper advocated voluntarism both in the use of the exchanges and in tackling the evils of casual labour, though warning that compulsory powers might be needed later on the latter front.

The decision to make the use of exchanges voluntary made the fifth issue – whether the trade unions and employers would support the new exchanges – all the more important. Churchill remarked: 'of course either side, employers or workmen, can bring the scheme to its knees by standing aloof at any moment'.[51] In particular, Churchill and Beveridge saw it as vital that the exchanges were not identified with vagrants and loafers but were used by the respectable working class. Great efforts were made to win the support of both sides of industry. In November 1908, it was arranged that four leading trade unionists should visit Germany to study social insurance and labour exchanges and this allayed their fears. The Labour Exchange Bill gave trade unionists a role on the local advisory committees in the management of exchanges (though 'workmen's representatives' would not necessarily all be trade unionists). But the crucial issue for the unions was whether the exchanges would handle 'blackleg' vacancies during strikes, and vacancies offering pay below the 'standard rate'. Beveridge argued against either accepting 'blackleg' and cut-price vacancies unconditionally or refusing to accept them, since in either case the exchanges would lose their neutrality. Instead, drawing on German experience, he recommended a middle way of accepting them but accepting also from unions notices for display about disputes and standard rates. Churchill put over this line persuasively to union representatives and this formula was later enshrined in the Regulations under the Act. In addition, Churchill introduced into the Bill in Committee a clause ensuring that under the regulations no worker should suffer a penalty from refusing these controversial vacancies. The outcome of all this diplomacy was that the new exchanges had some official support from the TUC though there would long be suspicions on the part of local trade unionists.

In August 1909, Churchill also met representatives of the engineering and shipbuilding employers' organisations. They feared that 'the Exchanges may be centres for the spread of discontent and will increase instead of alleviate the misfortunes of those they are intended to benefit'. They felt that their existing methods of recruiting labour were satisfactory – 'we have our own Labour Exchanges every morning'. Churchill sought to reassure them by stressing that employers' use of the exchanges would be voluntary. He promised that 'there will be no sort of loafing about at all... it is not intended that it shall be a sort of permanent club for the unemployed'. Churchill presented the 'neutral' line on disputes and wage rates: the exchanges would be 'a perfectly colourless soulless piece of communal mechanism'. By the end of the meeting, the employers had agreed to collaborate on the detail of the legislation.[52]

Meanwhile, the formidable administrative machine of the Board of Trade had been hard at work. In March 1909, a small committee, including Beveridge, produced a report on the organisation and finances of the labour exchange system.[53] With the help of the Office of Works, they developed a model plan for a 'first class labour exchange' in each big city. They recommended a national network of 227 offices, with a total of 863 staff. This exercise prepared the way for the legislation.

On 19 May 1909, in a debate on the Poor Law Commission Reports, Churchill spoke at length to the Commons about his package of labour exchanges and unemployment insurance.[54] He described unemployment as: 'this hideous crushing evil which has oppressed for so long the minds of every one who cares about social reform'. He recognised that the exchanges would not to any large extent create employment, but they would reduce friction in the labour market and so raise the standard of economic life. They would prevent useless tramping for work. They would make it possible to deal stringently with vagrants, by making it unnecessary to wander in search of work. The exchanges would make it possible to tackle casual employment – 'the original foundation of so many of the greatest evils in our social life'. They would permit the 'dovetailing' of seasonal occupations. He claimed that, drawing on experience in Germany and other lands, 'we may begin at a higher level and on a larger scale than has been done in any other country up to the present time'. Accordingly, his plan 'would be uniform and national in its character'. Last, but not least, it would institute machinery indispensable to a system of unemployment insurance, which the government would introduce later on. The labour exchange scheme would cost £170,000 per annum, rising to £200,000 to pay the capital cost of new buildings.

On 20 May, the Labour Exchange Bill was introduced into Parliament. This very short Bill enabling the Board of Trade to run labour exchanges received all-party support and became law on 20 September 1909.

Setting up the labour exchanges

In the words of Bonar Law, the Labour Exchanges Act was a 'blank cheque'.[55] It said nothing about the extent of the network or the speed with which it was to be established. The Board of Trade could have taken its time, consulted, experimented and gradually expanded its provision. But that was not the approach adopted. As Beveridge wrote later:

> *The actual policy of the Board was more audacious and more direct. They set out to establish as rapidly as possible a full-blown system under their own control. They took over and absorbed into this national system all the existing Exchanges with any life in them...; they secured the closing of all others.*

The Board saw this as desirable for labour market purposes. But there was an even more compelling pressure – the expected requirement to deliver unemployment insurance:

> *Machinery had to be established by which it would be possible by a given date in every part of the country to issue unemployment books for payment of contributions, to receive claims, to register the unemployed, and to pay unemployment benefit.*[56]

The first step was to set up a powerful central team. There was a reorganisation in the Board of Trade at Caxton House. There were doubts about giving Beveridge direct accountability for delivery but he resisted a suggestion that he should merely be an inventor of schemes.[57] The compromise was to appoint Beveridge director of a new labour exchange branch but to install a General Manager as well. Beveridge served in a new Labour Department, reporting for a year or two to Sir George Askwith – a high profile industrial relations conciliator within the Board of Trade,[58] who later was highly critical of the labour exchanges (pages 54–5). In August 1909, Beveridge visited Germany with Askwith and Llewellyn Smith in order to learn as much as possible from the practices of German labour exchanges. Beveridge and Askwith got on badly, with Askwith becoming increasingly hostile to the exchanges and in conflict with exchange officials over the handling of industrial disputes.[59]

Among the founding fathers of the exchanges, Beveridge has pride of place as the 'master mind' of the new system. But Charles Rey, the new General Manager, also played a key role. He was the antithesis of Beveridge, with no pretence to academic qualifications but 'excitable and most practically energetic. We had for ever to be raiding the Treasury for new staff and premises and Rey, always spoiling for a fight, was the spearhead of our forays'.[60] The Board of Trade at this time recognised the importance of strong central management – a lesson which was learned all over again in the 1960s and 1970s. The team also included three keen young 'Upper Division Clerks' – Thomas Phillips (later to become Permanent Secretary of the Ministry of Labour), Stephen Tallents and Humbert Wolfe (later to become Deputy Secretary in the Ministry of Labour and a distinguished poet and essayist). Beveridge summed them up: 'Tallents was the best of the three in judgement, Wolfe in speed and Phillips in mastery of detail'.[61] Stephen Tallents wrote in his memoirs that, while elsewhere in the civil service the team was regarded as engaged in 'a great gamble... a company of pirates', the young men saw themselves as 'high adventurers giving shape to one of the great social reform measures of the quinquennium'.[62] It was a time of intense activity, with Beveridge:

> *working for 14 hours a day, interviewing and cajoling employers, purchasing office sites, urging the Board of Education to take action on juvenile unemployment, and travelling about the country to explain and propagate labour exchange principles.*[63]

Beveridge recognised that everything could not be run from Headquarters. He wrote that the 'Divisional Chiefs' would be:

> *the brains and driving power...of the labour exchange movement ... They must be thoroughly responsible officers, combining initiative with business or administrative experience and able to hold their own with employers and workpeople.*[64]

Accordingly, below the General Manager was a tier of 11 powerful 'Divisional Officers' – reduced to eight with the introduction of insurance and later renamed 'Divisional Controllers'. These were the precursors of the Regional Directors of the modern employment service and indeed of many similar key posts in other departments and agencies today. Again, this reflected recognition of the importance of management. Even the divisions that were chosen are recognisable in the regional structure both of the modern employment service and indeed today's government offices.[65]

Another novelty was the extent of external recruitment of managers and staff, breaking through the established practice of selection by academic written examination, which tended to favour young inexperienced people. Churchill, keen to appoint managers with business experience, interviewed the prospective Divisional Officers himself. To avoid charges of patronage, Beveridge invented a written test in the form of a reply to an employer who criticised mistakes by the exchanges. The winning answer, by JB Adams, a former Antarctic explorer, included an invitation to the employer to discuss the matter over lunch. Adams became Divisional Officer in Leeds and later General Manager. He was a legendary figure in the service, who called everyone from the Permanent Secretary downwards 'skipper' or 'mate'. Other successful candidates included businessmen, trade unionists, a regular soldier, and an American gold speculator who claimed to have 'run a labour exchange in Chicago, with a revolver provided as part of the office equipment in the drawer of his desk'.[66] Selection of exchange managers was entrusted to a small committee, comprising the First Civil Service Commissioner, a leading trade unionist and a Conservative businessman. Adams later recalled:

> *practically all the staff were recruited from outside the Civil Service and a motley crew they were: trade unionists, Fabians, social reformers, men and women from factory and workshop and a sprinkling from the public schools.*[67]

Many of these were appointed on a temporary basis by a somewhat exceptional procedure. The policy of external recruitment did not last. It came under criticism in Parliament and from witnesses to the Royal Commission on the Civil Service in 1911–12. From 1911 onwards, senior officials were mainly recruited from within the civil service and Beveridge was highly critical of the salary limitations and the type of officials chosen.[68]

The number of staff in these early days was small by later standards – only 1000 in March 1912 when confined to employment work but rising to nearly 5000 in March 1913 with the introduction of insurance, and reaching 5250 in March 1914.[69] But under Treasury pressure Beveridge and his team, who included 'Inspectors', brought numbers down by simplifying procedures and measuring work volumes and the amount of time that processes took. The staff included some 600 women headed by a Chief Women's Officer.

Apart from recruiting the staff, the most urgent task was hastily to acquire premises and adapt them to their new function. It was a formidable achievement that as many as 61 labour exchanges opened their doors on 1 February 1910. By the end of 1912, when the insurance scheme came into full operation, the exchange organisation was extended to 414 labour exchanges and about 1000 local agencies of the unemployment fund.[70] (This extensive network – which has remained a characteristic of the British employment service ever since – was driven by insurance considerations; benefit claimants were to sign daily unless they lived more than three miles from an office.)[71] Churchill's vision of obtaining permanent premises, which could become 'industrial centres' in each town, was not fulfilled. The Treasury and the Office of Works insisted on the use of existing premises, which were often dismal and inconvenient and 'in the slummiest parts of the town'.[72]

On the opening day – 1 February 1910 – Churchill said to the *Daily Telegraph*:

> *People must not expect too much from these Exchanges. I have never claimed for them a higher position than they really can occupy, in fact. They are a piece of social mechanism, absolutely essential, I believe, to a well-ordered community...I am confident that fifteen or twenty years hence people would as soon do without telephone exchanges or electric trams as do without a national system of labour bureaux.*[73]

He pointed out that the new offices were 'painted green – the colour of hope'.

Unemployment insurance

Compulsory insurance was more controversial than setting up labour exchanges, even among Ministers. On 27 April 1909, Churchill wrote to his wife:

> *My Unemployment Insurance plan encountered much opposition from that old ruffian Burns & that little goose Runciman, & I could not get any decision yesterday from the Cabinet. Asquith however is quite firm about it, & I do not doubt that in the end it will come safely through.*[74]

Presumably, Burns wanted further reassurance about the protection of the insurance fund against malingerers, which Beveridge provided in a paper in May.[75] Churchill's confidence of Cabinet support proved justified. By 19 May, he was able to tell the Commons that the labour exchanges would be accompanied by a system of unemployment insurance: 'The exchanges and unemployment insurance were complementary. They were man and wife, mutually supported and sustained by each other.' He argued that compulsory insurance would benefit the exchanges by encouraging 'the higher ranks of labour – skilled workers, members of strong trade unions' to use the exchanges. Without insurance, there was a danger that 'the exchanges would only be used by the poorest and weakest in the labour market'.[76] There is support for this thesis in the way registrations and vacancies increased after insurance was introduced.

The main features of the unemployment insurance scheme were designed to avoid it becoming overwhelmed with bad personal risks as had happened in the St Gall scheme (page 16):

- Benefits would be confined to those who had made a sufficient number of contributions; there would be no benefit in the first week and no more than one week's benefit for every five contributions paid and no more than 15 weeks benefit in any year.
- Rates of benefit would be significantly below ordinary wage levels; they were set at seven shillings a week.
- There would be contributions both from the employers and workers (eventually set at $2\frac{1}{2}$ pence weekly from each), collected through the employer stamping an 'unemployment book' deposited with him by the workman and making a deduction from wages; this was based on German practice.
- There would be a state subsidy ($1\frac{2}{3}$ pence a week or one quarter of the total) to give the necessary stability and security.
- The scheme would cover only part of the workforce – building, construction of works, shipbuilding, mechanical engineering, ironfounding, construction of vehicles, sawmilling. These were trades that suffered from seasonal and cyclical unemployment and comprised 2.25 million workers, or 17 per cent of the workforce; Churchill envisaged extending the scheme after experience had been gained.
- State aid could be given to voluntary insurance run by associations in any trade.

The labour exchanges would provide the unemployment books in the first place, receive claims for benefit, ensure that they met the criteria and then pay the benefit.

As regards the criteria for receiving benefit, there was a major disagreement between Churchill and Llewellyn Smith about whether workers who had been dismissed for misconduct should be entitled to benefit. Churchill was against any disqualification. He did not like 'mixing up moralities and mathematics'. He went on: 'our concern is with the evil, not with the causes; with the fact of unemployment, not with the character of the unemployed'.[77] Llewellyn Smith, apprehensive about bad risks, was persistent and won the day. Workers who had lost employment through misconduct or had left it voluntarily without just cause were disqualified for a period of six weeks. (This remained the position until extended to a maximum of 13 weeks in 1986 and of 26 weeks in 1988.)

In order to protect ministers from answering endless questions on why individuals had been denied benefit, Beveridge devised an ingenious new system of adjudication.[78] These decisions would be made by statutory 'insurance officers' at Divisional Office (later, within the exchange). Disputed claims went to a Court of Referees (consisting of an employer, a workman and a chairman, usually of legal training) or ultimately to an Umpire appointed by the Crown. Much of this system has survived to the present day.

It was a condition of benefit that claimants registered for employment at the exchange; this was to remain the case until 1982. Claimants' inability to obtain suitable employment was tested substantially by whether the exchange could offer them a job or not. After their initial registration, they 'proved' their unemployment and capacity to work by signing an unemployed register *daily* at the exchange in working hours – an arrangement which Beveridge drew from the practice of trade union insurance schemes. A worker would not be refused benefit for declining a vacancy due to a trade dispute. Nor would a worker be disqualified for refusing a vacancy at less than the usual or recognised wages. This last provision survived until 1989 (page 270).

The designers of unemployment insurance built to last. Much of the framework they created has survived to this day, or at least until the 1980s and 1990s.

The main outline of the scheme was drawn up while Churchill was at the Board of Trade, but in February 1910 Churchill departed to the Home Office, to be replaced by the more self-effacing Sydney Buxton. There were tensions between the Treasury, under Lloyd George, which was responsible for health insurance, and the Board of Trade, which was responsible for unemployment insurance. During 1911, a bid by Lloyd George to take over unemployment insurance was turned down by Asquith. Instead, it was agreed that there would be two parts to a single bill.[79] The result was that the complexities of health insurance held up unemployment insurance. When a press leak appeared to this effect, it so enraged Lloyd George that he said he would 'smash to atoms Sydney Buxton and Llewellyn Smith'.[80] Despite these tensions, the National Insurance Bill passed into law in 1911. Part II of the Bill, which related to unemployment insurance, passed through Parliament with surprising ease, perhaps because it allowed the main existing interested parties – the trade unions – to continue their schemes under the Act if they wished.

There were intense preparations in the Board of Trade for the introduction of contributions on 15 July 1912 (known to Beveridge and his colleagues as 'Joy Day') and the introduction of benefits on 15 January 1913 (known as 'Judgement Day'). The pressure was such that in April 1912 Beveridge had a recurrence of athlete's heart, while in June Charles Rey had a nervous breakdown. Both men recovered, and the massive new system was introduced. In December 1912, Beveridge wrote:

> *All this once started must go on like clockwork and with absolute continuity for there will be a perpetual stream of applications for benefit ...never ceasing. Will the machine work? It's really as new in type as was the first steam locomotive and of course one has not been able to make experiments and trial runs...*[81]

This quotation shows Beveridge as a natural 'systems man', who would have been at home in the world of computers which arose in the service 50 years later. As it turned out, the manual machine of 1912–13 did work. Over 100,000 workmen – mostly from the building industry – qualified for benefit on the first day. On 15 January 1913 the first benefits were duly paid.

The labour market operations of the labour exchanges, 1910–14

In the years 1910–14, the procedures of the labour exchanges were introduced and tested.[82] Many of them were to last for the next 50 years and some of them are with us to this day.

'Applicants' (they would be known today as 'jobseekers') were urged to register and expected to review their registration weekly to prevent it lapsing. (If they were in the insured trades, they *had* to register to qualify for benefit.) All but 3–5 per cent of registrants were unemployed. Applicants could fill in an 'A form' themselves, in which case a clerk transposed the details to a 'B form'. Alternatively, a clerk filled in a 'B form' on their behalf. The 'B forms' on each registrant were then filed in a card index in occupational order, based on a list of 350 occupations. This was known as the 'live register'. When workmen in the insured trades claimed for benefit, they handed in their 'unemployment book' and their claim also counted as a registration. They received a grey receipt card known as the 'UI 40', which they had to produce when they signed daily to 'prove' unemployment. (A successor to this card, known as the 'UB 40', was still in use in the 1970s and 1980s, when it was adopted as the name of a pop group.)

The founders of the exchanges knew that they depended upon the goodwill of employers. They engaged in a 'large amount of propaganda work' (we would now call it 'marketing') with employers, including circulars, addresses at meetings and visiting employers' premises. The last was found to be the most effective. By 1914, 2000 employers had been persuaded to put up a notice on their gates saying that they only recruited through the exchanges. Vacancies were normally notified by phone and were kept in a card index, again filed by occupation.

When vacancies were notified, the exchange clerks would check the live register and, if they identified a suitable applicant, would either wait for him to call in or inform the applicant by postcard or messenger. The applicant was then interviewed to test suitability and, if thought suitable, was given a green card to pass on to the employer. It was for the employer to make the choice. Both employer and applicant had cards to send back to the exchange so that it could keep its records up to date.

In deciding on submissions, the dominating principle was 'to submit for any vacancy the applicant who appears *industrially the best qualified* for it'. The exchanges rejected earlier practices of the Distress Committees of selection according to domestic circumstances, personal character or duration of unemployment. At this stage, exchanges did not probe into personal circumstances. Moreover, Beveridge believed that managers would have been driven to the 'industrially best qualified' criterion in any case by the logic of operating on a voluntary basis.[83]

The exchanges took up a neutral stance on union membership, wages and strikes. They did not ask whether an applicant was a union member, though they would warn applicants if a vacancy was with a 'non-union' employer. The number of vacancies due to a strike or lock-out turned out to be very small and the number filled almost negligible. The 'neutrality' policy had the great advantage that exchanges did not have to decide whether a dispute was occurring. None the less, criticisms of the exchanges continued in trade union circles, fuelled perhaps by a feeling that their willingness in principle to accept 'blackleg' vacancies identified them as being on the employers' side.

One of the great advantages of a national system of exchanges was that it could facilitate geographical mobility. Initially, this depended on passing to a Divisional Clearing House details of vacancies that were hard to fill locally. But by October 1914 it was clear that it was better to group exchanges into compact industrial districts with a principal or 'clearing exchange' in each group. If the vacancy could not be filled within the group, it would be passed to a central or national Clearing House[84] and then might be circulated nationally in the weekly national *Clearing House Gazette*.

In looking at the performance of the exchanges in those years, it is important to remember that in 1912–13 'the whole staff was absorbed in the launching of unemployment insurance'.[85] The period up to August 1914 was too short for the peacetime potential of the exchanges to be fully developed. However, it was a time of exceptional prosperity, and it is in such conditions that labour market institutions can achieve the greatest economic benefits. Table 2.1 shows the business volumes relevant to employment work.

Table 2.1 *Labour exchange statistics, 1911–14*

Year	Registrations of workpeople (000s)	Vacancies	Vacancies filled, ie placings	Percentage of registrations filled	Percentage of notified vacancies filled
1911	1966	770	608	31	79
1912	2362	1034	810	34	78
1913	2836	1183	895	32	76
1914	3305	1437	1087	33	76

Source: JB Seymour, *The British Employment Exchange*, PS King, London, 1928, p269.

Table 2.1 shows that by 1914 the exchanges were responsible for over one million engagements a year. We do not know what proportion that was of total engagements, but Beveridge believed the exchanges were responsible for one third of all engagements in the insured trades – this is probably an overestimate, but none the less shows remarkable progress.[86] Moreover, the exchanges were consistently filling over 75 per cent of all the vacancies they received, which should have built up employer confidence. Remarkably, one in eight of all placings involved transference to other exchange districts[87] (5 per cent beyond five miles), representing the kind of improvement in mobility that Churchill and Beveridge were trying to achieve.

At the same time, there were also early signs of problems with performance measurement. One Divisional Chief later recalled that he was rebuked by Central Office at this time for the poor placing performance of his Division in comparison with Glasgow, which was achieving 600 placings a week. He investigated and found that Glasgow was placing large numbers of sandwich men for a few hours a day.[88] By 1913, there was a separate 'casual register', which kept separate records of 224,000 placings.[89]

Beveridge and his team endeavoured to tackle what he regarded as the most acute aspect of unemployment – the chronic underemployment in the casual trades – but met with limited success. As Beveridge said,[90] this was 'not for want of trying on their part'. They tried to achieve progressive decasualisation by negotiation in every considerable port in the kingdom and in other fields of casual work. They were unable to obtain the necessary cooperation from employers and workmen. As expected, progress could only be made by compulsion. So Beveridge worked hard in 1913–14 on securing the necessary powers for the Board of Trade, but he was frustrated by the continued resistance of the industry, the dilatoriness of the new President, John Burns, pressure of other Parliamentary business and the onset of war.[91]

Unemployment insurance operations 1913–14

On the insurance side, the brand new administrative machine proved effective. As might be expected in boom conditions, contributions up to August 1914 exceeded expenditure by £3 million. Beveridge reckoned that the fund was well on the way to being able to meet the kind of loss that might have occurred in a depression on the scale that had occurred in 1908–9. Even in the boom in 1913–14, there were surprisingly 1.1 million claims in respect of 0.55 million individuals – one in four of those insured. But most got back to work very quickly – on average within 15 days.

It is useful to look at the pattern of disallowances in 1913–14 in Table 2.2, as they may suggest reasons why the exchanges were to become unpopular in various quarters. It is interesting that as many as one in ten claims were rejected and that 43 per cent of all disallowances related to misconduct and voluntary leaving, where Churchill had wanted a more permissive regime. The second largest group related to trade disputes, where Beveridge had taken a hard line of excluding those indirectly affected in a works where there was a dispute. There was a large building dispute in London and another major dispute in Dublin at this time. The third group – not worked 26 weeks in the insured trades – reflects in part the problems involved in covering only part of a labour market in which people might move between occupations even within a day.

Table 2.2 *Disallowance of claims to unemployment benefit, July 1913–July 1914*

Reason	Number	Percentage of total
Not worked 26 weeks in insured trade	22,273	21.4
Not capable of work	300	0.3
Refusal of suitable employment	6137	5.9
Benefit exhausted	922	0.9
Trade dispute	30,328	29.2
Misconduct	14,113	13.6
Voluntary leaving without just cause	27,226	26.2
Other	2611	2.5
Total claims disallowed	103,910	9.5

Source: Beveridge's Report to July 1914, page 79.

Conclusion

What assessment can we make of the exchanges and unemployment insurance at the point in the summer of 1914 when Britain was about to face the rude shock of total war?

First, they were a remarkably radical incursion into what Churchill called 'the untrodden field of unemployment'. They represented the casting aside of long traditions of liberal *laissez faire*. It is true that, as was to become painfully clear after the war, these measures did not provide a bulwark against a recurrence of large-scale unemployment. But Churchill had made it clear both to the Cabinet and to Parliament that his measures would not abolish unemployment (pages 16 and 18). The aim of the reforms was more modest – to 'organise the labour market' in order both to improve national efficiency and to alleviate unemployment. If they are judged by this criterion, then one can see that solid practical progress had been achieved by 1914. The placing levels of the exchanges, including those outside the exchange's immediate area, suggest that already they were reducing frictional unemployment and the need for 'tramping' in search of work. Moreover, the unemployment insurance system, despite its limitations, was already cushioning the lives of the surprisingly large number who lost their jobs in the insured trades even in a boom. Certainly, the progress made by 1914 fell far short of the vision set out in Beveridge's book on unemployment – particularly as regards decasualisation – but it takes time to reform deep-seated practices, and there had not been much time.

Secondly, the administrative virtuosity of these social reformers was astonishing. Even now, with ample experience of change management in the public sector, the implementation of major administrative reforms can go seriously astray. By contrast, these elaborate plans went ahead with remarkable efficiency. They set up a new kind of network of government offices, both regionally and locally, which was to become the model for much of the welfare state in Britain. They set up systems and procedures which worked smoothly, and many of which survived to this day, or at least until the Thatcher era. Their model for adjudication and appeal outside the courts, but also outside direct Ministerial control, has also stood the test of time.

But were the concepts flawed in a way that spelt trouble in the long term? The most critical feature was the decision to combine employment and insurance in order to test the willingness to work of benefit recipients. Beveridge drew this idea from both German and trade union sources. Indeed, it was ironically from the trade unions that he derived the idea of daily signing, which helped to create the shuffling queues which were going to symbolise the despair of the 1920s and 1930s. The combination of employment and insurance created a curiously schizophrenic organisation. Churchill described employment and insurance as 'man and wife', but in reality they were an ill-assorted couple – one requiring entrepreneurial skills and adaptation to the local market, the other requiring uniform procedures and tight discipline. In 1930, Beveridge reflected that, even before the war, the exchanges had to subordinate their 'main function of organising the labour market' to the needs of insurance.[92] Desmond King writes:

> *The administrative decision to link the placement work of labour exchanges with the distribution of unemployment compensation produced an institutional bias towards the latter (though this policing role may not have been the primary concern of policy makers). This bias was more developed in Britain than in other countries whose governments were also concerned about the abuse of benefit by claimants...*[93]

But it is clear that, without this link as a secure defence against malingering, Churchill could never have got unemployment insurance through the Cabinet. Moreover, apart from the high level of disallowances which must have generated friction, it is not obvious that the insurance function *was* dragging down the employment function in these early years. On the contrary, the exchanges' penetration seems to have been much higher in the insured trades than elsewhere – not least among skilled workers.[94]

What is clear is the fundamental change in the role of government in Britain that these innovations represented. Bentley Gilbert writes: 'With the attack on unemployment, the national Government of Great Britain entered for the first time into the life of the ordinary, adult, male, able-bodied workman'.[95]

3

Time of Trial, 1914–18

'If the Exchanges had not existed before the War, the War would have invented them.' (Humbert Wolfe)[1]

Introduction

The First World War tested many British institutions to their limits. This was abundantly true of the labour exchanges. Britain was ill-prepared for war. Liberal tradition was antipathetic to the discipline necessary for total war and it was not until 1916 that conscription was introduced. Many assumed that the war would be over quickly. As it became clear that this was not to be the case, it was realised that one of the keys to survival, and indeed to victory, was the mobilisation of the nation's 'manpower' by the state on a scale hitherto remote from anyone's imagination. Indeed, it was during the war that the word 'manpower' first came into common parlance. This word remained popular until the 1980s, when it was finally overtaken by concepts of 'equal opportunities', but it was arguably a misnomer right from the start, since, of course, few things were more important during the war than the mobilisation of 'womanpower'. We shall use the neutral term 'labour'.

The mobilisation of labour did not take place in a highly organised, planned and rational fashion. On the contrary, as Humbert Wolfe said in his official history, it had more the character of a 'gigantic improvisation'.[2] One of the problems was the lack of a single manpower authority in the British government in 1914. Aspects of 'labour policy' rested with the Home Office and the Local Government Board as well as the Board of Trade. Moreover, in 1914 there was no overall government labour policy to constrain the recruitment efforts of the War Office and Admiralty. So labour policy during the war involved much experimentation, hesitation, inter-organisational conflict, the setting up of new organisations and their displacement by others. Among the new organisations to be created was the Ministry of Labour in December 1916, but ironically even this new creation did not become overall coordinator of the nation's labour. It was only from August 1917 that an institution approximating to such a role emerged, and this was the Ministry of National Service under Sir Auckland Geddes, working closely with the Cabinet Committee on Manpower.

It is obvious in retrospect that few, if any, organisations would be more practically useful to the mobilisation of labour than the labour exchanges. The exchanges offered a local instrument under central control for drawing labour into war work, for drawing additional labour, notably women, into the labour force, for transferring workers from one area to another and for providing information to the central planners on manpower deployment. None the less, particularly in the early stages of the war, one is struck by a hesitation about their role. Tasks which might have been theirs were entrusted to others. Military recruitment rested with the military authorities, not with the exchanges. The National Register of August 1915 (pages 37–8) was drawn up by the local authorities. The Tribunals which decided on appeals against enlistment were set up in October 1915 by the Local Government Board. Beveridge implied later that the reason for this hesitation about using the exchanges was that before the First World War the exchanges had been 'on trial'.[3] As the war proceeded, the centrality of the exchanges in labour mobilisation increased, and they were entrusted with ever more demanding, and more invidious, tasks.

Wartime management of the employment service

The management of the service went through four phases:

1. From August 1914 to May 1915: in this period, Beveridge as Director, and Charles Rey as General Manager, continued working under Llewellyn Smith as Permanent Secretary in the Board of Trade. Most of Beveridge's original labour exchange team remained to play important roles. An exception was Stephen Tallents, who joined the armed forces, to be invalided out later, when he became Director of Badges and Exemptions at the Ministry of Munitions.
2. From May 1915 to December 1916: Llewellyn Smith, Beveridge, Rey and Humbert Wolfe joined the new Ministry of Munitions under Lloyd George while retaining their old jobs in the Board of Trade. In May 1916, Beveridge became head of a new Employment Department within the Board of Trade, while still involved in munitions.
3. From December 1916 to September 1917: the 'Employment Exchanges' (as they were now called) were formally absorbed in January 1917 into the new Ministry of Labour under John Hodge. Charles Rey became Assistant Secretary in charge of the Employment Department. Llewellyn Smith and Beveridge departed from the labour scene.
4. From September 1917 to the Armistice in November 1918: Charles Rey was Director of the National Labour Supply Department in Sir Auckland Geddes' new Ministry of National Service, while retaining control of the employment exchanges.

This over-simplified outline suggests a command structure which was constantly changing amid the organisational turbulence of wartime Whitehall. In defiance of the Biblical injunction that 'No man can serve two masters', the exchanges were at two stages working in effect under two Ministries simultaneously. Charles Rey, for all his belligerence of character, emerges as a source of continuity in the management of the service. In addition, the Divisional Officers, who were in charge of the regions, played a vital role in keeping the machine steady.

The pressures within the service were vastly increased by the loss of key personnel to the armed forces. As early as September 1914, four out of the eight Divisional Officers had gone off to military service, together with 500 out of a total of 3000 male staff.[4] By July 1915, Beveridge was trying to resist further losses: 'the proportion actually enlisted is very large and we are suffering considerably from the unskilled work of the substitutes'.[5] But losses continued and, by December 1915, 1100 (36 per cent of the permanent male staff) were in the services. In November 1916, the pressures from the army were such that Llewellyn Smith, the Permanent Secretary, did a deal with General Macready, Adjutant General, that all fit men under 26 would be released to the services in exchange for the army returning all the men who were no longer fit for active service.[6] An early writer on the British employment exchanges commented that it was:

> a mistake on the part of the Government to allow the departure of so many of its most efficient exchange officials...They would have been of far more service to the country in carrying on their important duties at the exchange.[7]

The following table compares wartime staffing in employment exchange work with the numbers released to the armed forces.

Table 3.1 *Number of staff engaged in employment exchange work (including Central and Divisional Offices and finance functions), 1914–19*

	Total employed	With HM Forces or lent to other Departments (excluded from other column)
31 March 1914	5250	
1915	4789	624
1916	4784	1074
1917	5662	1157
1918	6342	1076
1919	19,384	247

Source: 1920 Committee of Enquiry on the Work of Employment Exchanges (Cmd 1054), Appendix 9, p439.

The table shows that total numbers were kept below 5000 in the early years of the war, reflecting a trade-off between a decline in benefit recipients and an increase in labour supply work. But numbers rose in 1917–18 with the extension of the scope of unemployment insurance (page 39) and the pressures from the Ministry of National Service. Because of the need to be able to reinstate those who had joined the armed forces, there was virtually no permanent recruitment during the war. An increasingly large proportion of the staff were temporarily recruited women, who were liable to discharge on two months' notice.

One other major management development of the wartime years was the centralisation of much of the clerical work to do with unemployment insurance at the Central Claims and Records Office at Ruskin Avenue, Kew (a location familiar to historians as the site of the Public Records Office). This centralisation had been planned before the war and came into effect in 1916. Llewellyn Smith described it as an 'immense economy'.[8] Kew was to become a legendary place in the service, with its own ethos and social life, exemplified in a social club called the Kew Klerks Klan.[9]

The outbreak of war

Beveridge did not share the general euphoria at the outbreak of war. Humbert Wolfe recalled standing with him watching 'the mob go roaring and cheering past brandishing flags...I of course shared the delirium, but Beveridge stood silent, fidgeting with his hands'.[10] Beveridge described the war as an 'incredible nightmare come true'; moreover, with his admiration for Germany, it was 'all against the grain to go in against Germans and with French and Russians'.[11] At the same time, he did not share the widespread inhibitions about using state power to mobilise the nation to the fullest extent and was frustrated by the lack of a coherent labour policy.[12]

On the declaration of war, Beveridge sent a circular to all staff urging them to 'render all possible help' to the military authorities but, subject to that, to 'regard it as a point of honour to maintain the punctual and orderly performance of the department's normal work'.[13] He activated a prior agreement with the War Office to provide labour to help the Expeditionary Force to get away; telegrams were sent to saddlers, bakers, blacksmiths and others, who then converged on Aldershot. He also responded to an Admiralty approach for shipyard workers to be sent to dockyards to hasten the completion of ships and be ready to repair war damage. Stephen Tallents and Humbert Wolfe organised an all-night service at Central Office, directing the movements of men.[14] Tallents afterwards recalled: 'For a few breathless days and sleepless nights, Humbert and I felt that we were the pivots of the war effort.'[15]

Responsibility for military recruitment lay with the War Office and the Admiralty, but Beveridge was keen that the exchanges should give every assistance. On 8 August, he went to see Sir Henry Rawlinson, War Office Director of Recruiting. Beveridge's Divisional Officer in Wales, OW Owen, went to see his War Office opposite number and reported: 'I found the office in absolute chaos and Major Lucas in a state bordering on distraction.'[16] Gradually, things took shape. By September, 32 exchanges were being used by recruiting officers as their base and the others were publicising the Services' recruitment arrangements. Beveridge was keen to help further. In particular, exchanges could help employers to find substitutes for men who enlisted. When it was agreed that MPs should engage in a recruitment campaign, Humbert Wolfe prepared a brief to assist them, emphasising the need for speakers to enlist employer and union support, to encourage employers to be flexible about substitutes and to guarantee reinstatement to men who enlisted.[17]

Wolfe was far-sighted enough to advise MPs that 'vital' workers from shipbuilding, munitions, saddlery, railways and food production should *not* be encouraged to enlist. This was a point that was largely overlooked in the disorganised enthusiasm which surrounded the outbreak of war. In the early months of the war, industries such as coal, steel, engineering, small arms, shipbuilding, chemicals and explosives lost to the armed forces between 15 and 25 per cent of their male workforce – a disastrous development for armaments production: 'From every shop men had gone suddenly and in large numbers, thus gravely embarrassing the machine at the very moment when it was to be called upon for unexampled effort.'[18] Following an initiative in Vickers, a system of 'badging' was introduced to protect vital war workers against the moral pressure to enlist.

Unemployment increased in the early months of the war owing to the dislocation of trade. But thereafter the pressures of labour supply pushed the country into unprecedented conditions of full employment and labour shortage. The numbers drawing unemployment benefit plummeted, building up the surplus in the unemployment fund.

Recruitment for the munitions industries

The most vital function of the exchanges in the early months of the war was to divert all the suitable labour they could to the government arsenals and the private sector munitions factories. Between August and December 1914, 18,000 work-people of all types were supplied to these establishments, but there was still a shortfall of 6000 armaments workers.[19] In January 1915, the exchanges ran a campaign to draw into the munitions factories engineering workers from firms engaged in commercial work. While the shortfall in the munitions factories went on increasing, only 942 men were transferred. This was not due to any dilatoriness on the part of the exchanges, which altogether had since the outbreak of war transferred not less than 100,000 work-people to engagements on national work.[20] The problem was that private employers did not wish to lose their skilled labour force but rather to participate in the munitions trade themselves. This failure led in the spring of 1915 to a major change of policy in which it was agreed no longer to confine munitions contracts to existing munitions companies but instead to distribute them much more widely and in addition to set up National Factories.

One of the problems arising from the shortage of labour in the munitions industries was the poaching of labour and the escalation of wages. Accordingly, in April 1915, regulations were introduced requiring employers in these industries to use the labour exchange when recruiting labour from more than 10 miles of their works and requiring labour exchanges to give priority to war work. This illustrates how the exchanges were increasingly becoming instruments of government direction of labour. In practice, however, the requirement upon employers proved unenforceable.[21]

In May 1915, the Ministry of Munitions was set up under Lloyd George, with Llewellyn Smith as General Secretary. Llewellyn Smith brought Beveridge over with him as Assistant General Secretary responsible for the supply and regulation of labour. Rey and Wolfe also joined the new ministry. All these importees retained their positions on the Board of Trade and their control of the exchanges – which was vital to their task of getting labour into the munitions industries and monitoring the overall labour position throughout the country. So the fate of the exchanges became entangled with that of this new ministry, which was itself an astonishing phenomenon, as Wolfe subsequently commented in his most exuberant style:

> *huge, industrious, all important, greatly directed by great men under the greatest of all. At one time, its staff outnumbered the population of Wakefield...it built factories in a day and forgot them in a fortnight, it did all the work that fell to its share and all the work that fell to everybody else's share...*[22]

Beveridge ceased to be responsible for the 'detailed working' of the labour exchanges from the beginning of 1915.[23] This was because he was increasingly drawn into fraught issues about state regulation of labour in the munitions industries. Beveridge favoured giving the Ministry of Munitions compulsory powers over munitions workers comparable to the powers of the War Office over army personnel.[24] Beveridge and Llewellyn Smith drew up the Munitions of War Bill, which became law on 1 July 1915. Even though toned down under union pressure, the Act was remarkably tough, including compulsory arbitration and the prohibition of strikes and lock-outs in factories engaged in war work. In 'controlled establishments', in order to stop poaching of labour, workers could not leave their jobs without a certificate proving their employer's consent – a provision that was deeply unpopular with the unions, modified in December 1915 and later abandoned. The Act also set up a War Munitions Volunteer Scheme to recruit additional labour from private employers.

As there continued to be a serious shortage of skilled men in the munitions industries, Beveridge went on pressing hard for 'dilution' (ie the large-scale introduction of semi-skilled labour, both male and female). His willingness to take legal action where necessary to enforce dilution gave rise during 1915–16 to the celebrated conflict between the Ministry of Munitions and 'Red Clydeside'. It also caused a fierce attack on Beveridge and his colleagues by the young Ernest Bevin, rising star of the trade union movement, at the annual conference of the TUC in 1916. Bevin claimed that 'behind Lloyd George there is another sinister crowd in the Civil Service who are preparing documents to be used against us. I refer to the chief officials of the Labour Exchanges'.[25] Jose Harris comments that 'the events of 1915–16 seem to have been largely responsible for a certain latent hostility between Beveridge and the union movement that lasted for the next quarter of a century'.[26]

There were two unfortunate implications of this affair for the exchanges. First, union hostility to Beveridge would reduce his involvement in government employment policies in the future – a loss for the exchanges, since Beveridge had the clearest vision of their potential role within wider employment policies. Secondly, the increased union suspicion of the exchanges made them more vulnerable once the war was over.

Tapping alternative sources of labour

The overriding priority of the exchanges during the war was to supply labour to meet the voracious needs of the munitions industries and other industries at a time when, altogether during the war, 5.5 million men joined the armed forces.

In his official history, Wolfe listed the following potential sources of additional labour:

- men engaged on inessential private work;
- retired men who could return to the labour market;
- boys of an age below that at which they would normally enter industry;
- women who were either not in work or who could move from inessential work;
- skilled men from the Dominions;
- aliens;
- enemy prisoners;
- men returning as unfit from the forces but able to work in industry; and
- persons capable of being trained up for skilled or semi-skilled work.

The process of diverting labour from inessential to essential work occurred partly through the awarding of contracts to munitions factories and partly through guidance by means of the labour exchanges. Government propaganda helped to draw retired men and boys into industry. But the really big source was female labour. Towards the end of 1914, the Board of Trade appealed to women to enrol for war service. Within a fortnight, 100,000 enrolled. But in the subsequent three months only 100 were placed in jobs. This reflected 'the prejudice against female labour that could not be killed by three months of war'.[27] Renewed efforts in 1915 were more effective. In March 1915, the

President of the Board of Trade appealed to women to join a special register at the labour exchanges. Employers were urged to send in their requirements for female labour. Government factories were required to recruit through the exchanges. As the war continued, the exchanges interviewed enormous numbers of women, arranged for their transfer to wherever they were needed, in many cases arranged reception at the end of the journey and even found them accommodation. The fact that the exchanges were a national network was invaluable for this kind of operation. The prejudice against female labour was largely broken down. The total number of women in employment rose by over 1.5 million between July 1914 and July 1918, predominantly in factories and offices. Between April 1916 and October 1917, the exchanges actually placed more women than men. At the end of the war, over 1.5 million women were substituting for men.[28]

Turning to overseas sources of labour, exchange officials were involved in missions to recruit skilled engineering labour in the Dominions. In the event, 7000 such workers were recruited, 5000 of them from Australia. It was a useful, though not vast, contribution. Recruitment of 'aliens' from the Continent was more fruitful. Altogether, 75,000 Belgians, Danes, Portuguese and Dutch were recruited. By far the largest numbers were Belgian refugees, who were encouraged to register at Folkestone labour exchange. At Birtley in the North East, a village was set up around a factory; it 'developed into a small but completely typical Belgian town...and had it not been for the Northumbrian climate the inhabitants might have believed that they were back in their own country'.[29]

Exchange officials also undertook the difficult task of trying to prise skilled men out of the armed forces in order to redeploy them in the munitions industry – a task which Lloyd George compared with 'getting through barbed wire entanglements with heavy guns'.[30] As the war progressed, they had the task of redeploying men from the forces who had been invalided out. This began to develop important expertise in the exchanges in the resettlement of 'disabled persons'.

Badging and reserved occupations

One of the key problems of wartime labour policy was that of reconciling the demand for additional men for the armed forces with the need to preserve skilled labour in the munitions industries. 'Badges', or exemptions, represented the first attempt to resolve this problem. This is not the place to set out the contorted history of this subject, which can be found elsewhere.[31] Here we focus on the role which the exchanges played in the developing system. Responsibility for 'badging' shifted from the employer to the Admiralty and War Office and then in July 1915 to the Ministry of Munitions. In August 1915, a National Register was launched. Local authorities issued forms to all males and females between the ages of 15 and 65 asking their occupation, whether they were on war work and any other skills they possessed. The names of all men of military age were to be recorded on pink forms – 'the Civil Service having a most inept sense of colour values' (Arthur Marwick).[32] In order to protect men in the munitions industries from enlistment, the labour exchanges marked with black stars the pink forms of men who were in occupations linked with munitions. It was found that, out of 5.2 million pink forms, 1.5 million were so starred.[33] In the Derby Scheme – the last attempt to recruit for the armed forces voluntarily – the 'starred' men were excluded, leaving a shortfall of recruits. At long last, in January 1916, Asquith introduced a Bill providing for conscription. Rarely can a clerical exercise by the exchanges have had such momentous consequences.

Grave misgivings on the part of the War Office and the Admiralty about the extent of 'badging' led in 1916 to a policy of 'debadging'. But there were continued problems as to which occupations, firms and industries should be exempt from military service, whether all men under 26 should be liable for military service and whether some form of conscription should exist for industrial workers as well as for military service. Some progress was made through a Reserved Occupations Committee of civil servants, set up in October 1915, to draw up a standard list of reserved occupations. Even so, the problems proved too difficult to resolve satisfactorily during 1916, whether by Cabinet Committees or by the trade unions under the Trade Cards Agreement.

Volunteer schemes

While there was hesitation about wholesale industrial conscription, there was mounting enthusiasm for special volunteer schemes under which people placed themselves voluntarily at the disposal of the government to be sent wherever their services were required, with the state paying travel and subsistence costs. This was a way both of harnessing patriotism and of getting labour to wherever it was required.

The first national scheme along these lines – and in some ways the most important – was the War Munitions Volunteer Scheme. It is also an interesting example of the way in which increasing authority was gradually delegated to the exchanges. It was set up in July 1915 under the Munitions of War Act. Wolfe states that Charles Rey's energy gave the scheme 'its first impetus'.[34] Enrolment was initially through special 'munition works bureaux' (half of which were in fact temporarily renamed labour exchanges) and then, after the bureaux had closed, through labour exchanges. In about 10 weeks, over 100,000 men enrolled. Placement under the scheme was ludicrously over-centralised, requiring the exchanges to send in the forms to Ministry of Munitions HQ along with any objections from employers. A committee of businessmen then had to consider 60,000 objections, using exchange staff and Home Office Inspectors to investigate the objections locally. By the end of September, 29,000 volunteers had been accepted by employers and 4500 had started work. The system was then decentralised, giving exchanges the duty of placing as well as enrolling. Also helpful was the introduction of 'dilution officers' to see that skilled labour was fully and economically used and to insist on release where appropriate. There was a serious shortage of housing in the armaments centres and, as the war was prolonged, service with the Volunteers became 'recognised as arduous and disagreeable'.[35]

One of the most remarkable volunteer schemes was the Liverpool Dock Labour Battalion, set up in 1915 by RF Williams, Divisional Officer for the labour exchanges in the North West. This unit comprised 1200 dockers 'all fully enlisted and subject to military discipline', employed in loading supplies for the front.[36] There were many other volunteer schemes involving the exchanges in enrolment. Altogether, the exchanges enrolled at least 435,000 people in special schemes during the war, including over 100,000 women, and even these figures may be under-estimates.[37]

Extension of unemployment insurance

In 1916, unemployment had fallen to 0.5 per cent, but there was concern about the serious risk of unemployment among munitions workers after the war had ended. Accordingly, in September 1916, unemployment insurance was extended to 1.25 million munitions workers. Beveridge favoured a much wider extension, but even this limited extension was unpopular since it imposed deductions from pay on workers for whom, at the time, unemployment seemed a remote prospect. Some workers caught up in the extension, such as the boot and shoe trades, successfully fought to be excluded. But with hindsight it can be argued that a much wider extension would have built up funds to alleviate the widespread unemployment that was to come.

The creation of the Ministry of Labour

Until December 1916, the exchanges, while in some ways a distinct service, or 'agency' to use modern parlance, were also very much part of the Board of Trade. From May 1915 onwards, the reporting lines of the exchanges had become more complex as their civil service chiefs also worked in the Ministry of Munitions. But their primary allegiance remained to the Board of Trade. However, at the end of 1916, all this changed.

In the political crisis of December 1916, the strains within the ruling coalition, between Asquith on the one hand and Lloyd George and his new Conservative allies, came to a head. The central issue was whether Asquith should continue to direct Britain's war effort, though the issues in contention included labour policy and the idea of 'National Service'.[38] Once Lloyd George emerged as the preferred alternative to Asquith, he needed Labour Party support if he was to have a secure majority in Parliament. His decision to create a Ministry of Labour can be seen, therefore, as designed primarily to win that support. The idea of a Ministry of Labour had a long history.[39] As early as 1892, Haldane had suggested the idea to Gladstone. Later the cause was taken up by the TUC and then by the Labour Party. In 1909, in the Minority Report of the Poor Law Commission, the Webbs gave a central role to a Ministry of Labour in their complex plans for tackling unemployment. There were repeated TUC and Labour Party proposals for such a ministry before and during the war. These culminated in 1916 in a TUC Resolution designed to give workers 'a direct, active and real part in the administrative affairs of the country' and a Labour Party plan for a Ministry of Industry and Labour. As Rodney Lowe has argued,[40] there were 'unresolved ambiguities' in the thinking about such a ministry. Was it to be a lobby for the working class in the corridors of power? Or was it to have the formidable powers necessary for the direction of labour in wartime and for tackling unemployment in peacetime? If the latter, what would be its relations with other departments, notably the Treasury? Would it be trusted with wide-ranging powers if it were seen as a working class lobby?

What emerged in December 1916 was more like a working class lobby in Whitehall. It was given responsibilities for industrial relations, reconstruction and the labour exchanges (now renamed employment exchanges). The first Minister of Labour was John Hodge, leader of the steel smelters' union, who lacked the prestige, imagination and administrative ability to establish the ministry on a sound foundation.[41] Like Bevin, he was suspicious of the labour exchange officials. As the first Permanent Secretary of the new ministry, Hodge chose David Shackleton, a respected former trade union official, Labour MP and National Health Commissioner, who lacked the administrative ability to carry weight in Whitehall. Beveridge, as Head of the Employment Department of the Board of Trade, suggested to Hodge that he should himself become joint permanent secretary. Hodge replied that he had wanted someone who had the confidence of the unions. He could not contemplate divided responsibility. He also felt that it would be too 'awkward' after this incident for Beveridge to serve in another capacity in the ministry.[42] Beveridge later learned that his appointment had been vetoed by certain trade unionists who felt him to be antipathetic to union interests. Beveridge commented sadly: 'I fear that the powers that now be are not very fond of either (Sir Hubert Llewellyn Smith) or me – we are out of Labour questions for a bit.'[43] He spent the rest of the war in food administration. The exchanges lost his unusual combination of vision, understanding of the labour market and administrative ability.

With characteristic irony, this most plebeian of ministries was:

> *palatially housed in Montague House, the ancestral home of the Dukes of Buccleuch, but palaces lend themselves to offices as little as offices are convertible into palaces. The magnificent reception rooms with their marble chimney pieces and their lofty painted ceilings were carved up into more or less spacious cells by hideous dun-coloured partitions... [the garden was] obliterated by a fungoid growth of unsightly huts... The whole effect was inexpressibly forlorn.*[44]

On 16 January 1917, the exchanges were formally transferred to the Ministry of Labour. They were now proportionally a much larger part of a much less weighty department. Hodge made Charles Rey the 'Assistant Secretary'[45] in charge of the employment exchanges. One of the effects of the creation of the new ministry was to reduce the autonomy of the exchanges. Under the Board of Trade, the Employment Department had been what we would now call an 'agency' – a 'self-contained unit responsible not only for general administration but for finance and establishments also'.[46] Now in the Ministry of Labour, the exchanges had to rely on the general finance and establishment departments of the ministry. While understandable in terms of the much smaller size of the new ministry, this would reduce flexibility, particularly when, after the war, these functions came under increasing Treasury pressure. The service would have to wait until 1974 before it would again have its own finance and personnel functions.

For all his limitations, Hodge had a commendable concern about the interactions between the state and the ordinary citizen, anticipating by 75 years some of the principles which John Major was to put forward in the Citizen's Charter. Hodge was deeply critical of the 'apparent lack of courtesy' of exchange officials towards the public. He decided on a programme of 'surprise visits' – a technique sometimes now known as 'mystery shopping'. At one exchange in Openshaw, Manchester, he stood at the counter for two or three minutes. There were a few officials behind the counter and none 'made a move to see what my business was'. Exasperated, he addressed one of them: 'Look here, young man, are you in charge here?' 'No.' When it turned out that both the manager and the under-manager were out, Hodge produced his card and said:

> *It will tell you who I am, and I am absolutely appalled. If this is the treatment usually meted out to workless men and workless women, God help them! ...In my opinion, each one of you behind the counter ought to be cleared out and live men put in your place.*

At the next Manchester exchange he visited, his experience was quite different, but he found that they had been warned on the phone. He then rang Openshaw to tell them that this was 'an abuse of the telephone and would be remembered against them'. He summed up:

> *a good many of the officials in the Exchanges were like wooden images, difficult to move, impossible to relax, with not an atom of the milk of human kindness in their hearts, nor that sympathetic feature which ought to be ever present in their dealing with their unfortunate fellow creatures.*[47]

Hodge's views about exchange officials were shared by some other trade union leaders at this time (page 42).

In August 1917, Hodge left for the Ministry of Pensions. His successor, GH Roberts, a printers' union leader, had even less weight in the labour movement than Hodge. The new ministry remained a Cinderella in Whitehall.

National Service

The Lloyd George Coalition Government created even more confusion in responsibility for labour mobilisation than had existed under Asquith. Far from giving the new Ministry of Labour the role of coordinating the distribution of labour, they gave that remit to a new Department of National Service, under Neville Chamberlain. But they failed to give Chamberlain a clear brief or the necessary authority over the other departments involved – the Ministries of Labour and Munitions, the War Office and the Admiralty. The result was a tragi-comedy of confusion and conflict. Chamberlain set to work with a will. He introduced tight control via the exchanges over all recruitment in key occupations. He also launched a National Service scheme designed to secure a mobile reserve of civilian labour – rather like the munitions volunteers. The government appealed to the whole male population aged 18–61 to enrol. It was for the exchanges to allocate individual volunteers to local vital war industries and to administer the system of travel and subsistence allowances. Local National Service Committees were set up. Chamberlain toured the country giving speeches. But against a target of 500,000 volunteers, only 273,000 men applied to the exchanges for enrolment, of whom 8842 were placed in employment.[48] Much effort had produced a small result. Many of those applying were already in 'protected occupations'. There was much criticism of administrative delays in following up applications. The impression that the scheme was a fiasco was reinforced by the information that three dukes, two admirals and a Director of the Bank of England had enrolled. It seemed unlikely that they would be interviewed for war work by the exchange clerks.[49]

From April 1917 onwards, Chamberlain concentrated on special appeals for 'substitution volunteers' to take the place of men called to war service. He formed a small Labour Advisory Committee of JH Thomas, Tom Shaw and Ben Tillett, who were highly critical of the exchanges (though this was by no means a unanimous view in labour circles).[50] On their advice, Chamberlain switched the interviewing and placing work away from the exchanges to his own staff. Privately, Chamberlain complained bitterly about Charles Rey, who 'makes trouble everywhere and is universally disliked because he is a mischievous chatterbox, always boasting, lying and intriguing'.[51] He believed that Rey leaked hostile stories about his department to *The Times*.[52] Chamberlain's decision to use his own staff intensified the conflict with the Ministry of Labour, but he none the less relied on the exchanges to provide vacancies for his own substitution officers to fill with volunteers. There were complaints that the vacancies were not made available, though by May he had to admit that the number of vacancies was very considerable.[53] During June

1917, relations between the two Departments 'dropped to a nadir from which they never recovered'.[54] This was partly due to a conflict over recruitment to the Women's Auxiliary Army Corps between Mrs Tennant and Violet Markham, who worked for Chamberlain, and Rey and Miss Durham of the Ministry of Labour, who maintained that they could supply all the women that the army needed without outside help. Lloyd George, Lord Derby and Milner were all involved in this imbroglio. Chamberlain described the conduct of the Ministry of Labour as 'perfectly insufferable throughout', but it was the ministry's line which prevailed.[55] In August 1917, an exasperated Chamberlain departed from office. Lloyd George later blamed Chamberlain's 'self-sufficient obstinacy' and 'rigid competency' for the failure[56] but Chamberlain understandably blamed Lloyd George's government for giving him an impossible brief.

The next attempt to coordinate labour was of a quite different character and proved remarkably successful. In August 1917, a Ministry of National Service was formed under Sir Auckland Geddes. From November 1917, this ministry was responsible for recruitment both to the army (taking over from the War Office) and to vital civilian war work. In contrast to Chamberlain's Department, the new ministry was integrated into the War Cabinet's overall war strategy through a powerful Cabinet Committee. Geddes saw how crucial it was for him to control the exchanges and tried to get them transferred to his ministry. But this was successfully resisted by Hodge, who pointed out to the War Cabinet that without the exchanges the Ministry of Labour would be a 'mutilated fragment with no very obvious reason for further existence'.[57] Geddes then tackled the problem in a different way. He persuaded Charles Rey to transfer temporarily to his ministry as Director of the National Labour Supply Department. In return, Rey persuaded Geddes to disband Chamberlain's 1000 remaining National Service Committees – seen as rival machinery to the exchanges. In this way, Geddes could use the exchanges both as instruments of recruitment and control and as sources of information on labour supply and demand. The information from the exchanges helped Geddes in his role of providing the War Cabinet with advice both on the allocation of labour to important industrial work and on military manpower issues. This was to prove invaluable to the War Cabinet in the acute pressures of the last year of the war.

None the less, inter-departmental battles continued. In March 1918, Geddes complained to Lloyd George that, 'Daily employers and trade unionists press upon me the need of improving the working of the employment exchanges.' When he explained to them that it was none of his business, they thought the whole government machine absurd. What was absurd was that Lloyd George had set up two ministries where only one was needed. But, despite these tensions, it was in this last year of the war that Britain came nearest to having a coherent approach to labour mobilisation.

Local Employment Committees

In 1910–11, Beveridge had set up 14 (later 16) Advisory Trade Committees of equal numbers of representatives of employers and work-people to provide advice on the new labour exchanges. But they covered too large an area to be effective, and during the war they 'became practically moribund'.[58] In 1917, a new system of Local Advisory Committees (later renamed Local Employment Committees or LECs) was introduced on a much more local basis and with the right to raise matters on their own initiative. Again, they consisted of equal numbers of employers' and workers' representatives – though not exclusively so. Hodge later said that he initiated this in order to help induce greater sensitivity on the part of exchange staff – and he encouraged Committee members to make 'surprise visits' themselves.[59] Other reasons for the setting up of the LECs were the prospective challenge of demobilisation and reconstruction and the elimination of Chamberlain's National Service Committees. By 1920, there were 302 LECs and this network of committees was to last for the next 50 years.

The 1920 Enquiry into the Work of Employment Exchanges was to hear numerous tributes to these LECs. For the exchanges, they were a valuable constituency of local support, an aid in some of the more invidious executive tasks of demobilisation, a useful sounding board and a curb on the insensitive behaviour which Hodge had detected among some exchange staff. At the same time, there was a risk of frustration on the part of the LECs since the exchanges were working under tight centralised instructions which the LECs could not influence. Various LEC representatives urged the 1920 Enquiry to propose that they should play a management role in relation to staffing and premises.

Conclusion

The exchanges had lost two of their founding fathers – Beveridge and Llewellyn Smith – in December 1916. At the end of the war, they lost the third – Charles Rey. After a period in 1919 in food administration on the Continent, he went to Abyssinia on unpaid leave to try his hand in business. The ministry did not want him back[60] and, when eventually he did return, it was to a fringe body – as Secretary of the Unemployed Grants Committee from 1927–9. Thereafter, true to his adventurous spirit, he became Resident Commissioner, Bechuanaland, for which service he was knighted in 1938. For all his belligerence of character, he had played an important part in building up the exchanges.

As the war had continued, the exchanges had become recognised as, in Wolfe's words, 'the machine upon which the whole Government system of labour supply rested'.[61] Table 3.2 shows how the activities of the exchanges built up during the war:

Table 3.2 *Business volumes of exchanges, 1913–18 (000s)*

Year	Registrations	Vacancies notified	Vacancies filled
1913	2836	1183	895
1914	3305	1437	1087
1915	3047	1761	1280
1916	3436	2017	1535
1917	3432	1974	1536
1918	3594	2040	1496

Source: 1920 Enquiry into the Work of Employment Exchanges, Minutes of Evidence, Appendix 3.

The wartime levels of registrations, vacancies and placings were all higher than peacetime levels. Placing work was more demanding in wartime. Exchange staff had to steer available labour into the munitions industries and to find suitable substitutes for skilled men. They had to take into account the increasing legal controls on employment. Much more of their work involved placing people away from their homes or enlisting and placing them on the various volunteer schemes. Above all, there was the task of integrating huge numbers of women into the world of work, often in occupations which up until then had been overwhelmingly male-dominated. The number of placings of women, which was only 193,000 in 1913, rose to 689,000 in 1916 and 700,000 in 1917 – in both years higher than the figure for men.

All this was achieved in a situation in which many of the exchange staff were on temporary contracts, replacing experienced men in the armed forces, and in which instructions from Central Office were changing with chaotic frequency as the government tried one expedient after another to resolve its labour problems. The 1920 Enquiry into the Work of Employment Exchanges concluded:

> *The Exchanges were an essential part of the machinery required for the mobilisation of the national resources for the purposes of the war; had they not existed, it would have been necessary to improvise some less adequate machinery for the purpose. It was fortunate that they were in existence and that Managers and Staff had acquired some knowledge of the psychology of employers and workmen and some experience of the transfer of labour... it would appear that the war work and the work connected with demobilisation was well done under adverse circumstances such as unsuitable buildings and improvised staffs, and that it must have involved immense strains on the Managers and other responsible officials.*

4

'The Ten Year Chaos', 1918–29

'In 1918...a report by one of the Committees set up by the Ministry of Reconstruction [pointed] to the prospect of widespread industrial dislocation and [urged] the generalisation of insurance. "Unless a scheme of general insurance is devised and launched at the earliest possible date it may be impossible to avoid the disastrous chaos of unorganised and improvised methods of relieving distress." Into that chaos, as nine months later the Armistice guns boomed out, the nation duly descended.'
(William Beveridge, 1930)[1]

Introduction

For the exchanges, the ten years after the war were dominated by a succession of desperate government expedients to deal with mass unemployment. As the quotation above indicates, Beveridge felt that, if the wartime governments had paid greater attention to the warnings that he and others were giving, much of the subsequent 'chaos', as he called it, could have been avoided. A more dispassionate observer might argue that no system of unemployment insurance, however much forward planning was exercised, could have coped with unemployment on the scale that was to hit the country from 1921 onwards.

The problems for the exchanges were all the greater because by the end of the war they suffered from widespread unpopularity. It might have been expected that their important wartime role would have consolidated their position as an indispensable public institution – no longer 'on trial', as Beveridge had felt them to be before the war. But this was not the case. After the war, many Conservatives and Liberals wanted to see the restoration of *laissez-faire* and saw the exchanges as part of the over-powerful state. Nor were the exchanges popular with the increasingly influential forces of organised labour. The conflicts between the 'labour exchange crowd' and the unions in 1916 (page 36) were not forgotten. Union members complained of officious regulation by exchange officials. By many on the left, the exchanges were seen as instruments of social control over the working class.

High unemployment was both the salvation and the bane of the exchanges. But for the huge problem which unemployment presented for the government, the exchanges might have been abolished in 1920–22. Instead, they were not only retained but expanded. They became indispensable state machinery for the payment, and regulation, of benefit to the great masses of the unemployed. To its credit, the Ministry of Labour did seek to develop the employment role of the exchanges, but they acquired a 'dole image' which would linger on long after mass unemployment had ended.

This chapter looks at the period up to the formation of the second Labour government in 1929. It starts with the Ministry of Labour's management of the exchanges. Then it follows through the dramatic sequence of events in the years after the war – demobilisation and the out-of-work donation, attempts to abolish the exchanges, the extension of unemployment insurance, the payment of unemployment relief to those without a contribution record and the conflicts surrounding the control of abuse. It goes on to describe the efforts of the ministry to build up employment work despite the unhappy image of the exchanges with unemployed clients.

The Ministry of Labour and the management of the exchanges

The previous chapter described the 'chaotic' wartime origins of the Ministry of Labour (pages 39–41). It continued to be seen by politicians as one of the 'least important ministries' right up to 1939.[2] There were five Ministers of Labour in this period:

- November 1918–February 1920   Sir Robert Horne (Coalition)
- February 1920–October 1922   T J Macnamara (Coalition)
- October 1922–January 1924   Sir Montague Barlow (Conservative)
- January 1924–November 1924   Tom Shaw (Labour)
- November 1924–May 1929   Sir Arthur Steel-Maitland (Conservative)

For the most part, these Ministers were not political stars. Only one of them rose to high office – Sir Robert Horne, who subsequently became Chancellor of the Exchequer. The others were not negligible figures but they did not match up to the magnitude of the problems confronting the ministry. Macnamara (1920–22), a Coalition Liberal, persuaded the Cabinet greatly to widen unemployment relief. Sir Montague Barlow (1922–24) stoutly defended the ministry at a time when many Conservative backbenchers pressed for its abolition. Tom Shaw, the first Minister of Labour in a Labour government, faced an almost impossible task in reconciling party policy with political reality.[3] Steel-Maitland, though knowledgeable as a former researcher for the Poor Law Royal Commission, lacked the incisiveness and political weight needed to win battles in Whitehall.[4]

The fact that the ministry survived the hostility of many Conservative backbenchers and threatened abolition by the Geddes Committee in 1922 was due in part to its role in industrial relations. But no less important was its role in relation to unemployment. Unemployment was discussed at Cabinet level with remarkable frequency and anxiety. The ministry was the main repository of expertise on the subject and in these pre-Keynesian days the main instrument of Government response. Indeed, Alan Bullock writes that at this time the ministry was 'mainly concerned with unemployment insurance'[5] and a former official recalled: 'it was widely believed in the office that unemployment insurance was a *sine qua non* for (promotion to) Assistant Secretary'.[6] The ministry was in this period more a 'social' than an 'economic' ministry.

The ministry built up an administrative team of remarkable calibre, many of whom played a key role in the Second World War, while after the war no less than 10 of them became Permanent Secretary or equivalent.[7] For all its lack of glamour, the ministry offered invaluable experience in sensitive political issues affecting huge numbers of citizens, in dealing with powerful interest groups and in organising provision for people throughout the country.

The ministry's first Permanent Secretary, Sir David Shackleton, was shunted off sideways in 1920 to become Chief Labour Adviser, being replaced by Sir James Masterton-Smith, with whom he had overlapped for a time. Masterton-Smith was a career civil servant, originally in the Admiralty, and was installed in the ministry to improve its efficiency, a goal which he pursued with such zeal as to suffer a nervous breakdown.

In 1921, Masterton-Smith was succeeeded by Sir Horace Wilson who was Permanent Secretary from 1921 to 1929. Of all the officials in the ministry's 80-year history, none to this day is better known than Wilson. He subsequently became Head of the Civil Service and Chamberlain's closest adviser at the time of Munich. He has been compared to Wolsey.[8] His background was in industrial relations and it is likely that, on issues to do with unemployment insurance and the exchanges, he relied heavily on Tom Phillips (later Sir Thomas Phillips). Phillips[9] emerges as the most influential official in the inter-war years from the point of view of the exchanges. Like Wilson, he came from humble origins – from a small school in mid-Wales to Oxford, where he proved academically brilliant. Entering the Board of Trade, he was one of Beveridge's key lieutenants and played an important role in the drafting of the National Insurance Act 1911. From this formative experience arose his lifelong love for unemployment insurance. For several years, he remained responsible for policy on unemployment insurance. By 1920, he was leading on the exchanges as well. Then he was promoted to Second Secretary in 1924 and to acting Permanent Secretary in 1929. He was a brilliant draftsman and was described as 'the best politician in Whitehall'. RA Butler described him as having 'an acute brain and a compassionate heart'.[10] But if it is the case that organisations take on the character of their leader, he was not the ideal role model for the employment exchanges, being 'curiously anonymous' and withdrawn. He was hardly the man to put the exchanges on the map and make them popular.

Moreover, his preoccupation with unemployment insurance reinforced the dominance of that aspect of the exchanges' work.

Other influential officials included Humbert Wolfe – also in Beveridge's original team, JFG Price and Wilfred Eady, who is described as having a quicksilver mind and radical instincts, though ultimately working within the system. He was interested in the underlying problems of the labour market and in developing the potential of the exchanges as labour market instruments. One of the strengths of the ministry at this time was its ability to harbour divergent views. At one extreme was FG Bowers, the Accountant General, who justified his massive Claims and Records Office at Kew on the grounds that it provided a bulwark against 'habitual shirkers'.[11] At the other was John Hilton, who was in charge of research and statistics and who carried out his own survey in order to challenge what he saw as oppressive policing of benefit (pages 64–5).[12]

In this period, the exchange service was losing its character as a distinct management unit and becoming absorbed into the overall Ministry of Labour machine. We saw in Chapter 3 that from 1917 it ceased to have its own finance and establishments functions (page 41). Then in 1920 Masterton-Smith's review of the organisation of the ministry's Employment Department (including the exchanges) led him to conclude that:

> *a division of work in HQ as between determination of policy and its execution is not practical and that the proper method of organisation is to place the whole of the Employment Department under the control of a Principal Assistant Secretary [Tom Phillips – see above] under whom should be an appropriate number of Assistant Secretaries and a Chief Inspector responsible for the practical efficiency of the Exchanges.*[13]

This rejection of an Agency concept for the service led to the abolition of the General Manager[14] post which Llewellyn Smith had installed and which had contributed to the exchanges' performance. The last holder of that post was JB Adams (page 21), who returned to being a Divisional Controller in Leeds. An inspection function was not new, but Masterton-Smith's review made the Chief Inspector a powerful figure with 'wide responsibilities for running the Exchange and Divisional Office machine'.[15] This substitution of 'inspection' for 'management' (reflecting both the dominance of insurance and Treasury influence) affected the culture of the service. It produced a huge and efficient regulatory machine rather than a decentralised management organisation which encouraged initiative among managers at all levels. Indeed, at this time exchange administration was exceedingly centralised: for instance, HQ had to be consulted if the washing of towels and dusters cost more than one shilling a dozen. In 1927, the Divisional Controllers secured some modest increases in delegation.[16]

Masterton-Smith's changes left the functions of the Exchange Service (apart from finance and establishments) concentrated in the Employment and

Insurance Department of ministry Headquarters. The Principal Assistant Secretary of that Department, Tom Phillips until 1924 and then JFG Price, could be seen as in effect the 'chief executive'.

The post-war atmosphere

Before looking at the role of the exchanges in conditions of mass unemployment, it is important to look at their role immediately after the war ended. This was a very unusual period in our history. Universal suffrage was almost complete,[17] making politicians more than ever sensitive to the shifts of public opinion. The Coupon Election of December 1918 did not stabilise the country but produced an uneasy Coalition Government combining a minority of Lloyd George radicals with a majority of Conservatives. Ministers were nervous of the public mood. George Orwell later wrote:

> *during and just after the war... England was nearer revolution than she has been since or had been for a century before. Throughout almost the whole nation there was running a wave of revolutionary feeling which has been reversed and forgotten, but which has left various deposits of sediment behind.*[18]

The Cabinet received regular reports of revolutionary discontent. It was against this frenetic background that the government determined its employment policies, in which the exchanges were to play a key part.

Demobilisation

1919 was an extraordinary year for the exchanges. It was the year when millions of British people moved back from war jobs to the civilian labour market. The exchanges were the key state instrument for achieving this transition and supporting people through it. Their staff built up from around 6000 in March 1918 to a peak of over 21,000 in June 1919.[19]

The government had long anticipated that the task of redeploying labour from war work to peace would be extraordinarily testing. They knew that the Napoleonic War had been followed by high unemployment and widespread unrest. In August 1916, Asquith, then still Prime Minister, commented in a discussion about demobilisation with a trade union deputation: 'I don't suppose a more complex problem has ever presented itself to any nation.'[20]

During the war, although its outcome remained uncertain, the government devoted much thought to 'reconstruction'. At the end of the war, they created a Civil Department of Demobilisation and Resettlement within the Ministry of Labour, under a Controller General, Sir Stephenson Kent. There was an array of new units concerned with various aspects of demobilisation, often staffed by former serving officers. The exchanges were 'placed at the disposal of this

Department to assist it in every way possible'.[21] Apart from Sir Stephenson Kent, who controlled much else besides, there does not seem to have been any single Director in charge of the exchanges at this exceptionally demanding moment in their history, though familiar figures like Tom Phillips and Humbert Wolfe were closely involved.[22]

The process of resettlement was governed by forms. Two-and-a-half million forms were filled in by men in the forces and sent into the exchanges' Central Clearing House for distribution to the exchanges. The exchanges received a further 2.5 million forms from employers. The exchanges vetted these forms and made recommendations on priorities to the new Local Employment Committees. The demobilisation plan made the speed of a man's release from the armed forces depend on the ability of industry to absorb him, with priority for the 'Pivotal men' – those vital to the industries of reconstruction – and then the 'Slip' men,[23] men who were both asked for by their former employers and who had themselves claimed an offer of employment.

Arthur Marwick describes the scheme as 'grotesquely misconceived',[24] mainly because it disregarded the claims of those who had been in the services for several years. Whatever its intrinsic merits, it was highly unpopular. In February 1919 Winston Churchill, as War Minister, abandoned it in favour of a first-in first-out system and speeded up the process of discharge. Over 2.5 million were demobilised in the first four months of 1919.[25] During 1919, the exchanges placed over 250,000 discharged ex-servicemen and assisted the resettlement of many others, eg by the provision of grants for tools. Fortunately, there was at the time abundant employment.

One of the most disturbing legacies of the war was the large number of disabled ex-servicemen. In September 1919, a 'King's National Roll' was set up for those employers who agreed to employ a given percentage of disabled employees (normally 5 per cent). The exchanges energetically promoted this scheme and by the end of 1920 23,500 employers were enrolled and 259,000 disabled men were provided for in this way.[26] They also steered disabled ex-servicemen into government training schemes, which were in addition provided for men whose apprenticeships had been interrupted by the war.

The release of munitions workers was controlled by a Demobilisation Board created by the Ministry of Munitions. The aim was again a gradual release to minimise unemployment, but there was also a need to prevent them from getting an unfair advantage over ex-servicemen. The exchanges helped people to move back to their home areas and sought vacancies for them.

A major problem in demobilisation was the displacement of women who had been working in munitions or replacing men in other industries. The number of women on the live register rose from 51,000 in October 1918 to 500,000 in March 1919. In tackling this problem, the Women's Departments of the exchanges were assisted by Women's Sub-Committees of the LECs. In 1919, they placed 342,000 women and in 1920 213,000. Some 300,000 of these placings were in domestic service, despite its unpopularity with many women who had tasted the greater freedom and remuneration of factory work.[27]

The exchanges' achievements in demobilisation led George Roberts, Minister of Labour up to November 1918, to comment that it was 'almost a miracle of organisation to have been able to release five million men on demobilisation and to resettle the larger proportion of them in civil life so smoothly and expeditiously'.[28]

The out of work donation

In 1916, Beveridge had anticipated the risk of unemployment at the end of the war and had wanted a big extension of unemployment insurance to cater for it, but against widespread industrial opposition the Board of Trade was only able to extend insurance to a small extent. In 1917, the Ministry of Reconstruction asked Beveridge to chair a sub-committee on unemployment insurance. In February 1918, the Sub-Committee recommended the earliest possible introduction of a scheme of general insurance. The Minister of Labour, George Roberts, was sympathetic to Beveridge's recommendation, but no action was taken for a further extension of insurance before the war ended.[29]

It had been decided quite early in the war that a non-contributory 'out of work donation' should be paid to ex-servicemen who were not immediately resettled in employment. But other preparations for peace were neglected by the War Cabinet. When in October 1918 victory suddenly and unexpectedly came in sight, Addison, the Minister of Reconstruction, hurriedly persuaded the Cabinet that the out of work donation should be extended to civilians. As Tom Phillips recalled a few months later, the government had suddenly 'woken up to the great amount of unemployment that was certain to occur'. Their primary objective was 'to prevent the dangers that would arise from the existence of great numbers of destitute unemployed'.[30] The Ministry of Labour had little or no warning of this vast extension of its responsibilities. There were only two or three weeks to prepare the scheme and get hold of the extra staff and premises before the donation became payable on 25 November 1918.[31] The expansion was achieved not by increasing the number of exchanges but, as in 1912–13, by the use of local agents, who became known as 'Branch Managers' and whose offices were renamed 'Branch Employment Offices'. Thus in 1919 there were 392 exchanges and 1019 Branch Employment Offices.[32]

Many of the conditions for receiving the donation were similar to those for insurance, such as daily signing and willingness to take suitable vacancies. This, as well as the lack of preparation, may have helped to cause criticism of the exchanges for the way they handled this work. For instance, female applicants were in most cases expected to take domestic service vacancies.[33] The scheme lasted only a year for civilians, but until the end of March 1921 for ex-servicemen.

The volumes of work were huge and unprecedented, amounting to over one million payments in a week at their peak in May 1919. Up to the end of May 1920, 2.25 million ex-servicemen and women and 2.5 million civilians had applied for donations. Senior ministry officials worried about the effect of the donation on the image of the exchanges. JB Adams, the General Manager, said:

> *Nothing has done the Exchanges so much harm in my opinion as the out of work donation because it brought everybody to us, it brought all sorts of people who in the ordinary course of events had never come to an Exchange at all, and we have had many complaints by organised labour of the kind of people who were receiving the out of work donation.*[34]

From the start of the exchanges, it had been a priority to get them used by the 'respectable' working man, and this was felt to be in jeopardy. It was at this time that the term 'dole' came into common use.

In view of press criticism of the way the exchanges administered the donation, an inquiry was set up under Lord Aberconway in May 1919. The inquiry report emphasised the scale of the task and said that 'on the whole the work of the staff has been exceedingly good'. It also said that the exchange premises were in many cases inadequate and unsuitable and there was a need to reduce reliance on temporary staff, who were continually leaving for other work.[35]

The Barnes Enquiry into the employment exchanges

In 1919–20, the exchanges were deeply unpopular. A virulent press campaign was waged against them and they came near to being abolished. The *Daily Mail* described the exchanges as:

> *a form of waste in view of the general condemnation of their uselessness by both workers and employers that ought to be stopped by a Chancellor of the Exchequer who does his duty to the country.*[36]

This may seem a strange public response to the extraordinary efforts the exchanges had made during the war and during demobilisation. But there were a number of reasons for their unpopularity. First, the service's role during and after the war had involved unprecedented interference with the freedom of employers and workers. After the war, there was a fierce reaction against government regulation and a wish to get back to the traditions of *laissez-faire*. Secondly, it was easy to point to examples of mistakes on the part of the exchanges, whether due to last minute changes of mind by politicians at the centre or to inexperienced staff in the exchanges. Thirdly, there was concern about the nation's post-war finances and a search for economies. Finally, there may have been an element of self-interest in the hostile press coverage about the exchanges. Newspaper profits depend in part on job advertising, which could benefit from the demise of the exchanges.

Office of Hope

Macnamara, then Minister of Labour, decided to hold a Committee of Enquiry – the first and in some ways the most high powered of at least half a dozen major reviews of the employment service that are chronicled in this history. The Chairman was George Barnes MP, a prominent Labour politician and former trade unionist, who had been Labour's representative in the War Cabinet and had thrown in his lot with Lloyd George in the Coupon Election of December 1918. The Committee included four other MPs, together with employers, Local Employment Committee chairmen, two women members and Professor Macgregor, a distinguished economist. Macnamara decided that the Terms of Reference should be: 'to examine the work and administration of the Employment Exchanges in Great Britain and to advise as to their future.' Macnamara explained to his officials: 'This makes it possible to recommend abolition – the policy is courageous; but I don't think we need to be afraid.'[37]

The Committee was established in June 1920 at a time when the Unemployment Insurance Bill (page 59) was going through Parliament. This overshadowed the Committee's work, since it proposed a massive extension of the coverage of unemployment insurance. So the overriding question facing the Committee became whether the extended insurance scheme could be administered in any other way than through the exchanges. The only alternative seriously considered was that it should be devolved to industrial bodies, building on the movement for Joint Industrial Councils launched by the Whitley Report in 1917.

In the Committee's lengthy public hearings, many witnesses gave hostile evidence about the exchanges. One of the most hostile was George Askwith, formerly Beveridge's superior in 1910 when the exchanges had been introduced. Askwith had retired from the civil service in 1919 after a major conflict with Lloyd George and the War Cabinet over industrial relations problems and had been made a Peer. He had become a fervent advocate of free enterprise and was later to form a Middle Class Union.[38] At the Committee hearings, he broke ranks with his former colleagues and delivered an astonishing diatribe against the exchanges, claiming that they were Germanic institutions:

> *It was this system, so suited to German ideas of organisation and so useful to a nation which wanted to know where every man was and what every man could do, which was hastily imposed upon this country... Its suitability to the United Kingdom and the effects it might have on relations of employers and employed were not thought out. German organisation seemed such an excellent ideal.*[39]

He argued that the cost of the exchanges with their 'army of officials' was 'out of all proportion to their value'. They had been a 'disintegrating force, rather than bringing classes together', since they allowed employers simply to divest themselves of surplus labour to the exchange, rather than taking responsibility for the unemployment problems in their own industry. The exchanges were run by 'officials who know little of industry' under a 'Minister who knows less'. He considered that industry bodies should administer extended unemployment insurance. Altogether, his criticisms were sweeping but imprecise, and Committee members picked holes in them.

Askwith's former colleagues defended the exchanges. Llewellyn Smith, now in a somewhat nebulous role as Economic Adviser to the Government, claimed that the primary purpose of the labour exchanges had always been to 'afford machinery for administering unemployment insurance' and that they remained essential for this purpose. As regards their subsidiary purpose of bringing together people and jobs, it was too early to determine their value in peacetime, though he praised their wartime service as 'wonderfully good...under very trying conditions'.[40]

Beveridge also gave evidence. He had not been involved with the exchanges since 1916 and was now knighted and Director of the London School of Economics. His defence of the exchanges was robust but lacked the compelling power of his evidence to the Royal Commission in 1907. He denied Askwith's charge about German methods – 'the actual methods are quite different'. For him, unlike Llewellyn Smith, unemployment insurance was a secondary object of the exchanges, even if important as providing the work test. Their first object was to 'diminish unemployment... by reducing...the intervals between one job and the next'. It was clear that 'with labour remunerated at something like 2s an hour, a very small average saving of time is sufficient to make the Exchanges pay thoroughly'. This was to become a favourite argument half a century later. He said that demobilisation alone more than justified the existence of the exchanges. Without them, 'chaos and disorder would have been unavoidable'. Current problems were partly due to government delays in introducing universal insurance. He dismissed as hopelessly unrealistic the idea that unemployment insurance could be entirely delivered by industry councils. Much of the criticism of the exchanges was ill-informed. The idea that skilled men did not use them was belied by the figures. Many big employers were unaware of the extent to which their firms used the exchanges. Nor were the exchanges simply his brainchild:

> *the return to old conditions is impracticable. The Exchanges were not started as the result of anybody's theory; they were recommended unanimously by the Poor Law Commission, which made the most complete study of unemployment as well as distress.*

Perhaps conscious that the achievements of the exchanges so far had fallen short of his earlier vision, he said that

> *the Exchanges have never yet had a fair chance of development. They have always been doing something else than their main job and there has never been time for a systematic overhauling of their administration.*[41]

Criticisms of the exchanges from both employers and union representatives included:

- claims that exchanges were not worth using because jobs could be obtained, and labour procured, more directly; and that the exchanges only handled the unskilled and 'riff raff'; these criticisms were not unanimous; for instance, the Managing Director of J Lyons praised the exchanges' role in recruiting catering workers for his company at the Crystal Palace;
- inadequate or unsuitable staff, too few with relevant technical knowledge, sometimes a lack of tact or 'too little humanness behind the counter';[42]
- undue bureaucracy; the workman was 'dragooned the moment he goes to an Exchange';[43] an 'obsession with forms'– some 2000 a year;[44]
- excessive costs;
- poor buildings;
- fictitious placing statistics; one journalist claimed that they were deceptive to the point of fraud but was unable to substantiate this to the Committee;[45] and
- claims that the Local Employment Committees should have executive power.

The chief Departmental spokesmen were Thomas Phillips, Head of the Employment Department, and JB Adams, the General Manager. Adams gave the more forceful defence. He claimed that Britain was in a much happier position than other countries after the war due largely to the efforts of the exchanges to secure the reinstatement of ex-servicemen. He complained bitterly of the 'entire absence of fairness in the campaign of the press against the Employment Exchanges which has had a very serious effect on the staff and on the public'. Chancing his arm as a civil servant, he deplored 'the absence of any support from our employers', ie the government.

The Committee was puzzled by the 'remarkable conflict of evidence'[46] before them, but their mind was made up for them by the Unemployment Insurance Act 1920, which came into effect in November 1920. In their report, they told Macnamara that the new Act 'has affected the whole problem before us and has vitally affected our conclusions'.[47] They concluded that the idea of 'contracting out' work under the Act to industry bodies and abolishing the exchanges was 'quite impracticable'. There was no actuarial basis for forecasting the level of unemployment by industry. Demarcation of industries would be very difficult. Industry was not ready for the compulsion that would be involved. Indeed, it was unclear how much permanent support there was for insurance through industries. Finally, such a fundamental change in the basis of National Insurance could not be seriously entertained so soon after the introduction of the Act. The Committee was 'forced to the conclusion that the Employment Exchanges must be retained as a national system and are a necessary corollary to the State system of unemployment insurance'.[48]

The Committee said that 'press complaints of incivility and lack of tact and patience were ... unfounded'.[49] They were more cautious about the value of the exchanges to industry. Current placing levels of about one million a year were not satisfactory. However, the exchanges 'had had little opportunity of perfecting their work as placing agencies'. The Committee concluded that it 'was in the interests of the national economy that they should be retained'.[50] They were 'capable of considerable improvement', including the following:

1. Premises should be improved and the exchanges should be centralised in each area, reducing the number of buildings in use.
2. There should be two channels of recruitment, one using civil service competitions and the other based on 'industrial knowledge and the ability to deal with men'.
3. Officers dealing with employers and workpeople should be named 'Registrars' rather than 'clerks', should be paid well enough to attract good candidates, should be promotable without a change of duties and should periodically visit industrial works.
4. Local Employment Committees should become more executive, with the ability to influence staffing, promotion, premises and unemployment measures.
5. Exchanges should not be available to employers or workpeople during a trade dispute.
6. Canvassing (in modern parlance 'marketing') should be curtailed.
7. Registration of still employed workers should be discouraged.
8. The number of branch offices should be curtailed, perhaps by use of post offices.
9. Central and Divisional activity and staff, and the number of forms, should be curtailed.
10. Responsibility for juvenile employment should rest with a single Department.

Masterton-Smith, the Permanent Secretary, welcomed the report as it gave a 'mandate for an immediate overhaul and scrutiny' of the service, which was what he had wanted ever since he came to the ministry.[51] However, in practice, the Barnes recommendations did not have much influence, apart from the main conclusion – that the exchanges were to survive. The main outcomes were:

- The recommendations on staff and premises were not strongly pursued (pages 68–70).
- The LECs did not become executive, mainly because this would cut across the minister's responsibility to Parliament.
- There was fortunately no ban on canvassing employers or on servicing still employed registrants.
- The number of branch offices did decline from 1049 in 1920 to 456 in 1939, but in general post offices were not found to be a suitable alternative.
- Efforts were made to curtail staffing at Central and Divisional offices, but these were overtaken by a vast increase in insurance work.

- Responsibility for juvenile employment was further reviewed and from 1927 policy responsibility was vested fully in the Ministry of Labour. Local education authorities retained a choice as to whether to provide a juvenile employment service themselves or leave this to the exchanges. In 1933, the exchanges still provided the service in 224 out of 368 exchange areas in England and Wales and everywhere except Edinburgh in Scotland.[52]

The report provided valuable support for the exchanges in the frenzied post-war atmosphere. It firmly adopted the 'benefit control' model of the service as its primary rationale. However, reflecting the *laissez-faire* atmosphere of the time, it was superficial in its analysis of the labour market role of the exchanges, ignoring much of Beveridge's original thinking on the subject. The Committee's discouragement of marketing and of registrants who were already employed betrayed a narrow view. On the other hand, the Committee showed good understanding of the importance and credibility of the front-line staff of the exchanges and the ministry should have taken these points more seriously.

The Geddes Committee on National Expenditure

It was not long before the issues apparently settled by Barnes were reopened in the context of government attempts to cut expenditure. In 1922, Sir Eric Geddes' Committee on National Expenditure proposed the abolition of the exchanges and their parent ministry. However, the Committee recognised the problem of the exchanges' responsibility for unemployment insurance. Their impression[53] was that

> *the real justification for the continuance of the Exchanges is not so much the finding of work for the unemployed, the original function of the Exchanges, but the fact that they afford a machinery for testing the validity of claims to unemployment benefit by offering to workpeople such employment as has been notified to the Exchanges.*

So the Committee asked the ministry whether there was a 'more economic means...for dealing with unemployment insurance'. None was found, and it was this which protected the exchanges and the ministry from an early demise. As Humbert Wolfe commented:

> *with a million and a quarter unemployed, with the universal system of unemployment insurance administered through the Exchanges and with no early prospect of insurance by industries, the Employment Department, by far the largest section with nine tenths of the Ministry of Labour, must remain, at least until some new system of insurance can be found.*[54]

The ministry could argue with justice that their insurance system based on the exchanges was economically and efficiently run and that it would be risky for the government to discard it in favour of some new and untried system. The Geddes axe hovered over the exchanges for a long time, causing great uncertainty and frustrating efforts to place more staff on a permanent basis. It was not until late in 1923 that the threat was lifted.

The extension of unemployment insurance

The survival of the exchanges in 1920–22 rested primarily on the Unemployment Insurance Act 1920. This Act represented policies that Beveridge had advocated since 1916, but more immediately it arose from the uneasiness of Ministry of Labour officials about the out of work donation. They felt that the lack of a contributory basis in the donation had led to its being exploited. It had been an *ad hoc* and unplanned response to the risk of unemployment, whereas what was wanted was a long-term approach. Unemployment insurance also had attractions for the Treasury, since it offered a source of revenue other than taxation. Thus the donation 'achieved the not unremarkable feat of uniting the ministry and the Treasury in a determined search for a workable scheme of contributory insurance'.[55]

In the summer of 1919, an extended insurance scheme was devised by an Inter-Departmental Committee, chaired by EC Cunningham, the able Second Secretary in the Ministry of Labour, and including Beveridge and Watson, the Government Actuary. Ministers, still deeply uneasy about popular unrest, agreed to introduce legislation. The Act extended unemployment insurance to some 11.75 million workers, comprising non-manual workers earning not more than £250 per year and all manual workers, except for those in agriculture, domestic service and certain groups in permanent employment such as public servants and railwaymen. It was hoped that many industries would contract out and run their own schemes, but due to the depression only the insurance and banking industries did so. The terms of the new scheme were largely based on the 1911 Act, safeguarding the actuarial viability of the scheme by such devices as a maximum of 15 weeks' benefit in a year and not more than one week of benefit for every six weeks of contributions.

The exchange staff had to work very hard to introduce the new scheme. They had to publicise the new provisions, and obtain a signed statement of particulars from, and issue an unemployment book to, each one of the eight million additional persons brought within scope of the scheme. These tasks were successfully accomplished by the due date – 8 November 1920.

The unemployment problem

By November 1920, when the extended unemployment insurance scheme came into force, unemployment was already rising, and then rose with 'fearful rapidity...from 5 to 15 per cent in four months'.[56] In 1921 it became clear that the nation faced a slump, with 1.8 million, or 17 per cent, unemployed out of those insured under the new Act. (Total unemployment has been estimated at some 2.2 million or 12 per cent altogether.) Moreover, the high unemployment of 1921 was not a flash in the pan. Table 4.1 shows that from 1921 and 1929 unemployment among the insured population exceeded 10 per cent in every year except 1927. (If one takes total unemployed as a percentage of total employees, then in every year except 1927 unemployment exceeded 7.5 per cent).[57] Even these high unemployment figures were considerable underestimates of the unused labour potential of the country, since one of the responses to the slump was to discourage married women from working altogether. The social impact of these high levels of unemployment was all the greater since they were not spread evenly across the country but concentrated particularly in the industrial regions of Wales, Scotland and the North, which had been traditionally dependent upon mining, shipbuilding, textiles and iron and steel. This concentration gave rise to severe problems of long-term unemployment in the 'depressed areas'. Table 4.1 shows that there were fluctuations in the level of unemployment, with some easement in 1923–24 and 1926–27, in each case followed by a rise.

Table 4.1 *Unemployment among the insured population, 1921–29*

Year	Number unemployed 16–64 (000s)	Insured unemployed as % of insured employees
1921	1840	16.9
1922	1541	14.3
1923	1292	11.7
1924	1152	10.3
1925	1289	11.3
1926	1441	12.5
1927	1141	9.7
1928	1267	10.8
1929	1276	10.4

Source: Office of National Statistics, *Labour Market Trends*, Jan 1996, Crown Copyright.

The unprecedented level of unemployment generated unrest. In 1921 there were meetings and demonstrations by the unemployed in many industrial areas, often held outside the local employment exchange. The TUC called for 'work or maintenance'. More extreme agitators, such as the Communist Wal Hannington, set up the National Unemployed Workers' Movement (NUWM) in order to mobilise the unemployed as a political force.[58] There were raids on workhouses to secure outdoor relief and on factories to bring overtime to an end. In the winter of 1922–23 there was the first post-war Hunger March of the unemployed to London and the NUWM was to organise a series of further spectacular marches.

The governments of this period did not believe that unemployment could be overcome by expansionist economic policies. Instead, they pinned their faith on economic orthodoxy, seeking balanced budgets and returning to the Gold Standard in 1925.

Thus the main government response to high unemployment was to provide financial relief to those affected by it. The Unemployment Insurance Act 1920 had been intended to ensure that contributions from employers, employees and the state would provide the necessary funding for unemployment benefit, but its rules were devised for short-term unemployment, not for long-term structural unemployment. Moreover, there had been no time to build up large reserves in the Unemployment Fund. This left a dangerous gap in government policy. Huge numbers of people now faced periods of unemployment far longer than the cover provided for them under the Act. Ministers were unwilling to consign all these people to the discredited safety net of the Poor Law. Rather than re-think the whole basis of unemployment relief, the government used – or rather misused – the system of unemployment insurance in order to relieve those who were not entitled to benefit under the rules of the scheme. Thus the responsibility for responding to the unprecedented and chronic unemployment crisis was thrust on to the exchanges.

The decline of insurance

This is not the place to describe the tortuous history of unemployment insurance in the 1920s, which is well described elsewhere.[59] In simple terms, what happened was that two types of benefit were provided by the exchanges – 'covenanted benefits' (those that were earned by contributions under the rules of the scheme) and 'uncovenanted benefits' (which were paid at the ministry's discretion to those who had exhausted their right to benefit). It was a sure sign of ministerial discomfort that there were constant name changes for the latter kind of benefit – 'extended benefits', 'transitional benefits', 'transitional payments' and finally 'unemployment assistance'. In November 1921, dependants' allowances were introduced. Until 1930, these provisions were financed from the 'Unemployment Fund' which plunged into deficit as a result. Under Conservative governments, though not under Labour, expenditure was controlled through a means test (from 1922–24 and from 1925–28). There were also requirements that first those on uncovenanted benefits and later all benefit recipients should prove that they were 'genuinely seeking work'. While the left attacked the system as ungenerous, the right-wing press attacked it as supporting 'scroungers'. For instance, on 18 April 1925, the *Daily Mail* printed an article with the following headlines:

THE VICIOUS DOLE
STAGGERING COST
£50,000,000 A YEAR
DESTROYING THE WILL TO WORK

In 1925, Sir Arthur Steel-Maitland, then Minister of Labour, set up the Blanesburgh Committee to sort out the muddle. An unnamed Ministry of Labour official (perhaps Tom Phillips) wrote as follows to Margaret Bondfield, one of the Committee members:

> *we have had a dreadful time in recent years on account of the fact that our fundamental aims have been in dispute. One section of the community have thought that we were not going far enough, and the other have treated us with little short of ridicule. It would be a great thing if we could work for the next ten or twenty years under the aegis of a unanimous finding from a Committee such as this...*[60]

Although the Blanesburgh Committee achieved unanimity (leading to virulent attacks by the left on Margaret Bondfield), their report did not resolve the problems. It led to a relaxation of contribution conditions for benefit, which was to contribute to a mounting financial crisis.

This series of desperate measures to provide relief to the unemployed had a huge impact on the exchanges. Firstly, staffing had to be greatly expanded, rising to a peak of over 25,000 in April 1921, though falling sharply thereafter (Table 4.3 below).

Secondly, the exchanges had to cope with the extraordinary volatility of government decision-making on unemployment. Between 1920 and 1926 alone, there were 15 new insurance Acts, two actually reversing legislation that had yet to become operative. This placed a heavy strain on exchange managers and staff, who faced the problem of explaining to bemused claimants why one kind of benefit had incomprehensibly ceased and another kind of benefit with different rules now applied.

Thirdly, the requirements for daily signing (now often reduced to twice weekly) meant that there were throngs of unemployed people passing through the exchanges every day, placing pressure on inadequate premises and causing queues of claimants which at times stretched right outside into the street. Again, the exchanges were handling large sums of public money. This meant collecting cash from the bank and paying it out accurately and efficiently. They were subject to close examination by inspectors and auditors.

Fourthly, the determination of eligibility to benefit involved exchange staff in highly controversial work, including means testing. But no less problematical were the work tests which had to be applied. These had been an important part of the exchanges' role since 1912 but their tightening in the early 1920s propelled the exchanges into a situation of acute controversy and conflict.

The control of abuse and the 'genuinely seeking work' condition[61]

Chapter 2 showed how Llewellyn Smith and Beveridge sought to prevent the insurance scheme from being exploited by 'malingerers'. In part, this was achieved by making benefit conditional on registration at the exchange and willingness to accept suitable vacancies. But even more powerful were the contribution conditions – no one could receive more than 15 weeks' benefit in any one year or more than one week's benefit for every five contributions paid.[62] These created an automatic barrier against malingering on benefit. The government decisions from 1921 onwards to relax the contribution conditions for benefit meant that this automatic barrier no longer existed. Moreover, benefit costs represented a huge addition to public expenditure at a time when there was intense political pressure for retrenchment and widespread suspicion of 'scroungers'. Thus there were arguments both of economy and of fear of abuse for introducing new safeguards against malingering.

Since 1911, it had been a condition of benefit that claimants were 'capable of and available for work but unable to obtain suitable employment'. This was now seen as an insufficient safeguard since it placed the onus of proof on the exchange officials and depended on their knowledge of suitable vacancies. But only about one-fifth of vacancies were actually notified to the exchanges. Thus, in 1921, a new safeguard was introduced in respect of applicants for 'uncovenanted benefits'. They had to prove to the Local Employment Committee that they were 'genuinely seeking whole-time employment but unable to obtain such employment'. The ministry's initial objective in introducing this clause was to prevent married women who had no real interest in a job from exploiting the relaxation of the contribution conditions. In 1924, Tom Shaw, Minister of Labour in the first Labour government, apparently unaware of the political risks he was taking, tightened up the safeguards on all claimants in order to win cross-party support for relaxations in other directions. Applicants for 'standard' (formerly 'covenanted') benefit had to be 'genuinely seeking work'. An applicant for 'extended' (formerly 'uncovenanted') benefit now additionally had to prove among other things a satisfactory employment record in the last two years, having regard to the circumstances, and that 'he was making all reasonable efforts to secure employment suited to his capacities and was prepared to accept such employment'.

In 1927, following the Blanesburgh Report, the provisions were simplified so as to remove time limits and the requirement for 'reasonable efforts'. But all claimants still had to prove that they were 'genuinely seeking work'.[63] What did 'genuinely seeking' mean? According to a famous Umpire's decision of July 1926, it depended on 'the state of the applicant's mind': 'if a person prefers benefit to wages, or is content to be without work so long as she receives benefit, it may be presumed that she is not genuinely seeking it'. In practice, the decisions depended on interviews with often inexperienced staff and very brief enquiries by LECs or later a Court of Referees, in which questions were asked to ascertain the extent of the individual's efforts in looking for jobs. Claimants might be expected to produce signatures from the employers they had visited in search of jobs.

There was a strong climate of opinion in the press and Parliament in favour of tightening up the system. This view was reflected within the Ministry of Labour. Indeed, the Committee on Unemployment Insurance Administration was known in Whitehall as the 'tightening-up committee'.[64] The ministry brought pressure on LECs through continual scrutiny of their decisions. Special staff at the exchanges examined a proportion of all cases. They visited claimants' homes and also, according to one Divisional Controller, interviewed neighbours, who were called upon 'ostensibly in error'; at such interviews, the 'life-history of a ne'er do well is readily volunteered'. There were large-scale 'special investigations'; one in 1925 led to 11,000 cases being referred back to the Committees.[65]

Altogether, between March 1921 and March 1930, nearly three million claims for benefit were refused because the claimant had failed to prove the necessary efforts to obtain employment. By 1927, one claim in ten was being disallowed because the claimant had failed to meet this condition.[66]

As the number of disallowances increased, there was an angry reaction on the part of the trade unions and the Labour movement. The National Unemployed Workers' Movement subverted the system by means of 'mass applications' to firms in Chesterfield and Sheffield. Nor was opinion on the 'genuinely seeking work' condition unanimously favourable within the Ministry of Labour. One sceptic was John Hilton, Assistant Secretary in the Statistics Division of the ministry and later Professor of Industrial Relations at Cambridge. His 'Reflections on a Tour of Certain Employment Exchanges'[67] of June 1929 is one of the most fascinating documents of the depression. He noted that in practice exchange staff tested whether men were 'genuinely seeking work' by asking them about the previous week's jobsearch activities, whereupon the men would reel off the firms they had visited each day. In Sheffield, Hilton 'put on an old suit and muffler and cap, abstained from shaving and went about, hands-in-pocket, looking rather miserable'. Starting at 6.30 in the morning, he toured the big works where unemployed men claimed to call regularly. To his astonishment, he found that the number of callers at these works was relatively small. He concluded that 'roughly 99% of the statements made at interview were not true... One cannot blame the men... It is not lying; it is a mere ritual required by the authorities...in a place like Sheffield, at any rate, the "genuinely seeking work" procedure is just a piece of ritual, an incantation into the substance of which one does not enquire'. Following the Umpire's formula, the real test was 'the capacity to tell a tale, remember it, and stick to it'. Moreover, employers would find it impossible to deal with callers on the scale that was claimed. Another problem was that interviewing officers had a 'groundless and dangerous faith' in their ability to spot a scrounger. He felt that the pressures on them from above were negative rather than positive:

If they were told to cease bothering about 'where you were last Tuesday', and to devote themselves to finding out what they could do to help the claimant in his quest for work, they would throw themselves into the work with real enthusiasm. They would, moreover, develop a real facility for guiding and helping.

While he exposed the fragility of the judgements about whether people were 'genuinely seeking work', Hilton was by no means complacent about the new benefit regime, under which, for the first time in British history, centrally prescribed cash benefits were paid to millions of unemployed people. Hilton wrote:

I believe that Unemployment Insurance and Health Insurance have between them virtually wiped out of existence hundreds of ways in which an industrially stranded man would have picked up a livelihood of sorts before these institutions came into being...

He recalled a visit to Newcastle in 1912 before unemployment benefit was widely available:

a crowd of young men...beset me each time I came into Newcastle station, wanting to carry my bag. I went to Newcastle on this present tour but no-one wanted to carry my bag. There are 6,000 unemployed men in Newcastle, but none wants to earn a shilling by carrying a bag...To 'be seen' earning a shilling is a terrifying prospect. The regulations may provide for such things but the unemployed man does not know what the regulations are and the last thing he wants is to stir up mud...There is also the barrier for the person who might think of employing him...Beyond this there is the barrier set up against a man working an allotment, keeping chickens...How far can he go while keeping his title to benefit?... No-one knows; better not to take risks...I am sure that here lies a good part of the reason why our present 'unemployment' stays put and does not cure itself. I cannot put any quantitative measure on it, but I feel fairly certain that, if the insurance schemes had not been in operation, a large part of the present unemployment would have by this time drained away along such channels.

Hilton was remarkably far-sighted in this analysis of how benefit systems cause 'inflexibility' in the labour market. But he condemned as inept many of the controls then being applied.

Chapter 5 will describe how the second Labour government got rid of the 'genuinely seeking work' provision. This and other control arrangements had caused huge numbers of people to be disqualified from benefit. Not until 1931 was an investigation carried out into the obvious question: what happened to people whose claims were disallowed? 2354 cases were followed up. The proportions who secured work were 32 per cent of the men, 44 per cent of the single women and 18 per cent of the married women. 29 per cent of the men and 4 per cent of the women drew poor relief. 82 per cent received help at some time from their family or from a wider circle, including landladies, reflecting the widespread reluctance to rely on the Poor Law.

Employment work

We have seen that it was their massively expanded insurance role that had protected the exchanges from abolition in 1920–22. Where did this leave their employment work? In the early 1920s, the emphasis was on its value in ensuring that benefit 'cannot continue to be drawn by persons for whom suitable work is available'.[68] But by 1925 the ministry was making public statements to the effect that, although the depression focused attention on benefit, the 'primary function' of the exchanges was 'to bring together employers requiring workpeople and workpeople desiring employment'.[69] This seems to have been a consistent ministry view thereafter.

It is a sign of the growing confidence of the ministry and its belief in its economic as well as its social role that it kept Beveridge's original vision for the exchanges alive in this period despite the apparently overwhelming pressures of unemployment relief. But this ministry line left a conundrum about how to test claimants' willingness to work. One answer was the 'genuinely seeking work' condition but, as we have seen, this proved highly controversial and was to be abolished in 1930. Another approach was to get more vacancies notified to the exchanges. Ministers and officials sent letters to employers' associations, but these brought a very 'meagre result'.[70] A more drastic option was to make the notification of vacancies compulsory. In 1923, Horace Wilson reported that this was being considered by 'a strong employers' committee', but on reflection the ministry resisted it. Eady commented that more forms would be unpopular and 'The real value of the proposal is not as great as it looks at first sight...'[71]

One of the consistent objectives of the ministry was to improve the efficiency of employment work, so as to raise employers' confidence. In the early 1920s, HQ officials drew on the criticisms by their Inspectors of the quality of placing work. For instance, exchanges had been responding to incoming vacancies simply by submitting someone who happened to be in the exchange at the time rather than checking registration documents to find the best candidate. HQ urged that, before making submissions, vacancy officers must carry out interviews and check qualifications. In 1923, Eady advised Phillips:

> If we are going to bring placing work up to anything like the standard that insurance work has now reached, we have got to prepare for an arduous campaign with the Divisional Controllers and the Exchanges and take a stricter view of the whole attitude of the Exchanges to the work.

In 1924, HQ initiated a big exercise in which Divisional Controllers or their staff were to review placing work in each exchange.[72] HQ sought to improve the calibre of employment sections and to have 'for each group of applicants an officer who knows all about them and is a kind of father confessor to them'.[73] In 1927, 'intensive clearing areas' were established in conurbations, so that all exchanges in an area exchanged information daily about vacancies and surplus labour.

Table 4.2 shows an improvement in placing performance during the 1920s after the nadir of 1921–23, so that placings reached 1.5 million in 1929. But there was no room for complacency. At the end of the 1920s, the National Confederation of Employers' Organisations informed the Morris Committee that manufacturers making use of large numbers of skilled men had little confidence in the placing efficiency of the employment exchanges.[74]

Table 4.2 *Vacancy and placing performance of the exchanges, 1919–29 (000s)*

Year	Vacancies notified (000s)	Vacancies filled (000s)
1919	1951	1290
1920	1312	942
1921	1025	842
1922	859	715
1923	1057	716
1924	1345	1144
1925	1481	1279
1926	1247	1083
1927	1436	1253
1928	1511	1327
1929	1781	1554

Notes: (1) Figures from 1919–21 are for the United Kingdom, including Ireland. Figures for 1922 are for Great Britain and Northern Ireland. Thereafter, figures relate to Great Britain only.
(2) Vacancies filled include 'Class B placings', where the work of the exchange was limited, eg because it simply involved obtaining former employees for an employer. Class B placings were around 250,000 in 1925 and 1926.
(3) Table includes juveniles, who comprise 150,000 of vacancies filled in 1923 and 310,000 in 1929.

Schemes to alleviate unemployment

The exchanges also played an important role in the local servicing of government measures to address the unemployment crisis. These were on a smaller scale than their successors in the 1970s and 1980s, when the term 'special measures' came into use. Examples included:

Office of Hope

- local relief schemes (run by the ministry of Transport and Unemployed Grants Committee);
- facilitating emigration to the Dominions (the Empire Settlement Act);
- transfers from the depressed areas, particularly mining areas, to more prosperous areas under the Industrial Transference Board from 1928 onwards; there were 32,000 such transfers in 1929 and 30,000 in 1930;
- Junior Employment Centres, later Junior Instruction Centres;
- Government Training Centres, primarily for skilled trades, from 1925 onwards;
- Instructional Centres;
- training for women under the ministry's Central Committee on Women's Training and Employment, initially for domestic service, but later extended to other vocations.

Even where the exchanges were not the prime organisers of these activities, they often helped to set them up and were often the channel through which unemployed people became involved in them.

Staffing

In the early 1920s, staffing in the exchanges was brought into line with the new template for the civil service as a whole. This was set out in the 1920 Report of the Reorganisation Committee of the National Whitley Council, which set up the three 'general classes' – Administrative, Executive and Clerical. The centralising tendencies of the Treasury in this period had some retrograde effects. For instance, in the early history of the exchanges, married women had been employed and men and women received the same salary, but in the 1920s the employment of married women was restricted and salaries for men and women were differentiated.[75]

The size of the employment service fluctuated astonishingly after the end of the war. Before and during the war, it had been a relatively small organisation with some 5000 staff. But in 1919 it expanded dramatically to a peak of 21,000 in June, as it handled the out of work donation, and again to another peak of well over 20,000 in 1921 with the extension of unemployment insurance and the growth in unemployment. It is impressive that the ministry, certainly under Treasury pressure, managed to bring staffing down sharply from these peaks. For instance, by September 1921, staff numbers had fallen away to 11,000.[76] Thereafter, staffing levels rose again with dependants' benefit, but the fluctuations each year were less marked. Table 4.3 shows staffing levels for the Ministry of Labour as a whole in the inter-war period. These are a good proxy for the employment service since most of the posts in HQ (and nearly all at Kew) were linked with the exchange functions.

Table 4.3 *Number of staff in the Ministry of Labour, 1919–1929*

Year	Total number of staff	Permanent staff
1 April 1919	26,308	3693
1 April 1920	18,869	4152
1 April 1921	25,277	5871
1 April 1922	21,299	6361
1 April 1923	16,205	6400
1 April 1924	14,991	6520
31 Dec 1925	14,718	7044
31 Dec 1926	16,163	7731
31 Dec 1927	14,482	8165
31 Dec 1928	17,469	8461
31 Dec 1929	16,481	8670

Notes: (1) Figures exclude staff of the Industrial Court and the Umpire.
(2) Figures up to 1921 include Ireland.
Source: Ministry of Labour Annual Reports.

The fluctuations in Table 4.3 reflect the volatility both of levels of unemployed claimants and of the measures to relieve them. It was these fluctuations and the uncertainties about unemployment in the future which explain the low level of permanent staffing, which was a major reason for the poor quality of much employment work in the exchanges. A perceptive observer commented that one of the greatest weaknesses of the exchanges was the use of temporary clerks in registration work.[77] There were recurring criticisms that the exchange staff lacked relevant industrial knowledge and experience. For instance, in 1930, Walter Citrine, General Secretary of the TUC, argued that the exchanges would never win confidence unless they could 'fit round pegs into round holes' and for this their staff needed 'actual industrial knowledge'.[78] The Barnes Committee in 1920 had recommended a separate channel of recruitment based on 'industrial knowledge and the ability to deal with men', but this was never implemented. For one thing, it did not fit in with the Treasury's new civil service model. For another, even within the ministry, there were doubts about whether staff with a technical background in industry would be flexible enough to cope with the constant changes in government policies with which exchange staff had to contend.[79] It was preferable to recruit well educated staff without an industrial background who could be trained in occupational and industrial knowledge than to take on specialists who might be less adaptable. Nor did the ministry accept Barnes' suggested job title – 'registrar'. But they did designate 'employment officers' at supervisory level, who played an important role in the exchanges.

Premises

One of the greatest problems for the service in the 1920s was its poor premises. In 1920 JB Adams, the General Manager, complained to the Barnes Committee that 'the whole prejudice against the Exchange Service is in the main caused by the fact that we have them in back streets; we are judged by outward appearance like all are in this world'.[80] The situation became much worse with the huge increase in unemployment in 1921. Many exchanges were hired shops, temporary wooden structures or ordinary dwelling houses with narrow passages which were quite unsuitable for dealing with large numbers of people. In Bradford, the exchange was in three buildings, with problems of overcrowding, defective natural light, poor ventilation and draughts causing sick leave.[81] In one extreme case, the exchange was in a former stable with a stench of liquid manure.[82] Barnes recommended improvements but, given the questioning of public expenditure by the Geddes Committee, Macnamara decreed that no new brick should be laid to provide accommodation for the exchanges, though he was prepared to use army huts.

After the Geddes threat had been removed, it became possible to tackle the massive task of improving the exchange estate. A programme of improvement was agreed with the Office of Works. By 1927 this had Parliamentary support, with the Select Committee on Estimates commenting:

> Now that the provision of Employment Exchanges has become a settled policy of Parliament, your Committee considers some form of classification (of those Exchanges needing replacement, improvement etc) most desirable...[83]

It was found that, out of 417 fully fledged exchanges, 268 were unsatisfactory and of these 128 needed urgent treatment.

Conclusion

The position of the employment exchanges in the 1920s was full of paradox. Many would see their role in very negative terms. Jose Harris writes that, in the 1920s and 1930s, they became 'a symbol of national despair and indifference to several millions of unemployed'.[84] Most of the exchanges were depressing places to visit. The unemployment benefits which they offered were a very inadequate substitute for a job. They were tied to complicated conditions which, as Hilton argued, both discouraged enterprise and could trap the less streetwise among the unemployed.

Yet it is possible to view their role in an entirely different way. It can be argued that of all the institutions of the state, it was the exchanges and their parent department, the Ministry of Labour, which did most to help Britain through the unprecedented problems which followed the First World War.

These problems began immediately after the war ended and, indeed, this was the time of highest risk. Archbishop William Temple wrote:

> *The special problem caused by demobilisation alike of soldiers and munitions-workers led to the establishment of what is unfairly called 'the dole', apart from which a revolution could hardly have been avoided.*[85]

Having played an indispensable role in the crisis of 1919, the exchanges were called upon from 1921 onwards to provide the financial 'maintenance' which was the state's main response to mass unemployment. The exchange service cannot be held responsible for the inadequacy of this response. Moreover, even if problems arose from the application of complicated insurance rules to the provision of relief, it remains impressive that 'between 1920 and 1929, more was done in this country than in any other to transfer spending power to the unemployed'.[86] This was a major contribution to social harmony for which the Ministry of Labour and the exchanges can take much of the credit. Moreover, the executive efficiency of the exchanges was remarkable. They delivered a succession of complex government relief programmes at short notice and with a level of cost effectiveness that compares impressively with such programmes in Britain's more recent history.

But where did this leave the original labour market rationale for the exchanges? In the early 1920s, the primary *raison d'être* of the exchanges was the delivery of benefits and the testing of claimants' willingness to work. In 1921, Neville Chamberlain commented that the Unemployment Insurance Act had thrown a great deal of work onto the exchanges – 'a new and perhaps more valuable function than that with which they started and one which it would now be very difficult to transfer to another body'.[87] However, the ministry moved on from this position. From 1925 onwards, it stressed that employment work was the primary function of the exchanges and it began to build up placing performance.

But the exchange service in 1929, for all its achievements, was weak both in its staffing and its premises and, in the next phase in its history, it would face an economic hurricane.

5

Office of Despair? 1929–39

'When as post-war Chancellor of the Exchequer, I turned on the apostles of old-style economics and said that "those who talked about creating pools of unemployment should be thrown into them and made to swim", I was still seeing in my own mind's eye the look of hopelessness in the eyes of the men of the thirties standing idly on street corners or queueing drably at the labour exchanges.' (RA Butler, Parliamentary Secretary, Ministry of Labour, 1937–8).[1]

Introduction

Chapter 1 records Philip Gibbs' description of a new labour exchange as an 'office of hope'. It is unlikely that any journalist in the 1930s would have described the exchanges in this way. 'Office of despair' would have seemed more appropriate. The exchanges became closely identified in the public mind with the national calamity of mass unemployment, as the quotation from RA Butler above indicates.

Ramsay Macdonald's Labour government which took office in June 1929 had little premonition of the economic hurricane that was going to destroy it. The new Minister of Labour, Margaret Bondfield, the first woman Cabinet Minister in British history, brought a fresh enthusiasm and drive to the ministry, including the running of the employment exchanges. But as Britain became engulfed in a world-wide slump, the Labour government faced impossible tensions between its wish to offer decent financial support to the unemployed and the demands of economic orthodoxy. As a result, in the crisis of August 1931, it was replaced by a National Government led by the former Labour Prime Minister, Ramsay Macdonald.

The National Government increasingly became a Conservative government. Macdonald was succeeded first by Stanley Baldwin and then by Neville Chamberlain. The government took some employment initiatives but conspicuously failed to find a remedy for mass unemployment. None the less, it managed to avoid the 'chaos' which had surrounded unemployment relief in the 1920s and instead built up more robust systems both of unemployment insurance and of unemployment assistance, while taking some steps to strengthen the employment work of the exchanges.

This chapter looks first at the leading Ministers and civil servants of the period, at the unemployment crisis of the early 1930s and at the resulting problems for unemployment relief and the way these problems were resolved in the mid-1930s, at the way in which employment work developed and the staffing and premises of the exchanges improved, and finally at attitudes to the exchanges.

Ministers and civil servants

The Ministers of Labour in this period were:

- June 1929–August 1931   Margaret Bondfield (Labour)
- August 1931–June 1934   Sir Henry Betterton (National)
- July 1934–June 1935   Oliver Stanley (National)
- June 1935–May 1940   Ernest Brown (National)

Margaret Bondfield showed commitment to the employment exchanges (just as the second female holder of this office – Barbara Castle – was to do 40 years later) and was very ready to intervene to improve their premises and to commend them to employers. There is an urgency and forcefulness about the communications from her office which may link with the story (perhaps apocryphal) of Humbert Wolfe missing his lunch hour in order to attend to her demands and later describing her as 'virago intacta'. Her successor, Sir Henry Betterton, drawing on his experience as the ministry's Parliamentary Secretary for much of the 1920s as well as on official briefing, managed greatly to improve Treasury plans for the Unemployment Assistance Board. Stanley had a brief and difficult spell as Minister. His successor, Ernest Brown, an ardent Baptist with a stentorian voice, was both the weakest of the four and the longest lasting. According to his Parliamentary Secretary, RA Butler, Brown 'as an ex-sergeant major was *simplicitas* itself, straight, loyal and running on pre-destinate grooves'.[2]

Sir Horace Wilson, Permanent Secretary since 1921, left the Department in 1929 to head up JH Thomas' secretariat in his abortive mission to tackle unemployment and much later to become Permanent Secretary of the Treasury. Tom Phillips (pages 48–9) became acting Permanent Secretary but, due allegedly to 'blackballing' by Wilson, he did not replace Wilson in 1930. Instead Sir Francis Floud – described as 'by no means bright or courageous'[3] – was installed. Phillips had to wait until 1935 to become substantive Permanent Secretary – a post which he held until 1944. A true expert on the ministry's affairs, particularly unemployment relief, he 'was able to achieve the remarkable feat of saving even Ernest Brown from regular Parliamentary embarrassment'.[4]

Office of Hope

In 1929, a major organisation review concluded that the Headquarters organisation of the Employment and Insurance Department of the ministry had 'outgrown the proportions and workable limits of a single unit of administration'.[5] Miss Bondfield accepted the recommendation to split its functions between three Departments:

- the Employment and Training Department, with Wilfrid Eady as Principal Assistant Secretary;
- the Unemployment Insurance Department, with JFG Price as Principal Assistant Secretary; and
- the Services and Establishments Department, with Humbert Wolfe as Director; this Department took over the common services of staff, premises and inspection and the executive control of the exchange machinery.

This review thus completed the process of absorbing the exchange service into the Ministry of Labour machine. There was no longer a separate entity with a distinctive mission that could be called the 'employment service'. The Departments headed by Eady and Price were 'policy' departments.

Another effect of this reorganisation was to make Eady and Wolfe influential figures at this time for the exchanges. Wolfe used his position in charge of establishments to push for better staffing and premises. He went on to become head of the Employment and Training Department from 1933–38 and then Deputy Secretary from 1938–39. (He died in 1940.) Wilfred Eady sought to build up the exchanges' employment work until in 1934 he became Secretary of the new Unemployment Assistance Board. From 1938–40, he master-minded the Home Office's critical Air Raid Precautions (ARP).

The role of the Divisional Controllers[6] remained vital to the efficiency of the exchanges. They were responsible for nearly all the ministry's services in their Division (though not Government Training Centres until 1943). Following the 1929 reorganisation, 'executive control' of the Divisional Controllers had passed to Wolfe as Director of Services and Establishments. The Controllers continued to meet monthly at HQ, but under Wolfe's chairmanship. These monthly meetings acquired a ritualistic quality which continued up to the 1970s. The Controllers would assemble the day before, having elected one of their number (usually the most senior) as chairman. They would discuss the agenda for the following day's meeting and agree a spokesman and a 'line' on each item. A former Controller said that minority opinions among Controllers were not concealed, but

> *if (Controllers) presented a united front, either for or against any policy, there can be expected to be a real difficulty to overcome... The more ...Controllers are taken into confidence and consulted, the more they can be expected to contribute and the better the results...*[7]

The unemployment problem

Table 5.1 shows the extraordinary increase in unemployment which occurred between 1929 and 1931 as a result of the world-wide slump. As in the 1920s, unemployment was concentrated particularly in the industrial regions of Wales, Scotland and the North, giving rise to severe problems of long-term unemployment in the 'depressed areas'. The table also shows a gradual improvement in the situation in the mid- to late 1930s, particularly after rearmament began to make an impact.

Table 5.1 *Unemployment among the insured population, 1929–38*

Year	Number unemployed 16–64 (000s)	Insured unemployed as % of insured employees
1929	1276	10.4
1930	2014	16.0
1931	2718	21.3
1932	2813	22.1
1933	2588	19.9
1934	2221	16.7
1935	2106	15.5
1936	1822	13.1
1937	1557	10.8
1938	1590	12.9

Source: Office of National Statistics, *Labour Market Trends*, Jan 1996. Crown Copyright.

There was deep despair about this level of unemployment symbolised, for instance, in the famous March in 1936 organised by Jarrow Town Council. The government response, apart from providing financial relief to the unemployed, remained small-scale. Programmes of labour transference and training continued as in the 1920s. In 1934, the government introduced the Special Areas Bill under which Commissioners were appointed in hard-hit areas to propose action that might be taken. While the work of the Commissioners was hedged around by restrictions, it led to a growing interest in pro-active regional policy in the latter half of the 1930s.[8]

One controversial Ministry of Labour initiative was the development of Instructional Centres.[9] They had antecedents in pre-war rural colonies. Moreover, the Webbs' 1909 plan for ending unemployment had included Farm Colonies for training the unemployed and 'Detention Colonies for the work-shy'.[10] The Centres originated from experience in 1928–29 with attempting to train and transfer men from the depressed areas. Many of the unemployed men were found to be unready for either the training or the work that was available. So in 1929 five 'Transfer Instructional Centres' were opened in rural areas to 'recondition' or 'harden' men from the depressed areas. The training was mostly outdoor work – forestry, road-making, excavating and levelling – designed to prepare them for employment on road works or relief schemes. Attendance was initially voluntary, but from March 1930 was enforceable by benefit sanctions. In 1932, they were renamed 'Instructional Centres' and compulsion was abandoned because the prospects of subsequently obtaining work were greatly reduced. In 1933, the programme expanded to 38,000 admissions, and the Centres included five tented camps operating successfully in the 'exceptionally fine summer' and a new non-residential centre in South Wales. In 1937, the task of inviting men to attend the Centres passed to the Assistance Board.

There were widely divergent views of this initiative. Those on the left saw the Centres as sinister instruments of social control. Wal Hannington of the National Unemployed Workers' Movement referred to them as 'slave camps' or 'concentration camps', arising from

> *that attitude of mind which regards the working classes as a lower species of humanity, which should be content to be merely an object of exploitation when working and, when unemployed, be grateful for being allowed to exist at all.*[11]

His greatest objection was that men worked for allowances rather than the rate for the job. He believed that pressures were placed on men to attend the Centres, even when they were supposedly voluntary. He reported riots and protests about poor food and lack of travel warrants to get back to families. Ministry officials saw things quite differently. The object was training or 'reconditioning', so a wage would be inappropriate. Strenuous physical activity in the fresh air was beneficial. When the Centres became voluntary in 1932, there was a most encouraging response from the distressed areas, filling all the available places. By June 1933, over half of those who had attended the Centres had been placed in employment – not a bad record in such a depressed period. This debate foreshadowed the arguments about unemployment measures in the 1980s and 1990s.

Unemployment relief: crisis and resolution

By 1929, the 'genuinely seeking work' condition (pages 63–6) was deeply unpopular with the labour movement. When Margaret Bondfield became Minister in 1929, she relaxed its administration and set up the Morris Committee to investigate the issues. This Committee came up with three separate Reports, but the Chairman's report recommended a fundamental change in the condition. After much argument, and vitriolic opposition by FG Bowers, the ministry's Accountant General, Ministers agreed that a claimant would be disallowed as not seeking work only if he or she refused an offer of suitable employment or failed to carry out the written instructions of an exchange officer. This was the end of the 'genuinely seeking' condition. The epitaph was appropriately provided by Beveridge, whose original case for labour exchanges had rested in part on ending the 'hawking of labour', which the condition had revived. He now commented that:

> *it was better to take the risk of an occasional loss to the fund by a few idle workmen than to drive all workmen on fruitless journeys and perpetuate the disorganisation of the labour market...The condition will not, it may be hoped, ever rise from its dishonoured grave.*[12]

As we shall see in Chapter 14, such a resurrection did take place 60 years later.

Bondfield and her colleagues continued to wrestle with the problems of the growing insolvency of the Unemployment Fund and the increasing numbers of unemployed people reliant upon 'transitional benefits' rather than contributory benefits. They switched the cost of transitional benefits away from the Unemployment Fund to the Exchequer. In 1930, they appointed a Royal Commission to address all these problems, but when in June 1931 it produced an Interim Report recommending various cuts in benefit, the most the government could agree to was legislation to address 'anomalies', which really meant depriving married women of benefit. By August 1931, the financial pressures both on the Unemployment Fund and on the Treasury were such as to precipitate the collapse of the government.[13]

With the establishment of the National Government in August 1931, the 'ten year chaos' in unemployment insurance (as Beveridge described it) finally came to an end. The immediate priority of the new National Government was to regain the confidence of the international financial community. Accordingly, they cut benefit levels and they introduced a new and more economical system of 'transitional payments' for the long-term unemployed who had exhausted their entitlement to benefit. These 'transitional payments' were to be paid as before by the exchanges, but would be subject to a 'means test'. The 'means test' was to be carried out by the Public Assistance Committees (PACs) which the Labour government had set up in lieu of the Poor Law Guardians.

In the years following the crisis of 1931, there emerged a new and lasting resolution of the fundamental problem with which governments had been grappling since 1921 – on what basis was unemployment relief to be paid to those who were not qualified through insurance contributions? In November 1932, the final report of the Royal Commission on Unemployment Insurance (appointed by the Labour government) appeared, recommending that the dual system of insurance and means-tested relief should continue and that the means tests should be administered by committees of local authorities. Neville Chamberlain, now Chancellor of the Exchequer, rejected this latter recommendation. He was unhappy with the decisions of certain Labour-controlled PACs about means-tested assistance and wanted such decisions to be taken in future by a new statutory commission insulated from the political process. The Ministry of Labour had long favoured devolution to local authorities, but now conceded defeat on this issue. However, the Minister, Henry Betterton, successfully challenged Chamberlain's idea that unemployment relief – one of the most controversial political issues of the day – could be insulated from politics. It was agreed that the new commission would be subject to Parliamentary scrutiny and come under the Minister of Labour and that its decisions in individual cases would be subject to appeal.

The decision to switch responsibility for unemployment assistance to a centrally-run body raised important questions of government organisation,[14] and the outcome was to have long-term implications for social welfare in Britain. Betterton favoured a single body to administer both insurance and unemployment assistance – in modern parlance, a 'one-stop-shop'. But he was persuaded by his officials to have two separate commissions – one for insurance and one for assistance. While the exchanges would continue to administer unemployment insurance, a separate network of offices would administer unemployment assistance. It might be supposed that, in recommending a separate network, the ministry was trying to prevent a reinforcement of the dole image of the exchanges. But apparently the decisive argument was put forward by the ministry's formidable Accountant General, FG Bowers, and was that having two separate organisations would create a barrier against Treasury pressure to shift the costs of assistance into insurance (which was part-funded by contributions). He also argued that a single commission would be too powerful in relation to the ministry itself. Rumour within the ministry had it that senior officials were simply pursuing their own interests – that having two bodies would provide 'for the poor and Eady and keep the Wolfe from the door'.[15]

These intense discussions led into the Unemployment Act 1934, which created two new statutory commissions reporting to the Minister of Labour:

- the *Unemployment Insurance Statutory Commission* (UISC) which was chaired by Sir William Beveridge; and
- the *Unemployment Assistance Board* (UAB), an executive body, which was chaired by Edgar Betterton, the former Minister; included on the Board were some prominent figures of the time, such as Tom Jones (formerly Lloyd George's secretary) and Violet Markham (page 43), with Wilfrid Eady as Secretary.

The UISC was in theory a purely advisory body but, with Beveridge as Chairman for the next 10 years, it became an influential policy-making body, whose recommendations were almost always accepted by the Minister. It succeeded in bringing unemployment insurance back to an actuarially sound footing. Furthermore, by bringing Beveridge back into the mainstream of social administration, it paved the way for his 1942 review of social insurance and allied services.

The UAB had a more formidable task than the UISC. It had to create its new network of offices. More critically, it had to decide the rates at which unemployment assistance would be set. Unfortunately, it pitched the new rates at a level which was significantly lower than many of the PAC rates. There was such a storm when the new rates were introduced on 7 January 1935 that Oliver Stanley, the Minister of Labour, introduced a 'standstill' under which applicants could choose between the old rates and the new rates. It was not until May 1938 that a uniform national rate was in operation.

What were the implications of this new structure for the exchanges? They retained their original dual role of filling jobs and administering insurance. Since 1931, they had been relieved of responsibility for means-testing those who were not eligible for insurance. This role now rested with the UAB, whose officers visited applicants' homes for means-testing. But these applicants had to register with, and sign regularly at, the exchanges. The exchanges paid them and retained the responsibility for the (now less stringent) work tests. The average applicant was probably confused about the relative roles of the two organisations. A Divisional Controller of this period commented that these duties 'brought to [the exchanges] a measure of the hostility which the 'means test' has in some measure always aroused'.[16] As in the 1920s, the exchanges were thus dealing with almost all the unemployed. At long last, the Poor Law was virtually abolished for the able-bodied unemployed, but there was a residue of some 30,000 able-bodied unemployed people who were vagrants or otherwise outside the scope of insurance and who continued to be handled under the Poor Law.[17]

Employment work

Chapter 4 showed that from 1925 onwards the ministry saw employment work as the primary function of the exchanges. This view was strongly endorsed in 1932 in the Report of the Royal Commission on Unemployment Insurance, which declared that

> *The primary functions of the Exchanges have remained to the present time, as defined in the Labour Exchanges Act 1909. They constitute a national service, organically whole and not necessarily dependent for its performance on the existence of an unemployment insurance scheme or any other form of provision for unemployed workers.*[18]

The report was much more positive about employment work than Barnes had been in 1920, pointing out that the exchanges speeded movement into jobs, offered employers a better selection of workers, increased the fluidity of labour across the country and could enable decasualisation of labour. It endorsed the policy of submitting to employers the 'industrially best qualified' workers. Any other course would lead to a loss of vacancies from employers. The report concluded:

> *offers of work cannot and should not be used primarily as a test of the bona fides of a claimant for unemployment benefit. Such services as the Exchanges perform in this respect will be incidental, and no more than incidental, to the performance of their primary function.*[19]

The Commission also considered a TUC proposal that employers should be required to recruit all their labour through the exchanges. They concluded that it would be premature to place this 'overwhelming burden' on the exchanges. Even the lesser proposal of compulsory notification of vacancies would cause an 'immense amount of unproductive work on the part both of employers and the Exchanges'. It was better for the exchanges to go on developing and expanding their services, subject to external competition.[20]

This recognition of the importance of employment work was due in part to the interest which Margaret Bondfield, as Minister from 1929 to 1931, took in this aspect of the exchanges' work. She saw the new Employment and Training Department under Eady as having the duty

> *to do away with the old criticism that the Employment Exchanges were merely benefit-paying offices, and never helped as they should do, in bringing employers and workers in touch.*[21]

In 1929, a pamphlet about the services of the exchanges was sent to employers. It had very little effect – perhaps because it looked like a government White Paper. One manager suggested that the ministry might try modern advertising techniques instead, but he was ahead of his time. In March 1930, Miss Bondfield wrote herself to many thousands of employers urging them to use the exchanges. Again, perhaps because of the economic downturn, the results were 'undeniably disappointing', bringing in only 637 vacancies. Officials gave up the idea of further propaganda at that time. But they included in the 1930 Unemployment Insurance Act a duty for the Minister 'so far as practicable' to arrange for employers to notify their vacancies.

The alarming increase in unemployment between 1929 and 1931 generated an anguished debate among key officials. Eady and his employment team saw a 'danger that the whole Exchange machine will clog up'. They pointed out that they had not been consulted about the new Staffing Basis Scheme and nothing in the Scheme prevented managers redeploying staff in any way they wished. As it was, managers responded to the pressures of mounting insurance work by deploying their most experienced staff to help them through. Eady urged that employment staffing should be ring-fenced and that emergency procedures (such as less frequent signing) be introduced in order to prevent employment work from being sacrificed. He was concerned that, with the imminent publication of the second edition of Beveridge's standard work on unemployment, 'the comparative inadequacy of the Exchanges as a placing medium may quite well come to the forefront of public discussion this Autumn'.[22]

In fact, as Table 5.2 shows, the exchanges weathered the storm and actually managed to increase their placings in 1931, though there was a decline in 1932, which was attributed to the loss of 133,000 vacancies through the discontinuance of relief works by the National Government. Thereafter, right up to 1939, placing work continued to build up steadily, with publicity direct to employers and at national exhibitions and targeted campaigns to publicise and fill particular kinds of vacancies, such as seasonal vacancies in holiday resorts and potato and tomato picker vacancies in Jersey. By 1937, some exchanges were reporting shortages of skilled labour in building, engineering and the hotel trade, a trend which increased as the rearmament programme got under way. Exchanges were trying where they could to supply workpeople with 'alternative experience', who in many cases proved adaptable and acceptable.[23]

Table 5.2 *Vacancy and placing performance of the exchanges, 1929–1938 (000s)*

Year	Vacancies notified (000s)	Vacancies filled (000s)
1929	1781	1554
1930	1931	1732
1931	2123	1952
1932	2016	1886
1933	2435	2201
1934	2627	2305
1935	2911	2512
1936	3103	2624
1937	3140	2625
1938	3153	2705

Notes: (1) Vacancies filled include 'Class B placings', where the work of the exchange was limited, eg because it simply involved obtaining former employees for an employer. Class B were around 350,000 in 1931, 415,000 in 1932, 524,000 in 1933, 511,000 in 1934, 494,000 in 1935, 451,000 in 1936, 382,000 in 1937 and 462,000 in 1938.
(2) Table includes juveniles, who comprise 310,000 of vacancies filled in 1929 and 445,000 in 1934.

The placing levels achieved in the 1930s are impressive, even if account is taken of the inclusion of youth placings and very easy 'Class B' placings (see Notes to Table 5.2). But a more critical test is the exchanges' share of total engagements in the labour market. Figures of total engagements are notoriously difficult to establish, but in this period the ministry found a proxy for them through adding to the placings figure the number of claimants moving into jobs without being placed by the exchanges. This probably overstates market share, since it is unlikely that the exchanges were aware of all labour turnover, but at least it provided a fairly consistent measure. Thus, whereas the exchanges' share of engagements was thought to be around 15–18 per cent in 1922–23,[24] by 1932 it had risen to 22 per cent and by 1937 to 29 per cent (35 per cent if workers

Office of Hope

returning to their former employer were disregarded). The share was much higher for women and juveniles than for men. The ministry also provided market shares by industry. For instance, in 1937, the exchanges' highest shares were in, or related to, the public sector, reflecting deliberate marketing efforts – national government (66 per cent), local government (60 per cent), public utilities (52 per cent) and public works contracting (50 per cent). Other strong areas were chemicals (43 per cent) and hotels (39 per cent). The lowest shares were in shipbuilding and repairing (19 per cent), mining and quarrying (20 per cent) and furniture-making (22 per cent).[25] The exchanges were evidently filling some service industry and white collar vacancies (at least in the public sector) at this time as well as industrial vacancies for manual labour.

Staffing

Table 5.3 shows staffing levels for the ministry as a whole, which are a good proxy for those in the exchanges. Chapter 4 noted that the large proportion of temporary staff in the 1920s had a damaging effect on the performance of the exchanges (page 69). The case for more permanent staff was supported by the Royal Commission on the Civil Service in 1931 and by the Royal Commission on Unemployment Insurance in 1932. Thereafter, the proportion of permanent staff did not fall below 50 per cent. The ministry gave preference in recruitment, other things being equal, to ex-servicemen and in particular to those who were disabled. These groups comprised respectively around 60 per cent and 20 per cent of the total workforce for much of the period.

Table 5.3 *Number of staff in the Ministry of Labour, 1929–1938*

Year	Total number of staff	Permanent staff
31 Dec 1929	16,481	8670
31 Dec 1930	22,797	9180
31 Dec 1931	24,506	9829
31 Dec 1932	24,588	13,022
31 Dec 1933	22,919	13,316
31 Dec 1934	23,469	12,470
31 Dec 1935	23,501	16,583
31 Dec 1936	24,541	18,744
31 Dec 1937	25,844	18,953
31 Dec 1938	29,754	Not known

Note: Figures exclude staff of the Industrial Court and the Umpire.
Source: Ministry of Labour Annual Reports.

The result of these policies was that, by the late 1930s, the ministry had a workforce which was ageing, predominantly male (58 per cent in 1938) and not particularly highly educated. It lacked real professionalism in employment work but was rich in practical experience and resilient and resourceful in implementing urgent measures with tight deadlines.

Premises

Chapter 4 noted that by 1927 there was Parliamentary support for improved premises for the exchanges (page 70). But the ministry was bitterly critical of dilatoriness on the part of the Office of Works, so that, over the 10 years 1919–28, only two-thirds of the money allocated for exchange improvements had actually been spent. Margaret Bondfield described this as a 'disgraceful state of affairs' and, in his last months as Permanent Secretary, Sir Horace Wilson deployed his formidable administrative skills to persuade his opposite numbers in the Office of Works and the Treasury to agree to implement an enlarged programme.[26] This intervention had the desired effect, and by January 1931 33 new premises were open, 38 had operations in progress and 120 cases were beyond the preliminary stage.

By 1939, there were 250 specially erected exchanges, adapted to the work but mostly in the dignified neo-Georgian architecture of the time. They were designed for unemployment at 4 per cent – an optimistic and unrealistic assumption, even if they could handle much higher levels with some relaxation of procedure. At the outbreak of war, there was still a large backlog of unsatisfactory premises.[27]

Attitudes to the exchange service

The improvement in vacancy notification (Table 5.2) suggests a marked improvement in employer perceptions of the exchanges between the early 1920s and the late 1930s. We lack systematic information about the perceptions of unemployed users of the service, but the anecdotal evidence is far from encouraging. A study of 200 working class autobiographies of the time led to the conclusion that

> *Autobiographers were predominantly hostile, sometimes violently so, to the procedures of unemployment benefit.*[28]

One unemployed man described the exchange as

> *dreary, dismal, gloomy, dirty and hopeless, painted in a typically standard olive, drab with clerical staff to match. Staff with little or no experience of life or work outside dole offices...Their main concern, it seemed, was to cut you down, to pay you as little as possible, not even your entitlements, to keep you at arm's length, by assuming you guilty of wilful idleness before you even opened your mouth...*[29]

Another found the inside of the exchange

> *dirty and repellent. There appeared to be a large number of notices forbidding me to do this and warning me of the penalties for doing that.*[30]

Others said that 'the clerks treated us like dirt' and that the police were often on duty to regulate queues, particularly when the NUWM organised demonstrations. In part, the unemployed were projecting their despair upon the representatives of the state who were closest to hand – the exchange clerks. But there was also a feeling of impotence in the face of 'the system':

> *'the administrative octopus' – the Employment Exchanges, Public Assistance Committee, Court of Referees, distant and potentially alien as they seemed to eyes dimmed by helplessness.*[31]

The process of obtaining benefit seemed like a 'devilish game of snakes and ladders'. On a Friday, a man would

> *have a short period of sickening anxiety lest the clerk should single him out and tell him that he is to be sent to the Court of Referees; then will follow a few days' consequent dread lest his benefit should be stopped and he be cast on the Poor Law.*[32]

One of the most revealing studies of the period was carried out by E Wight Bakke, an American researcher, who in 1931, on John Hilton's advice, immersed himself in the life of working class and unemployed men in Greenwich. He found that the unemployed claimant was impressed by the 'wonderful system' of insurance benefits operated by the exchanges, but uncomfortable with the 'apparent abruptness and even harshness of his treatment by the clerks'. He also noted 'an overwhelming lack of confidence in the ability of the Exchanges to find jobs. The estimate of placing work could be summed up usually in one of three phrases, "No jobs", "Poor jobs", "Low wage jobs".'[33]

There is an inconsistency between all this hostile feedback and the steady improvement in placings shown in Table 5.2. But the improvements in the exchanges in the 1930s were gradual and patchy and they continued to be identified with all the frustrations surrounding high unemployment. Many saw the exchanges just as 'instruments of state handouts; normally given, but (it appeared) grudgingly, and by hostile officials searching for any excuse to withdraw them'.[34] However, hostility to the exchanges was not universal among the long-term unemployed. One Nottinghamshire man commented: 'During four years of unemployment, I can honestly say that I have met with almost unfailing courtesy and much practical sympathy...the clerks show an interest in the men...'[35]

Conclusion

In this period, the Ministry of Labour and the exchanges continued to display remarkable executive efficiency. They coped at short notice with an extraordinary rise in unemployment in 1929–31. Moreover, the ministry secured an improvement in staffing and made some progress with the massive task of upgrading the estate. Placing figures improved. In 1937, a report on public social services by Political and Economic Planning (PEP) described the exchange system as 'one of our most successful public services', though it only dealt with about one quarter of the jobs placed each year and had not yet succeeded in establishing order in some sections of the labour market.[36]

Despite its achievements, the ministry totally failed to throw off the 'dole image' which the exchanges had acquired in the 1920s. Indeed, a well known journalist, Trevor Evans, claimed in 1946 that, 'The machine had developed into an apathetic negative sort of monster'.[37] While this comment may seem exaggerated, the 'dole image' was to prove so deep-seated in the public consciousness that officials were still concerned about it in the 1960s, long after mass unemployment had disappeared. In this sense the exchanges had become 'offices of despair'.

The exchanges had ceased to be 'on trial' and were instead an accepted part of the state apparatus. They were wholly integrated into the Ministry of Labour and so linked closely with Whitehall. Although this had its disadvantages, it could also be a source of strength, as was to be found in the next phase of their history.

6

Mobilising the Masses, 1939–45

'There has been a sudden switch over from being in the main a relief organisation to a great constructive Department spending its mind and energy in probably the greatest constructive effort the world has ever seen.' (Ernest Bevin, 6 March 1945)[1]

Introduction

There was a marked contrast between the position of the exchanges in the First World War and the Second World War. In the Second, the exchanges were recognised from the start as vital for the mobilisation of the nation. There was no need for them to prove themselves. This had been done already in the crises over unemployment of the preceding two decades. Moreover, the exchanges worked within a much stronger and more consistent framework in the Second War than they had in the First. In the First War, no central manpower authority existed until 1917, whereas in the Second War, from 1940 onwards, the exchanges' parent ministry, the Ministry of Labour, under the outstanding leadership of Ernest Bevin, organised the nation's labour force. The exchanges were its key executive instruments.

It was not inevitable that this should have been the case. Indeed, until just before the war started, the plans were very different.

This chapter looks first at the preparations for war and the steps taken during the 'phoney war'. It then looks at the advent of Ernest Bevin, the Ministry of Labour machine under his leadership, including the role of Godfrey Ince, and the progressive tightening of mobilisation to its peak in autumn 1943. It also looks at Bevin's vision for the exchanges, Beveridge's social security scheme, the services for highly qualified manpower and for disabled people, and the planning for demobilisation.

Preparations for war

From 1935–40 – a period longer than that of any of his predecessors – Ernest Brown was Minister of Labour. In Chapter 5, we noted Brown's limitations (page 73). One can imagine that, in the anxious and uncertain period before the Second World War and during its early months, he was very much in the hands of his officials. The leading officials involved in preparing the Department for war in the late 1930s were Sir Thomas Phillips and Humbert Wolfe. Both were extremely able, but they felt the lack of strong political leadership and were slow to develop effective strategies to deal with the extraordinarily threatening situation which confronted them.

It was not that war planning had been neglected. Contingency planning for the mobilisation of labour in the next war began in 1920[2] when the Committee of Imperial Defence set up a Sub-Committee to look at 'the question of national service in a future war'. The Chairman of the Sub-Committee was Sir W Graham Greene, uncle of the famous novelist and an *eminence grise* in the world of imperial defence. The Cabinet had advised that 'a ministry of National Service or similar ministry would be necessary to co-ordinate manpower requirements and prevent the confusion which had arisen in the early years of the Great War'. In 1923 the Sub-Committee reported, recommending that as soon as possible after a major war broke out, a national register should be compiled and conscription should be introduced for all men of military age, subject to exemptions for those on a schedule of reserved occupations. The Sub-Committee wanted a single authority to be responsible for mobilisation, but it faced a difficult dilemma as to which ministry should take on this role. The Ministry of Labour was the obvious choice, but it declined the role on the grounds that organising industrial conscription would conflict with the 'impartially neutral attitude' necessary for its industrial relations role:

> *its own preoccupations should be the representation of the labour attitude and advising the Government on labour questions... [the ministry] contemplated in the event of another Great War the transference of the Employment Exchange machinery both at HQ and locally to the body charged with the administration of the manpower machinery...*

Thus, in order to maintain the purity of its industrial relations role, the ministry was willing to give up the unique asset of its nationwide organisation. It had perhaps forgotten Hodge's comment in 1917 that without the exchanges the ministry would be a 'mutilated fragment with no very obvious reason for further existence' (page 43). Not only was this purist line adopted in 1923. It became seemingly immutable.

From 1936 onwards, doubts about this plan were expressed within the Ministry of Labour, particularly as the ministry acted as 'official parent' for a ministry of National Service. This included taking on its functions in advance, such as maintaining the vital Schedule of Reserved Occupations. When, at the time of Munich, offers of assistance flooded in from those with professional and technical qualifications, the ministry began its Central Register. After Munich, the ministry drew up the National Service Handbook and organised a successful campaign throughout the country to recruit volunteers for the armed forces and Civil Defence. National Service Committees were set up throughout the country. Following Hitler's occupation of Prague, the ministry was responsible for the Military Training Act of May 1939, which introduced compulsory military training for young men. In these activities, the exchanges played a key role.

Just before the outbreak of war, the ministry finally acknowledged the undesirability of a separate ministry of National Service. It was realised that the arguments about the incompatibility of the industrial relations and mobilisation roles had been overplayed and that coherence and continuity in labour organisation were more important. On 1 August 1939, the Manpower (Policy) Committee accepted a recommendation from Ernest Brown that his ministry should after all retain national service responsibilities in the event of war. On 8 September, shortly after the outbreak of war, the ministry was formally renamed the Ministry of Labour and National Service, a title which it would retain until 1959. In the nick of time, a divorce between the ministry and the exchanges had been averted, to the great benefit of the nation.

Another controversial issue was whether industrial conscription could be introduced at the start of a major war. This had been assumed by Graham Greene's Sub-Committee up to 1936, when Humbert Wolfe took over from Eady as the ministry's representative. Wolfe questioned whether public opinion would permit government to take such draconian powers at the outset of a war. It was 'futile and foolish to face a future war with a scheme based on assumptions wholly contrary to British history'.[3] In the first half of 1939, Wolfe's policy of gradualism was reflected in the ministry's discussions about war-time labour controls with the Employers' Confederation and the TUC. The TUC, deeply distrustful of the Chamberlain government, would only stomach some form of industry self-government, but this was unacceptable to the government. The ministry then came under criticism from the Committee of Imperial Defence, and from economists led by Lord Stamp, for failing to produce positive war plans. The ministry's response was the Control of Employment Bill, making it compulsory to engage workers through the exchanges, but this was watered down so much in discussion with the TUC and the Labour Party as to be ineffective.

The phoney war

On Sunday, 3 September 1939, war was declared, and on the same day the National Service Act was rushed through Parliament. The first eight months of the war were known as the phoney war. Hitler's expected aerial onslaught on

British towns did not take place. Nor was there fighting on the western front. The major achievement of the exchanges was to register some 450,000 men for the services.

With the outbreak of war, the ministry's War Book, which had been completed under great pressure in July, came into operation.[4] Instructions were issued relaxing the administration of unemployment insurance. As part of the great exodus from London for fear of bombing, the Claims and Records Office at Kew was closed down (never to reopen). The 2800 staff were dispersed to Divisional and local offices. Part of the ministry's Headquarters was despatched to Southport in Lancashire, and a skeleton Claims and Records Office of 400 staff established there (later in Acton). 'Refuges' for use in air raids were created at the London HQs at Montague House and Metropole House. (In 1941 the ministry moved to 8, St James Square.) Divisional Controllers were advised that, in the event of imminent danger or a breakdown of communications with HQ, they were to take their orders from the 12 Regional Commissioners who had been appointed. The number of Divisions was increased from nine to 12 to fit in with the Regional Commissioners. (The South East Division was later abolished.)

It was a time of hectic activity. In September, 'night duty' was introduced in exchanges so that they could receive instructions from the centre at any time, but in October this was reduced to ensuring the exchanges were manned on Saturday afternoons and Sundays. In January, top officials decided after some discussion that 'female staff might be employed at the counter (for registering men for military purposes) if circumstances rendered such a course inevitable'.[5]

But uncertainty continued on the question of the supply of labour to industries vital to the war effort.[6] It was in this connection that Humbert Wolfe rendered his last service before his sudden death, which shocked the ministry in January 1940. He led the first manpower survey of the war. He concluded that there was a need to increase the labour force in war-related industries by 2.2 million by July 1941 – a rate of increase far in excess of that achieved in the First World War. He also pointed to disturbing immediate shortages of skilled labour in engineering, which were slowing down the build-up of the munitions industries. Machine tools were particularly scarce and exchanges were instructed to give the machine tool industry overriding priority. By March, 150 placings had been achieved, but there were still 650 unfilled vacancies. Unemployment was slowly falling – from 1.23 million in September 1939 to below one million in April 1940. But the overall numbers in engineering still fell far short of the target, while there were alarming signs of the poaching of labour and wage inflation. The ministry remained reluctant to take on too much responsibility. It hoped to make progress by cooperation with employers and unions, but such cooperation was not easy to achieve. The unions remained suspicious of the Chamberlain government, while the employers blamed others for their problems. The ministry came under criticism again for letting things drift. On 4 May 1940, Mr Churchill, First Lord of the Admiralty, commented, 'we have hardly begun to organise manpower for the production of munitions'.[7] On 8 May, the supply departments urged that full responsibility for the control and recruitment of civilian labour should be vested in the Ministry of Labour, which should have the necessary powers. At this point, Chamberlain's government fell.

The advent of Ernest Bevin

May 1940 was a turning point in the war. Churchill became Prime Minister, while Hitler successfully invaded Belgium, Holland and France. British forces were evacuated from Dunkirk. May 1940 was also a turning point in labour policy. To general surprise, Churchill appointed Ernest Bevin as Minister of Labour, despite his complete lack of Parliamentary experience.[8] It was an inspired choice, reflecting Churchill's admiration for Bevin's patriotism and energy and also his recognition of the importance of union cooperation in the war effort. At a stroke, the appointment resolved the dilemma which had haunted the ministry from 1923 onwards – how to reconcile its role in industrial relations with responsibility for mobilising the labour force for war. Bevin, the leader of the Transport and General Workers' Union, was the very embodiment of the labour movement and could tackle wartime industrial relations problems with a directness that middle class ministers could not emulate. But it would be wrong to see him as a trade union 'fixer'. He was a man of extraordinary vision and creativity. Having thought he was nearing retiring age, he found himself to his surprise dominating the labour scene in Britain in a way no one has done before or since. Moreover, as he discharged his wartime role, he constantly had his eye on the task of building a better future after the war.

Bevin's appointment quickly changed the atmosphere in the ministry and the exchange service. From now on, there was no doubt who was in charge. Godfrey Ince later commented that Bevin 'knew what he wanted to do, knew where he wanted to go – and how to get there'.[9] Contrary to popular belief, civil servants prefer strong Ministers. Bevin provided strong leadership in abundance, but he was also prepared to listen and was deeply loyal to his civil servants. Bevin was initially mystified by Sir Thomas Phillips, the donnish Permanent Secretary, but soon grew to respect not only Phillips' famed drafting skills, but also his 'lucidity of mind and disinterested judgement'.[10]

The Ministry of Labour war machine

Bevin was taking over a Department which had formidable administrative strengths but which, up to his appointment, lacked a clear sense of direction about how best to use them in wartime. All this changed with Bevin's appointment. Alan Bullock writes:

> To treat Bevin's success at the Ministry of Labour as a virtuoso solo performance is to miss the point: the most important element

> *in it was his ability to weld together and inspire a team of men and women who, years later, without exception, still looked back on this as the most exciting part of their official careers.*[11]

Inevitably, the ministry had to expand. This expansion was partly at HQ, where the number of Deputy Secretaries rose from one at the outbreak of war to three by 1943 – Sir Frederick Leggett, Sir Frank Tribe and Godfrey Ince. The labour supply function rose from being relatively modest to comprise four large departments. The HQ ranks were enhanced by outsiders or 'irregulars', some from business or the trade unions and some from the academic world, such as Beveridge, Harold Wilson and HMD Parker. The expansion was also in the field, and the total staff of the ministry rose from 31,600 at the outbreak of war to a peak of 42,000, the vast majority of whom were in the exchanges.[12]

As Bevin gained experience in the job, he saw a need for a single official who, under his guidance, could direct the mobilisation of the entire manpower resources of the country: a Director General of Manpower. Beveridge, who was then an Under-Secretary in the ministry, longed to take on this role. He had many of the requisite qualities but was not an easy colleague with whom to work; moreover, he was known to be impatient with Bevin's caution in the use of compulsion. Bevin and Phillips wanted someone who was confident and decisive, but who would also ultimately work under their guidance. In June 1941, they chose Godfrey Ince.[13] A grammar school boy from Reigate, Ince graduated with distinction in mathematics and economics at University College, London, in 1913. After serving in the First War, he joined the Ministry of Labour. Later, with his 'phenomenal memory and mathematical brain', he became an expert on unemployment insurance and Chief Insurance Officer. In 1939, he was in charge of military recruitment. He was an excellent choice as Director General of Manpower. HMD Parker, historian and colleague, described him as 'a strong-willed man of action. In times of crisis, he was imperturbable and indefatigable'.[14] Bevin liked Ince's plain and direct advice which was 'not hedged about with debating subtleties'. As a result, 'there grew up between the two men a sense of mutual confidence and the fruit of their co-operation was the successful mobilisation of the manpower of the country'. His sense of leadership was reflected in his clear and challenging communications to the field. But Parker also pointed to Ince's 'innate streak of vanity and personal ambition' which made him enjoy his power and fame. Parker adds that

> *the strident tones with which he tried to dominate a conference tended to exacerbate where a little persuasiveness might have reconciled his opponents. But these defects, if betraying a lack of mental flexibility, reflected the fearless determination of his character.*

He was devoted to the ministry's staff but, Parker implied, sadly this was not reciprocated. Shy and taciturn, he neither drank nor smoked. He was 'a little intimidating to a stranger or junior. His fairly frequent visits to local offices tended to frighten rather than stimulate'. In the war, he was the right man at the right time. His weaknesses were more evident when he was Permanent Secretary after the war and faced the more subtle problems of peace.

One of the striking features of the war machine was the enhanced role of the Divisional Controllers (or 'Regional Controllers' as they were renamed in 1941.) It was for them (and their Regional Offices) to implement decisions taken at the centre, through the exchange service and through contacts with industry. Despite wartime disruption, they continued to meet almost every month at the ministry's London HQ, normally under Ince's chairmanship. This helped them to grasp what was required of them as the government's grip on the labour force tightened and also enabled HQ officials to learn what was happening in the real world. Bevin often attended these meetings himself, believing as he did that Britain was over-centralised and that 'the future course of development of government of this country would revolve largely around regional organisation'.[15] On this, as on much else, he was ahead of his time. Bevin wanted the Controllers to hold on to their strong contacts with industry after the war. A businessman from ICI who served in the ministry commented at the end of the war that the Controllers' role had developed 'beyond all recognition'.[16]

The pressures of work on applications for individual deferment of National Service led to the creation in 1942 of 44 District Manpower Offices – an administrative tier between the Regional Office and the local office. Linked with these offices were the District Manpower Boards, who reached decisions on deferment. The chairmen and officers of these new institutions were largely temporary officials of the ministry who were recruited externally. They built up 'a reputation for reliability, equity and courtesy'.[17]

The mobilisation process

On the day after his arrival at the ministry, Bevin presented to Phillips a four-page memorandum setting out his ideas.[18] He would accept full responsibility for labour supply and the use of labour, assisted by a large team of labour supply inspectors, and a Production Council to determine priorities. His Divisional Controllers should chair the 12 Area Boards established by the ministry of Supply to organise labour supply in each region. There should be 'bold and comprehensive training schemes'. At this stage, Bevin did not seek powers for industrial conscription or direction of labour. His union background made him cautious about such powers. But at the same time the question of direction of labour was being addressed by a Committee chaired by Neville Chamberlain, Lord President of the Council. Chamberlain produced a report for the War Cabinet recommending that, in a military emergency, the Minister of Labour and National Service, through designated National Service Officers, should have power to 'direct and require the services or labour of any person over 16 years of age'. On 20 May, both these papers went to a War Cabinet, perturbed by news of the disintegration of France. The Cabinet's decisions were an amalgamation of Bevin's and Chamberlain's proposals. On 22 May, the Cabinet obtained Parliamentary approval for the Emergency Powers Bill. The first Defence Regulation under this new legislation armed the Minister of Labour with the powers Chamberlain had recommended. Also on 22 May, Bevin secured the support of the National Joint Advisory Council representing employers and unions.

The momentous War Cabinet decisions of 20 May 1940 set the pattern for mobilisation for the rest of the war. Both the Production Council and the Labour Supply inspectors were established. Local offices were advised above all to look out for 'bottlenecks' in the mobilisation of labour and adopt every means at their disposal to remove them. On 5 June 1940, Bevin published an order requiring all jobs in key industries to be filled through the exchanges and banning advertising for labour. This gave the exchanges a better idea of the demand for labour and enabled them to persuade workers to take the most vital jobs. Other industries were also forbidden to recruit miners or farmworkers. In August, he required the registration of all workers with an engineering background who were working in other industries. All those unemployed for a month or more were interviewed, and it was found that 77 per cent of them were fit for work without rehabilitation, while 42 per cent were willing to take up work in other areas.[19] They were progressively integrated into work. At the same time, the Government Training Centres were expanded.

Bevin remained cautious about using his unprecedented powers over labour. He was a believer in what he called 'voluntaryism'. None the less, problems of labour shortage and excessive turnover persisted. Moreover, in the latter part of 1940, the second Manpower Survey of the War, carried out by Beveridge, assisted by Harold Wilson, produced results which were extremely challenging.[20] The armed forces were seeking almost two million additional personnel and the munitions industries nearly 1.5 million additional personnel by late 1941. These demands could only be met by big transfers of labour from the munitions industries to the Forces and from less essential industries to munitions industries, and by dilution and the mobilisation of large numbers of 'unoccupied' or under-occupied women. In January 1941, influenced by Beveridge, Bevin presented a paper called the Heads of Labour Policy to the War Cabinet. It was agreed that:

- workers could not leave, or be discharged from, establishments designated as engaged in 'national work', without the agreement of a National Service Officer; designation would involve checking that workers' terms and conditions, welfare and training were satisfactory;
- powers of registration of men and women at the exchanges would be used to ensure an adequate supply of labour for national work; and
- a more refined system would be introduced for defining who was exempt from call-up to the armed forces.[21]

It was this change of policy which enabled the ministry to mobilise the country's labour force so completely.

The first of these changes was embodied in the Essential Work Order of March 1941. By December 1941 it applied to 55 industries and 27,000 undertakings, covering 4.5 million workers.[22] The second enabled the ministry to call up successive age groups for registration and to identify those, particularly women, who were either not employed or were employed on low priority work and who could be moved, by direction if necessary, to national work. Up to 31 July 1941, only 2943 individual directions were issued.[23] However, the existence of these powers in the background enabled the exchange staff to persuade workers to move to, or to stay in, essential work.

By the summer of 1941, Bevin could feel some satisfaction that the Forces and munitions industries accounted for 37 per cent of the working population as against only 30 per cent a year before, when he had taken office. Moreover, it was in 1941 that both the USSR and the USA entered the war, offering the prospect of ultimate victory. But the third Manpower Survey of the War, which reported in October 1941, removed any grounds for complacency about manpower. It put the demand for additional manpower in the Forces and munitions industries by June 1942 at above two million. By December 1941, Bevin and Anderson, the Lord President, obtained the War Cabinet's agreement to

- lowering the call-up for young men to eighteen-and-a-half;
- removing reservation by occupation as grounds for exemption from military service and replacing it by highly selective individual reservation;
- a statutory obligation on all men and women from 18–60 to carry out some form of national service; and
- the conscription of women by age groups to the Auxiliary Services.

The last of these was the most controversial and was only agreed after intense discussion and agreement on safeguards, such as the exclusion of married women.

Against the relentless pressures of the war, Bevin was now much more willing to use compulsory powers, conscious as he was that the exchanges had built up the capacity to handle the problems inherent in such draconian powers. From this time onwards, powers of direction were used more extensively, building up to a total of one million directions in the war as a whole, which was still only a tiny fraction of total engagements. The registration of women went smoothly and by the end of 1942 over eight million women had been registered for war service. In many cases, this involved transferring young women from one region to another. Exchange officials handled this very conscientiously, seeing them off from their home area and welcoming them at their new area, organising meals, reception centres and accommodation. In July 1942, registration was extended to women up to the age of 51 – or 'grannies', as the press described them – causing a major controversy.

In Autumn 1943, the armed forces were still expanding in preparation for D-Day. But the peak of mobilisation had been reached. In four years, the number of people employed in the Forces, Civil Defence and industry had increased to over 22 million, a rise of over 3.75 million, of whom 2.5 million were women. Bevin warned the War Cabinet that there were no further reserves of labour on which to draw.[24] Any further demands could only be met by transfers.

The most intractable problem facing Bevin in the latter part of the war was the shortage of coal miners. In December 1943, he introduced a system of balloting to allocate one in ten of the young men called up for National Service to the mines. At HQ, 10 numbers – 0 to 9 – were put in a hat and one was drawn out in Bevin's presence. Those young men whose National Service number ended with the chosen digit became 'Bevin boys'. This system was deeply unpopular, but it produced 19,000 young men for the mines.[25]

Bevin and the exchanges

No Minister of Labour took a keener personal interest in the exchanges. This interest went back a long way. In March 1945, he recalled that in the inter-war years:

> *As a union official, I saw so many people in the Department who had great ability and yet always seemed to me so helpless and hopeless of doing the things that I felt sure they knew ought to be done.*[26]

He went on to say that grappling with the submerged tenth of the population must have been a soul-destroying job: 'I often wondered how it was possible to remain so courteous in spite of all the criticism from year to year.' Here he was perhaps being kind to his listeners. Like other trade union leaders, he had been uneasy about the way the exchanges operated. In May 1941, he said:

> *I have tried to humanise the labour exchanges and honestly, I think, with some success. I have appointed special people and have tried to create in them the idea that their prime duty as officials is not to pay out relief, but to find a clue in the occupation or the hobby of the men they are interviewing which would lead to the discernment of their capacity for assisting the war effort.*[27]

As part of his 'humanising' drive, he issued an instruction that exchange staff should say 'Good morning' to any member of the public coming for advice or an interview.[28]

Trevor Evans, then industrial correspondent of the *Daily Express*, gives a good account of how Bevin set about influencing the managers:

> *Into a regional centre would be invited all the managers of the employment offices in the area. Usually there would be about sixty present. Bevin would open the discussion by outlining his immediate programme. He would end: 'I cannot issue regulations which will cover all the contingencies you are likely to meet in the course of your day to day work. You must use your own initiative. If you make a mistake I will stand by you. One thing I will not forgive. That is inaction.*
>
> *That was a clever move on Bevin's part. It gave every local official a sense of playing a part in the national policy of his department.*[29]

By contrast with their regulatory role before the war, Bevin wanted the managers to 'be like a parish priest looking after the industrial welfare of their people and the Regional Controller like a bishop'.[30]

Bevin wanted to improve the way in which exchanges related to the public. Early in his period of office, he received many complaints from middle class women who were unfamiliar with the exchanges and had come to them to offer their services in the war effort. They felt they were treated in an off-hand fashion. In 1942, a woman officer, new to the civil service, was asked to investigate these complaints. She felt that the problem was that the exchanges were seen by many as 'places of last resort'. The worst of them 'reeked of unemployment and social defeat'. The key was for the staff to treat each woman as an individual, rather like the staff of a retail store.[31] But it was difficult for the exchange officials to get things right. In August 1941, Ince told Controllers that 'what women wanted was to be told what to do. A policy of firmness would produce the numbers'.[32] However, firmness, too, presented risks. Six months later, Controllers were warned that some staff were making too many directions and 'adopting a Hitlerite attitude'.[33] In July 1942, Ince upset the Regional Controllers when he reported a unanimous view among a group of industrial welfare officers that the exchanges were 'rude to the public', though he was able to reassure them later that these views were not universal in welfare circles.[34]

One response to these complaints was to encourage exchanges to arrange private interviews with people registering for national service, rather than snatched conversations over the counter with the waiting queue listening. This became the norm once the exchanges found themselves registering huge numbers of women from 1941 onwards. Bevin saw this 'interviewing system' as one of the most important innovations of the war and hoped that it would lead to a lasting improvement in exchange practice.

Another response was to improve the training of front-line staff, many of whom lacked interviewing skills. Arton Wilson, the Director of Establishments, with a wealth of experience of the ministry's services, was a key figure in giving effect to Bevin's wish to improve the quality of front-line work. From July 1942 onwards he gave high priority to staff training, starting with courses for front-line clerks, where he drew on Post Office experience. Later on, courses were provided for the supervisors of employment sections and managers and a staff training centre was established in London.

Bevin urged that the ministry should recruit trade union clerks and staff from the employment departments of large factories to work in the exchanges. This, like the similar views of Citrine in 1930 (page 69), was brushed aside. The Controllers did not want to recruit 'trade union clerks', while it was unrealistic to seek to recruit factory employment staff, who were overloaded.[35]

Bevin wanted to improve the appearance of the exchanges. He found them, including some housed in new buildings, 'extremely depressing':

> *Exchanges ought not to be so constructed as to make a man who is already depressed feel that the world is on top of him. They ought not to possess a uniform prison-like appearance, but should be built with some regard for local characteristics.*[36]

Arton Wilson was delighted with Bevin's approach, as compared with the 'old policy of dinginess and backwaters which had for long been imposed on the Department'.[37] In 1944, Bevin wrote to the Minister of Works urging a major improvement in the estate. The exchanges should be 'located in a central part of town, preferably in a quiet part of, or adjoining, a main thoroughfare'. They should be dignified but not institutional in appearance and the 'furniture and equipment must be of good quality and cheerful appearance'.[38] These views influenced post-war designs beneficially, though economic stringency held up any major improvement in the estate.

In his zeal to change the image of the exchanges, Bevin wanted the ministry to get rid of the term 'Employment Exchange' at the earliest possible moment.[39] But the subsequent search for a name that would 'trip off the tongue' proved abortive and the old name survived until marketing specialists came up with 'Jobcentre' in 1972.

In December 1944, Bevin's campaign to 'humanise the exchanges' was reflected in a major paper for Controllers about the post-war organisation of local offices. The objective was to satisfy the public with interviews carried out in 'an understanding manner' in an office where the premises were 'suitable and well located and the atmosphere 'dignified, friendly and attractive'. There was emphasis on good directional signs, a friendly enquiry point at the entrance and keeping the routine clerical work out of the public eye. The employment section should offer reasonable privacy for interviews with placing officers who specialised by occupation. It should be separated from the insurance section but should have good links with it. The insurance section must avoid congestion and an 'atmosphere of bustle and confusion'. Controllers welcomed these ideas, but remained concerned about 'the danger of unemployment insurance work overshadowing other duties'.[40]

The Beveridge Report on Social Insurance and Allied Services

From the beginning of the war, Beveridge hoped for a central role in organising the nation's manpower.[41] He was deeply frustrated by the reluctance of Ministers to make full use of his services. By 1941, the biggest task he had been given was that of leading a manpower survey (page 93). From December 1940 he was employed as a full-time Under-Secretary in the Ministry of Labour. Here his tendency to operate like a loose cannon did not endear him to his colleagues. One recalled Beveridge arriving uninvited and unbriefed at a tricky meeting with the Treasury and confusing the meeting with some dogmatic proposals.[42] Beveridge, insensitive to the impression he was creating, still hoped to be put in charge of manpower. Thus Bevin's decision in June 1941 to make Ince Director General of Manpower (page 91) came as an unpleasant shock.

Bevin now wished to get Beveridge out of the ministry. He seized an opportunity to achieve this by offering Beveridge the Chairmanship of an Inter-Departmental Committee on Social Insurance and Allied Service. It is said that Beveridge emerged from Bevin's room with tears in his eyes.[43] For the second time, a trade union Minister had pushed him out of the Ministry of Labour in wartime. For his new work, Beveridge would report to Arthur Greenwood, Minister without Portfolio, who was responsible for reconstruction, later replaced by Sir William Jowitt, the Paymaster General.

This is not the place to describe how Beveridge managed to transform what appeared to be a dry and technical exercise into the production of the most famous social policy document of the century. The account here will concentrate on the implications for the employment service of his report, which appeared in November 1942.[44]

At the heart of his report was the idea of creating a comprehensive system of social security under a new Ministry of Social Security. This meant that responsibility for unemployment insurance, which had been a central role of the Ministry of Labour since its creation, would pass to the new ministry. Unemployment benefit would continue broadly on the principles established before the war, but would be indefinite in duration, with no switch to means-tested unemployment assistance after contributions were exhausted. However, continued receipt of benefit after, say, six months, might be subject to attendance at a work or training centre. 'A minor reason' for this proposal was that:

> such a condition is the most effective way of unmasking the relatively few persons who may be suspected of malingering, who have perhaps some concealed means of earning which they are combining with an appearance of unemployment.

This is interesting as anticipating one of the arguments for forms of 'workfare' in the 1980s and 1990s. But more importantly, this requirement was part of a framework of reciprocal obligations between state and citizen:

> *The correlative of the State's undertaking to ensure adequate benefit for unavoidable interruption of earnings, however long, is enforcement of the citizen's obligation to seek and accept all reasonable opportunities of work, to co-operate in measures designed to save him from habituation to idleness...*[45]

On the administration of unemployment benefit, Beveridge said it needed to be co-located with employment work:

> *the administration of unemployment benefit depends on the test of availability for work which is the function of the employment exchanges: payment of unemployment benefit and placing in employment must in practice take place at the same local offices.*

This was consistent with his approach ever since his evidence to the Royal Commission on the Poor Law in 1907. But in 1942 he diverged from his previous thinking by recommending that this co-location might be achieved by transferring the 'registration and placing function of the Ministry of Labour and National Service to the Ministry of Social Security'. He was so absorbed in social security reform as to forget his earlier concern that the exchanges' labour market role could be damaged if they were associated too closely with the relief of distress (page 13). His alternative option was to keep them in the Ministry of Labour, but to house the staff in Ministry of Social Security offices – still a welfare-dominated approach.

When Beveridge's report came out, Sir Thomas Phillips was asked to chair an inter-departmental committee to consider the government's response. Phillips' report to Ministers[46] pointed out that Beveridge's tentative proposal to transfer the Exchanges to the Ministry of Social Security:

> *would place the wrong emphasis on their function as placing agencies by treating it as if it were primarily to administer an unemployment benefit test, very much as if the main function of a health service were to be that of giving certificates for disability benefit.*

Phillips' report also expressed doubt about the idea of indefinite unemployment benefit; there was much to be said in ordinary times for a man to face a move to assistance which was less welcome to many men. In other words, setting a limit to insurance-based benefit had a useful deterrent effect. (Bevin thought that, while insurance might contribute to unemployment relief, the Treasury should also contribute through unemployment assistance).[47] Another concern expressed by Phillips related to Beveridge's assumption of 8.5 per cent unemployment, given pre-war experience of much higher levels. If unemployment reverted to its pre-war levels, Beveridge's package could become impossibly costly. He asked Ministers whether the containment of unemployment 'is considered to be something which we intend to strain every effort to

Office of Hope

achieve'. An affirmative answer to this question was given in the White Paper on Employment Policy in May 1944.

Phillips suggested that detailed planning for implementing the Beveridge Report should be taken over by a full-time team drawn from relevant departments. Such a team was set up under Thomas Sheepshanks,[48] with Arthur Patterson as the Ministry of Labour representative. This team worked very effectively, reporting to the Ministerial Reconstruction Committee, chaired initially by Jowitt and later by Lord Woolton. Eventually, in September 1944, the White Paper on Social Insurance set out the government's conclusions on the Beveridge Report.

The White Paper rejected Beveridge's idea of indefinite insurance-based unemployment benefit, in favour of a limit normally of 30 weeks, after which people would be reliant on means-tested assistance. So the regime was to resemble that established under the Unemployment Act 1934. Moreover, the network of assistance offices was to remain, running alongside a new network of national insurance offices.

On the administration of unemployment benefit, the White Paper said that the employment exchanges would remain in the Ministry of Labour and that unemployment benefit would be paid, as at present, at the employment exchange. The reality was that, although the policy on unemployment insurance would now shift to the new Ministry of National Insurance, nearly all its delivery, apart from the collection of contributions, would remain with the Ministry of Labour on an 'agency' basis. In practice, the transfer of policy responsibility would 'make little practical difference in the Regions'.[49] This was the outcome of a lengthy debate initially involving the Ministry of Labour and Patterson in Sheepshanks' planning team.[50] The debate is interesting as it foreshadowed debates that occurred periodically in the subsequent 50 years. In April 1943, Patterson reported to Sheepshanks on a discussion with Arton Wilson, the Ministry of Labour's Director of Establishments. Three options were being seriously considered:

- To transfer unemployment insurance work to new local social security offices that were *not* co-located with exchanges. According to Patterson, many Ministry of Labour people favoured this, without considering it carefully, 'because they wanted to be rid of the great masses of unemployed workers coming to prove unemployment or to seek their benefit'. This concept of 'separation', in order to improve the image of the exchanges, was to become the ministry's objective under Barbara Castle in 1968. However, in 1943 there were seen to be two objections to it. First, there was Beveridge's argument that co-location was necessary to ensure that benefit recipients' availability for work was tested. Secondly, Bevin, sensitive to possible public reactions, 'felt strongly that applicants should not be sent from one officer to another'.
- To transfer unemployment insurance work to new local social security offices that *were* co-located with exchanges. This was favoured by Sir Thomas Phillips. Interestingly, this solution has affinities with that adopted

by John Major's government for the introduction of the Jobseeker's Allowance in 1996. Wilson and Patterson felt that the main objection was that it created divided responsibility for pieces of work that were closely interwoven and that it would be extravagant in small towns. Also, co-location was difficult to achieve in practice.
- To retain all the day-to-day work on unemployment benefit in the exchanges, for them to carry out as agents of the new Ministry of National Insurance.

It was this third option which was favoured by Wilson and Patterson and was the solution eventually adopted. It ensured co-location and kept all the intricate administrative work in the hands of a single department. The risk, which could not be anticipated in 1943–44, was that the Ministry of Labour's lack of any policy responsibility might in the long run affect their attitude to their delivery role.

In November 1944, the Ministry of National Insurance was established. Sir Thomas Phillips became Permanent Secretary of the new ministry and Sir Godfrey Ince took his place at the Ministry of Labour – an outcome that reflected Phillips' long-standing expertise in social insurance and also perhaps Bevin's preferences as between the two men. Harold Emmerson became Director General of Manpower for the remainder of the war.

On 1 April 1945, policy for unemployment insurance and assistance was formally transferred to the Minister of National Insurance. With the informality characteristic of British administration, the transfer was defined in a letter from Phillips to Ince.[51] Certain HQ personnel engaged in policy work would transfer to the new ministry, but the Ministry of Labour retained virtually all the work done at regional and local level, including adjudication by local Insurance Officers. The one point of contention was the extent to which the new ministry had the right to make enquiries direct to regional and local offices of the Ministry of Labour. The Ministry of Labour wished to restrict this right for fear of losing control of its own staff.

This was a curiously British revolution, involving a historic switch of responsibility for unemployment relief. It largely took away the Ministry of Labour's social role, which had been so important before the war. Yet the transfer was so organised that neither the public nor the staff would perceive any difference.

Technical, scientific and managerial personnel

During and after the war, the Ministry of Labour's role in the deployment of labour extended to those who were highly qualified whether by academic study or by experience.[52] This work was linked with, but not integrated into, the exchange service. It was not part of the war planning begun in the early 1920s but arose as a response to the spontaneous offers of service made at the time of the Munich crisis.

Thus from 1938 onwards, the ministry kept a Central Register of people with higher educational or scientific attainments and extended this by enquiries to the universities. In the early years of the war, it was found that those with technical and scientific expertise were greatly in demand, much more so than those with a managerial background. Technical personnel were drafted into the ministry to help match those on the register with the vacancies arising. From July 1940 onwards, all people with specified qualifications (eg engineers and chemists) were required to register their particulars.

In December 1939, it was decided to set up 16 offices in major towns to act as a register primarily for those whose qualifications were not such as to justify being on the Central Register. In March 1942, the ministry established an Appointments Department, divided into two branches – the Central Register, which focused on high-level scientists and engineers, and an Appointments Register for the rest, operating through 31 Appointments Offices.

In this way, the ministry had in effect set up a separate employment exchange system for the most highly qualified personnel whose expertise was most vital to the war effort. Between April 1942 and the end of the war, the Appointments Offices placed nearly 58,000 registrants.

Disabled Persons (Employment) Act 1944

It was characteristic of Bevin that he should seize the opportunities presented by the war to make a great improvement in the employment provision for disabled people. There was deep concern about those injured in the war, whether in the armed forces or civilians. From autumn 1941, it was arranged for ministry officials to visit those convalescing in hospital to discuss their future. Training was provided at colleges in Leatherhead and Exeter run by voluntary organisations.

In December 1941, Bevin set up an Inter-Departmental Committee chaired by his Parliamentary Secretary, George Tomlinson, with broad terms of reference. In January 1943, the Committee's final report was published as a White Paper, recommending far-reaching measures for the rehabilitation, training and placing of disabled people, whether they were victims of the war or had become disabled in some other way. Employers would be required to employ a prescribed quota from a disabled persons' register. This went far beyond the King's National Roll set up after the First War. In following up the Report, the Ministry of Labour decided to install specially trained Disablement Resettlement Officers (DROs) throughout the exchange network and to set up a specialist rehabilitation unit at Egham.

In 1944, the Disabled Persons (Employment) Act gave legislative effect to Tomlinson's proposals. Bevin showed his emotional commitment to this legislation when he said later that: 'One of the proudest days of my life was to stand in the House of Lords when the Royal Assent was given ...'[53]

Demobilisation and resettlement

It will be recalled that, following the First World War, the elaborate plans for demobilisation had to be scrapped in 1919 in response to popular clamour. Things were better handled at the end of the Second War. But planning was by no means straightforward, once it was realised that there would be two ends to the war, one in Europe and one in Asia. How these problems were resolved makes a curious story.[54]

In the summer of 1943, Bevin was persuaded to take a holiday in Scotland. In his absence, Churchill asked Sir William Jowitt to chair a new committee on demobilisation, on which the Ministry of Labour was not represented. Bevin was furious. When Jowitt's report came out in November, Bevin persuaded the War Cabinet to let him come up with alternative proposals. On returning to the ministry, Bevin told Ince to produce a paper 'yesterday', setting out the proposals the two of them had already discussed. Bevin banned the word 'demobilisation', which would be misunderstood, and instead referred to 're-allocation of man-power'. Call-up of new recruits would continue while others left the forces. Those released from the forces would fall into two classes:

- Class A – on the basis of age and length of service, and
- Class B – a much smaller group of men selected on the basis of special qualifications for work useful to reconstruction.

This very simple plan was agreed by the War Cabinet and formed the basis for the remarkably smooth process which followed. The ministry sent some of its officials to explain the resettlement plans to troops in the various theatres of war. These officials were carefully selected as they had to be able to 'stand up to vigorous heckling'.[55] The ministry also set up Resettlement Advice Offices in all the major towns throughout the country, staffed with officers chosen for their personal qualities and ability to present information on a wide range of subjects, including, for instance, housing and domestic problems as well as employment and training.

Conclusion

In May 1945, Churchill's Coalition Government eventually came to an end. During his last months at the ministry, in a remarkable and emotional speech to HQ staff,[56] Bevin said that

> When I came to the Department, I made up my mind to try and make it rank, before I left it, equal with the Treasury...The ministry is now regarded as making this tremendous contribution to the war effort and, whatever happens to me, I hope you will always keep your chin up and never lose the position you have achieved in the war.

Office of Hope

He talked of the 'quiet unruffled way in which millions of people have been moved about in this war'. He referred to many things that he held dear – better premises, 'the interviewing system', services for the disabled, links with industry, training. In reply, Ince praised Bevin for having raised the status of the Department and added, tempting fate, 'we have long since left the Treasury far behind'.

Ince later listed some statistics concerning the ministry's war effort:[57]

- 32 million people were registered for one purpose or another;
- 8.8 million interviews were carried out under the Registration of Employment Order;
- 22.5 million vacancies were filled by the exchanges and Appointment Offices;
- the unemployed were reduced to 54,000 by the end of 1944;
- from the 'non-industrial' classes, 0.5 million men and 2.5 million women were mobilised for full-time or part-time work;
- the armed forces were increased from 80,000 in mid-1939 to 5 million on D-Day;
- those employed on munitions and equipment for the Forces increased from 1.27 million in mid-1939 to 5.18 million in mid-1943;
- those employed in the 'less essential industries' were reduced from over 9 million in mid-1939 to 6 million in mid-1944.

It is important to remember how revolutionary were many of the steps taken by the ministry during the war, particularly as regards the mobilisation of women. Professor Postan commented that 'in the end, the Minister of Labour and the War Cabinet in general went further in this direction than the war governments of any other country, not excluding Germany and Russia'.[58]

It was in this period that the exchanges attained their strongest influence on British life. The exchange machinery was indispensable to the mobilisation of the nation for war, as Bevin recognised in a D-Day statement:

> ...*the ability it afforded us to keep in intimate touch with everything that was going on in the localities and at the same time co-ordinating it in a great national machine. From the clerk in the Employment Exchange to the manager, the Regional Controller, right up to the top, there has been demonstrated a great understanding of the people. The jobs have been very tedious and worrying and made more difficult by the fact that you had to get people to do things without always telling them the reason; the shifting of preferences; the changeover of priorities. But the great factor has been the enthusiasm of the staff and the flexibility of the machine.*[59]

7

Post-War Full Employment, 1945–60

'The Government accepts as one of their primary aims and responsibilities the maintenance of a high and stable level of employment after the war.' (White Paper on Employment Policy, 1944)

Introduction

After the remarkable achievements of the exchanges during the war, the following 15 years of peace proved to be an anti-climax. It was not clear at first that this would be the case. In the perilous years of economic weakness immediately following the war, the exchanges played a vital role in switching the labour force from swords to ploughshares and in mobilising it to meet Britain's economic priorities. This phase was then curiously extended by the rearmament prompted by the Korean War. But in reality, by the early 1950s Britain was already reverting to a largely unregulated peacetime economy. The surprising feature to anyone with memories of the inter-war years was the persistence of full employment and labour shortage. Less surprising were the government's equally persistent economic difficulties, which led to periodic bouts of cost-cutting. In this climate, the role of the exchanges began to look increasingly marginal.

This chapter traces the impact of the post-war Ministry of Labour on the exchanges, the inexorable decline in resources, the process of demobilisation and resettlement, the impact of full employment and the resumption of limited labour controls from 1952 to 1956. It goes on to look at the attempts to relaunch the exchanges, the trends in placing performance and the role the exchanges played in assisting special groups, such as disabled people, young people, the highly qualified and, most interestingly, immigrants from overseas.

The Ministry of Labour after the war

Chapter 6 indicated the importance both of the Ministry of Labour and the exchanges at the time when Bevin departed in May 1945. Even if the ministry was not in reality a rival to the Treasury as he had intended, it was a key domestic Department, in contrast with the 'least important Department' of the inter-war years. How did it come about that this strong position was not maintained after the Labour Party's triumph in the General Election of July 1945?

In peacetime, some decline in the ministry's position was inevitable. In the war, labour had set the ultimate limits of the war effort, so that the ministry responsible for mobilising it was in an inherently strong position. For several years after the war, economic conditions were such that the ministry continued to play a strong interventionist role in the labour market. But once the economic blizzard had subsided, the British preference for an unregulated economy diminished the role of the ministry, though arguably the chronic labour shortages of the 1950s offered more opportunities for a positive role than either the ministry or the government was ready to seize. Moreover, while the ministry had gained responsibility for the Factory Inspectorate, it had lost two of its most important pre-war policy functions – unemployment insurance, which went to the Ministry of National Insurance, and regional development, which went to the Board of Trade. Finally, Keynesian principles placed the overriding responsibility for the maintenance of full employment on the Treasury in its management of the economy, while government intervention in the supply side of the economy (eg on productivity) was at this time more for the Board of Trade than the Ministry of Labour.

Another factor was political leadership. The Ministers of Labour in this period were:

- May 1945–July 1945   RA Butler (Conservative)
- July 1945–Jan 1951   George Isaacs (Labour)
- Jan 1951–April 1951   Aneurin Bevan (Labour)
- April 1951–Oct 1951   George Robens (Labour)
- Oct 1951–Dec 1955   Walter Monckton (Conservative)
- Dec 1955–Oct 1959   Ian Macleod (Conservative)
- Oct 1959–July 1960   Edward Heath (Conservative).

Attlee's choice of George Isaacs as Minister of Labour for five-and-a-half years was a source of weakness for the ministry. Isaacs was a printing union leader, who had been in and out of Parliament between the wars, but had never held Ministerial office. In 1945, he was already in his sixties. His position as Chairman of the TUC General Council in 1945 may have led Attlee to appoint him as a way of cementing the new government's links with the trade unions. He was the kind of Minister who, when asked what Cabinet had decided, would tell his officials to await the minutes. His ineffectiveness was summed up by Fred Lee, his Parliamentary Secretary in 1950–51, who said that his policy of minimum intervention in industrial relations led others, notably Cripps, to seize the initiative on incomes policy. The Ministry of Labour became 'irrelevant to the main industrial strategy of the Government'.[1]

By 1950, Gaitskell, the Chancellor of the Exchequer, was urging Attlee to replace Isaacs with Aneurin Bevan, and in January 1951 Attlee 'at last' followed this advice.[2] But Bevan was at the ministry for only three months before his resignation. He was replaced by Alfred Robens, who served for six months. Neither of these short spells of office in a tottering Labour government offered new thinking on employment policy.

Nor was there any significant political interest in the future of the exchanges under the three Conservative Ministers of Labour of the 1950s. It was not surprising that Sir Walter Monckton (1951–55) should concentrate on the remit which Churchill had given him of preserving industrial peace.[3] The fact that Macleod (1955–59)[4] took no steps to halt the decline of the exchanges is perhaps more surprising. He was a much more dominant and decisive figure than Monckton and, moreover, had a keen interest in social policy and the maintenance of full employment. He did encourage fresh thinking on redundancies and recognised the importance of the exchanges in this context. But with economic crises before and after the Suez debacle it was not a good time to advocate additional expenditure. Ted Heath's spell of nine months as Minister (1959–60) was too short for him to make any impact on the issues discussed in this chapter.

Unfortunately, the top officials of the period did not make up for lack of Ministerial interest in employment policy. For most of the period, from 1944 to 1956, Sir Godfrey Ince was Permanent Secretary. His wartime prestige and strong personality made him a dominant figure, but the lack of mental flexibility which Parker detected in him (pages 91–2) stood in the way of him fundamentally rethinking the ministry's role in conditions of peacetime full employment. Even the emollient Monckton sometimes showed 'ill-concealed irritation' at Ince's 'lectures' at conferences.[5] Ince's successor, Sir Harold Emmerson, was drawing to the end of his career and, while giving staunch support to Macleod on industrial relations issues, did not offer new thinking on employment policy. Nor did the next Permanent Secretary, Sir Laurence Helsby, who lacked relevant experience and in any case soon moved on to become Head of the Civil Service.

The management of the exchanges

As had been the case since 1929, the exchange service was managed on a matrix basis. In 1945, policy responsibility for general employment work rested with the massive labour supply side of the wartime department. After the war, labour supply was reduced to a single Under-Secretary command under CWK Macmullan, who was followed by HMD Parker, both of whom incidentally were distinguished writers.[6] Also involved in the work of the exchanges in the late 1940s was Mary Smieton (DBE, 1949), who worked on employment policy and later in 1955 became a Deputy Secretary. By 1952, the labour supply function had been renamed Employment Services Department, led successively by Parker, JG Stewart and CJ Maston. These Under-Secretaries and the relevant Assistant Secretary (for a long time WH Hardman) struggled nobly and unsuccessfully to revive the general employment service. Meanwhile responsibility for disabled people, young people and military recruitment (still an important function until the call-up ended in 1960) generally rested elsewhere. But the official with the strongest grip on the exchanges was in reality the Director of Organisation and Establishments. It was to him that the Regional Controllers reported. Moreover, he controlled the crucial levers of staffing (including staff cuts exercises), premises work, inspection, and liaison with the Ministry of National Insurance about benefit work, which still occupied the largest proportion of staff time in the exchanges. It was an awkward structure in which management of the exchanges was widely shared and no one below the Permanent Secretary was in overall control.

Until 1948, the legislative basis for the work of the exchange service had essentially been the Labour Exchanges Act of 1909, though its work had been affected also by legislation concerned with unemployment insurance and the employment of disabled persons. The Employment and Training Act 1948 imposed on the Minister of Labour a duty to provide such services as he considered expedient for assisting persons to select, fit themselves for, obtain and retain suitable employment, of assisting employers to obtain suitable employees and of promoting employment for the community. In practice, however, the main change was in provision for young people (page 119).

The decline of resources

A striking feature of this period was the steady decline in the overall resources of the Department, and more particularly the exchanges, from the high point achieved in the war. This is shown in terms of staffing in Table 7.1.

While the ministry now had additional Factory Inspectorate staffing, the vast majority of the ministry's staff were still either in the exchanges or linked to them (eg in Regional Offices or in Resettlement Advice and Appointments Offices), so these figures give a good indication of the decline which occurred in the exchanges. The fall reflected the end of special provision linked to the war, the relatively low level of unemployment insurance work and a series of economy drives initiated by the Treasury. Staff levels fell in every year except 1958, when they increased temporarily because of a rise in unemployment benefit claims.

The consequences of this pattern of decline included a lack of promotion, an upwards shift in the age structure as relatively few young recruits could be taken on, and a morale problem because of a lack of opportunities for progression.

Not only was staffing drastically reduced. The ministry was totally unable to upgrade the exchange estate in the way Bevin had envisaged (page 97). The

Table 7.1 *Staffing of the Ministry of Labour, 1943–60*

Year*	Total staff	Year	Total staff
1943 (April)	44,427	1953	25,138
1946	43,354	1954	23,728
1947	35,830	1955	22,751
1948	33,711	1956	21,710
1949	31,327	1957	20,871
1950	28,466	1958	23,120
1951	27,309	1959	22,112
1952	26,388	1960	20,811

Note: * These figures relate to the end of the year in question in all cases except 1943, where they relate to April.
Source: Ministry of Labour Annual Reports.

restrictions on capital expenditure were so tight that hardly any new exchanges were built or acquired between 1945 and 1960 except where rehousing was unavoidable, eg because the owner wished to recover property on the expiry of a lease.[7] Money was spent on the internal refurbishment of exchanges, including the installation of cubicles to increase privacy during interviews. But overall the investment in the estate in this period was much less than it had been in the 1930s.

There was a considerable reduction in the ministry's extensive network. At the end of 1946, there were 11 Regional Offices, 35 District Manpower Offices, 1394 local offices, 367 Resettlement Advice Offices and 45 Appointments and Nursing Offices.[8] By 1960, there were still 11 Regional Offices but there were no District Manpower Offices, the number of local offices was reduced to 905 and the other offices no longer existed as separate entities (though some were incorporated into local offices).[9]

Treasury pressure for economies of course reflected the parlous state of the national finances immediately after the war and the periodic sterling crises throughout the period, which led to the 'stop' phases of the economic cycle. Even so, the Department might have avoided this degree of economic stringency if it had had Ministers like Bevin, who combined a dominant political position with a deep interest in services to the public. As it was, Godfrey Ince tried unsuccessfully to resist Treasury pressure for economies as wartime controls were relaxed. Parker writes, 'He had built up a departmental empire and was loath to accept any diminution of its powers'. Furthermore, he was devoted to the ministry's staff and was 'anxious to ensure that as far as possible they should continue in post till they reached the normal age of retirement'.[10] But the Treasury was too powerful for him. His jocular claim to Bevin that his ministry had overtaken the Treasury (page 104) may have had some germs of truth in wartime but was far from being the case in peacetime. Under the Attlee government, the Treasury resumed the powerful position it had held between the wars, particularly from 1947 onwards when Cripps took control of economic policy as well as finance.

Personnel and organisation

There is not space to discuss personnel and organisation matters in any detail, but two matters are worth a brief mention.

First, in May 1947 Arton Wilson, the Director of Establishments, reached an important agreement with the Staff Side, leading to the creation of a Special Departmental Class embracing all executive and clerical staff within the ministry. Previously, under the agreement reached in 1921, HQ staff had been in 'Treasury Classes' and this had acted as a constraint on movement between HQ and the field.

Secondly, in 1953–54, the ministry joined with the Ministry of National Insurance in a *joint local office experiment* in about 50 offices. This arose from the 1951 Report of a Committee chaired by Sir Arton Wilson. The report criticised the multiplication of local office networks which had occurred in the 1940s and called for measures to 'simplify the demands on the patience and time of members of the public' and to 'minimise the number of contacts the citizen has to have with Government offices'. The conclusion from the experiments was that there was no improvement in service to the public from jointly managed offices, largely because not much integration was possible between the different departmental functions. The Ministry of Labour had by far the most frequent contact with the public. The experiment was terminated, to the relief of Ministry of Labour officials who did not want their decisions about exchanges constrained by the need to fit in with other Departments. It was not until the 1990s that the idea of joint offices would again be seriously pursued.

Demobilisation and resettlement

The general principles of demobilisation, which had been determined by Bevin and Ince in 1943–44 (page 103), proved robust and effective and the whole process went much more smoothly than at the end of the First World War. From May 1945 onwards, a leaflet on resettlement began to be distributed throughout the Forces and soon ministry officials began their lecture tours of the overseas commands. 371 Resettlement Advice Offices were set up in major towns and late in 1945 were handling 30,000 queries a week. Following the recommendations of two Committees under Lord Hankey on aspects of the resettlement of highly qualified people, the Appointments Service of the ministry was strengthened (page 119) and a Further Education and Training Scheme was established. There was also provision for business training and vocational training and greatly improved provision for disabled people (page 118). At least in this period immediately following the war, the ministry's arrangements were well resourced, wide ranging and comprehensive.

'Mr Winston Churchill inspects the new Labour Exchanges in London and talks to an applicant at Camberwell Green' *The Daily Mirror*, 12 February 1910

'The popularity of the new government Labour Exchanges, and types of the applicants for work' *The Illustrated London News*, 12 February 1910

Winston Churchill, portrait taken when he joined the Liberals in 1904

William Beveridge: the young civil servant, 1909

Ernest Bevin, Minister of Labour, 1942

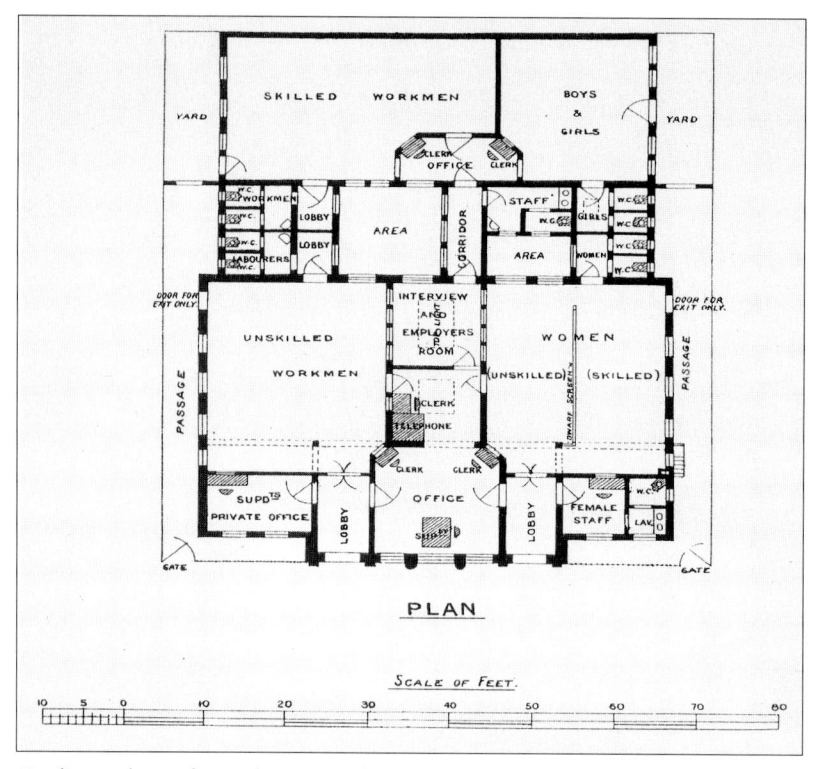

Earliest plan of a Labour Exchange, April 1909, Office of Works
(PRO LAB 2/211/15)

Opening day: 'The new Labour Exchange at Camberwell Green: the scramble for tickets' *The Graphic*, 12 February 1910

Exterior of Labour Exchange, 1910

'The Labour Exchange at Camberwell. Sixty of the new Board of Labour Exchanges opened their doors on the 1st of this month, and by the end of February over 100 exchanges out of the total of 250 will be at work in London and the Provinces.' *The Graphic*, 12 February 1910

Members of the Labour Supply Board at their first meeting at the Ministry of Labour, Whitehall. From left to right: Sir Thomas Philips, F W Leggett, Major General Appleyard, J C Little, Ernest Bevin, and F B Tribe were the men with the task of conscripting Britain's workforce during World War II

Interior of Middlesbrough Labour Exchange, 1946

March 1952, women cotton workers of Oldham, Lancashire queue for benefit at Oldham Employment Exchange. This was a scene to be found in most of the Lancashire cotton towns owing to the short time employment and increasing unemployment

Minister of Labour the Rt Hon Edward Heath accompanied by Lord Beveridge visits the Edgware Road Employment Exchange prior to the meeting to mark the 50th anniversary of the opening of the Employment Exchanges, 1910–1960

Barbara Castle, First Secretary of State and Secretary of State for Employment and Productivity, 1968–1970

Robert Carr, Secretary of State for Employment, 1970–1972

Ken Cooper, Chief Executive, Employment Service Agency, 1971–1975

The magnitude of the switch of labour from war to peace is illustrated in Table 7.2.

Table 7.2 *Demobilisation, 1945–48 (millions)*

	June 1945	end 1946	end 1948
Armed forces	5.09	1.46	0.81
Supply service	3.83	0.46 }	19.15
Civil employment	12.59	17.82 }	
Unemployed or on release leave	0.14	0.70	0.37
Total working population	21.65	20.44	20.33

Source: Alec Cairncross, *Years of Recovery: British Economic Policy 1945–51*, Methuen, London, 1985, p390.

That such shifts could occur with relatively little unemployment was a remarkable achievement for which the Ministry of Labour and the exchanges can take much of the credit.

Full employment

It was only in the last years of the war that official opinion came round to the view that Britain could avoid mass unemployment after the war. At the end of 1942, many officials thought Beveridge's assumption of 8.5 per cent unemployment after the war[11] too optimistic. In October 1943, Arton Wilson, Director of Establishments of the ministry, thought that post-war unemployment might rise to three million.[12] But during 1944 opinion shifted. In May 1944, in the White Paper on Employment Policy, the Coalition Government made its historic commitment to a 'high and stable level of employment after the war'. The White Paper foresaw no problem of general unemployment immediately after the war and predicted labour shortages. A year later, at the time of victory in Europe in May 1945, Bevin and his top officials warned the Regional Controllers to expect severe labour shortages, caused by the effects of a drop in the birth rate, the raising of the school leaving age, the need for continuing military recruitment, the likely withdrawal of many women from the labour force and the enormous demands for labour for reconstruction and the rebuilding of export industries.[13]

This advice was well judged. A remarkably low level of unemployment was achieved in the period following the war, as shown in Table 7.3. The one exception was a short-lived rise to over two million unemployed[14] in the fuel crisis of February 1947. But this was totally untypical. The nature of the labour market in these years and the ministry's response was summed up as follows in the ministry's *Annual Report* for 1955:

> *The general picture was of an industrial economy stretched to its utmost, which, with no reserves of labour to call on, was seeking on the one hand to heighten production by increased mechanisation and the redeployment of labour and on the other hand to maintain industrial peace through better co-operation and understanding at all levels and through improved methods of personnel management.*[15]

Table 7.3 UK unemployment, 1945–60 (annual averages)

Year	Per cent	Thousands	Year	Per cent	Thousands
1945	1.3	202	1953	1.8	380
1946	2.5	390	1954	1.5	318
1947	3.1	496	1955	1.2	265
1948	1.8	331	1956	1.3	347
1949	1.6	338	1957	1.6	347
1950	1.3	281	1958	2.2	501
1951	1.3	281	1959	2.3	512
1952	2.2	463	1960	1.7	393

Source: Office of National Statistics, *Labour Market Trends*, Jan 1996, Crown Copyright.

The main condition for full employment was probably the strong international economic framework, with the US willing to act as the engine of the world economy. Given the pressures on British governments of repeated crises over sterling and the balance of payments, another important factor was the government commitment to prevent mass unemployment by the use of Keynesian demand management.

But the exchanges also contributed to full employment. As in the previous boom period of 1912–14, there were still many people making fresh claims for unemployment benefit – there were three million fresh claims in 1953 alone. Following Beveridge's principles and their own well developed traditions, the exchanges were unwilling to let anyone receive benefit if there were jobs available which they could do. Placement came before payment: 'Whenever possible, potential benefit claimants are dealt with initially in the employment section, and when an individual can be placed in employment forthwith, a benefit claim is not taken'.[16] Moreover, those who remained on the register were followed up:

> *When it is clear that an applicant is going to be difficult to place, and in any event when he has been registered as wholly unemployed for a month, he is given a special interview known as a 'follow-up placing interview' by an experienced placing officer.*[17]

If after this the applicant remained unemployed – or had only brief spells of unemployment after the interview – then after three months he had a 'review interview' with a senior officer to see whether anything further could be done by the local office to find the applicant employment.[18] This was the tightly drawn system operating in 1950. It took advantage of the abundance of jobs to keep spells of unemployment as short as possible. It was probably a false economy that follow-up interviews were abandoned for a time as a result of the economies of 1952.

Labour supply and labour controls

Given the huge adjustments necessary in the labour force after the war, Bevin had advocated the retention of some controls over labour, but these should be 'narrowed to the strictest limits'.[19] Accordingly, most of the labour controls were relaxed during 1945, though they were retained in the cases of certain shortage occupations, such as nurses and midwives, building and civil engineering workers, agricultural workers and miners. Until 1947, there were controls to prevent an exodus of temporary civil servants from government departments. Even where there was no compulsion, the exchanges were expected 'to guide people to those industries where their services could most usefully be employed'.[20] Following wartime precedents, vacancies were placed in three categories by Regional Preference Committees, according to their importance to economic production:

- bottleneck vacancies;
- first preference vacancies;
- others.[21]

Exchange staff had to persuade suitable individuals to take vacancies in the first two categories. As a performance measure, the ministry would note that 12–13 per cent of its placings were in these categories.[22]

The exchanges were to retain this role of exhortation and persuasion until 1956. Strange as it may seem to later generations, this idea of pointing out to citizens their patriotic duty in the job market seems to have been acceptable to the public in the aftermath of the war, though its credibility gradually declined.

In 1947, acute economic difficulties led to the reimposition of many of the labour controls that had been relaxed. In August, the Prime Minister announced that most engagements would be required to take place through the exchanges 'so that workers leaving one job and entering another might be guided into that class of work in which they could best contribute towards overcoming the country's economic difficulties'.[23] In line with the puritan austerity of the time, workers occupied in amusement arcades, gambling establishments and night clubs had to register at the exchanges to shift to 'essential' work. George Isaacs made a broadcast appeal to women to take jobs in factories and agriculture and urged employers to adjust working hours to the needs of women with domestic responsibilities and to retain elderly workers. Coalmining and agriculture were designated as 'ring-fenced' industries. As in wartime, the ministry was sparing in its use of legal sanctions, preferring to keep these powers in the background as far as possible. But in 1948, the ministry issued 302 directions, 288 of which required people to remain in mining or agriculture.[24]

In 1949, controls were more generally reduced and there were only 162 directions. In 1950, the Control of Engagement Orders were lifted and employers and workers were free to enter into engagements without recourse to the exchanges. But the idea of the exchanges deploying labour so as to serve the national interest remained. It was important that the ministry 'justified the confidence of employers and workers in the free facilities of the Employment Exchange service for the distribution of manpower in accordance with the national interests'.[25] At the same time, the exchange service 'had to demonstrate its value as a placing agency in a free labour market'.[26] The implications of this situation for the exchanges are discussed below (pages 115–6).

The most carefully considered verdict on the labour controls of the late 1940s comes from Sir Alec Cairncross. He concluded that they enabled the undermanned industries to expand their labour force by 6.4 per cent, compared to a 4.8 per cent increase in total civilian employment. He commented: 'Such a result was worth a considerable effort'.[27]

In post-war politics, Labour was seen as the party of controls and the Conservatives as the party of the free market. Yet, strangely, in 1952 some limited labour control was reintroduced under Walter Monckton, a Conservative Minister of Labour. The background was the acute shortage of labour in defence and export industries in the period of rearmament following the outbreak of the Korean War. The Notification of Vacancies Order of 1952 required employers to use the exchanges for engagements. The idea was to enable exchange staff to gain a much wider knowledge of vacancies and to influence workers into first preference vacancies.[28] Following delicate negotiations with the influential Newspapers Proprietors' Association, Monckton amended the order to enable vacancy advertisements to continue in newspapers much as before, but with a prefatory notice that the actual engagement must take place through an exchange. This created a rather tedious bureaucratic formality at a stage when the worker was already committed to his prospective employer. Moreover, the ministry suspected there was widespread contravention of the order.[29] The order was used to give 'super-priority' to the production of certain weapons and military equipment and to reinforce a continuing persuasion role for the exchanges. The Order remained in force until it was revoked by Macleod in May 1956, partly in order to save 150 staff in a government economy drive. Macleod told the Commons: 'The employment exchanges will remain freely at the service of employers and workers and I hope that they will, for their own advantage, make the fullest use of this service'.[30] As it turned out, the revocation caused an immediate drop in placings from 237,000 in April 1956 to 162,000 in May.[31]

Relaunching the exchanges

In the period up to 1960, there were several attempts to relaunch the exchanges to meet the new conditions of post-war Britain, but these endeavours were frustrated by economy measures at each 'stop' phase of the 'stop-go' cycle, causing a good deal of cynicism within the ministry.

Chapter 6 showed that the first relaunch really began during the war, with Bevin's attempts to 'humanise the exchanges' and Arton Wilson's development of staff training (pages 95–7). After the war, Placing Officers were given rather tortuous advice on how to deal with people who now fell outside the labour controls. On the one hand, they should have constantly in mind the need to fill those vacancies which were 'the most important in the national interest'. On the other hand, they should not press people to take jobs against their will, since to do so would damage the prestige and efficiency of the service.[32] This dualism went on until 'first preference vacancies' reflecting the national interest were finally abandoned in 1956.[33]

In September 1949, the prospective abandonment of the remaining labour controls led to a debate with Controllers about placing work. The ministry would remain under pressure to fill first preference vacancies for undermanned industries, so that Placing Officers would need to point out which vacancies were in the national interest, but without putting on pressure. Controllers suggested offering applicants a choice. They felt that the exchanges' standing with employers was high and that the priority was to concentrate on the applicants.[34]

In May 1950, HMD Parker began a major review of placing work following the revocation of the Control of Engagement orders. In June 1950, he produced the first of a series of memoranda for exchange staff. It was called: 'The Employment Exchange Service in a Free Labour Market'.[35] It pointed out that the new situation of full employment with no labour controls was unprecedented and that success would depend on 'the initiative and personal approach of each exchange manager and his staff'. The memo encouraged staff to rethink their attitude to their clients after a decade of stressing the national interest. In future, it would be vital to satisfy both employers and workers. The policy was as follows:

> Every employer has the right to have the vacancies he notifies brought to the notice of suitable applicants irrespective of the importance of these vacancies in the national interest. Similarly, every person registering for employment has the right to have brought to his notice all vacancies for which he is suitably qualified.

The national interest was not forgotten. It was in the national interest to facilitate the mobility of workers necessary in a dynamic economy. (The exchanges were responsible both for transfer grants to other areas and for referring workers to training.) Moreover, the exchanges should do what they could – in a reasonable way and without pressure – to influence workers to take those jobs that were most important in the national interest. The memo concluded by emphasising the importance of making the exchanges attractive to workers and counteracting the idea that they were 'merely dole-paying agencies'. In some ways, this memo foreshadowed the agenda of the next 25 years.

With unemployment at such a low level, Parker and his colleagues believed that it was important for the exchanges to attract *'still employed workers'* – those in jobs who required advice, who wanted a new job or who foresaw redundancy. The National Joint Advisory Council accepted this policy, though employers had some reservations. It had to be handled carefully to avoid unsettling existing employees or creating the impression that the ministry was simply trying to boost its placing figures.[36] As still employed workers found it difficult to visit exchanges during working hours, many exchanges held open evenings on Tuesdays and Fridays.

Other initiatives at this time included the opening of commercial sections in 250 exchanges to increase their penetration of the growing non-manual labour market and publicity through display advertising and newspaper advertising. However, some newspapers refused to accept advertisements from the exchanges – which they saw as rivals to themselves in the job market.[37]

In 1952, there was a Treasury-led economy drive, which led among other things to the abandonment of development visits to employers, of follow-up work on vacancies and of follow-up interviews of those unemployed for some time. All these measures could be seen as perverse in relation to Parker's vision of a service that was adapting to a free labour market. In subsequent years, all these activities were resumed.

In 1953, JG Stewart took over from Parker as the Under-Secretary responsible for placing work. A new review was triggered by HR Whiteman, the Regional Controller for London and the South East. Whiteman argued that the service was giving too much priority to work for special categories of worker, such as disabled people, young people and the highly qualified at the expense of its work for the generality of workers. The service needed to attract more applicants who were 'good placing propositions'. Whiteman felt that the decline in the service was reflected in a recent estimate by a *Social Survey Report on the Mobility of Labour* that only one-fifth of the labour force obtained jobs through the exchanges – perhaps the first suggestion that the service might be in a downward spiral. Stewart cast doubt on this estimate of penetration since it implied a very high level of non-compliance with the Notification of Vacancies Order, but he was influenced by Whiteman's arguments.

In March 1954, Stewart held a major conference on placing work. This led to a renewed attempt to improve the service, known as the 'New Look', a phrase borrowed from the change in fashion brought about by the famous Paris couturier, Christian Dior. In November 1954 Stewart sent a memorandum to the exchanges called 'Meeting the Challenge of Full Employment'. The message was similar to that of Parker in 1950. It was important to attract the employed worker and to 'impress on the public that we run an employment and not an unemployment service'. The exchange should be 'a pleasant place to visit'. Exchanges should have vacancies on display outside and should be welcoming and well-signed for the new applicant. The exchanges should ensure that 'workers go into jobs which make the best use of their skills; jobs in which they will settle down to do good work'. Other memoranda followed. Development visits to employers were now encouraged. Registration and placing interviews were combined in a new employment interview. Exchanges should provide information and advice as well as placing. Follow-up interviews, now called 'Review Interviews', should be carried out on a discretionary rather than an automatic basis.

But the New Look in its turn was undermined by the major economy drive of 1956. Altogether, the ministry cut out well over 2000 posts, leading to bitter complaints from the Staff Side. The biggest impact was on general employment work, so that by 1958 the staffing allowance for this kind of work (as opposed to other local office functions such as unemployment insurance, disabled work or management and supervision) was only 2757 posts.

The 1956 economies also gave impetus to the 'aggregation' of men's and women's sections, thus gradually bringing to an end the segregation of men and women which had been a feature of the exchanges since 1910. It was later claimed that this had an adverse effect on women's placings, because some women jobseekers objected to sharing a counter with male manual workers.[38]

Table 7.4 shows the placing performance of the exchanges from 1947–60.

Table 7.4 *Placing performance of employment exchanges, 1946–60: Adults over 18 (000s)*

Year	Total	Year	Total
1947	2609	1954	2643
1948	4234	1955	2644
1949	4045	1956	1954
1950	2531	1957	1486
1951	2025	1958	1348
1952	2747	1959	1471
1953	2667	1960	1621

Notes: (1) For the years 1952–56, 'nominations' under the Notification of Vacancies Order have been excluded;
(2) Unlike Tables 4.2 and 5.2 above, this table excludes juveniles.
Source: Ministry of Labour Annual Reports.

Table 7.4 shows that placing performance was remarkably high in 1948–49, when extensive labour controls were in force. Placings fell away following the removal of the controls in March 1950, but rose again following the introduction of the Notification of Vacancies Order in February 1952. The full impact of the economy package, including the revocation of NOVO, of May 1956 was felt in 1957 when placings slumped to 1486 and then to 1348 in 1958. This fall was also influenced by economic conditions in 1957–58. Between 1954 and 1957, the average vacancies outstanding over the 12 months of the year declined from 281,000 to 185,000. Placings of still employed people also declined from 102,000 in 1954 to 55,000 in 1957.[39] By the late 1950s, overall placing levels had fallen below those for the mid-1930s.[40]

The various efforts to relaunch the exchanges had failed. By the end of the 1950s, the exchanges were in a downward spiral. Their resources had been squeezed repeatedly and they had been denied the investment necessary for them to keep pace with a rapidly changing labour market.

Employment of disabled people

Chapter 6 described the advances in services for disabled people linked with the Disabled Persons (Employment) Act 1944. After the war, the new provisions came fully into operation, including a National Advisory Council, 300 local Disablement Advisory Committees (DACs) and specially trained Disablement Resettlement Officers (DROs) at the exchanges. From September 1945, the registration of disabled workers (whether in work or unemployed) was introduced. The number registered under the Act reached a peak of 940,000 in 1950, but had declined to 700,000 by 1959.[41] Employers were required to employ a quota of their workforce from this register – initially 2 per cent and later raised to 3 per cent.

The ministry also built up its industrial rehabilitation facilities.[42] Following the establishment in 1943 of the Egham unit with 200 residential places, after the war the ministry established 14 further units, each with 100 places (mostly non-residential). These units had a busy atmosphere suggestive of 'the factory rather than the sick bay'. They offered a combination of preparation for returning to work and occupational assessment, with a multi-disciplinary team including medical officers, psychologists, social workers, instructors and DROs. Five-sixths of those attending were advised to change their occupation. It was a radical and resource-intensive concept which worked well. Not least of the benefits was the involvement of occupational psychologists whose role in the service in the future would expand.

The ministry also provided vocational training for disabled people and sponsored sheltered employment in Remploy Ltd for those so severely disabled that they were unlikely to get work in industry under normal conditions.

Altogether, the ministry's provision for the disabled represented a coherent investment in high quality provision which, as HR Whiteman had pointed out (page 116), presented a marked contrast to the general exchange service, which was increasingly starved of resources.

Young people

At the end of the war, Sir Godfrey Ince chaired a committee to review the arrangements for helping young people who were leaving education for the world of work. This had been a vexed issue ever since 1910 and the compromise reached in 1927 (page 58) had not proved entirely satisfactory. The Ince Committee recommended that the Minister of Labour should continue to be responsible to Parliament for what was now called the 'Youth Employment Service'. Administration would rest with a Central Youth Employment Executive, led by a Ministry of Labour Assistant Secretary, but including representatives of the Education Departments. Local authorities should be given a once-and-for-all option of providing the service in their areas, and would receive a 75 per cent earmarked grant from the ministry; otherwise the service would be provided by specially trained officers in the exchanges. These provisions were brought into effect by the Employment and Training Act 1948. By the scheduled date of January 1949, 128 of the 191 local authorities in Great Britain had opted to provide the service. This proved a workable system which survived until 1974.

Higher appointments

Earlier in this chapter (page 110), the role of the Appointments Services of the ministry in the process of demobilisation and resettlement was mentioned. Bevin had intended these services to be permanent, and in the early years after the war it looked as though this would be the case. They were high quality services, using psychological techniques and highly graded interviewers and achieving large numbers of placings. But inevitably, in the climate of economy that has been described, the number of Appointments Offices was gradually reduced to 14 in 1948 and to three in 1952. The 1956 cuts abolished the remaining three Appointments Offices and replaced them by a new Professional and Executive Register, with staff located in 48 of the larger exchanges. By providing much wider coverage, this improved the service. The centralised Technical and Scientific Register, which originated in 1938, survived until 1962, when it was merged with the Professional and Executive Register. Meanwhile, another legacy of the Bevin era, the specialist Nursing Appointments Service, remained important throughout the post-war period in addressing the serious shortages of nurses, achieving as many as 11,000 placings, for instance, in 1956.

Immigrants

In this age of labour shortage, one of the important contributions of the exchanges was to help incorporate overseas immigrants into the labour force. This had happened in the war, when, for instance, thousands of West Indians had joined the Air Force and European refugees and prisoners of war were mobilised to help the war effort. After the war, faced with desperate labour shortages, the ministry took advantage of every potential source of labour. The employment of German prisoners of war reached a peak of 350,000 in January 1947, but by then they were already beginning to return home and their numbers quickly diminished.[43] The ministry assisted in the formation of the Polish Resettlement Corps of 50,000 workers, which operated until 1949, and the European Voluntary Workers Scheme. The ministry set up a liaison office in Dublin to help bring over workers from Eire; 29,000 Irish workers came over in 1947. Large numbers of foreign workers came into the country on labour permits – 34,000, for instance, in 1953. Other influxes were generated by the turbulence of international relations. In 1956–57, the exchanges helped to place 15,500 Hungarian refugees and 1100 British subjects evacuated from Egypt. Altogether these flows of labour made a sizeable contribution to labour supply.

Rather different in character was the influx of Commonwealth immigrants. In the main, this was a spontaneous movement of people from poverty and under-employment in the West Indies, India and Pakistan to seek their fortune in Britain. They took advantage of the lack of immigration controls on Commonwealth citizens (until the Macmillan government introduced restrictions in 1962) and the acute labour shortages in Britain. However, but for the willingness of the exchanges to act as sponsors for the immigrants, they might have found it difficult to get established in the labour market owing to widespread colour prejudice. In 1955 a sociologist, AH Richmond, suggested that the British population was divided into three groups of roughly equal size: those who were tolerant of coloured people, those who were mildly prejudiced and those who were extremely prejudiced.[44] If colour prejudice was as widespread as this, then the sponsorship role of the Ministry of Labour and its exchanges was important.

It was in June 1948 that significant immigration from the West Indies began with the arrival at Tilbury of SS *Empire Windrush*, bringing 488 'coloured colonials' (as officials then called them). 204 of these were temporarily accommodated in Clapham in deep wartime shelters. Most of the new arrivals registered at their nearest exchanges and within three weeks 202 had been placed in London and a further 28 in North West Region.[45] This set the pattern for numerous further groups of immigrants who arrived by sea or by air – the immigrants would register at a local exchange quickly after their arrival and the exchanges would strive with considerable success to place them in jobs.

Senior officers in Ministry of Labour HQ quickly realised that this development raised some important issues – not only relating to employer and worker prejudice but also to problems of adjustment to the British urban labour market for immigrants from a quite different (largely rural) culture. There were reports of quarrelling, low productivity and casual turnover. Particularly sensitive to these issues was Mary Smieton, Under-Secretary in the Employment Policy Department in 1949, who had been involved in Bevin's welfare policies during the war. She advocated a policy of dispersal under which immigrants would be placed 'in small numbers in areas of good labour demand where the objections of employers and workers do not make themselves felt'.[46] This became Ministry of Labour orthodoxy for the next 10 years or so. In practice, it was by no means a straightforward solution. Immigrants understandably wanted to live with their own communities, while white communities were often sensitive to the appearance for the first time of a significant ethnic minority. The ministry's efforts helped to disperse the ethnic minorities a little more widely but they were still relatively concentrated. A survey in 1957 concluded that there was little scope for dispersing immigrants away from the main centres of employment.[47]

Smieton also advocated the introduction of 'coloured' members of staff to assist in placing immigrants in employment, because 'it was doubtful if we could understand properly the mentality of the coloured person'.[48] This idea was successfully resisted by regional representatives who felt that such appointments would imply segregation and might be resented and misunderstood. In retrospect, one can see that Smieton was right. Her approach would have improved understanding within the ministry and increased the confidence of ethnic minority clients.

In 1949–50, the problem of integrating Commonwealth immigrants into the workforce seemed small, but its scale gradually increased. Attitudes within the ministry were ambivalent. While officials generally briefed Ministers reassuringly about the exchanges' success in placing immigrants, they were also aware how widespread prejudice was. For instance, in 1950, 'definite prejudice' was reported in Yorkshire in wool, textiles, coalmining, iron and steel and building and civil engineering.[49] Behind the scenes, the ministry persuaded employers to take immigrants. In the early 1950s, public transport departments in cities like Birmingham began to recruit immigrants in large numbers. But the ministry's underlying anxieties led it to support the Colonial Office's efforts in 1950 to induce the Jamaican administration to discourage emigration to Britain.[50]

The ministry claimed to have no statistics of immigrant unemployment, because of its policy of non-discrimination, but in reality exchange managers in areas of immigrant concentration knew how many unemployed there were. When in 1954, Harold Watkinson, the Parliamentary Secretary, expounded the official line to the Commons, Sir Winston Churchill, the Prime Minister, who happened to be sitting on the front bench, murmured that such statistics should be collected, particularly in relation to 'coloured' immigrants. Thereafter, the ministry carried out regular counts. Table 7.5 shows the unemployment figures, including those informally collected before 1956.

Up to 1958, the figures were low and reassuring to Ministers. Indeed, in 1956, the ministry advised Lennox Boyd, the Colonial Secretary, and Sir Hugh Foot, the Governor of Jamaica, that there was no hard core of unemployed 'coloured' workers and that in London only six 'coloured' workers had been unemployed for any length of time. Sir Hugh paid high tribute to the work of the ministry.[51]

The official ministry view that the problems were manageable was not shared by all those working in the exchanges. Early in 1955, the Ministry of Labour Staff Association presented a memorandum to the TUC General

Table 7.5 *Unemployment among ethnic minorities (described as 'coloured'), 1953–58*

Week commencing	Men	Women	Total
15 June 1953	3096	270	3366
14 June 1954	2206	256	2462
18 July 1955	2217	636	2853
4 June 1956	3772	1431	5203
2 Sept 1957	5261	2305	7566
28 July 1958	13,043	4058	17,101

Council calling for an investigation into an 'increasingly acute problem'. They estimated that 65 per cent of West Indian immigrants were unskilled and often regarded manual work as degrading, while employers reported that they did not work hard. HQ officials rejected these views and briefed the press that there was no serious employment problem.[52]

From the mid-1950s, a pattern of large-scale immigration from India and Pakistan was established alongside the flow from the West Indies. The ministry's view that the problems were manageable persisted until unemployment among ethnic minorities increased in 1958 (Table 7.5). The *Manchester Guardian* reported that 'Redundancy in the Midlands falls heavily on West Indians'.[53] There were increasing reports of employers imposing quotas. Also in 1958, the Notting Hill riots shocked public opinion and Ministers intensified their efforts to persuade governments in the West Indies, India and Pakistan to restrain immigration.

Between 1955 and 1958, Sheila Patterson, a social anthropologist from the University of Edinburgh, carried out an intensive study of the absorption of immigrants in Brixton, including the role of the exchanges. She described how the exchanges interviewed West Indian workers and placed them in employment:

> *In practice, as in the case of all new and untried sources of labour, this involves intensive and far-ranging canvassing and cajoling of employers, few of whom...regard the prospect of employing any outsider with anything but reluctance and suspicion.*[54]

Exchange staff asked employers, 'Will you take coloured (West Indian) labour?' in order to protect the coloured applicant from the humiliation of rejection. The apparent discrimination 'sometimes brings unjustified odium on the employment exchange'. Patterson concluded that the exchanges were:

> *playing a considerable part in easing and accelerating the initial processes of the West Indian migrants' accommodation in local*

industry. The mild personal antipathy felt by a few officials was more than offset by the official policy of non-discrimination, by the professional desire for efficiency in placing applicants and in some exchanges by the very positive, sponsor-like attitude of the manager.[55]

Public employment services have a special importance for immigrants, who lack access to the networks which help the native community to get jobs. An important achievement of the exchanges in the post-war years was to facilitate the absorption of large numbers of immigrants into the labour market.

Conclusion

In 1960, Ted Heath, the Minister of Labour, decided to celebrate the 50th anniversary of the exchanges. Andrew Roth comments: 'These dreary offices hardly seemed a PR man's dream, but careful research produced some interesting facts...'[56] These facts about the role of Churchill and Beveridge in the foundation of the first Board of Trade exchanges are well known to readers of this volume. Churchill was abroad and not available. But on 1 February 1960 a remarkable ceremony took place at Edgware Road employment exchange which was attended not only by Heath himself but also by four former Ministers of Labour – Ernest Brown, George Isaacs, Alfred Robens and Lord Monckton. The main speaker was the 80-year-old Lord Beveridge who, in a brilliant and witty address, paid tribute to Churchill ('great fun to work with'), the Webbs ('the first really important people to listen to me'), Llewellyn Smith ('to work under him...was a liberal education'), Charles Rey, Wolfe, Phillips and Tallents. Beveridge concluded, 'We celebrate today an outstanding case of the British power for collaboration across party lines in a good cause. May that power never grow less'.[57] At the ceremony, a telegram of greetings from Sir Charles Rey, now retired in South Africa, was read out.

There was an irony about the celebrations of February 1960. It was right to celebrate the achievements of the exchanges over 50 years. But the reality was that in 1960 the exchanges had reached a low point. Their resources had been depleted. Their contribution to the labour market was diminished. They were in a time warp. They had not been adapted to the new conditions which had developed since the Second World War. Fortunately, within a couple of years, the Ministry of Labour would begin to address these issues.

8

The Stirring of Reform, 1960–70

'I am determined to make our new manpower services plan one of the key points of my activities this year and get it adopted before the summer ends. It may well prove to be my most important monument in this job...What fascinates me is the light this [note by Robin Keith] throws on the way government works in this country. Here was a group of officials who, independent of ministerial initiatives, initiated studies of their own department's inefficiencies and made suggestions, waiting for a Minister to pick them up.' (Barbara Castle's diary entry for 26 January 1970)[1]

Introduction

This quotation from Barbara Castle's *Diaries* sums up the story of the employment service in the 1960s. It was in the 1960s that the employment service moved from being an embarrassing legacy from the ministry's past to becoming the subject of major reform proposals from the First Secretary of State herself.

The moves to reform the employment service in the 1960s can be seen as part of a much wider attempt at that time to modernise British institutions. In the years following the Suez debacle, Macmillan's government began to reappraise Britain's place in the world, its institutions and its social and economic policies. The realisation that Britain's economic growth rate was lagging behind that of its continental neighbours was profoundly disturbing. The response in the 1960s, whether under Conservative or Labour governments, was one of radical intervention by the state.[2] Thus, whereas the Ministry of Labour had in the 1950s sought better personnel management and industrial training through consultations with the 'two sides of industry', in the early 1960s it introduced legislation to give workers clear contracts of employment and better training. This would help workers to accept change and end outdated industrial practices. Under a radical new Permanent Secretary, Sir James Dunnett, the new thinking within the ministry began in

1963 to extend to the employment service. But any reform required the investment of substantial resources. It took the support of a high profile minister, Barbara Castle, a major planning study and powerful endorsement from OECD before the government in 1970 appeared willing to provide those resources.

This chapter looks at the progress made under Dunnett before the 1964 Election and at the changes introduced under the Labour government between 1964 and 1968. It goes on to describe the major planning study of 1968–69 and the ministry's efforts to get wider government support for a reform programme, including the separation of employment and benefit work, culminating in the consultative document of May 1970.

Labour market background

As Table 8.1 indicates, the labour market background in the 1960s was similar to that in the 1950s – full employment and labour shortage. Unemployment continued to be very low by subsequent standards – between 1 and 3 per cent – but this did not prevent there being considerable concern when, as in 1962–63 and in 1967–70, unemployment went above 2 per cent.

Table 8.1 *Unemployment, 1960–70*

Year	Average number unemployed (000s)	Average percentage unemployed
1960	393	1.7
1961	377	1.6
1962	500	2.1
1963	612	2.6
1964	413	1.7
1965	360	1.5
1966	391	1.6
1967	599	2.5
1968	601	2.5
1969	597	2.5
1970	640	2.7

Source: Office of National Statistics, *Labour Market Trends*, Jan 1996, Crown Copyright.

Ministers and civil servants

The Ministers responsible for the department and the exchanges in this period were:

- 1960–63 John Hare (Conservative)
- 1963–64 Joseph Godber (Conservative)
- 1964–68 Ray Gunter (Labour)
- 1968–70 Barbara Castle (Labour) – Secretary of State for Employment and Productivity.

The Permanent Secretaries were:

- 1959–62 Sir Lawrence Helsby
- 1962–66 Sir James Dunnett
- 1966–73 Sir Denis Barnes

The last years of the Conservatives and the Dunnett Working Party

None of the Ministers of Labour of the early 1960s – John Hare, Joseph Godber and, after the 1964 Election, Ray Gunter – was a leading initiator of policy. None the less, it was in this period that the ministry's policy began to change, particularly under John Hare, whom Willie Whitelaw (his Parliamentary Secretary) later described as 'a most successful Minister and a very deceptive politician'.[3] The Contracts of Employment Act and the Industrial Training Act were examples of this new interventionist approach.

It was not until 1963 that this wind of change began to blow on the employment exchange service. In the early 1960s, the exchange service, although it accounted for the overwhelming majority of the ministry's staff, was an unfashionable and low priority area of the ministry's work. The HQ Employment Department was a backwater. The high profile area was industrial relations, which was not just about 'smoke-filled rooms', but also more constructively about ways of achieving long-term improvement in Britain's economic performance by 'positive employment policies'. To some of the policymakers in the cluster of old buildings in St James Square, where the Department had had its headquarters since 1941, the employment service did not seem very important. After all, with unemployment at 2 per cent or less, most people could move from job to job with no difficulty without using the employment exchanges. But others in the ministry were increasingly uneasy about the position of the exchanges. These included the Regional Controllers and some officials in Establishments, such as Robin Keith, an ex-Indian civil servant, who was to play an influential role. They felt rather like the inheritors of a family farm which was running to seed through years of neglect and which required a massive investment to put it on its feet. But they knew that their bankers in the Treasury would be most reluctant to make the necessary money available.

It was into this environment that a new Permanent Secretary, Sir James Dunnett, moved from the ministry of Transport in 1962. Restless, energetic, ambitious, a little morose and relatively young at 48, he was one of a new breed of reforming Permanent Secretaries.

The Stirring of Reform, 1960–70

Dunnett's interest was aroused by a discussion of placing work at the Controllers' Conference in May 1963. This discussion was held at the request of the Controllers and was the first time the Conference had discussed placing work since 1958 – indicating the prolonged lack of HQ interest in the subject. Jim Maston, Under-Secretary in the Employment Department, presented a paper which expressed concern at the downward trend in placings to only 1.29 million in 1962. The paper argued that placing levels needed to be compared with total engagements, but engagement figures were only available for manufacturing industry, where they suggested a market share for the exchanges of 20 per cent. It was clear that 'a large number of employers and workers prefer not to use the service'. The Controllers attributed this to lack of a clear lead from HQ about the priority of placing work, to the increase in white collar and more skilled jobs where the exchanges were not well equipped, and to weaknesses in front-line staffing. One of them said that the service was 'inspired by the traditional image of the dole queue ... and by the prevailing idea that the exchanges were for the rejects of the labour force'. There were interesting differences of view within the HQ team. Peter St John Wilson, the Deputy Secretary and son of a bishop, said that the service was set up to help those in difficulties – in terms of Chapter 1, the 'social welfare model'. By contrast, Jim Stewart, who had been responsible for the service's policy in the mid-1950s, said that the service was set up to relieve frictional unemployment as defined by Beveridge – the 'labour market transparency model'. It was characteristic of the ministry at this time that no one spoke up for the benefit control model. When Stewart said that the Treasury did not care how people got jobs provided they got them, Dunnett commented that this view was not self-evidently wrong.

The outcome of this discussion was a decision to set up a major review of the employment services, the first such review since the New Look of 1953–54. It was very significant that Dunnett decided to chair the Working Party himself. It was a very high level group, in which the intellectual initiative came from Robin Keith and the Establishments team.

At this time the total staffing of the employment exchange service as a whole was 12,000. Of these, only 3900 were directly engaged in employment work, with 770 on disabled persons work, 185 on professional and executive work and 215 on youth employment work, leaving only 2700 on work for able-bodied adults. (Additional staffing was provided for management and support.) The biggest proportion of exchange staff were engaged in benefit work. Benefit claimants had to sign twice weekly – normally on Wednesday and Friday – when they also collected their money. This created a great deal of congestion and pressure and distracted staff from employment work. The Working Party focused on ways of relieving this problem.

Dunnett asked the Working Party what kind of service they wanted. A paper by the Establishments Department offered a choice between a service for less than 3 per cent of the working population who were unemployed or one for the much larger group of people in jobs who wanted to change them. But, if it were for the latter, then they must discard the 'institutional stigma and the dislocation of the work of employment staff caused by benefit'. Experiments in separating the two functions were proposed.

Another way of reducing the disruption caused by benefit was to computerise the computation of benefit and to introduce payment by postal draft. It might take seven years to introduce this nationwide. Meanwhile, once a week signing was recommended. However, the ministry of Pensions and National Insurance (MPNI) had already turned down weekly signing, pointing out that unemployment benefit was a 'daily benefit' (sic). They regarded twice-weekly attendance as a minimum.

Premises were recognised as a key issue. As early as 1919, there had been aspirations for exchanges to be 'in a prominent position and in a central part of the town'. Between the wars, siting had been affected by a wish to 'keep queues from main roads and out of sight as far as possible', though the new buildings of the 1930s were generally located in good positions. In 1944, Ernest Bevin had asked the Minister of Works for central locations and dignified architecture (page 97). Current instructions in 1963 asked for central and accessible sites 'but not actually on a busy road or main shopping street'- a restriction which was queried by the Employment Department.

The group also discussed the competition offered by private employment agencies whose number was rapidly increasing – there were 1100 in London alone. In 1951, ILO Convention 96 had caused the government to undertake to regulate the agencies. But Parliamentary time had never been found and John Hare had discouraged a Home Office initiative to pursue the issue, arguing that there was no public pressure.

In May 1964, the Report of the Working Party[4] was sent to all staff, just in advance of the staff association conferences. In a foreword, Dunnett argued that the time had been ripe for a fundamental enquiry into whether the service needed major change:

> *55 years of service in peace and war have given us collectively immense experience of placing work and an unrivalled width of acquaintance among employers and employed. The question is whether we are exploiting these assets to the full.*

The report recalled the public view in the inter-war years of the exchanges having a 'strongly institutional and depressive atmosphere...a rather dismal inheritance' and went on to say that 'the association with the cash payment of unemployment benefit has had a more deleterious effect than any other'. It referred to the congestion caused by signing and payment and raised the ideas of a separation experiment and of piggy-backing on an MPNI experiment in automating benefit payments and of paying by postal draft. The report urged better staff training and greater industrial experience among the staff. It suggested that one of the most difficult practical problems would be improving the premises. Dunnett concluded by saying that the report was not a blueprint. Instead, it was to lead to the 'patient working out of these ideas and studies'.

Given Dunnett's ability and reputation, this may seem rather a cautious and disappointing outcome. But he was faced with an imminent election and was also aware that far more hard evidence would be needed to persuade the Treasury to put additional funds into the service. In a longer historical perspective, the Dunnett Working Party can be seen as the start of the reform process. It ended a period of stagnation and set in train a wide range of experimentation upon which eventually radical change would be based.

Rather late in the day, the draft report of the Working Party had been sent to the ministry of Pensions and National Insurance for comment. They were alarmed by its tone and content. One official commented that the report 'attributes so much to the malign influence of unemployment benefit work, that...the authors are moved to suggest desperate remedies'. Benefit was 'throughout spoken of in pejorative tones and cast as an administrative pariah'.[5] MPNI secured some amendments, including a recognition that there had to be 'close connections' between the employment service and benefit work. But MPNI remained highly critical of the report. Sir Eric Bowyer, the Permanent Secretary, called it 'a vague and superficial effort'. Sir John Walley, the Deputy Secretary who had served in the Ministry of Labour until 1945, felt that it did 'not really get to grips with the nature of unemployment benefit work'. Referring to idea of separation, he said that the report showed 'undue enthusiasm...for a pretty bad experiment'.[6]

Chapters 4 and 5 showed how in the inter-war years the Ministry of Labour had been the 'ministry of unemployment insurance'. The loss of policy responsibility for unemployment benefit in 1945 had over the succeeding 20 years gradually eliminated interest in benefit control among senior officers in the ministry, even if the controls continued to apply at local office level (pages 112–3). The ministry now saw itself as an economic ministry concerned with improving the working of the labour market. In conditions of very low unemployment, the problem of benefit control did not seem very significant. When policy makers investigated the system, they discovered disturbing anomalies; for example, that those disqualified from unemployment benefit moved on to supplementary benefit, sometimes actually receiving more than before. At that time, unemployment benefit was still flat rate and far from generous. It was unlikely that many would want to linger on it if jobs were available. In the eyes of Ministry of Labour administrators, the testing of people's willingness to work was bureaucratic and achieved little saving in public expenditure, but involved damaging side-effects for the employment service. These side-effects included overcrowding, the regular attendance at the exchanges of down-and-outs (who put off other potential clients) and distraction of the staff from employment work.[7]

MPNI, by contrast, stood by Beveridge's original concepts of benefit control (pages 4 and 98–9). The key condition for unemployment benefit was availability for work, of which the exchange officials were in effect the custodians, because they knew both the circumstances of people who had signed on and the local labour market. It was right that signing and paying should go together. Moreover, it was desirable that the state should offer a 'seamless' service to its citizens and not require them to visit additional offices unnecessarily. Finally, separation would require a major shift of work from one department to another and probably would not be cost-justified. For these reasons, MPNI was unconvinced by Ministry of Labour arguments for separation.[8]

A gap in understanding had arisen between the two ministries which would create considerable tensions in the coming years.

The new Labour government

The new Labour government which took power in October 1964 did not make a quick or dramatic difference to the position of the employment exchanges. The new Minister of Labour, Ray Gunter, was more interested in industrial relations and was quickly drawn into incomes policy problems. Officials were left to get on with the experiments and developments proposed by the Dunnett Working Party. The new government was more amenable to bids for resources than its Conservative predecessor had been and there were increases in staffing of over 2000 during the next few years, partly to take account of the rise in unemployment after the measures of July 1966.

In 1966, Denis Barnes took over from Sir James Dunnett as Permanent Secretary. Barnes was a career Ministry of Labour man, subtle and astute, whom Harold Wilson described to Barbara Castle as 'the best Permanent Secretary in Whitehall'[9] – which for all his ability seems an exaggeration. He was mainly absorbed in industrial relations, but he provided high level support for reform of the employment services. The Under-Secretary responsible for the employment service was Frank Pickford from 1964–66, followed by Robin Keith from 1966–69. Other officials involved in developing the service in this period included Barbara Green, Dorothy Kent and the young Geoffrey Holland.

There continued to be a high level Steering Group chaired by the Permanent Secretary. A series of innovative measures were introduced, including:

- *the introduction of Area Managers* – the managers of larger exchanges were given a lead marketing role for their Area, and a supervisory role in relation to the managers of smaller offices in their Area; this was a helpful measure in giving a coherent service since most exchanges did not serve a self-contained labour market;
- *the procedures for handling large redundancies* were improved and codified; this was at a time when industrial change was producing more redundancies and it is to the credit of the ministry that it was using its local machinery to take the opportunity for redeploying labour constructively;
- improvements in *staff training*, which Dunnett regarded as of 'considerable importance';

- improvements in *premises* and a major review of premises issues; in the next five years, the ministry invested in 120 new exchange buildings, a great advance on the previous 20 years, but according to Keith, there still remained over 350 'pre-Keynes local offices, mostly in places of first class industrial importance';[10]
- working on the *computer developments* recommended by the Dunnett Working Party; in the event this took much longer than expected (as was the way with big government computer projects);
- the introduction of the *occupational guidance service*;
- experiments in *self service*; and
- experiments in *separation* of delivery of benefit and employment work.

The last three of these were particularly important and will be described more fully.

Occupational guidance

The *occupational guidance service* seems to have arisen from a public lecture in September 1963 by Alec Rodger, a leading occupational psychologist, in which he criticised the lack of good vocational guidance for young adults. He asked: 'How many young adults nowadays would think of going to the Ministry of Labour for advice?' He went on to suggest that, if the Ministry of Labour could not rise to the occasion, then the job should be allocated to someone else like the National Health Service. He sent a copy of his remarks to St John Wilson, Deputy Secretary, who said that in all his 33 years in the ministry the need for a 'casualty ward' had been a bee in his bonnet but lack of resources had stood in the way of progress. The result of this correspondence was that the idea of a new occupational guidance service was fed into the Dunnett Working Party and in March 1966 it was introduced on an experimental basis in some of the larger offices. The service was conducted on the basis of personal interviews with carefully selected officers who had received a fairly intensive training from occupational psychologists. The purpose was to cater:

> For those who are facing an enforced change in employment; for those who feel they are under employed or who are judged capable of better work; for those who are unsettled in their work; and for those who are coming into the employment field for the first time or re-entering it after a break...[11]

By June 1968 more than 27,000 people had received guidance. By the end of 1968, 24 units were open and 72 guidance officers were in post. Feedback was good and OECD commended the initiative to other countries.

Self service

The introduction of *self service* was eventually to prove an even more important break from the traditional service, though in the 1960s it did not get beyond the pilot phase. Ever since 1910, the exchange officials had rarely put vacancies on display but had instead themselves decided which jobseeker to notify about each vacancy. In theory, this made possible an optimum match, though, when vacancies were scarce, it could give rise to suspicions of favouritism. Self service, on the other hand, enabled jobseekers to match themselves against displayed vacancies. Its origins lay in a new enthusiasm among officials for less bureaucratic and more consumer-orientated procedures. The new ideas seem to have occurred independently and almost simultaneously in the HQ Inspectorate, the Employment Service branch in HQ, in St Helens Employment exchange and in Sweden.[12]

In June 1967, Ron Stephenson, an able Inspector in the Establishments Department who was later to play an important role in the service, wrote a paper arguing that the questioning of jobseekers by employment officers was one of the reasons why 'the better type of jobseeker avoids our local offices if he possibly can'. Current procedures derived from an age of respect for officialdom. But a social revolution was in progress in which 'long established patterns of economic and social behaviour are breaking down and our captive clientele is diminishing in numbers and quality'. 'The motor car-owning generally emancipated jobseeker' mainly needed straightforward information provided by self service.

In September 1967, Robin Keith wrote a paper called 'The Employment Exchanges and the Unemployed Nexus'. It was inspired by some research carried out in North Shields (an area of relatively high unemployment) by Adrian Sinfield, then a lecturer at Essex University (and later Professor of Social Policy at Edinburgh University). Keith felt that Sinfield provided an explanation for the low esteem in which the exchanges were held. They were 'places of ill omen except under duress', because they were used by people who had lost their jobs and might be in a black, defeatist or domestically upset mood. The exchanges disciplined them as if they were workshy parasites; they were required to turn up twice a week and collect cash payments in full view along with shiftless unfortunates or misfits, for many of whom they had considerable personal contempt. Only one in four got a job through the exchange. The exchange's matching systems were secretive and they suspected favouritism in dispensing the jobs and victimisation in administering the work test. Beveridge's original theory that the exchange existed to save workers the misery of tramping after potential work was fallacious, because unemployed men took pride in taking their own initiatives, while employers respected such initiatives. Sinfield, as a sociologist, drew the moral that what was needed was a service for the hard to place. Keith turned this on its head and said that what was needed was to reduce the bureaucratic requirements attached to claiming benefit by the use of computers, to introduce more attractive modern offices

The Stirring of Reform, 1960–70

and, more radically, to run employment work *like a library* with vacancies on display. 'We should place greater faith in the bona fides and initiative of most workers than we do at present.'

Both Stephenson and Keith were challenging the paternalism and suspicion inherent in the traditional procedures of the service. They received support from Sweden – seen in the 1960s as the pioneers of labour market reform. The Swedes had just started experimenting with putting full details of all vacancies in a weekly magazine available to all jobseekers.

Not everyone welcomed these new ideas. Dorothy Kent, Head of Employment Service Branch at the time, was initially sceptical, believing that skilled selection by officials produced a better result for employers. Self-selection might cause a backlash from employers. Regional representatives thought that self service could undermine the Department's case to the Treasury for resources for a more 'professional' service. Fortunately, the HQ team persisted. One Controller volunteered Ashford in Kent for an experiment. But before this could get going, the manager at St Helens exchange in the North West began the first experiment in self service at the suggestion of his staff in September 1968. The motivation seems to have been very practical – a concern that most people registered on Monday when staff were too busy to place them; self service would enable them to place themselves. Vacancy levels at St Helens doubled and placings increased by 20–25 per cent. Ashford, which opened a year later, had similar success. Both the St Helens and the subsequent Ashford experiments differed from the Swedish model in that the name and address of the employer were *not* shown as part of the vacancy display. It was necessary to approach the receptionist for this information. This had several advantages:

- occasionally, the receptionist could prevent a highly unsuitable candidate from going forward;
- the exchange could monitor the number of candidates going forward and could call a halt if there were enough; and
- statistics of submissions and, through follow-up with the employer, of placings, could be maintained.

Remarkably, this model of self service has endured in the British employment service to the present day, despite various experiments with displaying full details.

In 1969, Ken Barnes, by then Deputy Secretary responsible for the employment service, recognising self service as a potential winner, suggested extending it to all low unemployment areas (assuming that it simply would not work where unemployment was high). But a Regional Controller advised him that there was no suitable space in most offices. In other words, the introduction of self service as a standard feature was dependent upon a national programme of premises renewal. By now Dorothy Kent too was a convert and she stimulated further experiments by the regions and asked the ministry of Public Building and Works to include space for self service in all new buildings.

The development of self service was a classic example of the value of the experimental approach encouraged by the Dunnett Working Party.

Separation experiments

The third major area of experimentation was the delivery of employment and benefit work in separate offices. The Ministry of Labour was determined to try this out, though they knew that they faced potentially bitter opposition from what was now the Ministry of Social Security under Margaret Herbison. They sought to overcome this both by pushing ahead regardless with an experiment in Warrington and also by pressing MoSS to agree to another six experiments. The new MoSS Permanent Secretary, Sir Clifford Jarrett, and Sir John Walley briefed Herbison to resist this because:

- 'the more difficult placing propositions would tend to remain out of sight, out of mind';
- it was implausible to suppose that this duplication of office overheads could ever be introduced throughout the country; and
- it would be better to rely on computerisation and postal payment to reduce the need for attendance at local offices.

Dunnett assured MoSS that there was no intention to neglect the hard to place and that split offices would only be for conurbations and large cities. Eventually, Herbison gave her agreement 'with the greatest reluctance'.[13] The experiments proved popular with managers and staff, though it proved difficult to get clearcut statistical evidence about their effects. At Blackpool, it was thought that better registrants might have been attracted because fewer people were 'loitering' at the office. Moreover, complaints from the public had been negligible, although the two offices were a mile apart.[14]

The advent of Barbara Castle

In April 1968, Barbara Castle became First Secretary of State and Secretary of State of a renamed Department of Employment and Productivity (DEP). She was the second woman Cabinet Minister to have these responsibilities and, like Margaret Bondfield, was energetic and enthusiastic. She was also one of the Prime Minister's closest allies. The Department now had more weight in Whitehall than at any time since the Second World War. Senior officials saw the opportunity for a step improvement in their dowdy inheritance of the exchanges. Barbara Castle proved willing to make this cause her own and to fight for it with her colleagues, even if she quickly became preoccupied with her White Paper on industrial relations – 'In Place of Strife'. The cause of reforming the exchanges was further helped by new evidence on employers' and workers' attitudes to the service and international support from OECD.

Employers' and workers' attitudes to the employment services

First, *employers attitudes*. PA Management Consultants had been commissioned by the Department in 1967 to carry out a survey of 800 firms. They found that employers used the service to fill 21 per cent of their vacancies. Usage was skewed towards unskilled manual vacancies (26 per cent) as compared with only 11 per cent of clerical vacancies and 4 per cent of executive vacancies. The service filled two-thirds of the vacancies it received, but well over half of the employers (53–58 per cent) were dissatisfied with the candidates produced by the exchanges – a figure which was thought to be 'shockingly bad'. Employers associated the service with the unskilled, the unemployed, the unemployable and the dole. Some, no doubt unfairly, branded its clientele as 'unemployable, workshy, misfits, the halt, the lame and the lazy'. It would make little difference to these employers if the service were to vanish overnight. Employment officers were not sufficiently selective – they were trying to find jobs for people rather than people for jobs. PA advocated setting up an organisation entirely separated from benefit, located in attractive modern premises and employing highly competent officers. The 'problem cases' should be hived off to another department.[15]

Senior HQ officials, who no doubt had worked with PA during the exercise, welcomed these ideas, but Regional Controllers were uneasy about divorcing the employment service from social insurance, fearing that it would undermine the viability of too much of the existing network.[16]

Also available were findings about *workers' attitudes* to the employment exchanges, derived from the Government Social Survey's Labour Mobility Survey of 1963. From a sample of 20,000, it was found that

- half commented favourably on the employment exchanges;
- 27 per cent complained of inefficiency or lack of courtesy or interest;
- 60 per cent said that no jobs were offered to them or those offered were unsuitable;
- 30 per cent complained of a lack of privacy;
- 24 per cent said that the staff were rather unhelpful;
- 41 per cent said that the staff did all they could;
- 18 per cent said that there was a long wait;
- 71 per cent of men had used the service, but less than half the women; the women who had used the service were less critical than the men;
- overall, the exchanges placed 19 per cent of those wanting jobs.[17]

These findings about workers' attitudes were consistent with those from employers and reinforced the Department's belief that radical change was required.

The OECD examination

Also influential were the pressures coming from overseas. In October 1968 the Department was 'examined' by a team of OECD examiners led by Professor J C Donovan of the USA. At this time, OECD was strongly influenced by the Swedish concept of active labour market policies designed to promote efficiency and economic growth. Like PA, the OECD examiners were unhappy about the close association of the British employment service with unemployment insurance administration. This had produced 'a vicious circle of low expectations about the value of the services to be received both among workers and employers'. The examiners rated the potential importance of the service very highly; indeed, in this respect their views were reminiscent of the young Beveridge (page 4). They said that 'the Employment Service is the single most important tool to ensure the proper functioning of the labour market and that it has a crucial role to play in revitalising the British economy.' They favoured radical reform – separation from benefit, moving into better premises, with more staff and better qualified staff. They pointed out that the Canadian, Swedish and Norwegian services were several times bigger than the British service in relation to total government expenditure. But they also thought that the British had far too many small local offices by international standards and advocated a much smaller network of larger offices.[18]

Although this report was not published until 1970, the thinking of the OECD examiners was well known to Department officials long before that and fitted in well with their own views. Indeed, these international opinions would be useful in debates with both the Department of Health and Social Security and the Treasury.

The Planning Unit study

From the Department's point of view, it was clear that radical reform of the exchanges was needed. But how could the evidence be brought together in such a convincing way as to overcome the resistance particularly on the resources front? A new mechanism was to hand. In June 1968, the Fulton Report on the Civil Service had been published. This followed the biggest enquiry into the civil service for a generation and was to have a profound effect on the employment service. It attacked the 'philosophy of the amateur' in government and called for greater professionalism. It criticised the lack of a managerial culture in the senior civil service. It proposed the creation of 'accountable management units' within government departments. Most usefully to Barbara Castle's officials in 1968, it also called for Planning Units in all departments to pursue major long-term policy planning.

In October 1968 Mrs Castle agreed that a Research and Planning Division should be set up in the DEP and that its first planning study should be on 'The Future of the Employment Services'. She asked the Department to make a searching examination of the service and to put forward proposals for such fundamental changes as might be thought necessary or desirable.[19] The study team was led by Jim Galbraith, head of the new division, supported by Rhys Robinson and Roderick Allison. This team set to work with a will to carry out what was in many ways the most searching and wide-ranging review of the service since its inception. They worked with the existing experts within the Department and drew on experience since the Dunnett Working Party.

On one central issue, however, Barbara Castle was already clear. She believed it 'essential that, at some stage, the Service should shed the responsibility for the payment of [unemployment benefit]'. She had already spoken to her old friend Dick Crossman, Secretary of State for Health and Social Security, who initially resisted strongly the idea of taking over unemployment benefit, but did conclude by saying that he accepted the logic of the arguments for a transfer. As we shall see, this was too optimistic an interpretation of Crossman's position. But these contacts with Crossman led to negotiations on the social security front which would run in parallel with the Planning Unit study (pages 141–3).

The Planning Unit took nearly a year to produce their report on 'The Future of the Employment Services'. The report began by setting out the manpower issues facing the country – recurrent shortages of workers with particular skills, the geographically uneven pressure of demand, the growing pace of technological change, causing the decline of some industries and the rise of others, the rise in educational expectations and the increase in women's role in the labour force. Government had been pursuing a range of radical policies to encourage training, to ease redundancies and to promote productivity and the report argued for radically remodelling the employment services in support of these initiatives. The report discarded two other options:

- *to keep the service at its present level.* But, largely as a result of its benefit responsibilities, 'a downward spiral has been operating: the less the service has been used by workers, the less it has been used by employers and vice versa'. It had become in effect 'an unemployment service' for unemployed manual workers. It could not stand still – only decline unless radical changes were made. This theory of the downward spiral has remained ever since a powerful motivating force for maintaining a respectable market position for the public employment service.
- *to abolish the service.* But 'a self-regulating market was inefficient in ways which, though not obvious, were important and costly'. It was estimated that, if the service did not exist, one quarter of a million fewer people might be in employment at any one time at a cost of £275 million in lost production and £88 million in extra benefits.

The line taken in the report is unsurprising. It brings together the long-standing wish of the Department to reform the exchanges with arguments likely to be attractive to a Labour government in favour of state intervention in this field – that it will both save money *and* support their industrial strategy.

The report suggested that the *strategic aim* of a 'national manpower service' should be: 'To contribute to the most efficient deployment and utilisation of the nation's manpower'. The *objectives* were:

(a) to help employers fill their vacancies as quickly as possible;
(b) to advise employers on methods of achieving better utilisation of manpower;
(c) to help workers develop their potential to the fullest possible extent and to find the most suitable jobs;
(d) to give workers who are at a disadvantage in the labour market the special help they are likely to need; and
(e) to collect and disseminate labour market information.

Two features are striking here. First, the phrase 'manpower services' is used instead of 'employment services'. There is an ambiguity running through the Planning Unit Report about whether it is just about the employment exchanges (its initial brief) or whether it also covers, for instance, local delivery of training services and advisory services. The term 'national manpower service' seems to imply this wider interpretation. This reflected concerns expressed by Robin Keith, now Director of Establishments, who complained that early versions of the report were 'oblivious of the DEP set up as a whole'.[20] This issue of whether to go for a narrow 'agency' approach or a broader, more comprehensive, approach was to be debated for years and eventually resolved in favour of the former. Second, the aims and objectives give priority to *economic* as opposed to *social* considerations, to use a dichotomy that was much used in the Department for many years. Only objectives (c) and (d) are predominantly 'social'. This report was dominated by the labour market transparency model of the service. Social welfare plays a secondary role, while benefit control does not even rate a mention among the objectives of the service.

The report advocated six principal changes, which we examine in turn:

1. to concentrate the Department's services to individuals in Manpower Centres in major urban centres;
2. to introduce unified control and responsibility for manpower services at HQ;
3. a professional standard of service to the public;
4. the Youth Employment Service to be fully integrated into an all-age guidance service;
5. more emphasis on experimentation and development; and
6. freedom from 'agency work' for other Departments, and in particular unemployment benefit work to pass to the DHSS.

First, *Manpower Centres* were proposed in about 40 major urban centres to concentrate a wide range of specialist functions under a high-powered director. This director would report direct to HQ, thus undermining the long-standing regional organisation of the Department. The present network would be pruned from 1100 outlets to about 700, with the retention of some 250 employment offices and 450 'satellites' and the closure of the remaining 450 offices, mainly in rural areas. This pruning of the network corresponded with the OECD recommendations and had affinities with other rationalisation exercises of the 1960s, affecting the rail network and cottage hospitals. Not surprisingly, all these proposals were strongly opposed by the existing Regional Controllers. They argued that HQ could not control 40 Centres, that there would be a loss of economies of scale in support services such as personnel and premises, that the new structure would not relate to the economic planning regions used by other Departments and that the rural closures went much too far.[21]

Secondly, there was to be a *General Manager* with unified control of manpower services including the field, the policy branches, staffing, inspection, R&D and the psychologists. This would remove the divided control of the exchanges between policy and establishments which had existed ever since the service had been progressively integrated into the Ministry of Labour between 1917 and 1929 (pages 41, 49 and 74). Jim Galbraith argued on the basis of 'modern management thinking' that 'diffusion of authority and a fragmented system of management makes increased efficiency difficult to achieve'.[22] These arguments accorded with the doctrine of 'accountable management' in the Fulton Report. There was some discussion about whether the service should be 'hived off', ie to an outside body. Galbraith saw some advantages in this as offering the 'major jolt to the total system' which he believed was needed, but on balance more cautious counsels prevailed as the civil service orthodoxy of the time was that hiving off was only appropriate when a function was commercial or self-financing. The report did propose a small advisory council, but, no doubt from bitter experience with the Department's existing advisory bodies, said that it was important that it was not 'dominated by special interests or pressure groups'. There was a debate between Galbraith and Keith about the scope of the General Manager's remit, with Keith inclining towards making the General Manager responsible for all the Department's operational and executive functions – rather like Ince's wartime role.

The third proposal was for a *professional service*, embracing

- higher grading (to executive officer equivalent) for adult employment advisory work, as already existed for disabled persons work;
- external recruitment of these advisers;
- greatly enhanced training of staff, particularly the advisers;
- the acquisition, probably by lease, of attractive convenient premises.

The fourth proposal concerned the *youth employment service*. It proposed ending the long-standing arrangement whereby careers guidance to young people was provided mostly by local authorities, but in a few cases by the Department (page 119). Instead, there should be an all-age guidance and placing service provided by the Department and integrated with the Occupational Guidance Service. This was justified by the increasing length of education, the difficulty of finding a suitable cut-off point for an education-based career service and the patchy quality of the present local authority service. Such integration into a national employment service would not be credible with the existing run-down exchange service, but would become so with modernisation. It was a highly controversial recommendation, which was rejected by 2:1 by the Department's National Youth Employment Council early in 1970, but it was none the less thought worth fighting for.

The fifth proposal was for *experimentation and development* – very much the style encouraged by the Dunnett Working Party. Self service came under this heading, as also did experiments in computerised matching of vacancies and registrants. The report showed remarkable foresight in recognising that at some point it might be necessary to choose between these developments; by the late 1970s, self service was to cast doubt on the cost justification of big computer matching schemes.

The sixth proposal, not surprisingly, was to *break out of Agency work for DHSS and other Departments* – 'to break out of this vicious circle, we must get rid of UB...our role should be limited to informing the DHSS that new claimants had registered with us for employment'.[23] The registration requirement should be retained for fear that some would otherwise 'take a holiday at the National Insurance Fund's expense while the Employment Exchange had a vacancy'. We discuss this further below.

The rest of the report cleared up various loose ends. It rejected the idea of reintroducing a requirement on employers to notify vacancies. It rejected charging employers except perhaps for new or specialised services. It deplored the resources devoted by employers to private employment agencies, noted the widespread dissatisfaction with these services and expected the reformed exchanges to compete effectively with the agencies.

The report discussed the problem of the '*socially disadvantaged*', noting an estimate by the statistician, RF Fowler, that 6.4 per cent of those unemployed were responsible for 50 per cent of the time spent on the register. It proposed a specialised service to help this group, either as part of the Disablement Resettlement Service or separately. But the Planning Unit did not want the modernised employment service to be identified with people at the extreme end of the spectrum. It recommended that 'the workshy – a category to which no one should be consigned without the fullest and most careful consideration – should be recognised as the responsibility of the DHSS'. 'The manpower service should only call in for interview those whom they need to see for employment reasons; it is a waste of time to call others to attend.' The long-term unemployed should not be out of sight, out of mind, but 'equally must not take up a wholly disproportionate share of manpower service time and resource' – a view which would be turned on its head 20 years later.

The report finished by trying to estimate the *costs and savings* arising from their recommendations. 1500–2000 extra staff would be needed, costing £3.5–£4 million a year. Premises would require an extra £500,000. The total would be £4–5 million a year, but the build-up in costs would be spread gradually over seven years.

Negotiations with the Department of Health and Social Security

Concurrently with the work on this report, the Department had suggested to the Ministry of Social Security a joint review of the proposal that they should take over unemployment benefit. Richard Crossman, the Secretary of State for Health and Social Security, in fact regarded Barbara Castle's ideas for reforming the employment services as dangerously elitist. His concerns, unlike those of his senior officials, did not relate to the potential weakening of benefit control but to the potential neglect of the employment problems of the disadvantaged – in other words, social welfare considerations. He was reinforced in his views by a discussion in September 1968 with Ron Hill, employment exchange manager in his own constituency of Coventry, who said: 'A lot of my staff would agree with Barbara. I don't. I don't think we want to turn our office in Coventry into a dolled-up employment agency cut off from the problem of poverty.'[24] Similarly, a group of supplementary benefit managers whom Crossman met in Manchester said that the transfer of unemployment benefit work to the DHSS would be 'an intolerable reform...we would be overwhelmed by the queues of callers'.[25] So in December 1968, Crossman wrote to Mrs Castle saying that he was most reluctant to add to the burdens on his staff, who had had a 'very hard time for the last two years. I would be courting disaster if I add to the burdens on staff by agreeing to a review'.[26] However, in January 1969, Barbara Castle broke down Crossman's resistance to a review by offering the *quid pro quo* of waiving her view on a separate bill for the preservation of pension rights.[27] Crossman thought he was kicking the subject into touch.

A joint working party was set up under two junior Ministers – David Ennals for the DHSS and Roy Hattersley – with terms of reference: 'To consider and report on the future administration of unemployment benefit, with particular reference to the desirability and feasibility of transferring this from DEP to DHSS.' In fact the two Ministers only attended the first meeting, no doubt finding the subject matter rather too arcane for their tastes. Future meetings were led by Mildred Riddelsdell for the DHSS and Ken Barnes for the DEP. (Ken Barnes – not to be confused with Denis Barnes – was a Deputy Secretary in the DEP.)

The joint working party's proceedings took a whole year. This reflected the wide gulf between the position of the two Departments which at times seemed unbridgeable. There was never a complete meeting of minds. But Miss Riddelsdell eventually suggested a compromise which enabled an 'agreed' report to be presented to Ministers in February 1970. The compromise was that the DHSS could not comment on the views of the various manpower experts in favour of separation, but would place on record the conditions under which any transfer could take place.[28] Even so, the report reads like the pasting together of two contradictory points of view.

This report recalled the decision in 1944 to allocate policy on unemployment benefit to the Ministry of National Insurance, while the Ministry of

Labour retained the day to day work (pages 100–1). It noted the OECD position:

> in the past the attitude in most countries, as in the Beveridge Report, has been to regard the safeguarding of unemployment funds as the main object of an [employment] service, but this is not the present view. Many Governments in advanced countries, including the US, Canada, Germany and Sweden, are improving their public employment services to attract and service a wide cross-section of the population, employed as well as unemployed. These policies do not imply neglect of the unemployed; on the contrary they may be combined with new special schemes for the socially disadvantaged. They do however usually involve some separation of UB and placing work.[29]

The report set out the usual DEP arguments about the 'dole image'. Then by contrast it presented the view of DHSS officials that nothing in their experience since Beveridge wrote in 1942 had cast doubt on his statement that 'the payment of UB and placing in employment must in practice take place at the same local office' (page 99). It was true that, in the case of supplementary benefit (SB), there was already partial separation, but SB recipients signed and were paid in the exchanges and at that time the majority of the unemployed were on UB anyway, as Table 8.2 shows:

Table 8.2 *Unemployed claimants receiving unemployment benefit (UB) and supplementary benefit (SB), November 1968*

Benefit category	Number (000s)
Registered unemployed	530
UB only	230
UB and SB	58
SB only	126

Both Departments agreed that, if manpower developments made separation unavoidable, then it was best to transfer benefit work to the DHSS, rather than to a distinct network within the DEP, though this was not ruled out as a 'transitional measure'. Separation presented two dangers:

- *the emphasis of employment work might shift away from the unemployed to their detriment.* The DEP considered that the more effective service would be beneficial to the unemployed, but the DHSS did not think this could be taken for granted and argued for systematic review interviewing of those remaining unemployed for more than a certain time;

- *the control of benefit might be progressively weakened.* Ultimate responsibility for benefit control would rest with the benefit administration. Fraud work was unlikely to be adversely affected. But there was a risk that voluntary unemployment would increase. The DHSS pointed out that separation in Canada had led to a steep drop in disqualifications for refusal of suitable employment etc. The DEP accepted the employment service's continuing responsibility to bring cases of doubt to the benefit administration's attention (for example, refusal of suitable employment and non-availability).

Finally, the report dealt with the practicalities of a transfer of benefit work to the DHSS. The problem was that the DHSS was engaged in integrating contributory benefit work with supplementary benefit work in the same local offices. This was a formidable task and it would take until 1975 to achieve it in two-thirds of their offices. Taking on unemployment benefit work would therefore be a major extra complication. For the indefinite future, there would be a 'complex patchwork of offices' at different stages of integration. There would also be inconvenience for the public in having to deal with more than one office. The conclusion was that 1975 was the earliest date when they might be able to cope with the transfer.

The Consultative Document

Now that the Department had the grudging acquiescence of DHSS officials to separation, the various building blocks seemed to be in place by early 1970 for a public pronouncement about reform of the employment service. Senior officials started to work on plans for developing the Planning Unit's ideas. It was too early for a General Manager: as one of the Controllers said, 'We are not yet ready to receive a Messiah – we first need a John the Baptist – a project manager'.[30] Ken Barnes took on Ken Cooper, an able Assistant Secretary, for this role.

Barbara Castle was increasingly enthusiastic about this whole project. Having suffered a grave rebuff in the Cabinet's retreat over her 'In Place of Strife' proposals, she thought that the 'manpower services plan' might prove to be 'my most important monument in this job' (see the opening quotation to this chapter). She was encouraged in this view by Robin Keith, to whom she had been introduced by Bernard Ingham, her Chief Information Officer, at his Christmas party. Keith provided her with his 'outstanding note' commenting on the Planning Unit Report. As a leading reformer of the service in the mid-1960s, he evidently felt that less than justice had been done to the achievements. But he recognised that so far they had failed to break the 'unemployment benefit nexus', to achieve a breakthrough on premises or to mobilise support from the TUC and the employers. He commended the Planning Unit Report as offering a new basis for a breakthrough. But, breaking ranks with his colleagues, he added that independence for the employment service within the

DEP might create 'a kind of apartheid in reverse in favour of a limited part of the DEP's purpose...fragmentation or split is neither workable, healthy or necessary'. He was also concerned about losing the Regional Controllers, whose jobs could be among the best and most useful in the country.[31]

In January 1970, Sir Denis Barnes chaired a meeting of Permanent Secretaries on the proposals. The main notes of concern came from the Departments of Education and Science and of the Environment about the proposal to remove the careers service from local authorities. Sir Clifford Jarrett, for the DHSS, said he had no objections in principle to the transfer of benefit administration but was concerned about the effects on the morale of his staff of an early announcement, given that the transfer would not take place for several years.

But officials had not allowed for a tremendous row at Ministerial level. Sir Clifford, and his Deputy, Mildred Riddelsdell, had not taken the elementary precaution of checking out the DHSS position with their brilliant but irascible Secretary of State, Richard Crossman. He was furious with his officials for having committed the Department without consulting him, and his diary records one 'tremendous row' after another as he took them to task. He recognised that they had agreed to a compromise 'out of sheer decency' – to accommodate Mrs Castle's ambitions – but the result was a compromise that was 'plain ridiculous'.[32] Crossman rang up both Mrs Castle and the Prime Minister to ensure that the proposals went through proper channels. He had a meeting with Mrs Castle and the two Permanent Secretaries which ended when Crossman expressed his fury at the 'conspiracy of the Permanent Secretaries' and stalked out of the room.[33]

There were two discussions of the proposals at SEP, a powerful Cabinet Committee normally chaired by the Prime Minister. However, on the first occasion, Harold Wilson was not keen to umpire a dispute between two of his oldest allies and spun out a discussion of the British Museum until he had to go, leaving the chair to Roy Jenkins. We have a vivid account of what occurred, as the diaries of both the main protagonists were subsequently published. According to Mrs Castle, Crossman was

> at his most outrageous...he made great demagogic play with the claim that it would not be to the benefit of the unemployed. All I wanted was to set up posh new offices and to deal with the easy cases. He was unctuous about the 'socially disadvantaged' who, he tried to make out, would be tucked somewhere out of sight under my policy. Weak with rage, I nonetheless hit back vigorously, pointing out that my policy was going to enable me to do something for these difficult cases for the first time – and in posh new offices.[34]

Roy Jenkins finally adjudicated that Mrs Castle should be allowed to put forward a consultative document but there should be no question of the government announcing its decision, least of all on timing, on either the transfer of UB or the transfer of the careers service. Crossman regarded it as an easy victory.[35] By the time the second SEP discussion took place on 13 May, it was agreed that the Consultative Document should propose separation of benefit from employment services, *but within DEP*. Barbara Castle felt this was a victory for her cause and that by now Crossman had become 'a little ashamed of himself'.[36]

In May 1970, the Consultative Document on the Future of the Employment Service appeared. This summarised the Planning Unit Report, but with some interesting changes of emphasis. As Keith had suggested, it was more positive about the service's recent achievements. On the new kind of service proposed, the document envisaged it becoming 'the first resort of employers making engagements as well as of people seeking jobs'. The document took a swipe at the private agencies – 'employers disliked having to rely on them...and would welcome a more effective public service'. It argued strongly for separation but, as had been painfully agreed, completely ignored the possibility of transferring the work to the DHSS and instead proposed separate benefit administration within the DEP. The scope of the service, including the proposed Manpower Centres, was broader than just running the exchanges and a bit like the OECD model; for example, it included 'mobilising resources for re-training' (but not running the Government Training Centres). On the vexed question of the future of the youth employment service, the document sat on the fence and invited wide public discussion.[37]

Conclusion

With the publication of the Consultative Document, the prospects for a major reform of the service were very promising. The stone had at last been rolled to the top of the hill. But in June 1970 the Labour government lost the General Election.

9

Modernisation, 1970–74

'a comprehensive public employment service should be maintained...and it should be modernised to serve its social and economic objectives.' (Tony Barber, Chancellor of the Exchequer, summing up the conclusions of the Economic Policy Committee on 16 November 1971)[1]

Introduction

The period of the Heath government was a decisive turning point in the history of the public employment service. At last, the political will and the resources were found for modernisation. Moreover, the service proved to be a testing ground for new ideas on the delivery of public services – both the Fulton Report's proposal for 'accountable units' or Agencies and the more radical idea of 'hiving off' government functions to bodies comprising employers and unions. The ferment of reorganisation within the Department of Employment anticipated debates in the late 1980s which were to revolutionise public administration in Britain.

But in June 1970, as the new government took office, the prospects of recovering the momentum for modernisation achieved under Barbara Castle looked bleak. Under the Conservative Party Manifesto, the top priority for the Department of Employment (it soon lost 'Productivity' from its title) was the Industrial Relations Bill. The Manifesto made no mention of employment services. Rather, it promised 'less government', with fewer civil servants, 'cost reduction plans' in every ministry and 'the widespread application throughout government of the most modern management, budgeting and cost effectiveness techniques'. In this climate, it seemed unlikely that the Department could obtain the extra resources essential for modernising the employment service.

This chapter shows how, after a hesitant and uneasy start, Robert Carr and his officials gained government approval for a modernisation plan that was in some ways more radical than that proposed by Barbara Castle. In particular, the marketing concept of the 'Jobcentre' was developed and the employment service was to become a performance-driven Agency. Under Carr's successor,

Maurice Macmillan, it was agreed that it should report to a new hived off body – the Manpower Services Commission.

Personalities

The new Secretary of State was Robert Carr, who knew the Department well, having been Parliamentary Secretary of the Ministry of Labour from 1955 to 1958. He was an able, perceptive and sensitive Minister. He had a business background and was keen both to improve the efficiency of government and to cushion the impact of economic change on the lives of ordinary people. He proved keen to modernise the employment service, though concerned to contain costs and ensure efficiency. He was disappointed to be moved from the Department in July 1972 to become Lord President and Leader of the House and then Home Secretary. He was succeeded by Maurice Macmillan, who in turn was succeeded by Willie Whitelaw in the dark days of the miners' strike in December 1973. All three Ministers were on the 'one nation' or moderate wing of the Conservative Party.

Sir Denis Barnes was Permanent Secretary almost throughout this period. Inevitably, in such a turbulent period, he was mainly preoccupied with industrial relations. But he continued to push for reform of the employment service, as did Ken Barnes, the Deputy Secretary concerned with 'manpower services' and John Locke, a lively and innovative character, who succeeded Ken Barnes during 1971.

Just before the 1970 Election, a new figure had come on to the scene who, more than anyone else, was to be identified with revolutionary change in the employment service. This was Ken Cooper, then aged 39, a career civil servant from the Department who had once been Robert Carr's Private Secretary. Cooper had remarkable talents for the job he was to occupy. He was strong, single-minded and dedicated – in no way the trimming mandarin, rather a natural leader who, unlike many senior civil servants, was keenly interested in management. He had his own vision of the service which he put over to managers and staff in tireless journeys around the network. On occasion, he would shout at those who seemed less than fully committed. His evangelistic oratory owed much to his experience as a teenager in the Salvation Army, speaking on street corners. This was a new style in the Department and the civil service, not universally popular, but formidable in its impact. In a period of five years, he was to put his personal stamp on the service to a greater extent than any senior official since Ince. Cooper came to the job as an Assistant Secretary but, as the Department gathered confidence that modernisation could be achieved, he was promoted to Under-Secretary in July 1971 and appointed Chief Executive late in 1971.

When the Election was called, Ken Cooper went on a six-week tour of the regions.[2] He visited unemployment blackspots like Liverpool and Glasgow and was appalled at the way the unemployed were treated, with 'long queues of men, women and children waiting to draw that week's unemployment cash'.

Office of Hope

He felt that it was it was important to 'treat people properly' and also to switch from cash to postal payment. He was also perturbed by the pettifogging inspection systems and instructions derived from benefit responsibilities, which since the 1920s had dominated the work of local office managers. More generally, he reflected on the experience of the large and high profile redundancies of the late 1960s. The exchanges had been expected to help those affected, but how much real help could they give if they were running a marginal operation in a secondary labour market?

The rise in unemployment

The Heath government was much affected by unemployment. Heath inherited a jobless total of around 600,000 in June 1970. But in 1971 unemployment began to rise dramatically, to reach one million by January 1972. The result was Heath's famous 'U-Turn'. During 1972, the Chancellor, Anthony Barber, pumped massive sums into the economy and, whatever its other effects, this had succeeded in bringing unemployment down to around 550,000 by early 1974.

The relatively high unemployment in 1970/71 put pressure on staffing in the exchanges. Relaxations in procedure permitted signing to be reduced from twice to once a week, review interviews to be deferred or waived and the use of self-registration forms by the public.[3]

Early days in the Heath government: the issue of hiving off

Despite the change of government, Barbara Castle's Consultative Document on the employment service was not forgotten. Many organisations sent in comments. But it was not clear that Ministers would want to implement Barbara Castle's proposals. Indeed, Ken Barnes, Ken Cooper and their colleagues were 'pawing the ground', uncertain of the government's intentions. It was not just that Carr was distracted by the Industrial Relations Bill. There were inherent contradictions in the government position. Before the election, Carr had made a speech in the Commons in favour of reforming the employment service and separating it from benefit. This suggested a continuation of the tradition of bipartisanship in relation to the employment service so much cherished by Beveridge (page 123). Indeed, Carr went further than Barbara Castle and advocated a hived off service under a national manpower commission representing unions, management and education.[4] But would Ministers be prepared to allocate the necessary extra resources, given the Manifesto commitment to 'less government'? Experience in the 1950s and 1960s had shown that reform without additional resources was futile. Moreover, the separation of employment from benefit work would require the agreement of Sir Keith Joseph, the new Secretary of Social Services, who was committed under the Manifesto to reduce abuse of the benefit system by 'the shirkers and the scroungers'. Was separation consistent with a drive against abuse?

Given these tensions, Ken Barnes did not press the issues about the employment service quickly but instead focused on Carr's apparent enthusiasm for hiving off. The Fulton Committee had briefly referred to the 'hiving off' of government functions to autonomous public boards but had said that the implications were outside their terms of reference and called for 'an early and thorough review'.[5] The new Civil Service Department, however, gave such ideas no encouragement. Chapter 8 showed that the possibility of hiving off the employment service had been considered briefly within DEP in 1968, but not pursued (page 139). Robert Carr saw 'hiving off' as a way of building a partnership between government and the two sides of industry – the other side of the coin to his attempt through the Industrial Relations Bill to counter irresponsible forces within the trade union movement.

Soon after the Election, Ken Barnes reported to Carr that, while there were some attractions in hiving off employment and training services,[6] the case was by no means clearcut, the main problem being financial control of some £70 million of public expenditure. Carr agreed to a further study involving the Treasury and the Civil Service Department.[7] This study involved visits to the two main European exemplars of hived off manpower services – Sweden and West Germany. Ken Cooper found that he was the first senior British civil servant to visit the Federal Institute for Labour in Nuremburg since the war, and he was greeted with open arms. Both the German and the Swedish models were impressive examples of cooperation between the 'social partners'. But the Treasury, represented by the formidable Leo Pliatzky, considered that a hived off body dependent upon public funds would be subject to the same controls and accountability to the Treasury and to Parliament as a government Department.

Ken Barnes' report to Carr of January 1971 argued that, given this Treasury line, the game of hiving off was not worth a candle and it would be better to concentrate on setting up 'better systems of accountable management' within the Department.[8] Carr disagreed:

> *I cannot help being a little disappointed at the conclusion coming down against the idea of a National Manpower Commission.*
>
> *Two of the most compelling arguments arise from the 'constitutional' position and would apply to all other proposals for hiving off, ie Parliamentary accountability and Treasury financial control.*[9]

He thought it important to get some policy consideration of these issues.

It was agreed to set up a Working Group chaired by Paul Bryan, the Minister of State, and including civil servants as well as politicians (an unusual arrangement) to consider:

> *what major changes might be proposed in the Department's policies for employment, training, the mobility of labour and the treatment of redundancy, and what changes in organisation these might call for.*

Members of the Working Group included David Howell, the Parliamentary Secretary of the Civil Service Department, and Ken Lane, the new Industrial Adviser, from Rio Tinto Zinc, as well as Ken Barnes, Ken Cooper and other officials.[10] This Working Group enabled Ministers to become engaged in the questions of employment service modernisation and training policy. Here we focus on two items from the Group's formidable agenda: hiving off and the employment service.

On hiving off, the Working Group came up against the same Treasury resistance as the previous exercise, now reinforced by a Civil Service Department representative – Tom Caulcott. He felt that bodies which were to be hived-off or made into 'accountable management' units needed to earn a considerable income and have effective ways of monitoring performance.[11]

The Working Group suggested that a hived off Commission might be financed by a manpower levy on employers. Pliatzky was not keen on this, presumably because of the Treasury's long-standing hostility to hypothecated taxation.[12] Caulcott argued that the debate got into

> *political concepts of what the government is about and what it should and could not do. This points to the need for Ministers to be able to control the affairs of any Commission to such an extent as to cast severe doubt on the possibility of granting the Commission real independence.*[13]

Chapters 11 and 12 will show that this was curiously prophetic about what was going to happen in the Manpower Services Commission in the early 1980s. The Working Group, however, were not persuaded by the central Departments. In May 1971 they reported to Carr that they remained 'strongly attracted as the ultimate solution' to a National Manpower Commission because it offered more 'forceful co-ordination' of services, it involved industry and a basis both for shaking up the employment service and eventually for replacing the industrial training boards.

In June 1971, Sir Denis Barnes, the Permanent Secretary, evidently perplexed by this awkward impasse over hiving off, consulted Sir William Armstrong, then at the height of his prestige as Head of the Civil Service. Armstrong felt that the best way to make progress was through a new executive body within the Department.[14] This led the Department to pull back from 'hiving off' and to propose that the employment service should instead be reorganised as a Departmental Agency.

As an interesting sequel to this debate, in September 1971, the CSD recommended the concept of the Departmental Agency to a meeting of Permanent Secretaries at Sunningdale. Such Agencies would have certain freedoms but be subject to performance indicators and accountable management systems. No doubt, the CSD saw this as a way both of following up Fulton and of escaping from the apparent ministerial predilection for hiving off. But they were also anticipating by 17 years the Next Steps Report of 1988 (Chapter 14). However, leaving aside developments in the DE, together with the creation of the Procurement Executive and the Property Services Agency, the 1971 paper was largely a stillborn initiative. Maybe Departments needed first to sharpen up their whole approach to management, as occurred with the Financial Management Initiative of 1982, before the idea of the Departmental Agency could become a reality.

The Programme Analysis Review (PAR)

In January 1971, the government introduced a new mechanism designed 'progressively to improve the analysis of public expenditure projects and programmes'.[15] This was Programme Analysis and Review or PAR – a product of the Conservative Party's new thinking while in Opposition.

In Ken Cooper's words, 'the PAR initiative was a godsend which we seized with alacrity'.[16] The Department proposed to the Treasury that its first PAR should be the study being carried out by Paul Bryan's Working Group. But the Treasury and CSD argued that the draft Bryan report was much too long and detailed to be a PAR.[17] Carr had in any case felt that more work needed to be done on training and mobility issues. So it was decided that the DE's first PAR – and the first PAR from any Department to be considered by Ministers – should focus exclusively on the public employment service. This decoupling of employment and training services for PAR purposes may have finally tipped the balance in favour of an employment service Agency, rather than an employment and training Agency. Chapter 8 showed how Robin Keith had fought a rearguard action against the notion of a narrowly based employment service Agency (page 138). The Report of the Departmental Study of January 1971 had recognised the attraction of the idea of an employment service Agency as its 'relative modesty and simplicity' as a largely executive body with well-defined responsibilities, concerned only at the margins with the Department's manpower policy. But it had also said that it would be retrograde to isolate services from one another:

> *The importance of the employment service does not depend solely on its placing work. Rather it is the pivot around which the various services for vocational guidance, training, mobility, rehabilitation, redundancy payments and market intelligence should turn.*[18]

Despite this pivotal role in relation to other services, the PAR would lead to the employment service becoming a separate and distinct Agency.

Ken Cooper spent most of 1971 in refining the ideas from the Research and Planning Report of 1969 into a costed and practical plan which could be sold first to the Bryan Group and then through the PAR to the government generally. The key problem was the government's wish to spend less rather than more.

One possible route out of this dilemma was through charging. Ken Lane, the Department's business adviser, analysed the employment service as having

Office of Hope

three objectives, which resemble the three models of the service discussed in our Chapter 1:

- 'disciplinary' – ensuring benefit recipients sought work;
- aiding the socially disadvantaged;
- economic – where the scale of the service depended on cost benefit – or, if there was charging, on normal commercial criteria.[19]

Lane thought that charging could help determine the extent of the economic activity of the service, but other members of the Group pointed out that, if managers were excessively motivated by revenue considerations, this could go against the interests of the less competitive workers who used the service. It was impossible to disentangle the economic aspects of the service from the social aspects. It was agreed to restrict charging for the time being at least to professional and executive recruitment, where it could help to recover the costs of improvement.[20]

But in other areas Cooper had to bid for extra resources. He gave the first priority to:

- separation of employment and benefit;
- training and regrading of staff;
- a general manager; and
- a new network with better premises in the right locations.

The second priority items were expanding occupational guidance, area management in London and introducing fee-charging into the professional and executive register. The third category items were services for the socially disadvantaged and experiments with 'manpower centres'. The Bryan Group Report was in principle in favour of all these items but recognised that those in Category 3 might need to be delayed.[21] In practice, the idea of 'manpower centres' was dropped; nor did officials think it realistic to press for any substantial resources for a service for the socially disadvantaged.

Cooper offered compensating savings of about 250 staff and £0.5 million a year through the closure of some 450 small local offices out of the current network of 1100. This was consistent with the views of OECD (page 136) and the 1969 Planning Report (page 139). But it did not take into account the political aspects of closure of local services – whether cottage hospitals, post offices or employment exchanges – and in the event nothing like this number of closures was achieved.

At the time, the employment service for non-disabled adults employed some 7000 staff and cost £17.5m annually. The main item of extra cost in the PAR Report was improved premises, estimated to cost an extra £2m a year in rents at the end of 10 years, together with extra capital expenditure for adaptations of the order of £150,000 to £200,000 a year during the 10-year period. In addition, the new service would need about 150 extra staff a year for five years, which would be found by staffing economies elsewhere in the employment and benefit services.

When he saw the Bryan Report, Robert Carr was evidently anxious about the expenditure implications. He wrote: 'I simply will NOT accept that reorganisation per se requires either more money or more manpower – on the contrary, it should produce savings'.[22] But he accepted that increased output might require more inputs and this was presumably how he squared the proposals for increased expenditure on the employment service with his conscience.

Another obstacle to be overcome was that of persuading the DHSS to acquiesce in the separation of employment and benefit work. Again Sir Denis Barnes enlisted the help of Sir William Armstrong. On 22 July 1971, Sir William chaired a meeting with Sir Denis, Sir Philip Rogers and Mildred Riddelsdell of the DHSS. Sir William said the PAR needed to examine the implications of separation. The meeting discussed three problems raised by Miss Riddelsdell:

- not being able to divert employment staff to benefit work in a crisis; the PAR would look at this;
- the likely slackening of the existing controls over abuse of benefit (in Canada, after separation, disqualifications dropped by 90 per cent). DE accepted that the service would have continuing obligations and argued that improved vacancy penetration should make it easier to test willingness to work;
- the danger that ordinary unemployed people might be neglected in favour of the better qualified, leading to more people on benefit; again DE accepted a responsibility to ensure that the service did not neglect the unemployed.

Miss Riddelsdell did not think the DHSS would oppose separation in principle, but the internal management problems for the DHSS in taking over unemployment benefit work now looked worse than they had in 1969/70 (page 143) and the earliest time for transfer would now be the very late 1970s.

The result of these consultations was that the PAR Report included the following paragraph:

> *Separation is not seen as a means of relieving the employment service of its present responsibilities for the proper control of unemployment benefit and for protecting the National Insurance Fund against abuse. In the event of separation, care will be taken to ensure that this function continues to be discharged as effectively as possible. DHSS nevertheless consider that increased preoccupation with employment work consequent upon separation would inevitably, at least in the short run, result in some relaxation of the control of unemployment benefit and consequently some increase in expenditure.*[23]

At the end of October, Locke and Cooper submitted the completed PAR Report to Robert Carr. The report argued that the employment service had the following objectives:

(a) *economic* – to improve the efficiency of the labour market, eg by speeding up and improving the matching of jobs and workers; by giving guidance on the best use of abilities; by channelling people to training opportunities; by attracting labour into employment and assisting useful mobility of labour.
(b) *social* – to help people who have difficulty in obtaining or retaining satisfactory employment, particularly those with special handicaps.

These objectives overlapped considerably. As a matter of practical politics, there was no alternative to providing a basic public service to help find work for the unemployed. It was playing a significant role, filling 1.5 million jobs a year, and, unlike other forms of job-filling, it was linking disparate local labour markets through its national network, offering advice and guidance and links with training and mobility schemes and helping with redundancies. But the service operated in a vicious circle. It was regarded as a service for the unemployed and primarily for manual workers. It was short of vacancies – 4.5 million registrants against two million vacancies had been typical of recent years. It needed to operate in the clerical and executive markets. It was hard to see how the needs of unemployed people could be totally ignored, whether they were blue collar, white collar or executive, though the latter could be served by a fee-charging service. Overall, there were risks that the efficiency of the service would decline and lead to more intractable problems of unemployment unless it was fundamentally modernised, as a Departmental Agency, with improvements in the training and grading of staff, a new network of employment offices and separation from benefit work. Although the Department 'had not yet succeeded in satisfactorily measuring the value of the service in reducing unemployment', there was a broad economic case for modernisation in terms of improving the operation of the labour market.

Carr commended the report to his colleagues at a meeting on 16 November 1971 of the Economic Policy Committee, chaired by Tony Barber, the Chancellor of the Exchequer. Carr argued that, for the service to be able to fulfil its social obligation of placing those in difficulty, it needed a stronger place in the market. Fears were voiced, no doubt by Sir Keith Joseph, that the interests of the unemployed and those in difficulties might be neglected, but Carr was reassuring on this. The Committee agreed that hiving off the service would be premature pending effective arrangements for Treasury control and Parliamentary accountability, but the possibility of hiving off in the future was not ruled out. Separation *within* the DE was agreed, subject to satisfactory safeguards against abuse. There was some concern that individuals might have to go to three separate offices. (In reality, this was a direct consequence of what Ministers were deciding – those needing supplementary (or means tested) benefit would have to attend a DHSS office as well as two DE offices.) Postal payment of benefit was also agreed, subject to a continuation of weekly signing.

(Locke thought such weekly attendance completely unnecessary but acquiesced in it in view of the DHSS's attitude.)[24] At the end of the discussion, Barber summed up the main conclusion of ministers that 'a comprehensive public employment service should be maintained...and it should be modernised to serve its social and economic objectives.'

Ministers were self-critical about this first ever discussion of a PAR Report. Maurice Macmillan, Chief Secretary, reporting to Ted Heath, noted that Carr himself, one of the originators of the PAR concept when in Opposition, had said that this first PAR Report did not live up to his expectations. Macmillan himself felt the report contained too much prose and too little rigorous cost-benefit analysis. Nor had there been enough vigorous cross-examination. None the less, the analysis had led to a conclusion and pointed to areas of further work.[25]

Whatever the shortcomings, this first PAR was a historic success for the Department of Employment. At long last, there was a firm government decision to modernise the employment service. The agreed modernisation package was quickly turned into a booklet entitled *People and Jobs*, which was published in December 1971.

The dilemma of services for young people

There was however one major disappointment. Chapter 8 showed that the 1969 Planning Unit Report had advocated introducing an 'all-age guidance service' within the employment service to replace the existing arrangement under which in 85 per cent of the country the youth employment service was provided by local education authorities, and in 15 per cent by the exchanges (pages 139–40). Like Barbara Castle, Carr was initially strongly in favour of an all-age guidance service.[26] But when the idea was floated to other Departments, there were pained reactions both from the Education Department and the Department of the Environment. The latter Department pointed out that the proposals 'run counter to the Government's declared intention to increase the responsibilities of local authorities'.[27]

Rather than getting distracted in a prolonged dispute, Carr decided on a graceful retreat. At the same meeting of the Economic Policy Committee in November which considered the ES PAR, he presented a paper proposing that local education authorities should continue to provide a youth employment service, perhaps in future on a compulsory basis. Moreover, instead of the current dividing line between the youth and the adult service at the age of 18, he suggested a 'more natural dividing line of entry into the labour market after the first placing in employment'. This was broadly agreed.

It can be argued that a valuable opportunity was lost. Combining the careers service with the employment service would have created a richly professional service, strong both in its understanding of employers' vacancies and in its understanding of occupations and career patterns. But responsibility for youth employment had been a highly contentious issue ever since Beveridge's struggles with education officials in 1909 (page 15). In 1971, Mrs Thatcher was Minister of Education. Maybe Carr was right to judge that it would have been a difficult battle to win.

The employment service management team and the action plan

During 1971, Ken Cooper built up a radical and energetic management team, including David Richardson as policy lead (later succeeded by Alan Brown), Jim Thomson and Frank Pyne on management and organisational issues, and Norman McGlynn on statistical, network and many other issues. Their main task was to plan how to implement the big structural changes set out in *People and Jobs* and to produce the *Action Plan for a Modern Employment Service*, which was published towards the end of 1972.

Cooper did not have a completely free hand. Robert Carr chaired the monthly meetings of the Employment Service Board until his departure in July 1972, after which the chair was taken by John Locke, who largely gave Cooper his head. By November 1972, Cooper's team had produced a draft Action Plan, which was submitted to Maurice Macmillan for approval. Ken Cooper described its main features as follows:

1. Organisation. A new management structure of 18 Areas separated from the unemployment benefit service and from the Department.
2. Premises. A 7 year rehousing programme based on a new network plan, introducing new-style Jobcentres, the first of which would open in April/May 1973.
3. New job structure. First line assessment and advice for jobseekers done by executive level employment adviser.
4. New approaches.

Ken Cooper explained:

> The employment service is not just a welfare service of last resort: it is a key part of labour market machinery and it makes its contribution as it succeeds in being more efficient than other means of job filling and job finding. This calls for a new emphasis on marketing in the planning, provision and presentation of the service and closer association and control of performance (both costs and results) – hence the management budget, the setting of objectives and the planning for fuller systems of accountability.

Cooper went on in characteristic style:

> The programme will entail big changes for staff. It will take time, effort and inspiration to develop understanding and commitment to the new methods of working. But there is goodwill for

modernisation among the staff and no lack of ability at middle management levels. We ought to succeed.[28]

The Action Plan was published in December 1972 and was the basis for the most radical overhaul of the employment service since its foundation in 1910. The main structural changes took place in 1973 and 1974, though the crucial introduction of Jobcentres was spread over the next decade. It is worthwhile to look at the main changes in turn, starting with the revival during 1972 of the idea of hiving off.

Hiving off again – the Manpower Services Commission

We have seen that in 1971 Robert Carr had been persuaded by the combined forces of the Treasury and the Civil Service Department to drop the idea of hiving off manpower services (page 150). Instead, Ministers agreed to make the employment service a Departmental Agency. But this was not the end of the story.

Early in 1972, Carr published 'Training for the Future', a policy document proposing a massive new adult training programme, the Training Opportunities Scheme (TOPS), the end of the levy/grant system and also a National Training Agency, which might be departmental, running alongside the employment service, or 'preferably' might be 'separate' and outside the civil service. (In the summer, Maurice Macmillan appointed John Cassels Chief Executive of the new Training Agency. From then on, Cooper and Cassels were known in the Department as the 'terrible twins'.)

In June 1972, Carr's proposals stimulated the TUC and the CBI to send to Maurice Macmillan an unusual joint letter expressing concerns about separating the new training body from the employment service. They proposed a new body involving representatives of employers and employees to coordinate the activities of both employment and training services.[29] The initiative for this demarche no doubt came from the TUC, which had long argued for a national manpower commission, whereas the CBI had never previously shown any enthusiasm for such ideas.[30]

In normal times, this proposal from industry might have been swept aside by the Treasury and CSD, just as they had scuppered similar proposals from Robert Carr. But by the summer of 1972 times were far from normal. Edward Heath, the Prime Minister, was desperate to reach agreement with the TUC and the CBI on a voluntary incomes policy to prevent the government's reflation of the economy from generating inflation. In July, John Locke briefed the Prime Minister to say to the TUC and CBI that Ministers saw considerable attractions in the general concept of running employment and training services in association with industry and suggesting tripartite discussions conducted by the Department of Employment.[31] In the talks which followed, Locke found that the TUC

> *discounted (rather more than I would do) the risk of major divergencies about policy issues between the Secretary of State and the Commission, suggesting that in the last analysis some compromise would be found.*

There were tensions between, on the one hand, the TUC's wish for executive responsibility for a new body in which they would participate, and on the other hand Treasury and CSD concerns about hiving off a body that was dependent upon public funds. Locke's fertile mind produced the new concept of 'partial hiving off' under which the new Commission would be responsible to the Secretary of State. Drawing on his experience of passenger transport bodies, Locke proposed a two tier structure with the employment service and training agencies reporting to a relatively small Commission of 10 members – an independent Chairman, three from the TUC, three from the CBI, two from local authorities and one from education. The Commissioners would need to retain the confidence of the organisation nominating them but would not be delegates. The government would remain responsible for the general policy objectives and the budget. Indeed, the Secretary of State would provide both the staff and the finance.[32] Staff would lose their formal civil service status, but their terms and conditions would be such as to enable them to transfer in and out of the Department.[33]

In October 1972, this new version of hiving off was agreed by Ministers, though Sir Keith Joseph expressed some fears about 'the implications for the control and payment of unemployment benefit', since the new Commission would be somewhat distanced from government. On 22 November 1972, following further talks with the TUC and the CBI, Macmillan announced his intention to introduce legislation to set up the new Manpower Services Commission.[34] Sir Denis Barnes wrote to all Departmental staff advising them of the intention that MSC staff should not be civil servants, but promised consultations with the staff side with the intention of reaching a concordat ruling out variations from civil service terms and conditions.

Ironically, by this time, the original intention to use the MSC as a bargaining counter to encourage the TUC to accept a voluntary incomes policy had already failed. On 2 November, the Downing Street talks had finally broken down, and on 6 November the Prime Minister had announced legislation enforcing a 90-day freeze. But the idea of an MSC had a momentum of its own and there were no second thoughts. Despite all its difficulties with the trade unions, the Heath government had no qualms about 'corporatism' in government.

In 1973, the Employment and Training Bill was introduced in Parliament and passed into law, enabling the Secretary of State to set up three 'bodies corporate' – the Manpower Services Commission, the Employment Service Agency and the Training Services Agency. The duty of the Commission was:

> *to make such arrangements as it considers appropriate for the purpose of assisting persons to select, train for, obtain and retain*

> *employment suitable for their ages and capacities and to obtain suitable employees...*

It proved a remarkably flexible piece of legislation, which did not require amendment when the two Agencies were abolished in 1977 or even in September 1987, when the Commission ceased to be responsible for the employment service, though legislation was subsequently introduced.

Ken Cooper would have been content with a Departmental Agency. But now that there was to be an MSC, he and his colleagues were keen to escape from the rigid manpower ceilings operated by CSD and to facilitate the recruitment of staff from industry. They were therefore prepared to risk antagonising staff and unions by removing civil service status. Surprisingly, however – bearing in mind what happened two decades later with Next Steps Agencies – they made no attempt to relax the tight grip that the Treasury and CSD had on civil service terms and conditions of employment. Instead, they promised adherence to these terms in order to soften the blow of losing civil service status and to ensure transferability between the MSC and the Department.

The broader policy implications of setting up the MSC were very difficult to predict in 1972. Chapter 10 will show that the MSC proved a dynamic body with ideas of its own and a willingness to lobby for the services for which it was responsible, as well as offering its senior staff unusual opportunities for initiative.

The philosophy of 'hiving off' was nowhere so zealously pursued as in the Department of Employment. In 1974, most of the functions of the Department were hived off to external bodies – employment services and training to the MSC, conciliation and arbitration to ACAS and health and safety to the Health and Safety Commission. The term 'Department of Employment Group' was coined to describe the new federal structure. Of all the changes, hiving off the employment service had the most profound impact in breaking up the multipurpose matrix organisation of the Department which had existed since the 1920s, when the employment exchange service became fully integrated into the Ministry of Labour.

Separation of employment and benefit work

The second major change was separation from the unemployment benefit service. This had been an ambition of the senior officials of the Department since the time of the Dunnett Report in 1964. As *People and Jobs* argued in December 1971:

> *The Employment Service has come to be regarded by many workers and employers as catering primarily for the* unemployed *and as having a poor selection of jobs and of workers seeking them. Thus if the Service is to improve its quality and reputation for satisfying a wide variety of needs, its 'dole image' must be removed.*[35]

It was further argued that the two functions required different qualities in the staff and different kinds of premises.

We have seen that the DHSS was consistently uneasy about this whole line of argument, though in the last analysis not prepared to make a stand against it. For the DHSS, hiving off made matters worse. In October 1972, AG Beard of the DHSS wrote to Ken Cooper to express concern that the employment service's much greater degree of independence, particularly under the new MSC, might 'erode the essential part the service plays in benefit control'. He urged that the MSC should be obliged to provide information for this purpose to the benefit authorities. Ken Cooper wrote back reassuringly that 'we accept without equivocation the duty to cooperate with your Department in protecting both unemployment and supplementary benefit from abuse'. He believed that the improvements in the service would in fact lessen the burdens on the Fund.[36]

In 1971, Sir Keith Joseph had followed up the Manifesto commitment to reduce abuse of the benefit system by setting up a Committee chaired by Sir Henry Fisher. In March 1973 Fisher reported. His report expressed fears that modernisation would increase the employment service's reluctance to submit long-term unemployed people to employers and declared:

> *The obligation to serve such people should in our opinion be kept high in the attentions of the employment exchanges. We should deplore any change in personnel, premises or attitudes which adversely affected the service given to such people.*[37]

In January 1974, Ralph Howells, a Conservative MP who was to focus on the link between benefit and unemployment over the next two decades, asked the Secretary of State how benefit control would be assured after separation. He was assured that

> *The Employment and Training Act 1973 requires the MSC to provide information necessary for the determination of claims to benefit. The arrangements for transmission of information between the employment and training services of the MSC and the benefit service of my Department will be broadly the same as those operating now, where the functions are separately performed.*

This answer referred to the trials in separation which had been running since the mid-1960s and to the transit card arrangements and other procedures that had been devised to ensure the necessary flow of information.

Chapters 13 and 14 will show that, by the mid-1980s, it was seen as a mistake to have separated the two functions. This requires us to consider carefully the separation decision of 1971. The DHSS's criticisms were from two angles – benefit control and social welfare. Chapter 8 showed that DHSS officials were most worried about the impact on benefit control, whereas

Crossman was more worried about the impact on those who were socially disadvantaged (page 141) – a view that was shared by some academic writers, such as Brian Showler[38] as well as by the Fisher Committee. Sir Keith Joseph seems to been concerned about both aspects.

It is important not to over-simplify the arguments about separation. It was clearly not essential to benefit control that the employment service should actually administer the benefit system. After all, in the system that was running from 1945 to 1974, the employment service administered unemployment benefit, but supplementary benefit was administered by the DHSS and in 1971 was received by as many as 37 per cent of the unemployed.[39] So the key issues relate not to overall administration but to the employment service's involvement in benefit controls and whether, as Beveridge had argued in 1942, it was essential that payment of benefit and placing in employment should take place in the same office (page 99). In the 1960s and early 1970s, Department of Employment officials fundamentally were not interested in benefit control. Unemployment was still low by later standards and long-term unemployment had not become a major national problem as it did later. But they recognised that some commitment to benefit control was necessary if the DHSS was to be persuaded to go along with their modernisation plans. Thus they accepted that the employment service would be obliged to continue reporting cases of non-availability and refusal of suitable employment (though there was scepticism about the wisdom of sending reluctant workers to an employer to 'test them out'). They appreciated that benefit control would not work so well if regular attendance for signing was not in an office concerned with employment. But for the DE it was all a question of priorities. They believed that they could never achieve major cultural change in employment service offices so long as these offices were identified in the public mind as benefit-paying institutions. They were committed to the labour market transparency model of the service, but prepared for some compromise to safeguard DHSS interests.

The compromise reached in 1971–72 did not anticipate the way in which the ethos of the new Employment Service Agency was to develop. Priority was given to building up penetration of the labour market. A powerful new system of performance objectives or targets (pages 165–6) was introduced, which emphasised maximising placings, with no differentiation between those still in a job who wanted a change and the unemployed – whether short term or long term. Protection of benefit funds played no part of management rhetoric at this time. ES management would have welcomed extra resources for a special service for the 'disadvantaged'. Failing this, it was assumed that 'the disadvantaged' would benefit not through targeting services directly towards them, but through a sort of 'trickle down' from the much stronger service that would emerge. Senior managers were trying to achieve a massive turn-round in attitudes. Some over-simplification of the message may have been unavoidable. But a price was paid later.

Management structure

We now look at the decision to organise the new service into 18 Areas. This too proved highly controversial. In 1972, the Department had seven English Regions, plus Scotland and Wales. The Employment Service Management Team initially argued for 25 Area Managers in a tier immediately below Head Office so that they would be closer to community needs and market knowledge and with a more consistent span of control than in the existing regional structure. There was also an unspoken belief that a radical break from the old regional structure would facilitate a change in culture. These proposals were vehemently opposed by the existing Regional Controllers, led by AAG McNaughton, Regional Controller for Yorkshire and Humberside. He argued that the 25 Areas would be still be fairly remote from the front line (indeed, another tier of management, eventually called District Managers, was proposed between it and the local offices), they would be very costly and would not integrate well with other Departmental services, such as training and industrial relations.[40]

This dispute came to a head at the Regional Controllers' Conference on 21 September 1972, with John Locke in the chair, deputising for the Permanent Secretary, Sir Denis Barnes. The issue was whether the employment service should be organised into 'regions' or 'sub-regions'. Locke and Cooper rejected McNaughton's argument that the organisation of the employment service had to be integrated with that of the rest of the Department. Subsequently, Cooper trimmed a little, but stuck to the essence of the plan. The 11,000 ESA staff were deployed in 18, rather than 25, Areas. Beneath the Areas were 106 District Managers and 950 local offices.

The Department itself, on the other hand, retained nine Regions for its remaining regional functions, which were the unemployment benefit service (UBS), the employment aspects of economic planning, the wages inspectorate, work on redundancy payments, statistics and industrial relations (though in 1974 this last function was handed over to ACAS). The UBS was by far the biggest element, with 13,500 staff in local Unemployment Benefit Offices (UBOs) reporting to a high ranking Regional Benefit Manager in each Region, who had a dual reporting line, both to the Regional Controller and to the Head of the Benefit Service in HQ. Training went to the new Training Services Agency, which retained the traditional regional structure. Rather surprisingly, the Civil Service Department agreed to the retention of Regional Controller posts at Assistant Secretary level, although these posts were mere shadows of their former selves.

The organisational structure for which Cooper and his team fought so hard in 1972 was neat and logical but it suffered from two defects. First, it was costly and could only be resourced by withdrawing resources from the front line – contributing to the industrial relations problems which hit the organisation in 1974. The relatively high management overheads came in for continuing criticism until they were eliminated in the early 1980s. Secondly, coordination in the Regions was made more difficult by having ESA operating with a different structure from the other services of the Department. Again, this proved a continuing bone of contention until the reversion to nine Regions in 1983.

The Jobcentre

The third area of modernisation was the concept of the Jobcentre and it was here that Ken Cooper and his management team made their biggest breakthrough. They drew both on existing strands of thinking and experimentation and on a new marketing approach. Influenced by Ken Lane, business adviser to the Department, and by the Heath government's emphasis on new styles of management, Cooper's team had the imagination to apply modern marketing ideas to the provision of a public service. Cooper recruited Keith Williams from IBM as Director of Marketing.

Most important was self service. Chapter 8 showed how experiments in self service were launched in the late 1960s (pages 132–4). In February 1971 Ken Cooper wrote:

> *at least three of the schemes – Ashford, Coventry and York – have achieved quite striking results in terms of increases in the number of callers, the number of notified vacancies and the number of placings achieved ... Self service needs no further validation by experiment. It should accordingly be introduced as a normal part of our employment service ...*[41]

Self service not only increased volumes and outputs. It represented a revolution in the way customers were treated, through enabling customers themselves to take the initiative. It also opened up to public view what was available in the local labour market. But self service could only thrive in suitable premises.

So the next key feature was a premises revolution. Self service was to be set in an *attractively designed, open plan environment* which replaced the cubicles and counters of the old service. Moreover, the siting of offices was emphasised as never before: 'The accepted aim now is to get Jobcentres sited in a town's shopping centre, with a street level presence for self service...'[42] Thus managers now had among their top priorities the acquisition of attractive retail premises for Jobcentres. It was reckoned that 80 per cent of all offices would need to be rehoused.[43] A programme of 100 new Jobcentres a year was developed right up to the end of the decade. Extensive discussions took place with the Department of the Environment – soon the Property Services Agency – and over the years they gave the programme a great deal of support. The Treasury agreed to the allocation of an extra £1.7 million a year for the rehousing programme.[44]

Modernisation was bound to be gradual. Cooper noted that:

Office of Hope

> As far as the public is concerned, modernisation of the Employment Service will only be realised as we open Jobcentres – that is, offices sited, designed and equipped to the latest standards and offering self service facilities and new style advisory services.[45]

The first Jobcentres were opened in Reading, Havant and Wakefield in the summer of 1973. By September, Cooper was able to report that Reading in particular was a remarkable success, with a big overall increase in placings and a sharp increase in the proportion of self service placings.[46] The team had found a winning formula. Over the next few years, in shopping precincts and high streets up and down the country, attractive new shop-fronted Jobcentres appeared in a highly conspicuous orange and black decor. The term 'Jobcentre', which had been concocted by Cooper's marketing specialists,[47] passed into the English language and soon appeared in the *Oxford English Dictionary*.

In planning the new network, the Management Team consulted the Regions about the bold claim made to Ministers in the PAR that as many as 450 small offices might be closed (page 152). The team set a criterion of 600 placings in each office a year. This caused great concern in the Regions and eventually the team backed off and the closure programme became much more modest. The Action Plan in December 1972 said that 'it should be practicable to withdraw several dozen of the smallest offices by the end of 1974'.[48] Some small offices were closed in 1973–74, but thereafter under the Labour government the closure programme was not pursued.

Changes in services and staffing

Along with the premises change went important changes in services and staffing. The idea of a *three tier service* was devised:

- self service – information on specific jobs in the local labour market or beyond;
- advice on labour market opportunities from trained employment advisers;
- expert assessment or guidance for particular clients with special problems or needs, such as the Occupational Guidance Service, the Disablement Resettlement Service and the Industrial Rehabilitation Units.[49]

The introduction of employment advisers at executive or junior management fulfilled one of the major objectives of the 1969 Research and Planning Report. The aim was to raise the quality of advice to members of the public by installing employment advisers in every local office, whether a new style Jobcentre or not. Some of these were recruited externally, under special arrangements agreed with the Civil Service Commission, but most were promoted from within the service. They all received extensive training in such things as interviewing, the operations of the service and industrial and occupational knowledge. The plan was to complete the introduction by 1978, by which time there would be some 2750 advisers, including 1200 upgraded posts.[50] The large staff training programmes for Jobcentre managers, employment advisers and clerical staff were crucial both in increasing professionalism and changing attitudes.

Managing the service

From his appointment as Chief Executive in December 1971, Cooper was concerned not just with planning structural changes, but also with changing the whole ethos of the service and the attitudes of managers and staff. This service had great achievements to its credit but over 60 years had accumulated complex rules and customs and had been subject to a complicated matrix structure of senior management embedded in the Department. Now it had a single leader, who was determined to transform it into a highly motivated, market-sensitive, fast-moving organisation, esteemed by jobseekers and employers alike. He conveyed a sense of urgency and heady excitement. He introduced a regular *Newsletter* to managers and staff to put over what he expected of the service as well as the progress being made with central changes.

Cooper's outstanding management innovation was the introduction of performance objectives or targets. He was influenced by the Fulton Report and by the view of the Treasury and CSD in the hiving off debate in 1971–72 that one of the prerequisites of 'accountable management' was a means of monitoring performance (page 150). Fortunately, WR Joslin had introduced a system of operating statistics for the employment exchanges in Wales and later this was adopted nationally. From 1968 onwards, the Wales management had pioneered the use of these statistics as a tool for planning and monitoring the workload and outputs of each management command.

Cooper and his team wanted to replace detailed control by central instructions and inspection with the setting of performance objectives, combined with considerable discretion as to how objectives would be achieved. Cooper built on the experience in Wales and at regular meetings with senior regional representatives began to monitor the management control statistics, Region by Region. In July 1972, following 'a somewhat turbulent discussion', he set objectives for 1973 for placings, vacancies, training applications and moves under the Employment Transfer Scheme.

In this first round of objective-setting, the regional targets were largely set at Head Office, though subsequently a greater element of negotiation entered into the process. The exercise represented a major cultural change. Some line managers felt very uneasy. Within the Head Office Management Team there were intense debates. Would an emphasis on quantity devalue quality? Cooper replied that top management's views on service values, qualities and priorities needed to be as explicit as possible. The crudity of the measures themselves was widely discussed. Would the system lead to the neglect of people who were more difficult to place? Was it right to treat all placings as of equal value? The economists worked on ideas about 'shadow pricing', but these techniques, even if interesting to Head Office, were too complex and sophisticated to be used as part of the overall performance management system. More promising seemed the idea of adopting a more sophisticated model of 'Management by Objectives', and Chapter 10 discusses how this was pursued.

For all its faults, this new system of objectives had a profound effect in raising the level of management motivation and initiative. Table 9.1 shows that the targets of 2.5 million vacancies and 1.6 million placings set for 1973 were exceeded, with 2.75 million vacancies and 1.65 million placings – the highest figures since 1956, though admittedly 1973 was a year of buoyant demand. The use of numerical objectives proved an effective way of managing the service and anticipated the widespread introduction of performance management in government following the 1988 Next Steps Report (Chapter 14).

Table 9.1 *Placings and vacancies, 1969–74*

	1969	1970	1971	1972	1973 (53 weeks)	1974
Vacancies notified	2145	2207	1897	2147	2757	(2453)
Placings	1532	1485	1305	1407	1650	(1557)
Average unemployment %	2.5	2.7	3.5	3.8	2.7	2.6

Professional and executive recruitment

We have seen that, in the early days of the Heath government, Ken Lane, the Department's business adviser, had come up with the idea of introducing fee charging into the specialist professional and executive service (page 152). The service cost £1 million per year, but its share of engagements in its market was only about 5 per cent. Without charging it would be difficult to find the resources to develop it into an effective service. Ministers were advised that

> These proposals are designed to enable the P&E Register to increase its share of the market but it would be moving into a vacuum rather than competing with or duplicating the activities of private agencies.[51]

Lane argued that, for fee charging to work, this service would have to be completely restyled and managed separately from the rest of the employment service. These proposals were included in the PAR and approved by Ministers in 1971. This was, as the PAR pointed out, 'quite an innovation. No other country is known to charge for any material part of the public employment services'.[52] Indeed, the UK government had to denounce an ILO Convention forbidding charging for such services to enable the new service to be set up.

In March 1973 a separate subsidiary of ESA, known as PER, Professional and Executive Recruitment, began operating under Dewi Rees, a Director recruited from industry. It had a network of 40 offices and a computerised matching system. It charged fees to employers on a sliding scale ranging from only £30 for jobs under £1000 a year to 8 per cent of salary for jobs over £4000 a year. It would receive a 'social subvention' (amounting to £600,000 in 1974/75) for its non-commercial role in assisting unemployed people, but apart from this the aim was to achieve financial self-sufficiency by 1976.

Chapter 10 will show that it was an uphill struggle for PER to achieve financial self-sufficiency, while the aim set out in *People and Jobs* of 'securing a substantially larger share of the placings in this field' was an imposssible dream.

Conclusion

The rest of the story of the service under the Heath administration can be told briefly. Progress with setting up the two Agencies and the MSC was curiously unaffected by the government's disastrous conflict with the miners. Late in 1973, Sir Denis Barnes was appointed Chairman of the new Manpower Services Commission, handing over the onerous role of Permanent Secretary of the Department to Conrad Heron. Nine new Commissioners were appointed after consultation with the CBI, TUC, local government and the education world. The Commission had its first meeting on 9 January 1974. In February, Ken Cooper gave the Commission a full presentation on the modernisation of the employment service. It was well received. Commissioners welcomed the more 'consumer orientated' approach and thought the introduction of employment advisers of 'critical importance'. The TUC expressed their scepticism about PER, as they were to do many times.[53] The Commission did not take formal responsibility for the employment service until 1 October 1974. During the spring and summer of 1974, managers and staff went through the 'options exercise' to determine whether they would join the UBS or the ESA, and then appointments were made at all the various levels. The process went remarkably smoothly.

We now take stock of what was achieved under the Heath government. By a careful process of discussion and perhaps by not rushing things, senior officials had persuaded Ministers to agree to the modernisation of the employment service and to the necessary additional resources – on a scale that was sufficient, but by no means extravagant compared to the remarkable increases in expenditure on other public services that were occurring at the same time.[54] After tortuous discussions and changes of mind, Ministers also added the extra ingredient of 'hiving off' to the Manpower Services Commission – a 'wild card' with unpredictable consequences.

Cooper and his team could not have achieved all this without drawing on the studies and experimentation in the Department from Dunnett's time onwards. But they also improved on the ideas of the 1960s. In particular, they introduced a new and aggressive marketing approach and devised the concept of the Jobcentre, which set a new standard of market-sensitive public service. Cooper also broke new ground in his approach to management and in particular in his introduction of performance targets. This fundamentally changed management style in the employment service and in the long term was an influential model for the civil service more generally.

At the same time, these changes contained the seeds of some serious problems. The overwhelming focus on 'maximising placings' was to raise questions about the role of the service in relation to benefit control and services to the disadvantaged. In 1976, an academic writer, Brian Showler, criticised the modernisation programme as follows:

> *the new Service, while making enormous progress in terms of its organisation, scope and staffing, is tending to ignore the employment problems of those of its clients needing the greatest help in finding and keeping jobs.*[55]

Moreover, despite the emphasis on marketing, the culture which developed in the service seemed to outsiders rather introverted. Cooper told his managers to be 'single-minded but not bloody-minded'. Some outsiders thought that the Agency *was* 'bloody-minded' and not cooperative enough with other public bodies engaged in related tasks.

But these qualifications should not obscure the remarkable achievements of those years in transforming the market standing of an old-fashioned public service. Without this change, the service would have been trapped in the declining low-skilled manual sector, with little to offer the increasing numbers of unemployed.

10

The New Model Employment Service, 1974–79

'You look at the new Jobcentres. They're very different things from the old employment offices, not just in appearance but also in their approach and method of doing work. And... in the results they are getting in a time of very difficult employment.' (Lord Carr of Hadley, formerly Robert Carr, 1980)[1]

Introduction

In October 1974, the employment service became the Employment Service Agency (ESA) of the Manpower Services Commission (MSC). It was a public service in an unusually favoured position. The battle for radical reform had been fought and won under the Heath government. The Labour government which came to power in March 1974 backed the new style of operation and provided the service with more resources, even at times when, under international pressures, other public expenditure was being cut back. Moreover, the organisation of the service had been disentangled from that of its parent Department for the first time since the First World War. The new MSC was supportive, despite some hesitations among employer Commissioners. Both the Department and the MSC gave the new Agency a considerable degree of autonomy.

In this period, the *labour market transparency* model of the service was pursued with remarkable rigour and consistency. Separation from the delivery of unemployment benefit had been achieved for the first time since the introduction of unemployment benefit in 1912. This freed the service to build up its role in the labour market. The dramatic rise in unemployment which occurred in this period, far from undermining confidence in the labour market goal, if anything reinforced it.

This chapter looks at the framework within which the Agency worked, at its plans and programmes, staffing and management and computer systems, at the impact of rising unemployment and the vexed question of benefit control, the fortunes of PER and finally at John Cassels' major review of the service in 1979.

The Labour government and the new Commission

Chapter 9 showed that, while it was the Heath government which had set up the Manpower Services Commission, the initiative for its creation had come from the two sides of industry and notably from the TUC. In March 1974, the new Labour government under Harold Wilson came into power at a time of crisis and on the basis of a wafer-thin majority. It looked to the TUC, through a 'social contract', to help it avoid inflation and industrial unrest. The new Secretary of State for Employment, Michael Foot, therefore was predisposed to work closely with the TUC and readily accepted the new role of the MSC. As a keen Parliamentarian, Foot probably had some anxieties about the constitutional position of this great new quango and was insistent that the Commission was answerable to Parliament through Ministers and that MPs had every right to question its activities. But in practice he and his successor from 1966, Albert Booth, were prepared to work in partnership with the Commission, to entrust to it important new tasks but not to interfere with its internal affairs.

The Permanent Secretary of the Department was Sir Conrad Heron until 1976, when he was succeeded by Kenneth Barnes (knighted in 1977). Much of the Department's relationship with the MSC rested with Donald Derx, the Deputy Secretary, who, as the indefatigable Chair of the inter-departmental Manpower Group, became the coordinator of increasingly ambitious packages of 'special measures' to deal with unemployment. Like their Ministers, these officials left considerable autonomy to the Commission, though Ken Barnes did lead a major review of organisational structure in 1976/77 (pages 173–4). In these years, an important preoccupation for the Department was the establishment of the unemployment benefit service as a distinct organisation in its own right, which had to expand rapidly in response to rising unemployment. In time, this responsibility led senior officials like Ken Barnes to an interest in benefit control

The new Commission saw its role as mainly strategic and did not attempt the detailed management of the Agency. The Commission consisted of a Chairman – initially Sir Denis Barnes, former Permanent Secretary of the Department, succeeded in 1976 by Richard O'Brien, who had an employer background – together with three representatives of the TUC, three representatives of the Confederation of British Industry, two members representing local authorities and one member representing education. The Commissioners rapidly became a cohesive group. Formally they 'reported' to the Secretary of State for whom they delivered programmes. But they also became a powerful lobby, pressing, for instance, for measures to alleviate unemployment. Moreover, they soon sought a role going beyond running their two Agencies. In July 1974, they resolved to seek Michael Foot's agreement that they should develop a 'general manpower strategy' (later described as a 'comprehensive manpower policy'), buttressed by a manpower intelligence function.[2] Michael Foot agreed to this enhanced MSC role.

Chapter 9 described how Ken Cooper introduced Commissioners to ESA's work (page 167). They became protectors of the employment service when the government tried to cut its forecast expenditure. For instance, in July 1975, they resolved to see the Chancellor and the Secretary of State to press that cuts in the Jobcentre programme be restored.[3] However, in the major economic crisis of 1976, CBI Commissioners became 'increasingly critical of MSC expenditure'[4] of which the new Jobcentres were a conspicuous element. ESA had to convince them that the Jobcentre programme should be continued (page 175). By April 1977, the CBI assured the MSC Chairman of its support for the improved Jobcentre service, but stressed the importance of demonstrating cost-effectiveness.[5]

The senior management team of the Agency

The senior managers on the Executive Committee of the Employment Service Agency (ESA) were highly committed to Ken Cooper's vision of the Agency of 1971–72. Indeed, later on, some felt they were too committed. But in the mid-1970s they had strong political and civil service support in their efforts to develop ESA's role in the labour market and its position as a new style public agency.

Consistency of purpose was assisted by continuity of personnel in senior posts. Ken Cooper remained Chief Executive until December 1975, when he became Chief Executive of the sister Training Services Agency. He was replaced by Alan Brown, who had been one of the key planners of the new-style service in 1973–74; quieter than Ken Cooper, Alan Brown was astute and no less committed to the cause. There were two Deputy Chief Executives – posts filled at different times by Rhys Robinson, Keith Williams, a marketing man from IBM, Dewi Rees, the founder of PER, Jean Collingridge and myself. But much of the tone at the top of ESA was set by the three top line managers – the Divisional Directors (later Executive Directors), each responsible for one third of Great Britain. These initially were Ron Stephenson, Tony Dechant and Jim Potter (succeeded in 1977 by Jim Thomson). Their presence on the Executive Committee helped to ensure that new policies were practical and deliverable. The Divisional Directors flung themselves into delivering the new dispensation with enormous energy. But some of their Head Office colleagues were critical of their influence and drew analogies with King John and the Barons. Jack Teasdale, the Chief Psychologist and a former boilermaker, accused them of being arrogant and heartless in their resistance to doing more for unemployed jobseekers. The Divisional Directors stood for the labour market transparency model of the service and insisted that the reforms set in motion in 1971/72 should be carried through for the long term without distractions along the route.

'Plans and Programmes'

In October 1974, the Agency set out its vision for the next five years in *The Employment Service: Plans and Programmes*,[6] a skilfully drafted document for which Alan Brown was primarily responsible. The Commission endorsed its emphasis on increasing market penetration, but also said that the needs of the disadvantaged must not be overlooked and might require extra resources from government.[7] The document defined the 'aim' of the employment service as 'to help people choose, train for and get the right jobs and employers to get the right people as quickly as possible'. The service acted as a 'catalyst' in the numerous labour markets that it served. It had an equal responsibility to employers and jobseekers and had to serve both in a balanced way. It was dependent on its market share for its effectiveness. While it was expected to serve all-comers, without distinction, in practice it faced awkward choices in the deployment of its resources, particularly whether to do more for the disadvantaged. There was no easy or permanent answer. The document said that at that point in time it would be wrong, and not in the long-term interest of the disadvantaged, to divert resources from building up a credible service in the high street. It concluded: 'In short, if the Agency is to fulfil its "social" as well as its "economic" responsibilities, it cannot afford, in either case, to neglect the market.'

Plans and Programmes set out four 'immediate objectives' for the general employment service:

- to sustain a programme of Jobcentre openings of at least 100 each year up to 1980;
- to increase the Agency's share of the labour market so that its 'placing and job-filling performance improves by at least 25 per cent overall';
- to 'restructure' employment advisory work by the introduction of well trained employment advisers and more self-service facilities throughout the service by the end of 1978; and
- to achieve savings which could be used to provide services to those in need of special assistance.

This document said little about unemployed people but, according to Ken Cooper, this did not indicate any lack of concern. Unemployed people were 'embraced by the portmanteau term "jobseeker"'.[8] But undoubtedly the dominant message was about new Jobcentres and increasing market share.

The Sex Discrimination Act 1975

For most of its history, the employment service had dealt with men and women in separate men's and women's sections. From the mid-1950s onwards, there was a trend towards combined sections, though there were later suggestions that this might have reduced women's placings (page 117). The new Jobcentre design envisaged combined services in modern and attractive surroundings. In 1975, the Sex Discrimination Act was passed, making discrimination on grounds of sex or marriage unlawful. This meant that the employment service:

- could not accept vacancies in which employers illegally tried to confine recruitment to either men or women;
- should not differentiate between men's and women's vacancies in vacancy displays; and
- should close down the remaining separate men's and women's sections.

The Divisional Directors reviewed the position in each office in their territory and ensured compliance with the new Act. Commissioners welcomed the legislation as a contribution to combating the under-utilisation of women in the British labour market.[9]

The management review of 1976–77

Chapter 9 showed that the Employment and Training Act 1973 created the Commission as a distinct entity from its two Agencies – the Training Services Agency and ESA (pages 158–9). As the Commission built up its strategic role in 1975–76, it secured Michael Foot's agreement to the creation in 1975 of two key posts – first that of Director of Manpower Intelligence, filled by Graham Reid, and then the more senior post of Director, filled by John Cassels. But there remained unresolved questions about the regional structure of the Commission and of the Department. In November 1976, a major management review of the Department of Employment Group was set up to consider this, with a project team, including Clive Priestley, Roderick Allison and Jenny Bacon reporting to a Steering Group, chaired by Ken Barnes, the Permanent Secretary.

This was the first review of the organisation of the Department as it had emerged from the changes made in 1974. The 1974 settlement had replaced the old unitary structure of the manpower side of the Department with three parallel hierarchies – the ESA, the TSA and the unemployment benefit service, with the first two reporting to the new MSC and the third to the Department. It had left an anomalous post of DE Regional Director in each region. The key issue in the review was whether to create powerful Regional Director posts in the MSC, with responsibility for both employment and training services. This idea was strongly opposed by the senior team in the ESA as it would undermine the direct line of accountability within the ESA from the 18 Area Managers, through the three Divisional Directors to the Chief Executive. The ESA argued that such a change would be entirely premature and unnecessary after only two years' experience and that the ESA's new structure was delivering well, with success in opening new Jobcentres and encouraging placing performance.

In the end, after a few months of controversy, Ken Barnes' Steering Group decided to retain the employment and training services' distinct lines of accountability in the regions. Leading figures in the Steering Group such as Ken Barnes and John Locke had been heavily involved in the earlier controversies about a separate command structure and must have felt that the case was not proven for reverting so soon to something that looked like the pre-1974 *status quo*. However, new posts of Regional Manpower Services Director (RMSDs) were created within the MSC, replacing the DE Regional Directors. The new RMSDs would not have line control over the employment service Area Managers (who would continue to report via Divisional Directors to the ES Chief Executive). But the RMSDs would have a 'coordinating' role and would chair a Manpower Service Board in each Region. At national level, it was agreed that the Agencies should be replaced by Divisions under Chief Executives, reporting to the Director, John Cassels, rather than, as before, direct to the Commission. Head Office support services (such as personnel and finance) for both employment and training would be amalgamated under a new Director of Corporate Services. These proposals were accepted by Ministers and the Commission in June 1977 and came into effect later in the year.

The senior team in the employment service was relieved. The essential features of the 1974 employment service structure remained in place, with a strong line of accountability running from the local Jobcentre manager up to a dedicated Chief Executive and an Executive Committee in which three Divisional Directors (now renamed Executive Directors) continued to play a powerful role.

The Jobcentre programme

Chapter 9 drew attention to the Jobcentre as Ken Cooper's most notable innovation. The key target in ES Plans and Programmes was to open 100 Jobcentres each year up to 1980. The total programme of 1000 Jobcentres was expected to take 10 years. Line managers set about implementing the programme with a will. A Design Guide was issued and the Property Services Agency was engaged to work zealously on the programme. While the PSA came in for some criticism, the programme could not have advanced so rapidly without a strong contribution on their part. An opportunistic approach was adopted to the sequencing of the programme. While ideally it would have been preferable to start with Jobcentres in places of key industrial or commercial importance, in practice this was not feasible. Instead, opportunities for suitable sites had to be seized wherever they arose, provided they fitted in with overall network plans. The result was a rather uneven pattern of development, with rapid progress in some rural areas, while the programme in London lagged behind because of a shortage of suitable sites.

The programme had aroused little opposition when it was first agreed, but as the attractive new Jobcentres with their bright orange decor started to appear in high streets and shopping arcades up and down the country, questions began to be asked. Some people resented paying taxes to provide well sited and attractive public offices for the unemployed. The Federation of Personnel Agencies, representing private employment agencies, saw the new Jobcentres as potential threats to their own business and began agitation against the programme. The Public Accounts Committee was critical of the use of high street sites. By December 1976, Richard O'Brien, the new Chairman of the MSC, reported on a meeting with James Prior, the shadow employment spokesman: 'the Opposition were by no means convinced of the value of the Jobcentre programme. A sophisticated defence of the whole concept of the Jobcentre will have to be prepared'.[10] The CBI also were concerned about MSC expenditure (page 171).

The available evaluation evidence about the Jobcentre programme was quickly put together by Ray Phillips in an Interim Report to the Commission meeting in February 1977, which was presented by Rhys Robinson, the Deputy Chief Executive. The report showed that the performance noted in the early Jobcentres had been maintained, with a 30–40 per cent improvement in placings. It was accepted that Jobcentres cost about 14 per cent more to run (with capital costs amortised). But their unit costs per placing were less than those of traditional offices (down by about 5 per cent)[11] and staff productivity was up 20 per cent. This report was accepted by the Commission and was published to coincide with the opening of the 300th Jobcentre.

The Jobcentre programme had survived its most serious challenge so far, but not everyone was convinced. Ken Barnes, a Permanent Secretary well versed in employment service matters, felt publication was premature. It was not clear whether a new Jobcentre benefited the local economy. This turned on speed of vacancy filling or providing more suitable candidates than other market mechanisms. Greater usage might merely reflect the fact that the service was free. John Cassels defended publication to counter ill-founded criticism. While the case was not conclusive, the report showed that Jobcentres were a better market mechanism than the employment offices, which were also free. In any case, the service had always been free, so the fact that it was now gaining ground against other mechanisms was significant. The service could not be judged by purely economic criteria; also important was its effectiveness for young people and older workers and its role as the MSC's key point of contact with the public for all its activities.[12]

Staffing and industrial relations

The ESA had found a winning formula for the external marketing and delivery of the service, but it faced difficult problems in its staffing and industrial relations.

The first problem was whether its staff were to retain their civil service status. Soon after he became Secretary of State, Michael Foot was urged by the trade unions representing staff in the Department of Employment to secure the repeal of the provision in the 1973 Employment and Training Act which deprived the staff of the new MSC of their 'civil service status' (pages 158–9). The Commissioners, including those from the TUC, advised Foot to reject the unions' plea for fear that it might limit the Commission's autonomy and lead to tighter control of numbers by central government. However, Foot sided with the civil service unions and included the necessary amendment in legislation in 1975. For practical purposes, it did not make much difference, as there had already been undertakings that MSC staff would be on the same terms and conditions as Departmental staff.

A far more contentious issue was the level of staffing. The ESA emerged from the separation process with over 13,000 staff, of whom 10,900 were in local offices.[13] Separation from the benefit service protected the employment service from being raided to staff up benefit work as unemployment rose sharply from 1975 onwards. But separation and modernisation also removed economies of scale as one network of about 1000 offices was turned into two networks with a total of 2000 offices. It also required the diversion of staff resources from local offices to District, Area and Head Offices.

The service might have swiftly adjusted to these new patterns of staffing but for another factor – the increasing militancy of the civil service trade unions. Traditionally, there had been a close – almost cosy – relationship between the Department of Employment and its 'Staff Side', which comprised representatives of all the recognised unions. Management tried to reach accommodation with union leaders over major changes, with the help of rising administrators like Ken Cooper, who acted for a period as Chairman of the Staff Side. For their part, the two principal unions – the Ministry of Labour Staff Association (representing clerical staff) and the Association of Officers of the Ministry of Labour (representing junior and middle management) – were like house unions, strongly committed to the Department.

This tradition was now under threat. One influence was the increasingly turbulent industrial relations climate in Britain as a whole. Another influence came from militants in other parts of the civil service, such as the DHSS, particularly after the MLSA and the AOML were absorbed into national unions covering nearly all the major departments – the Civil and Public Services Association (CPSA) and the Society of Civil Servants (SCS) respectively. This brought greater professionalism among full-time officials, but also less concern than hitherto about the impact of industrial action on the Department's image. Young militants from a remarkable variety of left-wing groups began to lead many local branches – particularly in the North West, the Midlands, Scotland and London – and proved very effective in getting themselves elected to union executives.

These ingredients combined in the autumn of 1974 to create an industrial dispute which was one of the formative experiences of the new ESA. In October 1974, the argument about the staffing of the new Agency erupted into a novel form of industrial action, when CPSA branches in West Midlands Area banned work on the unemployment count, with the support of the CPSA nationally. At the same time, the CPSA throughout the civil service banned work and statistics connected with Management by Objectives (page 180). In December, the CPSA extended its ban on statistics nationwide and called for 900 more staff. In this trial of strength, the CPSA proved to have widespread support: no statistics were collected in 730 out of 950 offices.

With hindsight, it may seem surprising that no sanctions were applied to union members who abstained from performing part of their normal duties. But senior managers in the ESA, the Department of Employment and the Civil Service Department were cautious about sanctions[14] because of a reluctance to put relationships throughout the ESA at risk by a punitive response, and anxiety that the dispute might spread to the unemployment benefit service and to the DHSS. Moreover, compromise rather than confrontation was a characteristic management response in the mid-1970s. Accordingly, in January 1975, ESA management negotiated a settlement with the CPSA, under which some staffing increases in local offices were brought forward from the following financial year and the unemployment count was resumed.

But ESA management tried to go beyond mere compromise. For the next four years, stimulated by this dispute, it was in the vanguard of efforts in the public sector at a highly participative approach to management. This produced some successes as well as some disappointing failures.

One example of this participative approach was the joint review of the complementing system, which was now urgently pursued. The 'complementing system' determined the number of staff by function nationally, regionally and in each local office. Its history went back to 1929, when the Ministry of Labour had introduced a *staffing basis scheme* which differentiated between *fluctuating* and *non-fluctuating* elements. Unemployment benefit staffing fluctuated with the number of claimants. But most employment work was 'non-fluctuating' and it was extremely difficult to find satisfactory principles to determine what the levels of staffing should be. Indeed, in 1962, the ministry's Inspectors had concluded that the amount of effort made 'depends to a considerable extent on the amount of time available' and that the extent of staff resourcing was 'a matter for policy decision'.[15] But ESA management still needed a rational basis for allocating staff to Regions, Districts and local offices and for determining the staffing implications of changes in policy or programmes. They reached two crucial decisions:

- the new system should be based on workloads rather than outputs (such as placings), since a system based on outputs would unduly penalise areas of high unemployment; and
- the new staffing pointers should be based on the actual allocation of staff time as established in an activity sampling exercise, rather than, as some argued, on centrally prescribed work standards. This reflected the freedom Ken Cooper had given to managers to experiment with new methods of work. Line managers now regarded most Head Office instructions as advisory rather than prescriptive (with the exception of those which were statutory or statistical).[16]

Thus the findings of an activity sampling exercise formed the basis for a new system. There were four pointers for general placing work – registrations, the live register (ie the level of unemployment), orders (ie vacancies) and self service submissions. It was then possible to calculate a *pointer product*, ie the level of staffing produced by multiplying the relevant statistical volumes by the pointers. But the problem with the new system was that, right from the start, this pointer product exceeded the staffing available – reflecting both rising unemployment and the dynamism of the ESA in taking on new business as more Jobcentres opened. This 'deficit', as it came to be called, was an obstacle to an agreement with the unions on staffing.

During 1976, further industrial relations difficulties arose from the Lord Privy Seal's exercise to cut civil service staffing. Following pleas by the MSC Commissioners, Michael Foot in July 1976 restricted the impact on the ESA to a cut in planned growth of 780 staff for 1978/79[17] – surprisingly lenient treatment at a time of economic crisis. But as part of their national campaign against cuts in public services, the CPSA called for industrial action on 1 November in the whole Department of Employment Group, including bans on overtime and statistical work.

Despite this dispute, management and unions in the ESA were near agreement by December 1976 about a new complementing system. The 'deficit' problem was referred to Michael Foot and he advised the staff side that 'ESA's overall staff ceiling should not be regarded as open-ended. Within the agreed ceilings, therefore, tasks had to be matched to the staff which have been allocated.' However, he accepted the high priority of the work of the ESA and would 'wish to review the overall staffing provision if there were substantial changes in workload such as might occur with rising registers'. The choice then would be between 'some curtailment of desirable activities or services, or reconsideration of the planned ceilings'.[18] On this basis, the Staff Side eventually agreed to the new complementing system.

Meanwhile, on 12 January 1977, the CPSA called off its industrial action in the Department of Employment Group, including the ESA. As in 1974/75, management had not resorted to sanctions. But the tactics adopted by Catherine Andrews, who was in the lead in the Department on industrial relations, had proved highly effective. Management had pointed out to staff the weakness of the CPSA's rationale for the dispute in the DE Group. In addition, ordinary CPSA members were disturbed to read in the *News of the World* on 9 January, or subsequently in other newspapers, how many members of the CPSA Executive belonged to the Communist Party or other extreme left-wing groups. The Executive decision to end the dispute was in part due to a large number of phone calls and telegrams from moderate members. There were limits to the readiness of the rank and file to follow the left-wing lead, though left-wing candidates continued to prove successful in CPSA elections.

The new complementing system, linked to operational planning, proved a useful tool for the distribution of staff resources. But its apparent ability through the 'pointer product' to indicate a 'correct' staffing level placed a continuing uncomfortable pressure upon senior management, not just from the CPSA but also from the middle managers and their union, the SCPS. This pressure increased as the estimated 'deficit' rose from 375 staff units in August 1977 to over 1000 in September 1978.[19] But it was not clear that the deficit was valid as a barometer of workload pressures. Area Managers complained of heavy pressures,[20] but Civil Service Department Inspectors, who visited six local offices, reported that staffing was 'reasonably generous' and were also critical of the number of employment advisers as compared with clerical officers.[21] John Cassels criticised the complementing system, suggesting that it needed a factor for annual increases in productivity. Employment service senior managers contemplated breaking down the pointers into narrower tasks, some of which could be dropped if resources were tight, but the unions resisted a further review of the complementing system unless the 'deficit' were removed first. The two sides had reached a stalemate.

These struggles about staffing under the Labour government 1974–79 were typical of the public sector in this period and full of irony. In reality, the employment service was treated generously with an increase of over 1000 staff in local offices (10.5 per cent) between 1974 and 1978/79.[22] But the trade unions – and to some extent management – persuaded themselves that they were hard done by. Experience under the next government would put this into perspective.

Planning and management systems

Chapter 9 referred to Ken Cooper's major innovations in management in the early 1970s (page 165). Here we look at how this important management agenda was pursued between 1974 and 1979.

The new ESA quickly became a laboratory in which the latest ideas on management in the public service were tried out. Following the ideas in the Fulton Report, the Employment Service Action Plan of 1972 had envisaged making

> units of organisation in the ES Agency accountable for their performance by applying a discipline of planning and controlling against plans. This will provide a framework within which maximum delegation of authority and responsibility can be achieved...planning and control would be based on an integrated management information system...

These principles would later be applied much more widely in the civil service, but at this time the employment service was unusual in pursuing them.

Alan Brown developed these ideas further into a framework for a major consultancy exercise by a Coopers and Lybrand team led by Peter Burnham. In December 1974, the consultants produced a massive report on a new *management information system* for the fledgling Agency. Some felt that their approach was too ambitious. Ron Stephenson described it as 'a blanket which may suffocate us all'. It did not prove practicable to introduce the full recommendations. But important progress was made on three fronts:

- the work of the Agency was divided into *programmes and subprogrammes*, for the purposes of planning and financial control; Head Office specialists were seen as 'programme co-ordinators';
- a computerised *Financial and Management Accounting System* (FMAS) was developed, designed to meet not only Treasury requirements but also modern management accounting concepts, including accruals and prepayments, so that expenditure and outputs for a particular period could be compared and, where appropriate, unit costs calculated; the system met Treasury needs, but worked less well for management purposes because of the amount of work required to improve the quality of data;[23] some Management Accountants were recruited to help with these problems; and
- an *Operating Statistics Project* was launched (page 183).

The most successful management innovation of this period was the development of the *operational planning system*, which was championed by Ron Stephenson and first introduced nationally for the planning year 1976/77. The Executive Committee issued a Planning Memorandum which set out the national priorities for the coming year, the resource position, the economic climate and special features of particular programmes. On this basis, Area Managers would submit to senior management for approval their proposed Area plans and targets (by then known as 'estimated levels of performance') for the next year. Performance was then reviewed against plan. From 1977/78 onwards, complementing became integrated into the planning system. This kind of planning system proved valuable and has persisted in the employment service to this day.

Less successful were attempts to introduce Management by Objectives (MbO). Chapter 9 described Ken Cooper's introduction in 1972 of performance objectives or targets (page 165). While this encouraged managers to be more results-orientated, it was also criticised as being too crude and authoritarian. To meet these criticisms, Cooper decided to shift to a more participative and sophisticated model of Management by Objectives (MbO), which at that time was being advocated by the Civil Service Department (CSD).[24]

The idea was that, with the help of management advisers and with the involvement of their staff, managers should identify their 'key result areas', clarify their objectives and performance measures and then be held to account in periodic reviews. In a sense, it was a further elaboration of operational planning. But it came up against strong opposition. The CPSA opposed MbO throughout the civil service, perhaps because they did not want management to by-pass the union by discussing objectives directly with staff. Furthermore, many middle managers already felt threatened by the new management style and did not want it carried any further. Despite lengthy discussions with the unions, promising pilots and many changes of name, management failed to secure the necessary consensus for extending the approach nationwide. Indeed, in 1977 union opposition seemed to have been fostered by certain Area Managers in the North West – an example of the way in which management and trade union roles could be confused in the strife-torn 1970s. The Executive Committee gave up the idea of a centrally devised MbO template and instead, during 1978, encouraged Area Managers to appoint 'management advisers' to coach managers.[25]

The unions' success in frustrating these initiatives may seem surprising. It would not have happened in the 1980s. However, the unions were reflecting genuine managerial concerns, illustrated by the complaint of one Area Manager: 'We are in a very simple business, but we have made it all very complicated.' The Executive Committee felt that this process of management education was too sensitive to be introduced by executive action. The investment was not entirely wasted. Along with other powerful influences on managers at this time, notably operational planning and the Jobcentre managers' training courses, it helped to improve the quality of management. In this period, managers adapted to a management style radically different from anything they had experienced in the past.

Computerisation

As early as 1964, the Dunnett Report had recognised the important potential of computers in the work of employment exchanges, giving impetus to a massive project to computerise the assessment and payment of unemployment benefit. The resulting system – NUBS (National Unemployment Benefit System) – was rolled out during the 1970s and made it easier for the new unemployment benefit service to cope with a huge increase in claims. The Department was also interested in the potential of computers for employment work. Possible applications included vacancy circulation, statistics, registrant information, employer information, matching people and jobs, career information and instructions. Ken Cooper's planning team were aware of developments in Japan and the US in using computers to provide banks of job information and to help match applicants to vacancies. But in the early 1970s, they focused on vacancy circulation in large conurbations and decided to introduce facsimile transmission (Mufax) rather than computers in all conurbations except London – arguably a mistake, as Mufax was not a satisfactory system.

London's labour market was so vast and complex that Bruce Graham, from PA Management Consultants, was called in to study the problem. In May 1973, Graham recommended piloting a comprehensive real-time computer solution, incorporating not just vacancy circulation, but also full information on registrants and vacancies together with matching and statistics. Following the pilot, the roll-out throughout London might be completed by 1976, with subsequent extension to other conurbations.

The employment service decided to proceed with the proposed pilot and enlisted the necessary support from the MSC, the Department of Employment, the Treasury and the Central Computer and Telecommunications Agency. It seemed a compelling case, though it was to present ES management with some serious problems. The project was well managed by Brian White, who led an expert team which grew to over 60 staff. It was named CAPITAL – Computer Assisted Placing in the Areas of London. Some of the London managers were initially cool about the project, which they saw as HQ's intellectual conception, but they joined in a large steering committee. Honeywell was commissioned to provide computer bureaux services for the pilot. After intensive efforts, the pilot in 15 offices in a rather depressed area in North-East London became operational in 1977 – three years later than the Feasibility Report had suggested.

The switchover to this new system was remarkably smooth. Technologically, CAPITAL was an instant success. Visitors came from all over the world to see it – the most eminent being the Deputy Prime Minister of Sweden. A technical expert from the French employment service described the reponse times as *'incroyable'*. In 1979, the project won the British Computer Society's award for social applications of computing.

In value for money terms, the case for CAPITAL was less clear. The Treasury, unlike its counterparts in many other Western nations, insisted on elaborate cost-benefit justification for large computer projects. In order to maintain the momentum of the project, the evaluation report was produced in July 1978, only a few months after the project went live, but managers had had no time to work out the best way to use the system.

Another problem was that employment service operations had changed dramatically in the four years since Bruce Graham's original report. In 1973, the potential for considerable performance gains from computerised matching had seemed clear. But since 1973, self service, in which jobseekers matched themselves against displayed vacancies, had been extended to the point where it accounted for 70 per cent of all London placings. Moreover, in those parts of London outside the pilot area, self service had been facilitated by the introduction late in 1977 of Message Switch. Message Switch combined a mini-computer with telecommunications links to terminals in local offices. Unlike CAPITAL, Message Switch did not offer a database of information on vacancies and registrants or any scope for matching. But it did offer rapid vacancy circulation, so that jobseekers using self service had rapid access to vacancies from other offices. CAPITAL had now to be evaluated not against the inefficient systems prevailing in 1973 but against the much more efficient Message Switch.

The evaluation estimated that CAPITAL would still increase placings by 10 per cent and reduce vacancy duration by 20 per cent or three quarters of a day (later reduced to half a day). In addition, CAPITAL saved about 20 per cent of the staff time. The proposal was to extend CAPITAL to the whole of London by 1982/83, at a cost of £11 million; thereafter, the annual running cost would be £1.7 million. The benefits in the form of the savings to employers through faster vacancy filling, combined with the saving to the exchequer through fewer staff, exceeded the costs by a comfortable margin.[26]

Top management in the MSC and the Commissioners themselves supported the extension,[27] though Richard O'Brien, the Chairman, and others were worried about the shakiness of the evidence and about the achievability of the staff savings given union attitudes in the employment service. Negotiations with the unions began in August 1978 and soon got bogged down. The unions did not object to the project as such but did object to trading technology for jobs, bearing in mind the 'deficit' of 1000 under the complementing system (page 178). They rejected a management offer of a compromise on the staff savings. Management was reluctant to proceed against union opposition, since staff goodwill seemed necessary for such a fundamental change in office procedure. Nor were TUC Commissioners likely to support executive action. The CBI Commissioners argued for threatening to abandon the project – following Sir Michael Edwardes' tactics in the motor industry – but this was unlikely to change the union line. So there was a stalemate right up to the 1979 Election.

While CAPITAL was by far the highest profile computer development, progress was being made with other computer projects. Coopers and Lybrand's study in 1974 of the management information requirements of the ESA (page 179), led to a proposal for computerising both the labour market statistics and the performance statistics produced by the employment service. The ESA consulted the statisticians of the Department of Employment, as the highly sensitive monthly unemployment figures were derived from employment service data about registrants. Eventually, in May 1977 the DE statisticians astonished the employment service team by proposing a 'claims based count', ie deriving the unemployment figures from the computer record of those who were unemployed and claiming benefit. This, they argued, would both be cheaper and more accurate. Following further study, senior officials in the DE and MSC decided in March 1978 in favour of a 'Joint Unemployment, Vacancy and Operating Statistics' (JUVOS) system to be introduced incrementally and completed by 1984 and to incorporate the claims-based unemployment count. In the event, the claims-based count was introduced in 1982 following the decision of the Thatcher government to abandon compulsory registration for unemployed claimants (Chapter 11). Some interpreted this as a cynical move to reduce the unemployment count. But the original plans for this change were laid in 1977–78 under the Callaghan government and derived from the concerns of Department of Employment statisticians about the accuracy and cost of the registrant based count – and perhaps its vulnerability to industrial action.

In April 1979, the Executive Committee agreed an 'Interim Computer Strategy'[28] drawn up by Norman McGlynn, an experienced systems expert. The strategy assumed CAPITAL would go ahead in London but avoided commitment to its extension elsewhere. Meanwhile, Message Switch offered a cheap, quick and effective alternative way of addressing the key problem of vacancy circulation in conurbations, with the potential for enhancement to provide vacancy and placing statistics as well. So it was agreed to provide computerised vacancy circulation and statistics, in every travel-to-work area outside London'. This became known as the VACS Project, which eventually became a nationwide system in 1983. This strategy was called 'interim' because of the uncertainties about the potential for achieving a breakthrough in the computerised matching of registrants and vacancies. Neither the CAPITAL evaluation nor some psychologists' experiments in the use of job preference checklists for matching were encouraging. The problem was that only 20–25 per cent of all placings were achieved through matching: the rest were achieved by self service or on the basis of skeleton temporary registrations. So computerised matching did not seem to offer the scope for achieving a major leap in performance comparable to that achieved by self service. This conclusion left a gnawing doubt about the prestigious CAPITAL project.

The impact of rising unemployment

Table 10.1 shows the alarming trend in unemployment in this period. When the Labour government took over in March 1974, unemployment was below 3 per cent, thanks to the Barber boom, but this could not last. Rocketing inflation and efforts to restrain it caused a recession which lasted from 1975 to 1978, during which unemployment rose to more than 6 per cent or 1.4 million in 1977/78. It then fell slightly to around 1.3 million at the time of the 1979 Election. Long-term unemployment also increased sharply: those unemployed for over 52 weeks rose steadily from 132,000 in April 1974 to 347,000 in April 1979. Among Ministers, there was much discomfort that under a Labour government unemployment had reached the highest levels since the 1930s.

Table 10.1 *Unemployment, 1974–79*

Year	Numbers unemployed – yearly average (000s)	% unemployed
1974	619	2.6
1975	978	4.2
1976	1359	5.7
1977	1484	6.2
1978	1475	6.1
1979	1390	5.7

Source: Office of National Statistics, *Labour Market Trends*, Jan 1996, Crown Copyright.

The rise in unemployment was not unexpected. Indeed, in January 1974 the newly appointed MSC initiated 'contingency planning' for a potential increase in unemployment.[29] They sought the advice of Santosh Mukherjee, a labour market economist, who reported in June 1974, recommending a *job creation scheme*.[30] When the expected upsurge in unemployment occurred in 1975, with unemployment rising to over 1 million for the first time since 1940, urgent discussions took place between the government and the MSC about 'special measures'. The government set up the Manpower Group, a powerful interdepartmental group of civil servants, to advise it on special measures and on the ideas coming from the MSC. In September 1975, the first of many packages of 'special measures' to tackle unemployment was announced, including a work creation scheme. The Commission set up a Committee under Geoffrey Holland

The New Model Employment Service, 1974-79

to investigate guaranteed opportunities for work experience for all young people under 18. In March 1977, the Committee recommended a 'Youth Opportunities Programme (YOP)', which the government approved.

What was the response of the employment service to this mounting unemployment crisis? Of all government agencies, it was closest to unemployment, since all new unemployed claimants had to register with the service and the great majority of its clients were unemployed. The main job of its employment advisers was to advise the unemployed on getting back to work. Finally, the ESA was the source of the unemployment statistics, the announcement of which was an increasingly disturbing monthly ritual for the Secretary of State.

ESA senior management did not, however, consider that this rise in unemployment demanded a fundamental change in ESA strategy. After all, that strategy had been decided in 1971/72 when unemployment was approaching 1 million. The ESA's priority was to carry through the modernisation of the service, to introduce Jobcentres and to attract more vacancies. This programme in itself was so demanding that the ESA decided, perhaps unwisely, against bidding to run the new Job Creation Programme. Modernisation, through increasing the ESA's labour market penetration, would, it was argued, benefit the mounting numbers of unemployed people by opening up to them more vacancies. But there remained a problem about the pressures on staff time, given that the number of unemployed people on the ESA's books was increasing so fast. In 1975, Cooper secured an increase of 600 staff brought forward from 1976/77 and extra money for the Jobcentre programme.[31]

But these measures were not enough in themselves to ease the pressure on staffing. In May 1975, Frank Harrison, the Area Manager for East Midlands, presented a paper on rising unemployment at a senior management meeting. He argued that the best way to help the unemployed was give *priority to finding and filling vacancies*. In order to find enough staff time for this, managers should abandon 'six point plan' registration interviews in favour of much shorter interviews – something that was already tending to happen. Similarly, there was unlikely to be much time for 'review interviews' for people who were long-term unemployed. This policy, known as 'find and fill', followed on logically from the modernisation programme and became deeply embedded in managerial attitudes in the employment service right up to the mid-1980s, when Ministers required a change.

Inevitably, the 'find and fill' strategy was widely questioned, for instance, by the Department of Social Security (page 188) and, closer to home, by the Department of Employment, the TUC Commissioners and some MSC colleagues. But the ESA could point to the unhappy example of the US in the 1960s, where a policy of giving priority to helping unemployed jobseekers over filling vacancies had led to a severe fall in placing performance. The ESA argued along utilitarian lines that their policy helped the greatest number of people.

One of the implications of 'find and fill', and indeed of placing targets themselves, given tight resource levels, was that managers tended to identify the 'good placing propositions' from among the huge numbers of registrations and focus matching efforts on them. Employment advisers would have a 'hot box' of the most placeable people to match against vacancies as they came in. This pre-dated modernisation, but was encouraged by it. It came into public view as a result of the plans for the CAPITAL computer system in London (pages 181–2). London management wanted to identify jobseekers by four 'job categories' and focus matching effort on the top categories. The CPSA protested and leaked the story to the press, leading to a *Guardian* editorial entitled 'The ABC of Injustice'. The matter was discussed by Commissioners, who accepted the approach, and a compromise was eventually reached with CPSA.

ESA management recognised that 'find and fill' was an incomplete answer to the needs of those who faced increasingly long spells of unemployment. Such people might well need guidance, counselling and special help with jobsearch if they were to get back to work; after all, such specialist help was available for disabled people and there was a case for extending it to others who faced many of the same problems. In 1973, 'Resettlement Trials' had been set up in four locations as experiments in ways of assisting 'socially disadvantaged people with special employment problems'.[32] By 1977, it was concluded that:

> *The resettlement trials...point towards a new service based on a case-work approach with an Employment Adviser undertaking both in-depth counselling and intensive placing action...this service should be developed separately from the present DRO service'.*[33]

This new service was called the 'Special Employment Needs' (SEN) service and was launched on an experimental basis in autumn 1977. By 1978/79, 48 SEN advisers (about half in inner city areas) were engaged in this experiment and achieved 2053 placings – less than one placing per adviser per week. This illustrates the difficulty at that time of placing people, most of whom were only a few months unemployed. This was and remained a modest experiment, because of other pressures on staffing and a fear of putting employers off the service.

The employment service Executive Committee's caution about the long-term unemployed persisted right up to the 1979 Election. In April 1978, ideas from the Department of Employment for subsidies to employers who took on the long-term unemployed prompted concern that this could 'cut across our fundamental strategy'. Any large-scale involvement of the service in such a scheme 'would endanger the credibility with employers which had been painstakingly built up over the last five years'.[34] In August 1978, the Executive concluded that the service could best help people by *preventing* them becoming long-term unemployed and 'that undue attention to the long-term unemployed was unlikely to assist this group significantly, but that it would have a detrimental effect on the remainder of the service'.[35] In September 1978, the employment service contributed along these lines in a paper for the Commission on long-term unemployment, which suggested that a commitment to offer opportunities to all the long-term unemployed would be difficult and expensive.[36] The paper was submitted to the Secretary of State, Albert Booth. But political interest in the long-term unemployed persisted. Jim Callaghan announced an urgent study to the 1978 Labour Party Conference. Moreover, the 1979 Labour Party Manifesto promised to introduce a commitment that all those unemployed for more than a year would receive the offer of either a job or training. It can be argued that the employment service was too absorbed in its existing agenda and not responsive enough to the strong new currents flowing outside it.

The concerns within government and in public opinion about mounting unemployment were in part about what we have called 'social welfare'. But alongside these, and growing in intensity, were mounting concerns about the cost to the taxpayer of benefits for the unemployed and about whether there was adequate control of this vast benefit expenditure.

Links with the DHSS and with the DE's new unemployment benefit service

Chapter 9 showed that the decision in 1971 to separate benefit from employment work had been taken against the DHSS's better judgement. The DHSS had only acquiesced in the decision as a result of undertakings from Ken Cooper to cooperate with the DHSS in combating abuse (pages 153 and 159–61), requirements on the MSC to provide the Government with any information it needed for social security purposes[37] and the decision that separation should take place *within* the Department of Employment.

Separation meant that, by October 1974, alongside the MSC's new Employment Service Agency, was a new unemployment benefit service (the UBS) within the Department of Employment, led initially by Meg Green. In 1974, the UBS had some 11,500 staff in some 400 large or medium-sized offices and a similar number of smaller limited benefit offices. As unemployment increased, UBS staffing increased to reach around 19,000 by 1978/79. (The Treasury had always accepted that benefit staffing, unlike staffing for employment work, had to rise with unemployment.) It was an unsung achievement of the Department of Employment to maintain the efficient and regular payment of benefit to this greatly increasing population. The UBS was not exempt from staffing constraints. The Lord Privy Seal's exercise in 1976 to cut civil service staffing led to a decision that claimants should sign fortnightly rather than weekly from 1978 to achieve a saving of 800 posts, despite some Treasury worries about potential increases in benefit expenditure.

The UBS was assisted in coping with the increase in claimants by the introduction at this time of the National Unemployment Benefit System (NUBS). The DE was many years ahead of the DHSS in introducing computer terminals into front-line offices. Another helpful feature was the releasing of space in the benefit offices as employment staff departed to new Jobcentres. Even so, there were severe problems of overcrowding.

There were difficulties in establishing the new arrangements for benefit control. These depended on cooperation between the employment service on the one hand and the UBS and the Supplementary Benefit Commission (SBC) on the other, as follows:

- Transit cards needed to flow between the ESA offices and the UB Offices to ensure that claimants had registered for employment and to notify movements off the register and other significant changes.
- Employment service staff were expected to notify the UBO of cases of abuse of the benefit system, where people were working while drawing benefit (fraud) or avoiding taking jobs that they could perform (refusal of suitable employment – RSE) or placing unreasonable restrictions on their availability for work; and of cases where they were incapable of work.
- Employment service staff were expected to take similar action in respect of claimants receiving supplementary benefit and to co-operate with the Unemployment Review Officers (UROs) of the SBC.

The UBS issued its instructions on these liaison issues at the time of separation in October 1974, but the ESA still had not done so two years later. The drafting had got bogged down in argument. Moreover, the number of referrals for refusal of suitable employment or neglect to avail of suitable opportunities had plummeted since separation (Table 10.2). By the autumn of 1976, Alan Brown, the Chief Executive, found himself assailed with criticism on several fronts. One critic was the Exchequer and Audit Department, to whom Brown explained in September that the pre-1974 instructions 'for the most part remained in force', though they needed updating. He gave an assurance that staff were trained in benefit liaison. As regards the decline in referrals, Brown argued that this was due to high unemployment, the low level of vacancies and the fact that 60–80 per cent of submissions were now made in self service. He argued against submitting unsuitable or unwilling workers in order to test them. This would undermine employer confidence. 'To provide the maximum service to the generality of jobseekers, ESA must carry the full confidence of employers.' None the less, the ESA would continue to report 'flagrant' cases of abuse.[38]

In October 1976, the pressure was intensified. Mrs Kent, the Under-Secretary in charge of the UBS in the Department, urged Brown to get the new instructions out quickly. She referred to concerns about alleged benefit abuse not only in the Public Accounts Committee, but also among Ministers, including the Prime Minister, Jim Callaghan, who felt the subject deserved some priority.[39] Alan Brown told his team to speed up their work and the new instructions eventually appeared in February 1977.

In November 1976, Brown faced a further onslaught, this time from Geoff Beltram of the SBC. Beltram complained of ESA reluctance to submit long-term claimants to vacancies, on grounds of their concern about employer attitudes; it was 'unfortunate when ESA staff automatically assume that a long-term claimant is *ipso facto* unsuitable for any vacancy whatsoever'. Some ESA

The New Model Employment Service, 1974-79

Table 10.2 *Referrals for refusal of suitable employment, neglect to avail of suitable opportunities and restricted availability, 1968-78*

Year	Refusal of suitable employment or neglect to avail of suitable opportunities Referrals	% of referrals resulting in disqualification	Restricted availability Referrals	% of referrals resulting in disqualification
1968	28,270	78	18,242	41
1969	25,452	78	16,450	41
1970	24,219	79	15,946	42
1971	19,647	79	15,315	38
1972	20,743	79	15,555	42
1973	18,947	83	11,902	46
1974	13,248	81	10,251	44
1975	6858	75	11,049	41
1976	5603	68	10,955	42
1977	8423	69	13,489	40
1978	7696	64	15,835	38

Source: Report of Working Group chaired by Jim Lester, Parliamentary Secretary, 1980. DE file 3/ET 207/80.

managers had even objected to the Unemployment Review Officers (UROs) encouraging people to use self service and had refused to provide vacancy information to UROs or to support UROs in submissions to employers. Beltram concluded with a catalogue of quotations which the SBC had picked up from ESA managers and staff:

- 'We are not interested in your sort of people; we have our image to consider.'
- 'Our duty is to the employer, not to the employee.'
- 'ESA will not put its image at risk with an undertaking to assist with evidence of voluntary unemployment by a job submission – no matter how rare the request or how sympathetic the employer.'
- 'UI 195 action (ie submissions to employers to test out willingness to accept suitable employment) is a 'waste of time' (ESA Manager).
- 'URO specifically requested not to send claimants to the Jobcentre.'

The ESA's reply acknowledged that their policy was to submit the most suitable people to employers' vacancies and to prevent clearly unsuitable people from being submitted through self service. But staff did not automatically exclude long-term unemployed people. The Operational Plan for 1977/78 would encourage managers to take account of 'the needs of people on the register' as well as the need for speedy vacancy filling. In the ESA's view, the problems raised by the SBC arose from very high unemployment, which intensified competition from the more able. The new instructions would clarify procedures.

Table 10.2 shows that, following the issue of the instructions in February 1977, referral rates for potential abuse increased, though not dramatically. Fundamentally, however, the employment service continued to give very low priority to 'benefit liaison'. Thus, although benefit liaison had featured in the seminal documents of the early 1970s – *People and Jobs* and the *Action Plan* – it is virtually unmentioned in strategic or operational plans thereafter. The SBC's catalogue of quotations represented genuine ESA managerial attitudes at the time. Ken Cooper and his senior team had succeeded in re-orienting managers towards maximising labour market penetration. Managers knew that this depended on employer attitudes and that employers were in a buyers' market as unemployment rose. Employers did not want to be sent potential 'scroungers' to test them out. In this climate, only very clear and authoritative messages from Head Office could have ensured that benefit control was taken seriously. But Head Office itself was divided. The Divisional Directors shared the views of the other line managers. It took heavy external pressure even to get out the basic instructions, and even then benefit control had no real priority.

This could be seen as common sense at a time of high unemployment. If there was a grave shortage of jobs, should you not encourage the keen jobseekers to get them, rather than harrassing the workshy to go after them? This worked with, rather than against, the grain of the labour market. However, there were counter-arguments about the risks of growing welfare dependency among the long-term unemployed. Moreover, the Canadian government, which had pioneered separation, had decided to re-integrate benefit and employment work on precisely the same arguments about abuse of benefit that were beginning to be advanced in Britain.

Professional and Executive Recruitment (PER)

Chapter 9 described the setting up of PER as a fee-charging subsidiary of ESA (pages 166-7). The target was to achieve financial self-sufficiency by 1976, apart from the 'social subvention' (which in 1975/76 covered 25 per cent of its costs). Despite remarkable vigour and panache, this target was not achieved, partly because of the decline in the labour market (which caused losses among private agencies at the time) and also because of the constraints imposed by civil service rules on staffing and grading. In April 1976, despite continued TUC misgivings about a commercial service, the Commission decided to maintain the commercial operation for another three years, with a revised fee structure and more external recruitment.[40]

Commercial self-sufficiency was achieved in 1977/78 and placings rose to 8800.[41] But, in response to continued scepticism on the part of the Public Accounts Committee, Richard O'Brien, MSC Chairman, led a further review of PER[42] which reported to the Commission in October 1979. The Commission again endorsed PER as a commercial venture – this time for another five years. PER's commercial performance had greatly improved, though there were still staffing difficulties. It was agreed to pursue a proposal from Geoff Crosby, the Director of PER, to rebuild PER operations around a weekly jobs newspaper (rather than on computerised matching, which had not been very successful). This newspaper – *Executive Post* – was to prove PER's outstanding success.

PER is interesting as an example of applying a commercial model to a public employment service. Predictably, there were problems with the constraints of the civil service regime and at this time, long before the Next Steps Report, there was little scope to vary this. Moreover, it took time and experience to adapt to the commercial market, but commercial success was eventually achieved with clear savings for the taxpayer. But there were also adverse effects:

- Charging created a service strongly orientated towards employers. Until *Executive Post* was introduced, many jobseekers who went on the PER's register heard nothing more from the organisation. It is true that some training and self-presentation courses were pioneered, but the advisory services for jobseekers were relatively weak, at a time when rising numbers of unemployed executives were coming on the market;
- Charging also constricted PER's market share, thus further limiting the help available to jobseekers; admittedly, PER faced tougher competition than the general service, particularly from newspaper advertising; but, in contrast to the general service, the reforms of the early 1970s at the professional and executive level did not boost market share; placings were 13,000 in 1970 before commercialisation[43] as against 9300 in 1978/79, though in a less favourable labour market.

The commercialisation of a public service tends to be a one-way street. Any move back to providing a free service is bound to be costly, since the taxpayer will have to make up for the lost commercial revenues. The 1978/79 Review did consider the alternative of using self help facilities and packages in Jobcentres, but without a placing service.[44] But even this would probably have entailed extra cost, and the retention of a commercial operation was preferred.

Services for disabled people

In the post-war history of the employment service, the disabled services were unusual in that they continued to enjoy a high level of commitment and resourcing even when other services were in decline. So it is interesting to see how they fared now that the general service was being modernised on the basis of an agenda that was more economic than social in its philosophy.

The MSC and its Employment Service Agency treated this area of social responsibility very seriously. They inherited from the Department of Employment not only some 500 Disablement Resettlement Officers (DROs) and a network of 26 Industrial Rehabilitation Units, but also from 1976 policy responsibility for the employment of disabled people, for the funding of sheltered employment and for the administration of the 'quota' (page 118). During the period, some 60 Senior DROs were appointed to lead a drive to encourage employers to adopt 'positive policies' towards the employment of disabled people. The training of DROs was improved. A scheme was introduced to fund special aids to employment. Two policy dilemmas emerged. First, the future of the 'quota', which was increasingly cumbersome and difficult to administer, but equally difficult to replace. Experiments in stricter enforcement demanded by Ministers did not result in additional placings.[45] The second dilemma was whether it made sense for all disabled people to receive a separate specialist service. Officials sought experiments under which some disabled people would be dealt with by the general service.[46]

The 1979 review of the employment service

In May 1978, it was decided to hold a major review of the 'aims, objectives and priorities of the employment service'. Such a review might have been expected in 1979, five years after *Plans and Programmes*. But it was brought forward because of disquiet on the part of the two senior officers of the MSC – Richard O'Brien and John Cassels – at the stance taken up by the Employment Service Division in the MSC's strategic planning round in 1978. ESD had stuck to its goal of increasing its market share (though not as an end in itself) and its scepticism about diverting resources to the disadvantaged, lest this should undermine the service to the ordinary registrant.[47] Moreover, Richard O'Brien was uncomfortable about the apparently 'inexorable onward march' of the Jobcentre programme.[48] These concerns were shared by senior people in the Department of Employment and had been voiced by the Public Accounts Committee.

The review was carried out by a Steering Group, chaired by John Cassels, with a small secretariat led by Jeremy Walker from the ESD. The Employment Service Executive was strongly represented on the Steering Group. While Cassels ensured that there was some hard questioning, it was very much an internal review. By the time it reported to the Commission in July 1979, the Thatcher government had taken office. But it reflected the philosophy which the MSC had developed since 1974, rather than that of the new government – or even the old government. Indeed, early in the review, John Golding, the Minister of State, had expressed scepticism about the 'numbers game' in which he felt ESD was engaged and advocated a service more like the careers service, with a focus on developing individuals – in other words, the 'social welfare' model of our Chapter 1. But the review did not follow this lead.

The Review Report[49] began with an emphatic endorsement of the achievements of the service since 1974. It noted that three of the four objectives in *Plans and Programmes* (page 172) had been achieved:

1. *to open at least 100 Jobcentres a year up to 1980*; by 31 March 1979, there were 555 Jobcentres out of a network of 1000 offices and 62 per cent of the staff were employed in Jobcentres;
2. *to improve job-filling performance by at least 25 per cent overall by 1979*; Table 10.3 shows that, by 1978/79, vacancies had risen to 2.68 million and placings to 1.8 million, the highest figure recorded since the compulsory notification of vacancies order was revoked in 1956 and despite a massive rise in unemployment; market share had risen from 16 per cent in 1973 to over 20 per cent by 1979, an increase of 25 per cent;[50]
3. *to introduce well trained employment advisers and self service facilities throughout the local office network by 1979*; this had been achieved;
4. *to achieve savings which would justify and permit giving more help to jobseekers in need of special assistance and support*; less progress had been made here; while self service had improved productivity, the increase in unemployment had 'prevented advisory and guidance services from being developed as fully as had been hoped'; however, modernisation had benefited the long-term unemployed since Jobcentres achieved more submissions and placings of long-term unemployed people than other ES offices (even if the actual number of such submissions was low – around one or two per registrant).

Table 10.3 *Vacancy and placing performance, 1973/74–1978/79*

Financial year	1973/74	1974/75	1975/76	1976/77	1977/78	1978/79
Vacancies notified (millions)	2.62	2.42	1.91	2.13	2.36	2.68
Placings (millions)	1.60	1.56	1.29	1.48	1.61	1.81
Unemployment (April) %	2.90	2.60	3.60	5.40	5.80	6.00

The report argued that Jobcentres were more *cost effective* than other offices (unit cost of placings, including premises costs: £36.30 and £38.10 respectively) and offered an advantage in terms of *speed of vacancy filling*. The ES filled vacancies faster than other market media; also, Jobcentres saved about one and a half days compared with other ES offices. At current levels of placings, this reduced unemployment at any given time by 12,000, saving nearly £40 million per year in the public sector borrowing requirement. These calculations were to prove an important battleground in the early 1980s.

The report defined the main rationale of the employment service as

> *to make the labour market more 'transparent' so that employers and jobseekers can obtain and use the information they need and the market can therefore function as effectively as economic circumstances permit.*

It gave six reasons for a public service:

1. Economies of scale in linking jobseekers and employers; avoidance of abortive search.
2. Employer-financed services would not cater for the needs of many jobseekers.
3. Speed of vacancy filling, with gains to national output and the exchequer.
4. Access to other manpower services such as training.
5. Extra help for jobseekers who might face discrimination.
6. Potential to draw attention to vacancies of national importance.

Labour market transparency was the overwhelming thrust of these six points and of the whole report. But the report made some modest response to the mounting clamour for tighter benefit control. After listing the six points above, it acknowledged, almost as an afterthought, that the service 'enables a check to be kept on the willingness to work of those in receipt of state benefits'.[51] Later, it argued that increased post-registration action was desirable in its own right and also the 'most effective way in which the service could assist in checking abuse of benefits'. But the service

> *was not asked to operate a 'test', that is to submit doubtful candidates to its vacancies solely to test their availability for work. To do that would run the risk of alienating employers and thus reducing the ability of the service to place the unemployed. At the same time it is important that the employment service should discharge its obligations to follow up cases where people seem to be unreasonably refusing employment.*[52]

On the key issue of *labour market penetration*, the report suggested that there was 'a point at which each increase in market share will cost more than the benefits it brings and be more likely to displace a relatively efficient alternative'. This was difficult to apply in practice, but criteria might be that the service was faster and cheaper than other alternatives and achieved high levels of customer satisfaction. At national level, these criteria suggested that it was right to continue with the modernisation programme. Cassels gave some support to the ESD 'find and fill' philosophy: 'It is above all the share of vacancies which it handles which determines whether the service is able to function effectively.' Without this 'grip on the market', the ESD could not fulfil all its other roles. Moreover, modernisation had to be completed because the current Jobcentre network was patchy and London and the West Midlands had less than their share of Jobcentres. The conclusion, endorsed by the previously sceptical O'Brien and the rest of the Commission, was that: *The first priority for the next five years should be to complete the modernisation programme by 1983/84.*[53] This should itself boost the ESD's national market share to the range of 25 per cent to 28 per cent by 1983/84.

Cassels wanted to limit the pursuit of market share in local labour markets, once a Jobcentre had established a 'basic service' against tests of speed, cheapness and customer satisfaction. At that point, 'the next priorities should be the provision of additional help to job-seekers with special employment difficulties and to employers with particular problems over recruitment'.[54]

Cassels rejected the proposals of the Federation of Personnel Services that the ES should leave the non-manual market to the private sector. The ES had to provide a service to all who sought it, including the increasing proportion of non-manual registrants. Private agencies were not evenly spread either geographically or occupationally, and their fees greatly exceeded the unit cost of a placing.[55]

Cassels supported experiments in 'open display' in self service (ie displaying full details of the employer) and for developing information services, such as Joblibraries and job information points. He wanted a 'minimum level of service' to registrants. The absolute minimum was:

- simple registration, with self-registration as far as possible;
- immediate provision of self-help material, information about jobs, training etc through self service;
- sufficient matching to achieve early submissions where possible; and
- response to individuals seeking further help.

But desirably there would also be continued matching, a full assessment after four or five weeks and periodical review thereafter. Admittedly, resources would not permit this for every registrant, nor would it always be productive, but there should be experiments with post-registration activities to see what could be done.

Cassels rejected employers' calls for the 'close screening' of every jobseeker submitted as too expensive and also unfair to some jobseekers. Local offices should limit the numbers submitted to a given vacancy and job specifications should be improved.

The MSC approved the report and it was published under the optimistic title *The Employment Service in the 1980s* shortly after the Thatcher government had taken office. In view of the delicacy of relations between the government and the MSC, it was not strongly promoted, though it was noted that 'low profile publicity had been successfully achieved'.[56] The report belonged to the 1970s and could not anticipate the radically changed political climate of the 1980s. None the less, it was valuable in providing the Commission with a clear analysis on which decisions on priorities could be based.

Conclusion

This chapter has described how the vision for a new-style employment service as an instrument of labour market transparency was put into effect. It is striking how faithfully this vision was followed. That there was such continuity in the service in the 1970s under first a Conservative government and then a Labour government reflects a remarkable bi-partisanship and also a common readiness to devolve power to the MSC.

The central achievement of the service in this period was the introduction of more than 500 new Jobcentres. Along with this went a shift to a results-orientated approach in managers and staff, so that placing performance held up remarkably well in a bleak economic climate. The new-style employment service was well planned and organised and highly motivated, but it also ran the risk of rigidity. This could be seen in its reluctance to take on an increasing role in relation to people who were unemployed for a significant period. Admittedly, the introduction and training of employment advisers raised the quality of information and advice to unemployed people. But in those years the service was so concerned about damaging its image as to preclude any significant targeting towards the long-term unemployed. As Chapter 11 will show, this laid it open to some biting criticism by Professor Layard that it was 'a service which increasingly services the easy to place'.[57]

None the less, the achievements of these years were truly remarkable. As the 1979 review report commented:

> *From being a run-down service often poorly regarded by both employers and jobseekers, the employment service has secured the respect of both and has become a stronger and more positive force in the labour market. Underlying the statistics is the reality of the transformation of the search for work from a depressed back-street operation to a normal activity conducted in businesslike conditions in which those concerned – employers, jobseekers and employment service staff – have the tools to do the job. The rise in unemployment underlines how timely this transformation has been.*[58]

11

The Challenge of Thatcherism, 1979–81

'The right definition (of "Thatcherism") involves a mixture of free markets, financial discipline, firm control of public expenditure, tax cuts, nationalism, "Victorian values" (of the Samuel Smiles self-help variety), privatisation and a dash of populism.' (Nigel Lawson)[1]

Introduction

The advent of Mrs Thatcher's Conservative government in May 1979 was a turning point for the employment service, as it was for all public services. The Conservative Manifesto for the 1979 Election reflected the themes set out by Nigel Lawson in the quotation above. It emphasised 'the reduction of waste, bureaucracy and over-government' and restoring the incentive to work in the social security system. There would prove to be three elements in Thatcherite policy affecting the public employment service:

- public expenditure: how much the service could be cut;
- the public versus the private sector: whether these activities need to be done in the public sector at all; and
- self-help versus dependence on benefit: whether the service should give priority to 'benefit control'.

While all three themes were under discussion during these early Thatcher years, in practice it was the public expenditure issue that was dominant. The employment service faced a succession of cuts exercises which forced it into a defensive mode, and also tested out what should be its real priorities. But its strategy remained focused on labour market transparency, until David Young became Secretary of State in September 1985.

It is difficult to interpret the course of events between 1979 and 1985 without attributing to the Prime Minister herself a view that the modernised employment service was one example among many of the 'waste, bureaucracy and over-government' which her Manifesto had promised to reduce. But the politics of the situation meant that the challenge to the employment service was gradual and progressive rather than swift and lethal. For one thing, with unemployment soaring to heights unprecedented since the 1930s, some sensitivity was needed in reforming institutions serving the unemployed. For another, Mrs Thatcher's government was initially a coalition between the new right, which she represented, and the traditional 'one nation' Conservatives such as Jim Prior, whom she appointed Secretary of State for Employment. But the biggest complication was the position of the employment service as a division of the Manpower Services Commission. The government decided to make use of the MSC rather than abolishing it, and this constrained its handling of the employment service. This chapter focuses on the efforts to cut the employment service early in Mrs Thatcher's term of office.

1979 was a turning point for the employment service in two other ways. First, in June 1979, there was a change of Chief Executive. Alan Brown departed to become Chief Executive of the Training Services Division and was succeeded by Jean Collingridge, an energetic and lively woman, whose background was in the Department's personnel management advisory service and conciliation work, particularly in the West Midlands.

Secondly, it was in July 1979 that the Prime Minister finally confirmed that MSC Head Office was to move to Sheffield. This dispersal had been agreed under the Labour government, with Commissioners deciding that Sheffield was the best destination of six cities that were considered.[2] But the Thatcher government, encouraged by Ken Barnes, the Permanent Secretary, decided to review the decision, on grounds of its cost and the communications damage that would result from it. Richard O'Brien, the MSC Chairman, and John Cassels, the MSC Director, said that it was too late to reverse the decision: some civil servants had already moved, it would produce cost savings in the long run and – the clinching argument – the government was committed to the major new Moorfoot building, which was already under construction. The MSC's view prevailed and ESD was the first part of MSC to re-locate. On the whole, dispersal was a success. MSC staff liked living in Sheffield and communications damage was kept to a minimum by a great deal of travelling for senior staff and the use of the latest technology for meetings. But dispersal also contributed to the tensions between Ministers and the MSC. Ministers felt, perhaps rightly, that Sheffield-based MSC staff were less sensitive to Ministerial concerns and pressures than the civil servants who surrounded them in London.

This chapter looks at the political framework within which the service operated in the early Thatcher years, the unemployment problem, the early cuts in staffing and public expenditure, the concerns about benefit control, the Rayner recommendation to remove the requirement on claimants to register in Jobcentres and the demise of the CAPITAL project.

The interplay between Ministers, the Department of Employment, the MSC and ESD

Soon after taking up office, the new Secretary of State, Jim Prior, reassured Richard O'Brien, the MSC Chairman, that the future of the MSC was secure and had never been in doubt, but that the government was keen to control public expenditure.[3] In reality, the situation was more complex than this. As their respective memoirs show,[4] there was a profound philosophical gulf between Prior and the Prime Minister. Prior was comfortable with the idea of involving the TUC, CBI and local authorities in government manpower programmes. By contrast, Mrs Thatcher had little time for the views of the TUC or the CBI, let alone those of local authorities. Like many to the right of the Conservative Party, she was suspicious of the MSC as the biggest quango of all, which had greatly expanded under the Labour government. Thus the government's decision in September 1979 to have a searching review of quangos may have been an indirect challenge to the MSC. Moreover, the official asked to carry out this review was none other than Sir Leo Pliatzky, who, as Chapter 9 recounted, had successfully led Treasury resistance to hiving off manpower services in the early days of the Heath administration (pages 149–50). In the event, Pliatzky's report gave the MSC a relatively clean bill of health. He noted that there had been 'problems associated with rapid expansion, but orthodox financial systems have been preserved and should be adequate for the adjustment to a climate of greater financial stringency'.[5] He also noted that MSC's future role presupposed continuing separate administration of employment and benefit work. He argued that the existence of three separate networks was less burdensome than it appeared since, even if unemployed people might visit a Jobcentre every day, they made 'much more spaced-out visits to the other offices'.[6]

The Prime Minister proved remarkably pragmatic in her attitude to the MSC. Her initial unease about the Commission was perhaps reflected in the disproportionately large cuts imposed on the MSC in December 1979 (page 202). Moreover, as time went on, she took steps to ensure that the Commission was controlled by people who shared her view of the world. But she also proved willing to entrust it with increasingly demanding tasks.

The employment service was seen as one of the more vulnerable parts of the MSC. Just after the Election, the *Sunday Telegraph* ran an article arguing that the separation of employment and benefit work had involved substantial bureaucratic duplication, 'although it must be conceded that one can be unemployed in more luxurious surroundings'.[7] Moreover, the private employment agencies, which resented state-funded competition from both PER and Jobcentres, felt that at last there was a government which might understand their point of view. In August 1979, Alec Reed of Reed Executive wrote to Prior suggesting that his company should take over some of the Jobcentres. The Earl of Gowrie, Minister of State, turned down this offer. The Federation of Personnel Services lobbied Ministers and Richard O'Brien to get PER abolished and some large Jobcentres closed. But the MSC in its reviews of both the general service and PER turned down these suggestions.

In September 1979, Jean Collingridge invited Ken Barnes, the Permanent Secretary of the Department of Employment, to meet her Executive. Barnes was central to the various cuts exercises. He welcomed the improved image of the employment service, but was critical of extravagance, quoting as an example the Piccadilly Jobcentre – an embarrassing white elephant. He doubted the economic justification for pursuing the Jobcentre programme further and felt the service should instead do more for benefit control. He concluded, 'Remember, a poor country cannot afford a Rolls-Royce employment service…', to which Jean Collingridge retorted, 'We wouldn't claim more than a Ford Cortina.' This exchange illustrated how the Department of Employment, which had launched modernisation in the early 1970s, had become increasingly sceptical about it in the later Callaghan years and now wanted to call a halt. It was the MSC, not the Department, which stood in the way of any swift reorientation of the service in the new government climate. The Commission's decision in July 1979 to publish the Report on the Review of the Employment Service (page 195) reflected its continued support for existing employment service policy, including the completion of the Jobcentre programme, albeit with some hesitation on the part of the CBI.

The unemployment problem

The new government had inherited unemployment at about 1.3 million or 5 per cent and in gentle decline. But in 1980, as a result of a world-wide recession and of government efforts to combat inflation at home, it began its spectacular rise to reach 3 million or over 13 per cent in 1982 (Table 11.1)

Table 11.1 *Unemployment, 1979–85*

Year	Numbers unemployed – yearly average (000s)	% unemployed
1979	1390	5.7
1980	1795	7.4
1981	2734	11.4
1982	3119	13.0
1983	3105	12.2
1984	3160	11.5
1985	3271	10.5

Source: Office of National Statistics, *Labour Market Trends*, Jan 1996. Crown Copyright.

The increase in unemployment caused great public disquiet, with investigations by Select Committees in both Houses of Parliament and some popular demonstrations including the People's March for Jobs in 1981. The Thatcher government, unlike the Heath government in 1972, decided against Keynesian measures to reflate the economy. None the less, Ministers were concerned about unemployment and looked for ways of alleviating it. This may well have kept the MSC in being, for, as we shall see later, it was expected to deliver massive programmes designed to reduce unemployment. Ministers were also appalled at the mounting costs of benefits for the unemployed and from 1980 onwards took a series of measures designed to contain these, such as the abolition of earnings-related benefit, the taxation of benefit, tighter conditions for unemployment benefit and less generous uprating than hitherto.[8] Mrs Thatcher later noted that Ministers were not only seeking to contain public spending but also trying 'to deal with the "Why work?" problem (namely, the disincentive to work created by the small disparity between in-work and out-of-work incomes)'.[9]

Early cuts in staffing and public expenditure

From the earliest days of the Thatcher government, there was a succession of exercises to cut both money and staff. For the employment service as a labour intensive organisation, the most demanding exercise was that concerned with 'reducing the size of the civil service' under which 'options' for cuts at 10 per cent, 15 per cent and 20 per cent over the next three years were required. On Prior's advice, the Commission skewed the cuts against the ESD in order to protect the Training Opportunities Programme and avoid closing skillcentres.[10]

The money cuts were achieved mainly by big cuts in the Employment Transfer Scheme (which subsidised geographical moves for jobs). The ESD lacked faith in this scheme, though it was stoutly defended by the TUC Commissioner, Ken Graham. There were also lesser cuts in the Jobcentre programme, in rehabilitation and in plans for extending CAPITAL outside London.

When the Employment Service Executive considered staff cuts, Ron Stephenson, now Deputy Chief Executive, suggested the analogy of medieval soldiers defending a castle and said that they must 'defend the keep', by which he meant the ES's capacity for 'finding and filling vacancies'. Accordingly, the Executive resolved that, if cut at the 20 per cent level:

> the essential requirement would be to continue to provide a basic vacancy finding and filling service which was appropriate to the needs of the largest number of jobseeker clients.[11]

The corollary was heavier cuts on the more specialised services, which tended to have more of a social welfare orientation, and on the administrative superstructure:

- the Occupational Guidance Service was abolished. This was an innovation of the 1960s (page 131) designed to provide careers advice to adults. It produced less tangible outputs than the general placing service and its role was difficult in a deepening recession. But the clinching argument for abolition was that resources were better deployed in giving small amounts of direct advice and placing assistance to many people than more intensive guidance to a few people;
- the Special Employment Needs service (page 186) was abolished for similar reasons;
- it was proposed that the Disablement Resettlement Service should be cut, with the general employment service handling the less seriously disabled people; this proved unacceptable to Prior and was strongly criticised by the Commons Select Committee on Employment, much to the Commission's irritation;[12] the Commission set up the Review of Assistance to Disabled People, under Jean Collingridge to resolve these issues (Chapter 11); and
- there were disproportionately large cuts on Area Offices, in order to minimise the impact on the front line.

Officials in the Department of Employment and DHSS were uneasy about this policy of abolishing in-depth help to those in employment difficulties. It was certainly a difficult policy to present and justify. But against a background of dwindling resources, the Executive probably was right to preserve maximum flexibility in responding to the growing unemployment crisis. Their policy became more defensible from 1981 onwards, when Jean Collingridge required a specific allocation of resources to the long-term unemployed (page 206).

In December 1979, it was announced that the MSC was to lose 3400 staff, of which the ESD's contribution was 2000 staff. The MSC's cuts were around 13 per cent, compared with less than 5 per cent in the civil service as a whole – a disparity which the Commission noted with some chagrin, particularly at a time when the labour market prospects were 'daunting'.

In March 1980, a further reduction of 300 staff in the ESD was required. Then, on 13 May 1980, the Prime Minister announced her intention of reducing the civil service to 630,000 by April 1984, which meant a further cut of 8 per cent in MSC staffing. Commissioners doubted whether they could discharge their responsibilities if they had to sustain so large a further cut at a time of rapidly rising unemployment. TUC Commissioners wanted a public protest, but the majority of Commissioners thought that this would alienate Jim Prior, who understood their position. It was agreed to address the further cut in the next Corporate Plan.[13] For the employment service, this further cut raised the question of whether some major change in procedure or strategy was required. This became the big debating point of 1980.

The link with benefit and the Layard Thesis

The 1979 Conservative Manifesto said that 'the rules about the unemployed accepting available jobs will be reinforced and we shall act more vigorously against fraud and abuse'. In August 1980, Jim Prior, with Richard O'Brien's consent, set up a Working Group of ED and MSC officials under Jim Lester, Parliamentary Secretary, with the following terms of reference:

> *To consider what could be done, within the existing statutory framework, to improve the liaison between the MSC and the UBS on the application of the rules about the unemployed accepting jobs which are suitable and available.*

Jean Collingridge could see the need for a shift of emphasis and in August 1979 gave instructions to her line managers to ensure that there was an increase in referrals to the benefit authorities.

Early in 1980, the Working Group reported. It was mildly critical of both the ESD – for an alleged lack of commitment to benefit control – and of the unemployment benefit service (UBS) because 'there has been a growing feeling that the UBS's prime concern is with payment of benefit rather than control of abuse'. The report focused mainly on making the existing system work more smoothly, but also urged ESD to consider experiments in systematic review in areas where there was still a high level of vacancies as well as of unemployed.

MSC officials were content with the report, though Ken Barnes, the Permanent Secretary, would have preferred a large-scale introduction of review interviews. However, even the modest proposal for experiments in 'systematic review' proved a stumbling block for the TUC. In March and April 1980, the Commission stood by the more modest shift towards tighter benefit control in the Review of the Employment Service (page 194). But it was 'highly undesirable that any impression should be given that the Commission regard unemployed people as malingerers who ought to be harried into leaving the unemployment register'.[14] The TUC ensured that the Commission did not agree to experiments in systematic review and 'dissociated itself from an essentially policing approach'.[15]

This was the beginning of a long-running tension between the Commission and the government about the role of the ES in benefit control, which would eventually contribute to the demise of the Commission. The TUC Commissioners were reflecting a profound unease among their own constituents about the tendency of the right-wing press to identify unemployment with 'malingerers' and 'scroungers'. Most other Commissioners were relatively relaxed on the subject, but were content to let the TUC make the running.

During the proceedings of the Lester Committee, a much more radical critique of the employment service had appeared, which came to be known as the Layard Thesis as it came from the fluent pen of Richard Layard of the London School of Economics. In November 1979,[16] Layard produced both a detailed paper and a popular *Guardian* article arguing that the modernisation of the employment service had contributed to the rise in unemployment. In terms of the analysis in Chapter 1, he rejected the pre-eminence of the labour market transparency model of the service established by the modernisers in the 1960s and 1970s and called for the reinstatement of the benefit control model.

Layard argued that systems of benefit administration could influence the level of unemployment. He drew on the figures in Table 10.2 (page 189) to conclude that 'many fewer people are being denied benefit on the grounds that they are workshy'. He then pointed to three features of 'Jobcentre reform':

- separation had drastically reduced communication between the job matchers and the benefit payers; these two groups had once had shared objectives, but now the job matchers aimed simply to provide employers with suitable applicants;
- self service favoured the newly unemployed as against the long-term unemployed; in 1976, two-thirds of all those who had been out of work for a year had *never* been submitted to a job;
- the employment service's use of targets emphasised volume of placings rather than placing the long-term unemployed, who, it was felt, might damage the image of the service.

Layard summed up:

> *Thus we have a service which increasingly serves the easy to place. Those who are workshy are not offered jobs and because they are not offered jobs, no sanction can be used against them; it is very difficult to force someone to help himself.*

This explained a fraction of the post-1973 rise in unemployment – 'probably small but enough for me to worry about'. He went on to argue that the number of jobs is not given:

> *If more people are forced into active jobsearch, real wages will tend to be pushed down and more jobs will thus be provided.*

His solutions were:

- to house the Jobcentre and Benefit Offices together again;
- to divert more jobs to the long-term unemployed. Where unemployment is high, leave jobs out of self-service;
- judge Jobcentres by their placings of the over-one month unemployed;
- introduce earlier systematic review interviews for those on unemployment benefit;
- reintroduce weekly signing in place of fortnightly.

In November 1979, Jean Collingridge wrote a spirited letter to the *Guardian* in reply to Layard. In June 1980 the MSC submitted a more considered response in a paper to the House of Lords Select Committee on Unemployment, which was chaired by Baroness Seear, a veteran expert in employment issues, and which included among its members Lord Carr of Hadley, who, as Robert Carr, had been the Minister responsible for employment service modernisation in 1971. The MSC argued:

- the level of referrals for refusal of suitable employment and non-availability had always been minuscule in relation to total movements on and off the register;[17] moreover, referrals were bound to decline with fewer jobs on offer;
- self service, now responsible for about half the placings, reduced the scope for referrals, but self service benefited the long-term unemployed as well as other unemployed people;
- modernisation had increased market share, so that 0.4 million more unemployed people were placed in 1978/79 than in 1975/76;
- the MSC had strengthened liaison with the benefit authorities and were alert to the need to protect National Insurance funds; and
- research showed that Jobcentres submitted and placed more long-term unemployed people than traditional employment offices and that, where unemployed people got jobs, the ES's contribution was much the same proportionally for long-term as for short-term unemployed.

The MSC rejected Layard's proposal to reunify the employment and benefit services. They saw no reason why benefit control should override all other policy considerations and pointed out that France was introducing separation. They felt that the proposal to judge Jobcentres by their placings of over one month unemployed ignored the diversity of Jobcentre services and that systematic review interviews of the unemployed were desirable in principle but costly in staff resources.

In its report produced in May 1982, the Lords Select Committee, representing as it did the pre-Thatcher establishment, sided on the whole with the MSC. They rejected Layard's proposal for the re-integration of the employment and benefit services. They were not convinced that there had been a serious falling off in vigilance to check abuse. They believed that:

> *most unemployed people want to work and many will accept virtually any job that is available. Where people are not looking for work, it is generally because they have come to believe in the inevitability of unemployment as a result of age or disability. With the ratio of jobseekers to notified vacancies standing at 28:1, the Committee considers it unlikely that malingering is contributing significantly to the level of unemployment. We believe that the employment service should be shaped by the need to assist the unemployed, not to protect the benefit system from abuse.*[18]

At the same time, the Committee expressed concern at the cuts imposed on the employment service, they recommended thorough interviews with the unemployed after six months and 12 months and they thought that Jobcentres should be 'judged on a dual scale, according to overall rate of placings and achievements with the hard-to-place'.[19] Layard's arguments had had some influence on their conclusions.

Responding to criticism of the employment service's provision for the growing numbers of long-term unemployed, Jean Collingridge decided to introduce from April 1981 onwards a long-term unemployed initiative, which continued for several years. Local offices had to devote to the long-term unemployed not less than 10 per cent of their net staff resources for the general employment service. DHSS welcomed this as ESD's 'death-bed repentance'. In 1983/84, it was claimed that this initiative was responsible for 87,700 people obtaining jobs, training or rehabilitation.[20]

The Registration requirement and the Rayner Scrutiny of the delivery of benefits

During 1980, both the MSC and the government were reviewing the requirement dating back to 1911 (page 23) for unemployed people seeking benefit to register with the employment service.

The MSC's interest arose mainly from the proposed further cut of 8 per cent in MSC staffing (page 202). There were two options:

(a) 'Voluntary registration', under which use of ES services by unemployed people would become entirely voluntary; and
(b) 'Deferred registration', under which registration with the ES would only become a condition of benefit after a month of unemployment, reflecting the fact that many unemployed people find themselves a job in the first month.

Opinions within the Employment Service Executive differed widely.[21] But in September and October 1980, in the context of the draft Corporate Plan, John Cassels and Jean Collingridge put forward proposals to the Commission for deferred registration, arguing that many existing registration interviews were a waste of time and the change could release 340–750 staff. Some Commissioners, however, were uneasy that people would stop using the Jobcentres and the matter was left unresolved.

Meanwhile, the registration issue was also being addressed by a 'scrutiny team' under Sir Derek Rayner, Managing Director of Marks and Spencer and the government's efficiency adviser. Rayner's method was to recruit young high-flying civil servants in rapid investigations designed to eliminate inefficiency and waste in central government. The team of Young Turks would report to a Permanent Secretary or other very senior official to cut through middle layers of possible obstruction. The Prime Minister and her colleagues and, of course, Sir Derek himself took a keen personal interest in progress.

In March 1980, Jim Prior and Patrick Jenkin, Secretaries of State for Employment and Health and Social Security respectively, announced a Rayner Scrutiny: 'To report on whether the organisation and methods by which unemployment benefit and supplementary benefit for unemployed people are delivered can be made more effective'. The team consisted of Ian Johnston and Leigh Lewis from the Department of Employment and Gerald Johnson from the DHSS. They had six months in which to discharge their huge remit, relating to three networks of government offices (Social Security Offices, Unemployment Benefit Offices and Jobcentres) and the work of some 40,000 staff.[22] Ministers asked the team to suggest improvements in efficiency and effectiveness in a system which had grown like Topsy. Particular concerns were the need for a claimant to visit three offices, the duplication of work and flows of paperwork between the offices and the complexity of instructions to local office staff.[23] Whether such a rushed exercise with no outside experts on social security or the labour market was the best way to tackle such massive issues is questionable. But the team was remarkably energetic and radical.

The team's report looked at the relationship between the Jobcentres and the DE's unemployment benefit offices (UBOs). Their analysis initially seemed to follow that of Richard Layard, but then diverged sharply from it:

> *A weakness in the systems which struck us lay in the application of benefit controls, by which we mean the initial checking of a claimant's availability for work and the continuing of the claimant's willingness to take suitable employment. The weakness is that the controls seem to fall into a void between UBOs and Jobcentres...in the Jobcentres we visited the controls seemed to be given a low priority by managers and staff. Given the other important objectives of Jobcentres, not related to benefit, it is not perhaps surprising that benefit objectives receive low priority there. This led us to question the involvement of Jobcentres in benefit matters at all.*[24]

They acknowledged Layard's arguments for re-integrating the employment and benefit networks but did not advocate such a solution:

> *The rationale for a state employment service and its location are outside our terms of reference – but ... if the state wishes vacancies to be notified so that they can be made available to people ... then the self service aspects of well-situated Jobcentres seem an effective and fast method of doing this. However, nothing we saw indicated that registration of all unemployed claimants was an essential part of that function, though having claimants' addresses can help some other Jobcentre activities.*
>
> *Thus one of our aims is to disengage Jobcentres from benefit matters. The route to this seems to be to make registration*

voluntary and not a condition for receiving benefit, and to absorb the control functions into the benefit administration.[25]

In support of making registration voluntary, the team argued that:

- Jobcentres were an unlikely instrument of benefit control; only 3 per cent of claimants said that the Jobcentre was putting any pressure on them to find work;
- registration was a waste of time for those not looking for work, those who already had a job to go to soon, those for whom Jobcentres did not normally carry vacancies, those who wanted to look for work in other ways and, more generally, those who were unemployed for very short periods; and
- registration was costly and making it voluntary would, in the team's view, save 2000 staff, assuming only 50 per cent would then register.

The team rejected the alternative of deferring registration for one month on the grounds that it would still involve a waste of time for many claimants, it would not provide any effective benefit control and the savings would be much less (only 600 staff).

The team also recommended that:

- responsibility for initiating availability tests be transferred away from Jobcentres to Unemployment Review Officers (UROs) and to UBOs;
- control of availability should be tightened by introducing a formal test at the initial claims stage, as in West Germany, and by expecting claimants to broaden their choice of occupations after three months of unemployment;
- Review interviews, while hard to justify on labour market or social grounds, were desirable on benefit control grounds. (The team's survey had shown that 16 per cent of claimants were not looking for work.) ESD's review interviews (half a million a year with no vacancy in prospect, absorbing about 150 staff) should cease. Review interviews should be the responsibility of UROs in both DE and DHSS, whose numbers should be enhanced from 940 to 1250 so that most claimants would be reviewed about 16 weeks after claiming.

The rest of the report mainly affected UBOs and social security offices rather than Jobcentres. However, it is worth noting two important conclusions:

- in the long term, unemployed claimants should have to deal with only one network of offices on benefit matters and that should be the DE's network of UBOs, because the DE has a wider geographical network than the DHSS; and because, for reasons of size and industrial relations, 'innovation, experiment and work measurement are harder to achieve in the DHSS';[26]
- roughly 8 per cent or more of unemployed people might be unlawfully working and claiming benefits; this needed further investigation and an

additional 750 staff to carry out special fraud drives.

The team claimed that its recommendations could ultimately save some 5000 staff and £75–80 million.

When early drafts of the report appeared, the Rayner team was supported by the DE Permanent Secretary, Ken Barnes, who felt that the employment service no longer needed compulsory registration as 'a recruiting sergeant' and would gain from being cut loose from the bureaucracy of benefit. But there were strong adverse reactions from officials in both the DHSS and the MSC. The DHSS were disturbed by the notion of making the DE's UBOs a single office network for unemployed claimants. This cut across the 'whole person' concept being developed as part of the government's social security operational strategy. The DHSS argued that many unemployed people were receiving a variety of social security benefits, and also pointed out that the 1945 'agency arrangement' (pages 100–1) under which the DE administered unemployment benefit was intended to link benefits with placement and questioned whether it was right now to remove the MSC's responsibilities altogether to the UBOs, which were not a placement service.[27]

MSC officials, as we have seen (page 206), favoured deferred rather than voluntary registration, since for many unemployed people the registration interview was valuable in offering information and advice and a basis for subsequent matching. MSC officials feared that the report could lead to Unemployment Review Officers becoming a parallel employment service. They questioned review interviews for benefit control purposes after 16 weeks: 'Why should the ordinary unemployed citizen be interviewed as a potential suspect?'[28] Above all, they deplored the proposed cut of 2000 staff. ES staffing was a source of great anxiety, with general placing staffing already due to fall to 6600 in 1984, so this further cut would amount to over 25 per cent.

The scene seemed to be set for a prolonged Whitehall dispute. Moreover, it seemed by no means clear that Ministers, and above all the Prime Minister, with her preoccupation with benefit control, would accept voluntary registration. Would she not see it as a 'scroungers' charter'? But here events took an unexpected turn. Rayner and his team gave a presentation to the Prime Minister and the two Secretaries of State, Patrick Jenkin and James Prior. Mrs Thatcher was delighted by this new radical thinking. She thought the report was 'of first class quality and great importance'[29] and asked Jenkin and Prior to produce urgently a joint programme of implementation.

An inter-departmental committee, chaired by Donald Derx of the DE and Peter Oglesby of the DHSS, drew up a draft government statement to be issued along with a public version of the report. There continued to be a good deal of disagreement, and at one point the Prime Minister offered to chair a meeting to sort out the differences – an offer which had the desired effect.

In March 1980, the government published the Rayner Report, with a preface setting out the government's response. Fifty-five of the recommendations had been accepted, 24 were being considered further and two were rejected. On the main issues, the government's view was that:

- subject to consultation with the MSC, there was 'a very strong case for abolishing the statutory requirement for unemployed adults to register for employment';
- if registration were made voluntary, then the government would also accept the recommendations on availability tests and also the proposal to have 300 additional Unemployment Review Officers; however, flows into unemployment were such as to rule out interviews of all after 16 weeks and instead UROs should focus on those whose attitude to work was suspect and those who needed special help for personal or family reasons;
- on statistics, existing plans for a benefit-based unemployment count entailed a discontinuity of some 50,000 at current levels of unemployment (2 per cent of the unemployed); voluntary registration would affect these plans, notably causing problems in producing statistics on the occupational and disablement status of the unemployed; and
- unemployed claimants should have to deal with only one benefit office and that should be the DE's UBOs.

As regards this last point, the DHSS continued to resist the idea of the DE UBO becoming the 'one office' for benefits for the unemployed and, by playing the issue long, managed to prevent this from happening. It is interesting to compare the stance of the two Departments on this organisational issue in the early 1980s with that in 1969–72 (pages 141–3 and 153). In the earlier period, the DE's priority had been employment service modernisation, in the interests of which it wanted to get rid of benefit work to the DHSS. It was only the turbulence in the DHSS offices which prevented the DHSS from taking it on, so that DE instead formed its own network of UBOs. Now the positions were reversed. Emboldened by its success in running the UBOs, the DE was making a takeover bid, with Prime Ministerial backing, to handle supplementary allowance as well as UB for the unemployed. By contrast, the DHSS now saw grave dangers to its own departmental position and to the coherence of the social security system in Rayner's ideas for locating all benefit work for the unemployed in the DE. This conflict would re-surface in the mid-1980s (Chapter 13).

Returning to voluntary registration, Prior adopted the Rayner assumption that 50 per cent would register voluntarily and proposed to O'Brien that the MSC should sustain a further staff cut of 1250 on top of the 1710 already required under the 8 per cent cuts. MSC officials felt this was still too high.

Among MSC and ESD senior officials, debates about voluntary registration continued. Some saw it as healthy in completing the divorce of Jobcentres from benefit control which separation had begun. Others saw it as socially desirable that the ESD should continue to play a role in benefit control and also felt that without any such role the organisation was extremely vulnerable to further cuts or to privatisation. John Cassels' view was that the question of compulsion was essentially for the government, which had responsibility for benefit control, rather than for the MSC, which did not. But the MSC should resist excessive cuts.

There followed a remarkably public row between the MSC and its parent Department. It may seem surprising that MSC officials went public to bring pressure on Ministers, but they saw themselves as working for an organisation that was distinct from government. As early as November 1980, the MSC had held a press lunch for influential correspondents in order indirectly to counter the pressure for cuts. On the day of the publication of the Rayner Report, MSC officials issued a press briefing critical of the report, setting the record about Jobcentres straight, as MSC saw it. Press coverage favourable to the employment service appeared in *New Society* in an article by Bill Daniel of the Policy Studies Institute on his research on the 'unemployed flow' (page 215),[30] and in the *Observer*[31] in an article by Robert Taylor which reported the concern of 'manpower officials' about the effect of the Rayner proposals on 'those least able to help themselves' and fears that the work of the Commission could be put back by a decade.

The Commissioners were split. The TUC, despite their aversion to benefit control, were against voluntary registration and believed that the government's proposals would reduce services to 'an intolerable level'. The CBI thought that voluntary registration would improve services and remove an administrative burden; staff savings were a separate issue but should be achieved where possible. Other Commissioners were unhappy about the government enhancing the policing of benefit at the expense of cuts in constructive placing efforts. John Cassels and Jean Collingridge argued that the judgement on compulsion was for the government to make. O'Brien only managed to get decisions from the Commission by splitting the policy issue from the staffing issue and getting a separate majority on each.[32]

Despite the embarrassing disunity of the Commission, O'Brien wrote a strong letter to Prior on 22 May and issued a Press Notice under the heading 'MSC says "yes" to voluntary registration and "no" to still more staff cuts'. Commenting on this 'bitter attack' on 'Thatcher's axemen', John Fryer in the *Sunday Times* said that it was unusual for the civil service to fight so viciously in public. On 23 June, Prior met the Commissioners. O'Brien said that it was 'the most difficult issue he had had to deal with in his term of office so far'. He was puzzled that the situation had arisen. Surely, the rising numbers of unemployed people had to be treated with dignity. The effects of Prior's proposal would be to push up the total cut in the ESD since 1979 from 19 per cent to 29 per cent. Jobcentres would be ill-equipped to service the increased vacancies expected by 1984 and would place 300,000 less people. Prior said that voluntary registration was right in principle and that the ESD was not demonstrably understaffed, but that he would consider the matter further with his colleagues.[33]

Rather surprisingly, Prior relented and on 30 July announced that the extra cut for voluntary registration would be 550 instead of 1250. This decision had been influenced by fears of the MSC breaking up, by Bill Daniel's view that more than 50 per cent would register voluntarily and by a DHSS decision to forgo 250 extra UROs in order to preserve staff in the ESD who could assist existing UROs. Prior had agreed his concession with ministerial colleagues.

Lord Soames, Lord President of the Council, who was responsible for civil service staffing, wondered about a further scrutiny of the employment service in the following year.[34]

Voluntary registration was introduced as one of the provisions in the 1982 Social Security Act[35] and came into effect in October 1982. The employment service's strategy was to encourage 'usage' rather than registration and early on it was found that registrations were down 60 per cent – nearer to the Rayner teams's estimate than that of the MSC – while substantive usage was down 6 per cent, but submissions were up 2 per cent. In the first full year after the change, Jobcentres had 34.5 million contacts by letter or phone or in person,[36] so that the MSC's fears of a serious falling-off of usage were not fulfilled. Ironically, voluntary registration pushed the Jobcentres closer to the UBOs because the former looked to the latter for publicity to newly unemployed people.

With the benefit of hindsight, these government decisions in 1981 are surprising. Here is the most right-wing government since the war abolishing a historic condition for unemployment benefit, opposed by the TUC. The implied message to unemployed claimants was that the state was reducing pressure for active jobsearch at the Jobcentre. Moreover, the UBOs faced inherent difficulties in benefit control as they were remote from the labour market. These decisions were reversed within a few years. But it is important to understand the context of the time. The Rayner team wanted to tighten benefit control and to challenge fraud, but felt that the Jobcentres were ill-suited to these tasks and that their reporting line to the MSC was a major obstacle to change, so what emerged was an alternative route to the same goal.

The dispute was a climactic event both for the MSC and for the ESD. It was the biggest and most public conflict the Commission had with the government and may well have stimulated the government to impose tighter control upon the Commission, notably through replacing the Chairman (page 218).

The effect on the ESD was to reinforce the labour market transparency model of the 1970s and to delay any reconciliation with government concerns about benefit control. This increased the insecurity of the ESD's position, since Ministers did not in their hearts accept the labour market transparency model and instead saw the organisation as offering easy pickings in their drive to cut the civil service. Reflecting on this situation in September 1980, John Cassels ruminated on the idea of bringing employment and benefit together under the MSC:

> *The objections seem to have much more to do with politics than with efficiency. So long as the MSC exists, it would be the obvious organisation to take on this responsibility (cf Germany, Sweden) but it is not a notion that has much current political appeal.*[37]

Ken Barnes' reaction was:

> *Organisationally, I agree that there is much to be said for the employment and benefit networks being under the same direction. For one thing, the old facility to shift the staff between the two to*

> *meet changes in workload seems to me thoroughly sensible. But I do not think that the considerations which justify Ministers in delegating to the CBI, TUC etc. a measure of responsibility for manpower services apply in the same way to benefit.*[38]

Cassels still felt that there was 'in principle a strong case' for having benefit run on an agency basis by the MSC, with benefit policy firmly retained by Ministers. Within Whitehall, there was at the time no interest in such an idea.

Computerisation and the demise of CAPITAL

Chapter 10 described how the extension of ESD's prestigious CAPITAL project in North East London to the rest of London was held up by union opposition to the staff cuts necessary to justify the investment (page 182). The unions stuck to their position after the 1979 Election. In July 1979, the Commission seriously considered abandoning the project – the CBI's preferred course – but eventually agreed to put off a decision until November.[39] Jean Collingridge launched a 'communications exercise' to outflank the unions and bid for support direct from managers and staff. Ian Marshall, the Controller of CAPITAL, and his team carried out with great gusto over 100 audiovisual presentations up and down the country, with live access to a computer terminal provided. Those who attended were impressed and this favourable reception convinced line management for the first time that it would be possible to proceed by 'executive action' (ie without union cooperation) if necessary.

At the Commission, the TUC was strongly against executive action but, under pressure from the CBI, offered their good offices to try to resolve the issue. On 21 February 1980, all three TUC Commissioners had a tough session with the civil service unions. At this point, SCPS, the managerial union, agreed to cooperate with CAPITAL, but the clerical union, CPSA, remained adamantly opposed. This enabled the TUC at last to swallow its scruples about proceeding by executive action and to join other Commissioners in a unanimous decision to proceed with the project.

The next task was to sell the project to government. There were doubts within the Department of Employment, particularly about the rather marginal balance of benefits over costs, and the MSC was warned that Prior would not be willing to take on the Treasury for CAPITAL. But the case none the less was submitted to the Treasury, who put off a decision until the autumn in view of wider public expenditure considerations.

By November 1980, ESD management was having second thoughts about this £15 million investment project, because

- voluntary or deferred registration would remove a significant part of the staff savings;
- placing performance in the pilot area had been poor and there were doubts about the benefits to be gained from computerised matching;

- line management in London doubted whether projected staff cuts would leave them enough staff time for computerised matching; and
- CPSA was still proposing industrial action to resist extension.

ESD senior management decided to recommend the replacement of CAPITAL by a new job bank project, ie to computerise the vacancy side of ESD operations only and to give up the idea of computerising the registrant file. One option was to achieve this by a major modification of CAPITAL, but this did not seem straightforward and there were attractions in a fresh start that would allow a more unified and more economical approach to computerisation throughout ESD. On balance, it was decided to go back to the drawing board.

This dramatic change of policy was agreed by the Chairman's Management Committee, with Alan Brown dissenting, and presented to the Commission on 16 December 1980. Here it caused one of the worst rows in the Commission's history. The TUC Commissioners felt badly let down, having been led earlier in the year to put their credibility on the line with the civil service unions for the sake of the project. Some other Commissioners were upset at abandoning a high profile new technology project, while others accepted that such hard decisions sometimes had to be made. Despite the heated reaction, the proposals were accepted.

CAPITAL was by no means unique as a big computer project that ran into difficulties. But there was a great sense of disillusionment at the abandonment of a project apparently of such promise, into which so much dedicated work had been invested. Very few in the able project team joined in the new Job Bank project. It was not until 1987 that a major new pilot using visual display units was introduced in Jobcentres. The UK ceased to be seen internationally as the leader in the computerisation of employment service functions, though it adopted a prudent and carefully evaluated approach. One of the ifs of history is whether a truncated version of CAPITAL would have been technically successful and whether it would have survived the further cuts to be demanded by Peter Morrison. Ironically, the full CAPITAL facilities, including the registrant file, would have been a useful instrument of benefit control when the strategy of the service changed fundamentally in the mid-1980s. But no one could anticipate this in 1980.

Among the lessons of the project were:

- there were inherent perils in very large projects with long timescales; requirements changed over time and there was a difficult obstacle course within government in getting financial approval; a modular approach stood a better chance of success and might also offer time to learn how best to use a new system;
- more needed to be done to ensure ownership of major projects of this kind by line management; and
- the ESD needed to handle industrial relations more firmly and effectively, even if it had special problems at Commission level in taking executive action.

Thanks to Norman McGlynn's work in the late 1970s (page 183), the ESD had a viable computer strategy which was independent of CAPITAL. The VACs project, combining Message Switch vacancy circulation with vacancy and placing statistics, was cheap, effective and uncontroversial, partly because it could be justified without staff savings. The first VACS system was introduced in 1979 and by 1983 had been extended to all regions. In addition, at Jean Collingridge's suggestion, a national database (NATVACS) of highly specialised vacancies was set up to facilitate geographical mobility of labour.

The Job Bank feasibility study team was set up soon after the demise of CAPITAL. The concept was of a system comprising visual display units in Jobcentres connected to a computerised job bank, enabling computer sifting of the bank to identify those jobs satisfying specified search criteria.

Conclusion

The employment service had changed a good deal in the first couple of years of the Thatcher government. By spring 1981, it had:

- nearly 2000 fewer staff;
- still about 1000 outlets;
- the Jobcentre programme still proceeding, if more cautiously;
- plans for a reduced role at the point where people become unemployed;
- a greater emphasis on the long-term unemployed; and
- a much less ambitious computerisation programme.

Placings had fallen, but this was due more to the deepening recession than to the cuts. Indeed, the service's share of a rapidly contracting recruitment market was probably still increasing quite sharply.

The research for the 1979 review had shown that the service did more for the long-term unemployed than its critics supposed. Moreover, Bill Daniel's research on a group of people who became unemployed in May 1980 led him to draw the following conclusions:

- the service had established itself as the principal method of job search for people becoming unemployed;
- 47 per cent received some job suggestions within the first six weeks of becoming unemployed;
- nearly two-thirds of jobseekers felt that the service was very good (17 per cent) or fairly good (45 per cent);
- among those back at work, 26 per cent heard of their jobs through the service; and
- new Jobcentres scored better than traditional employment offices on virtually all measures of the service.[40]

Office of Hope

While this information was encouraging, it was not going to avert further fundamental questioning by the Thatcher government. The first two years were just a beginning.

12

The Era of Peter Morrison, 1981–85

'Peter was a remarkable Minister. When he first came to the Department he rapidly became extremely unpopular with most of the officials who dealt with him in the Commission… He was very enthusiastic and a workaholic. He looked into detail in a way that few Ministers did. He called civil servants Martians, beings from another planet…Gradually, as time went by, attitudes towards him changed.' (Lord Young, Chairman of the MSC 1982–84)[1]

Introduction

During 1981, unemployment continued its inexorable rise to reach three million in January 1982. Far from being deflected from her course, Mrs Thatcher consolidated her grip on power by appointing people who shared her views to key positions. One such appointment was that of Peter Morrison as Parliamentary Secretary in the Department of Employment in March 1981. He was to remain in the Department for four-and-a-half years, an unusually long time for a Minister. During that time, he gave more concentrated attention to the employment service than any Minister before or since.

In this chapter, we trace Morrison's influence in stimulating another major review of the service. Then, after examining the service's increasing involvement in special measures to combat unemployment, we look at the attempts by a new Chief Executive, Bryan Emmett, to pursue Morrison's reform agenda.

Peter Morrison

Morrison was MP for Chester. An old Etonian, he came from a wealthy and highly political family. His father, the Earl of Margadale, had been Chairman of the 1922 Committee of Conservative MPs. His brother, Charles, was a fellow MP. His sister-in-law, Sarah, had been close to Ted Heath as Vice-Chairman of the Party. Peter Morrison was the 'driest' or most right-wing of the family and the closest to Mrs Thatcher, having helped to organise her leadership campaign. In 1990, he was to be her Parliamentary Private Secretary at the time of her fall from power.

Morrison was engagingly frank. When invited to take the job, he had been told by the Prime Minister that his mission was to 'sort out the MSC', a body of whose existence he had previously been unaware. Within the MSC, his prime target was the ESD, reflecting the lobbying of the private employment agencies and recent discussions about the Jobcentre programme in the Select Committee on Employment. He was an idiosyncratic character, a great man for nicknames. He called civil servants 'Martians', because of their curiously regimented behaviour. He was impatient with the high-minded theorising of the MSC about the labour market. For him the employment service was an example of the public waste which his Party had been elected to rectify. His instincts were not those of a strategist or conceptual thinker but rather of an aristocratic inspector. With a curious combination of charm and ruthlessness, he sought to control the affairs of the employment service. All this was regardless of the provisions of the 1973 Act, under which the Heath government had placed manpower services under a hived-off Commission, thus supposedly distancing them from direct day-to-day intervention by Ministers.

Other changes in the top team

During 1981, other key changes took place among the people at the top of the Department and the MSC. In September 1981, Mrs Thatcher carried out her major reshuffle, which shifted the overall balance in the Cabinet sharply to the right. This shift was particularly notable in the Department of Employment, where Jim Prior was replaced by Norman Tebbit. In April 1982, Tebbit appointed David Young to succeed Sir Richard O'Brien as Chairman of the MSC. Young had had a highly successful business career, had served in the influential right-wing Centre for Policy Studies, and then had become Industrial Adviser at the Department of Trade and Industry, where Tebbit had been a Minister. He approached his new job in a critical frame of mind. In his memoirs, he says that the Commission 'had evolved over the years into a Kafka-esque bureaucratic nightmare'.[2] Despite these sentiments, Young proved remarkably skilful in handling the complex politics of the Commission, including the preoccupations of the TUC. He was destined to play an even more important part than Peter Morrison in the story of the employment service.

The MSC was a curious survival from another much more consensual era. The government found it useful because of its remarkable capacity for the rapid delivery of new programmes, but was much less happy when it adopted a campaigning or policy role, as it had done over voluntary registration. No doubt Tebbit hoped that Young would ensure that the Commission focused on its delivery role.

There were also changes in the key civil servants. In 1982, Sir Kenneth Barnes, well-informed but uneasy about the modernised employment service, was succeeded as Permanent Secretary of the Department of Employment by Michael Quinlan from the Treasury.

At the MSC, in October 1981, John Cassels was replaced as Director by Geoffrey Holland, described by Lord Young as 'a most unusual civil servant'; Young saw himself and Holland as 'two hyper-active enthusiasts'.[3] Holland had worked in the employment service in the late 1960s, had been the main architect of the Youth Opportunities Programme, and in 1981 was leading the design of the Youth Training Scheme. Now that he was Director, he was keen to 'bring the service out of the cold'. At the same time, he worried about the ESD being too bureaucratic.

The challenge from the private employment agencies

Before Morrison became Minister in March 1981, a formidable campaign critical of the employment service had been launched by the Federation of Personnel Services (FPS), which represented private employment agencies, such as Reed's, Alfred Marks and Brook Street Bureau. With the help of Patrick Cormack MP, their Parliamentary consultant, they lobbied not only the Prime Minister and other Ministers but also the MSC Chairman, the Select Committee on Employment and senior ESD officials. Their thesis was that the crisis facing their industry, in which many agency branches were having to close, was due not just to the recession, but also to unfair competition from the Jobcentres. They asked why the MSC – a 'juggernaut out of control' – should use public money to open large new Jobcentres in the high street and to advertise vacancies for temporary staff.

ESD top management argued that the FPS's claims were exaggerated and failed to recognise the ESD's distinctive role in serving a mainly unemployed clientele. Morrison initially sought a rapprochement between the ESD and FPS and in October 1981 chaired a meeting between them. He accepted that the ESD had to be in the short-term engagement market, but suggested that both sides needed to think about their use of the 'temps' label to avoid confusion. It was also agreed to have experiments in the cross-referral of vacancies.[4] This was a useful advance but by no means resolved the problem.

The Rayner Scrutiny of the employment service

Soon after his arrival, Morrison suggested an enquiry into the ESD, an idea welcomed by the Prime Minister and, nearer to home, by Sir Kenneth Barnes. After some debate, it was agreed (with TUC Commissioners dissenting) that there should be a Scrutiny into the 'general employment service' (ie not the disabled services or PER), which would report to Sir Derek Rayner (and his new deputy, John Cassels) and the MSC Chairman, rather than to Ministers.

The terms of reference were to 'examine the organisation, methods of work and deployment of resources' of the service.

The Scrutiny Team was led by Bryan Winkett, former Head of Planning in the ESD (known by Morrison as the 'Headmaster') and, at Morrison's suggestion, included two business representatives – Michael Kempson from Boots and Tony Smith from Barclays Bank. The fourth member, Paul Read, represented ESD interests. The team worked very hard indeed, visiting over 100 local offices and consulting many experts, including Professor Layard.

The team faced the problem of widely differing expectations. Morrison wanted drastic cuts in staff and in the Jobcentre network and a move out of expensive high street sites and out of some occupational sectors to leave them for the private agencies.[5] Sir Derek Rayner thought the Scrutiny was about 'the essential minimum level of service to employers and jobseekers'.[6] The Treasury and the Management and Personnel Office (which had replaced the Civil Service Department after its abolition in November 1981) thought it was about the scale of service needed and the relationship between the public and private sector.[7] Jean Collingridge said that she looked for advice on how the service could contribute to labour market transparency and serve the unemployed.[8] But in reality she wanted an objective basis for resolving the tensions between Ministers and the service once and for all.

In April 1982, the team produced their report, *The General Employment Service in Great Britain* – a remarkably thorough and detailed document, quite different in character from the more strategic reports of 1969, 1971 and 1979. It sought to answer conscientiously every question put to it. Its overall effect was one of damage limitation. To Ministers, it offered cuts of around 600 posts and around £11 million, amounting to 8 per cent of resources. But these were achieved through numerous detailed proposals, none of which should undermine the modernised service.

Ministers – and the private agencies – had wanted to reduce the market share of the service. The report said that modernisation had pushed up the market share from about 16 per cent in 1973 (20 per cent for manual occupations and 6 per cent for non-manual) to about 23.5 per cent in 1982 (30 per cent for manual and 15 per cent for non-manual).[9] On the economic value of the service, the report commented as follows:

> *The service involves a net cost to the exchequer. Its quantified economic benefit depends on the assumptions used – which are very uncertain. However, it seems probable that the service overall confers economic benefits at least equal to its cost. However, in so far as a marginal change in the service's share of the engagement market might be at the expense, or in favour of, informal mechanisms, some reduction in it would be likely to benefit the economy. However, it is important that the service should not enter into a spiral of declining usage, otherwise the loss of benefits would probably outweigh the costs forgone.*[10]

The argument seemed to be that 'informal mechanisms' (getting a job through direct contacts with employers) were cheap and, at least in a recession, quick, so that a modest switch away from Jobcentres into informal mechanisms would be beneficial. However, the report acknowledged that there might also be 'some loss of efficiency',[11] as informal mechanisms often do not find the best qualified person available; nor do they ensure equal opportunities.

The report poured some cold water on the speed of vacancy filling arguments on which the MSC had heavily relied to justify the service. In a recent survey of employers, the great majority of employers had said that it would not have mattered to them if a new recruit had started work a week later.[12] Employers could often adjust overtime or make temporary improvements in efficiency or intensity of work or draw down stocks, without a serious effect on production. On the other hand, increased speed of vacancy filling *did* benefit exchequer finances, because it reduced benefit payments and increased receipts from taxation. The service also offered the advantage of avoiding labour turnover, because it was much more likely than other market mechanisms to favour the unemployed, and so avoid a costly chain of vacancies and engagements.

The main conclusions of the Scrutiny were:

- fee charging to employers was rejected as it would adversely affect the balance of ESD activity;
- the minimum level of service was: receipt of orders, selective circulation, order-based matching, registration of those jobseekers for whom this would be useful, giving minimal advice and recruiting for other labour market programmes;
- the desirable level of service involved in addition particular help to the long-term unemployed and a higher level of usage and registration by jobseekers; this could be achieved with 360 fewer staff than were planned for 1984;
- less marketing should be carried out;
- the number of job libraries should not exceed 37;
- the ESD had contributed to the halving of the private agencies' share of the market over the last five years; the ESD had to stay in the short-term engagement market, but it should stop using the term 'temps' and should cease separate marketing of 'temps' services;
- voluntary registration would increase the importance of close cooperation with the unemployment benefit service; the UBS would advertise Jobcentre services and should also display vacancies and provide Jobcentres with lists of those unemployed more than, say, six months;
- the ESD should not run 'nursebanks';
- premises modernisation should continue, but use of expensive ground floor accommodation should be restricted; in rural areas Jobcentres should be co-located with the UBO, DHSS etc, where possible; 42 high cost/low performance offices and 125 small rural offices should be reviewed but there should not be a major closure programme of rural and small town offices;

- the 'executive content' of placing related work (ie the proportion of work done by the executive officers as opposed to clerical officers) should be brought down from 46 per cent to 30 per cent by October 1984;
- the number of Districts should come down from 100 to 60–65;
- the number of Areas should come down from 14 to nine to conform with training regions and in three or four years there should be a review to see if there should be full integration of MSC services at regional level.

The Employment Service Executive was relieved by the damage limitation approach but was concerned about the questioning of the economic case and the cuts proposed to achieve the 'desirable level of service'. Line managers did not like the cuts in senior management posts. The proposed cut in executive content provoked a powerful letter from Dorothy Kent, one of the architects of modernisation, now retired. She recalled employers' criticisms of the 'ignorance and inefficiency of the staff' before modernisation. In those days, 'the Department abounded with the stories of the appalling service received by any friends and acquaintances who were so ill-advised as to call in at an exchange for employment help'. In overseas employment services, interviewing the public and dealing with employers were regarded as executive functions. The proposal was 'very understandable but disastrous'. Despite this formidable onslaught, the ES Executive held a grading review which confirmed the Rayner recommendation, and executive content was lowered considerably.

Morrison was disappointed – apparently 'hopping mad' – with the report which, for him, did not go far enough. He had been hoping for drastic cuts in the Jobcentres. So, for him, the Rayner savings were 'only a start'. Clearly, Jean Collingridge's hope that the Scrutiny might get Ministers off the ESD's back was not to be fulfilled. At the same time, Tebbit declared that the MSC's speed of vacancy filling arguments were a 'load of nonsense'. He was looking for the full £11 million savings.[13]

The Federation of Personnel Services shared Morrison's disappointment: the report 'fell far short of the radical proposals now needed'.[14] Fundamentally, they sought not a continuation of the competition between the private and public services but the carving out of 'spheres of influence' in which the public service would focus on the unskilled and semi-skilled unemployed, leaving the skilled, managerial and professional sectors to the private agencies. But the Rayner team had refused to push the employment service back into the declining unskilled and semi-skilled sector, since this would not have provided the service which its overwhelmingly unemployed clientele needed. Moreover, the coverage of the private agencies was extremely patchy, with a strong presence in the great cities but less elsewhere.

Sir Derek Rayner himself commented on the report. He was sceptical about the employment service's use of 'business jargon', since it was 'not a 'business' in the commercial sense, '...we are here dealing with a government agency staffed by civil servants and operating by the rules of Whitehall, not those of the market place'. He noted that the ESD suffered from such common Whitehall defects as 'lack of cost-consciousness and responsiveness'. None the less, 'Some of ESD's "business approach" is not to be despised. The emphasis on providing good service for "clients" whether jobseekers or employers is what the general taxpayer is entitled to expect.' He drew on his retailing experience to urge a greater use of part-timers to meet times of peak demand without overstaffing at other times.[15] This was a useful practical insight, as Jobcentres face peaks and troughs of jobseeker demand at different times in the day and on different days in the week. One of the consequences of this Scrutiny was a far greater usage of part-timers ever afterwards, contributing incidentally to a historic shift towards a predominantly female workforce.

In July 1982, the Commission, with the TUC and Roy Thwaites (Association of Metropolitan Authorities) dissenting on the major issues, accepted the Rayner package, though also agreeing that the service needed sufficient resources for a 'decent service to jobseekers' and enough engagements to contribute to the operation of the labour market and to help the disadvantaged.[16] At the same meeting, the Commission approved the recommendation of the Review of Assistance to Disabled People (RADP) that much assistance to disabled people could in future come from the general service. However, this review concluded that the staff saving of 170 in disabled work envisaged in the 1981 Corporate Plan could not be met without undue risk to the level of service. The reality was that such a cut was politically unacceptable to Ministers. Young persuaded Ministers to treat these new Rayner cuts as offsetting those originally sought from disabled services. The RADP also led to the setting up of District teams to encourage employers both to recruit disabled jobseekers and to retain disabled people already in their organisations.

Arguments between Morrison and the ESD about the follow-up of the Rayner Report took months to resolve. But the main changes were carried through. For example, by October 1993 the number of Areas had been reduced to nine (renamed 'Regions' to conform with the Training Regions) and the number of Districts (renamed 'Areas') brought down to 69. Savings of £860,000 on 'high cost offices' had been implemented. From the first review of rural and small town offices, the Commission agreed, after considerable debate, in July 1983 to close nine offices and reduce the opening hours of 11 offices.

Jean Collingridge retired in September 1982 after three turbulent years as Chief Executive. As a result of Ministerial pressures and cuts, the service had changed a great deal under her leadership. She had preserved the fundamentals of the modernised service, but she had not been able to persuade Ministers that it was time for that elusive 'period of stability'.

The Community Programme

Unemployment reached three million in January 1982, with the number of those unemployed for more than a year reaching 865,000 in February 1982. The unemployment crisis increased the tensions between the Commission and the government. The Commission wanted to expand to 60,000 places the Community Enterprise Programme (CEP – the adult job creation programme which was now administered by the employment service). But the government decided to restrict it to 30,000 places. In January 1982, the TUC Commissioners wanted the Commission to declare that they were 'appalled at the lack of government response' to the high level of unemployment.[17] This was rejected as too political. But the whole Commission shared the concern, including the CBI which had set up a high powered committee on unemployment. The Commission agreed that the ESD should carry out a study of long-term unemployment but, in view of government sensitivities, David Young persuaded the Commission to publish it as a low key 'Occasional Paper' in the Summer.[18] Meanwhile, the government and the Commission had become engaged in a tense discussion about a massive new programme for the long-term unemployed.

In March 1982, Sir Geoffrey Howe, the Chancellor of the Exchequer, announced in his Budget that £150 million would be available to the MSC for 100,000 places in local community projects, in which participants would receive their benefit plus £15 per week. Ministers did *not* want this money to go to CEP, as they considered that CEP wages, based on 'rate for the job', were too high. Economists advising the government, such as Professor Alan Walters and Professor Patrick Minford, were arguing that rising unemployment was linked with a lack of flexibility in wages. Ministers therefore believed that this new programme for the long-term unemployed could serve a dual purpose – it would both provide useful work for the unemployed *and* exert a beneficial downward pressure on wages.

There followed three months of intense negotiations in which Young, Holland and senior employment service officials sought to find a *modus vivendi* between on the one hand Howe and Tebbit and their officials and on the other hand the TUC, the local authorities and the voluntary sector. The local authorities, particularly the Labour-dominated Association of Metropolitan Authorities (AMA), were of key importance, as experience suggested that they were likely to provide many of the programme places, but they, like the TUC, favoured 'the rate for the job'. All sorts of devices were considered, but each of these was rejected by one side or the other. Tebbit took a tough line. He told Young that the MSC did not exist in its own right or have a life of its own. It existed during Her Majesty's pleasure, which would continue so long as it carried out the government's will. Various adjustments could be made, but expanding CEP was outside the rules of play.

After a couple of months of frustrating impasse, Young had a brainwave. What about *part-time CEP*, which would combine the tight unit cost constraints imposed by government with retaining much of CEP as desired by the TUC and the AMA? He managed to sell this to Howe and Tebbit. However, at the June Commission, Young was dismayed to find that Roy Thwaites for the AMA was unwilling to accept two-and-a-half days a week part-time work. Young and Jeremy Surr of the ESD then met the AMA at Sheffield Town Hall. Young recalls that:

David Blunkett, now a prominent Labour MP, suddenly suggested that we should offer the rate for the job for the number of hours worked. I jumped at this and quickly sketched out a scheme which would continue to have as many full-time places as the existing Community Enterprise Programme and allow a large number of places to be made up of part-time jobs paying the appropriate hourly rate.[19]

Young cleared this latest variant successfully with Tebbit. Then it was found that the National Council of Voluntary Organisations (NCVO) was unhappy. At a meeting of some 50 representatives chaired by the Council's President, Peter Jay, on 19 July, there was a majority of voices for non-cooperation on the grounds that the new proposals offered low pay and too much change and complex administration. On 27 July, the Commission approved Young's deal with the AMA, subject to the TUC clearing it with appropriate unions, which they succeeded in doing. Despite threats of an NCVO boycott, the voluntary sector overcame their reservations and supplied about half the places under the new programme, which Young entitled the Community Programme (CP).

This was a classic example of the way in which the MSC manoeuvred between government and outside organisations; it would be recognisable to those in other countries which operate a consensual model, such as Sweden, Austria and Eire. Such a process is frustrating to those who believe that they know the answers and simply want to impose a quick decision. But the success of programmes often depends on gaining the commitment of interested parties and agencies and on building into the programme design the features which they from their experience see as necessary.

People in the employment service took on their new task of running CP with great zest. They were delighted to have something new and positive to run and to have opportunities to offer to the constantly increasing number of long-term unemployed. The central team was led by Jeremy Surr, who with David Main, Tony Potter and others went to enormous efforts to launch the new Programme in October 1982 and to achieve the expansion, with the help of an advertising campaign by Saatchi and Saatchi. They had started with 30,000 filled places inherited from CEP, and their task was to build up to 130,000 by April 1984. The objective was to provide temporary employment of community benefit for unemployed people over 18. The target groups were those aged 18 to 24 and unemployed for six of the last nine months, and those over 25 unemployed for 12 of the last 15 months. In practice, because of the predominance of part-time work (84 per cent by 1986) and relatively low pay (an average wage of £60, rising to £63 in October 1985), the Programme was attractive mainly to younger single people. The over-25s comprised 45 per cent initially, falling to 34 per cent by 1985, as the real value of the average wage fell with inflation.

The Programme was delivered through a large number of managing agents, who might be national bodies such as NACRO (the National Association for the Care and Resettlement of Offenders) or local bodies, including local authorities. In order to avoid substitution and displacement, they were required to provide work of community value which would not otherwise be done over the next two years. The work done was extraordinarily diverse, including environmental, construction, social service, health, educational and even artistic and theatrical projects.

Ironically, ESD was so successful in marketing the Community Programme that late in 1983 it had temporarily to rein in the expansion to avoid an overshoot on the target of 130,000 places by April 1984 and an overspend on the available expenditure. Later, more money was provided, but there was also an enquiry into how the overrun had occurred and into the systems of financial control. But Ministers evidently regarded CP as a success, as they expanded the Programme in the 1985 and 1986 Budgets, and the Programme peaked at nearly 250,000 places in the spring of 1987 – at the time of the General Election.

The most uncomfortable element in CP was the funding of TUC Centres for the Unemployed, which also illustrates the curiously ambiguous role of the MSC at this time. In January 1981, Jim Prior had reluctantly agreed to fund posts in these centres under CEP, provided that they were jointly managed by unions and local authorities and that political activities were banned. Tebbit and Morrison, inheriting this situation, were deeply suspicious of these Centres, particularly when they received information from Conservative activists suggesting that the Centres were hotbeds of anti-government propaganda. MSC officials steered an uneasy course between the pressures from Ministers and the TUC Commissioners. When the TUC held a Day of Action on 22 September 1982, it was found that 30 out of 80 funded Centres were mysteriously closed. In certain cases, such as Sheffield, funding was withdrawn. Negotiations with the TUC to ensure tighter control of political activities reached an impasse and in March 1983 the MSC imposed a moratorium on new Centres, but funding for existing Centres continued until the demise of CP in the late 1980s.[20]

In 1986, the Department of Employment completed an evaluation of the Community Programme, known as the 'Normington Report', after its principal author, David Normington. It found that 27 per cent of participants went straight from CP into a job, training or further education, and 48 per cent had had one or more jobs between leaving CP and the follow-up survey. The evaluation found weaknesses in some projects, 'reinforcing the lack of skills of participants' and tolerating too low a pace of work. It also found a failure to monitor projects rigorously enough to ensure value. The evaluation recognised that the Programme had fulfilled its primary aim of providing temporary employment but endorsed the call from Tom King, Secretary of State from October 1983, for greater concentration now on the 'secondary objectives' of improving employment prospects of participants and getting maximum community benefit.[21]

Looking back, CP remains a remarkable achievement. The MSC turned a highly controversial government proposal into a practical and acceptable programme. The employment service managed the delivery with great energy and drive. Many hundreds of thousands of people benefited from the Programme, at a time when the numbers of long-term unemployed were continuing to rise (to 1.2 million by April 1984). It was the biggest special employment programme ever launched by a British government until Labour's New Deal came in 1998.

The Enterprise Allowance Scheme

This was another highly innovative programme which the employment service pioneered in this period. It originated from complaints about the withdrawal of social security benefits if unemployed people tried to set up their own businesses. Jim Prior asked the Commission to pilot an 'enterprise allowance' scheme to provide support while people established their business. In June 1981, Commissioners turned this down as an unpromising idea – reflecting the TUC's suspicion of self-employment.[22] But Prior pressed for further consideration and Jean Collingridge bid strongly to run such a scheme. In September 1981, the Commission agreed, with the TUC dissenting, to a 'qualified experiment'.[23]

The task of devising the scheme fell to Roger Lasko in the ESD, and he made it as simple as possible. Anyone who had been out of work for 13 weeks and whose new business met some very broad criteria, including available capital of £1000, could receive £40 per week for 12 months. The pilots were very successful and the scheme was introduced on a national basis in August 1983. By March 1988, 94,000 were receiving the allowance and over 320,000 people had been through the scheme. The criteria were so broad that some strange businesses received state support and led the *Daily Mail* to describe the MSC as the 'ministry of Silly Jobs'. There was also inevitably some deadweight: one-third would have set up at the same time without EAS, but it was found that 63 per cent were still self employed two years after leaving EAS,[24] which is impressive, given the high mortality rate of new small businesses.[25]

Bryan Emmett

In November 1982, Bryan Emmett, aged 41, took over as Chief Executive. He was to prove very different from his three predecessors. He had started work as a clerical officer in Wimbledon employment exchange. He had been promoted to Assistant Principal in the Department of Energy, where he had been Private Secretary both to Thomas Balogh and to Tony Benn, before becoming Principal Establishments and Finance Officer. He and his wife moved up to live near Sheffield, where they acquired not only a house but also a field for their two horses. He was an engaging and flamboyant character.

As a perceptive newcomer, he could see perhaps more clearly than the old MSC hands around him how fictitious the position of the Commission was becoming under such strong interventionist Ministers as Tebbit and Morrison.

Office of Hope

His instinct was to find out what Ministers wanted and seek to deliver it. Indeed, he seemed to work more closely to Morrison than to his official boss, Geoffrey Holland. Unlike his predecessors, he did not feel the need to 'defend' the service. Early on, he told Area Managers that, if Ministers said that they wanted to abolish the ESD, he would say: 'This year, next year or in five years, Minister?' Impatient of the Executive Committee that had hitherto been the key decision-making body in the ESD, he replaced it by a more flexible 'Group of Six', making it clear that he would outvote his five senior colleagues whenever he wished. He made it clear that his decisions would be governed by 'the three Es' – 'economy, efficiency and effectiveness', together with what Ministers wanted, rather than on MSC concepts such as 'transparency of the labour market'.

In his first week in his new post, he recommended to Morrison the abolition of the Job Bank project, which Jean Collingridge had pushed strongly following the abandonment of CAPITAL (pages 213–5). Emmett knew that Ministers were uneasy about Job Bank as a project justified in part by what they saw as dubious arguments about speed of vacancy filling. Morrison gratefully agreed to abandonment, leaving Emmett's MSC colleagues resentful of the lack of consultation with them. Job Bank was replaced by the Supervacs Project, which enhanced the existing VACS system with VDUs and additional functionality, but did not enable the vacancy database to be searched for matching purposes. This jobsearch facility, increasingly common in overseas employment services, was going to have to wait until the early 1990s. Supervacs was justified entirely by saving some 450 staff. In favour of Emmett's approach, he now had wholehearted Ministerial backing for a major project which could therefore be seen through to its completion. Like other large government projects in this era, its implementation took many years: the first live pilot in a 'vanguard region' began in 1987/88 and nationwide coverage was not achieved until 1991.

Emmett also secured Morrison's support for a smaller pilot of the jobsearcher system, under which a terminal was placed in a supermarket or even in the high street and passers-by could interrogate this to find out about local vacancies. Though an attractive idea, which later was introduced on a large scale in the German employment service, this particular pilot did not lead into any widespread implementation.

Bearing in mind Morrison's views, Emmett pulled back on key strategic objectives. He deleted any reference to 'maintaining market share' from the MSC's 1983 Corporate Plan. In the 1983 COMIS exercise (an elaborate review of all MSC programmes in response to the government's Financial Management Initiative), he cast doubt on the concept of 'finding and filling vacancies' which was still the Ark of the Covenant to many middle managers. He argued that the emphasis on volumes encouraged cheap, easy placings which were often of poor quality – 'strawberry-pickers' were a favourite example of his. Instead, he said the service should aim at 'quality placings'. But this healthy questioning did not lead to a new long-term approach to performance management apart from the separate identification of placings lasting less than five days. Following a complaint from Edward du Cann MP, he also discouraged Jobcentres from writing to registrants to check if they were still seeking a job. As a result, Jobcentres ceased to hold large numbers of registration documents. He introduced a new bidding system as a basis for the distribution of staff resources, which led to some useful reallocation of resources from North to South.

In July 1983, in response to Ministers' wishes, he ran a pilot of Saturday opening of Jobcentres. It did not produce much in the way of results, but it was not easy to establish whether that was due to civil service union picketing, lack of middle management enthusiasm or the practical problem that most employers were not available on Saturdays to take submissions on the phone. He also ran an experiment in the open display of vacancies – an idea which had been around since the introduction of self service (page 133) and which Rayner had recommended. This did not produce sufficiently positive results to be replicated. Employers wanted more, rather than less, screening, while jobseekers often sought help from staff.

'The Development of the Employment Service'

Emmett's highest priority was to prepare proposals for radical change in the service for Tebbit and Morrison. In his first few months, he produced for them a confidential 'Report' which proposed limiting the service's main outlets to some 230 and franchising the remaining outlets to the private sector. Though Emmett probably did not realise it at the time, there were historical precedents for this in the early history of the employment service. Chapters 2 and 4 showed how in the early days of the service there were around 1000 local agencies (later Branch Employment Offices) run by 'local agents' (solicitors, accountants etc) running alongside around 400 exchanges manned by civil servants (pages 21 and 52). Subsequently the balance in the network shifted towards far more exchanges and far fewer agencies, but as late as 1956 28 local agencies still survived.[26] Anyway, in 1983, this franchising proposal became linked with the precondition of moving the employment service (now known as the 'Employment Department' (ED) of MSC) back into the Department of Employment. In the event, these ideas were overtaken by the June 1983 Election, which the Conservatives won resoundingly.

Just before the Election, Morrison said his final farewells to the MSC. But after the Conservative triumph, to everybody's surprise, including his own, he was back, now promoted to Minister of State. Within a few days, he travelled to Sheffield and addressed all senior staff in the MSC. He noted that 'last week ...the trendy *Guardian* readers who do nothing but pontificate were laid to rest'. The electorate had decided 'that we should continue with a market economy'. He promised that he would 'continue to take a very close interest in every detail of the MSC's work'. Credit would go to any official who came up with sound practical ideas for cutting waste. It was not the job of officials to come up with ideas for spending more of the taxpayer's money. Far from being the 'greatest sceptic about the MSC', he was in fact their 'greatest ally'. He believed in the need for a public employment service; it must be cost effective and the development of information technology made it necessary to think how best the service could be delivered.[27]

After the Election, Tebbit also returned to the Department of Employment for a few more months before handing over to Tom King in October 1983. Clandestine discussions were resumed about ideas for big changes in the employment service and shifting it back to the DE, alongside an even bigger debate about the future of education. As is clear from his autobiography, David Young's real passion was to reform the educational system.[28] Already, as a first massive MSC venture into education territory, he had launched the Technical and Vocational Educational Initiative (TVEI). Now he was seeking a much bigger transfer of vocational education to the MSC, or to a new national training authority.

The two issues about education and about the employment service were curiously intertwined. One argument was that the bigger the transfer of educational funding to a new-style MSC, the stronger the case for transferring the employment service to the DE, to avoid too much concentration of power in an already massive quango. Morrison was attracted by the idea gaining hold of direct control of the employment service by removing it from the Commission. Senior Commission officials on the other hand were worried that this might lead not only to unacceptable changes to the employment service, but also to a TUC walk-out and the unravelling of the Commission itself, and its key programmes like YTS and CP. It might even be worth some sacrifice to prevent this from happening. The Whitehall advice to Ministers was to avoid battles on too many fronts at once. The idea of returning the employment service to the Department in 1983/84 does not seem to have been driven primarily by Layard-type arguments about benefit control, though Morrison may have seen the scope for economy in some reintegration with the benefit service.

This is not the place to attempt a definitive account of the way in which these issues were resolved. There is a clue in Tebbit's autobiography, where he says: 'David Young and I worked well together, although I had to be firm over his ambitious and expensive plans vastly to increase the size of the MSC'.[29] In the early months of 1984, Ministers' decisions began to emerge:

- in January 1984, it was announced in the White Paper 'Training for Jobs' that the MSC would be given some £200 million per annum, about a quarter of the annual spend on non-advanced further education;
- the idea of shifting the employment service back into the DE was quietly dropped, at least for the time being; and
- Bryan Emmett's 'Development Plan' suddenly hit the headlines on 5 April 1984.

'The Development of the Employment Service' (called here the Development Plan) was a major reworking of 'the Report' produced 12 months earlier. It was less radical in that it did not explicitly propose the franchising of part of the service (though it would make such an option easier to carry out later if desired). To put it very briefly, it laid great emphasis on the contribution of technology and proposed reorganising the present network of roughly 1000 Jobcentres into:

- 350 full Jobcentres
- 350 self service outlets, and
- 400–500 information outlets in post offices, supermarkets and other premises.

This part of the Plan would save 800 staff, Supervacs would save 450 staff and the Plan as a whole would save 1400 staff.

Before the proposals became public, there was much anguished discussion within Emmett's Group of six and at the Chairman's Management Committee at a meeting in late February 1984. The Plan was criticised as having a misleading title, as a doomed effort to popularise a cuts package and as lacking any sense of strategy, any analysis of the market or any discussion of the effect of the reduction in service, particularly the elimination of advisory interviews in two-thirds of the network. The Plan had few friends within MSC, but by late February Emmett had already successfully cleared it with Morrison and King.

On 4 April 1984, Emmett met the trade union side in Sheffield to explain the Plan to them. The unions were shocked by the news. They then seized the initiative with remarkable skill, creating a public relations coup for themselves and an acute public relations problem for the Commission. While Emmett was in a train going to London for his press briefing, the unions told the BBC and other media that two-thirds of the Jobcentres were to be closed. This became the first item on numerous BBC bulletins and headline news the next day. The unions had played down the fact that formally these were *proposals* due to go the Commission at its next meeting and that, under the proposals, self service and information would still be available in at least as many locations as present. But the Plan had been drawn up in a way which invited this kind of distortion.

In the storm which followed, Emmett was in an isolated position. Top management in the Commission kept their heads down on the grounds that the Commission had not yet discussed these proposals. Morrison had been worried when the news broke, but then relieved that it was out in the open. He was willing to intervene in public, but was advised not to do so, as formally these were matters for the Commission. So it was Emmett who appeared on 'Newsnight' to defend the proposals against an attack from John Smith, Shadow Employment Minister – an awkward position for a civil servant.

Emmett did a tour of the Regions and presented his Plan to groups of managers. The sessions were adversarial in tone, with managers asking aggressive questions and receiving sharp replies from Emmett. In one Region, the managers maintained a sullen silence and refused to ask any questions. In another, the Regional Manager flatly refused to lead a press conference on the Plan. In a third Region, no sooner had Emmett left the managers' meeting than union representatives were welcomed in to join managers in criticism of the Plan. There was general dismay among managers at the way in which the announcement had been made and suspicion of the role of senior management. Meanwhile, union propaganda was targeting Emmett personally, with the CPSA headlining their circular 'Emmett Armageddon' and trying to organise strikes wherever the Chief Executive went. It did not help that this was a time of civil service union indignation about the banning of unions at GCHQ.

The next problem was how to handle the Commission discussion on 26 April 1984 in such a way as to avert a walk-out by the TUC, which might bring the Commission's existence to an end. Unfortunately, in addition to the 'Development Plan' there were two other divisive issues – the switch of further education funding and the abolition of Graham Reid's post as Director of Manpower Intelligence and Planning – which marked the end of the Commission's role as an independent commentator on the labour market. In the event, the debate on the Development Plan went better than had been feared. The CBI supported it. The TUC were very critical of the way the announcement had been made but were prepared to tolerate extensive consultation on the proposals and pilots of the proposed information points. It was uncomfortable that the most detailed critique came from Wilson Longden, the education Commissioner who occupied the pivotal position on the Commission between left and right. On this occasion, Longden remarked that the employment service's much-vaunted computers had advised him to become a sewing machinist, which caused general hilarity and lightened the atmosphere. As happened many times with the Commission, a dangerous corner was negotiated without the vehicle going off the road.

The Development Plan, which had been conceived in such secrecy, was now the subject of a remarkably open and widespread consultative process. Regional Employment Managers drew up network plans on the basis of the three categories of outlet in the Plan and discussed them with Area Manpower Boards, local authorities, unions and employers. 3000 organisations and individuals commented and there was extensive criticism of the proposed staff cuts and the loss of service in certain offices.

In November 1984, Emmett came back to the Commission with a radically revised Development Plan. There would now be 1065 Jobcentre outlets altogether (compared with a current figure of 991). Whereas the original Plan had envisaged only 350 main Jobcentres with the full range of services, there would now be 530 of these. The three distinct categories of outlet were dropped. Instead, in the remaining 535 outlets, the range and level of service would be 'determined flexibly to suit local circumstances'. Where individuals had to travel more than three miles to get help from a specialised service, their fares would be paid. The staff savings arising from these changes were reduced from 800 to 530. Implementation would take three years.

Presiding over this discussion was a new MSC Chairman, Bryan Nicholson, from Rank Xerox. He was very managerial in style, more interested in efficiency than Young. Despite the degree of movement since April, the new Chairman found after two-and-a-half hours discussion that the revised Plan did not command a majority. Again, the CBI were in favour, and the TUC vehemently against. The 'third world' of education and local government was split. A decision was deferred to the December meeting at which the revised Plan went through with the TUC dissenting.

Emmett returned to the Department of Energy a few months later and was succeeded in May 1985 by Steve Loveman, a former management trainee in the Department of Employment who had worked in the MSC for most of his career, most recently in the troubled Skills Training Agency. He had a steadying influence on a service in which middle management remained unsettled.

Conclusion

It is strange that the history of the employment service between 1979 and 1985 should have been so dominated by issues of resources and efficiency. One might have expected the dominant theme to have been how best the employment service might use its resources to respond to the alarming rise in unemployment to three million by 1982 and its subsequent stubbornness in remaining at this level. The resources absorbed by the employment service were not vast – around £128 million in 1978–79 – and the government soon found itself spending much more than this on special measures to alleviate unemployment.

This criticism, however, ignores the dynamics of Thatcherism. Thatcherism was all about challenging examples of apparently unnecessary and ostentatious state expenditure and refusing to be deflected by difficulties along the way, such as the extent of unemployment or the legal position of the MSC. This chapter has shown how increasing pressure was placed on the MSC to secure cuts in the employment service, culminating in the Development Plan of April 1984. This was the high water mark of the cuts strategy and it was instructive, since it showed that Ministers had under-estimated the public concern that might be generated by cuts in Jobcentre services. There followed an orderly retreat to a reduced cuts package similar to its many predecessors.

Another factor was the personality of Peter Morrison. He lacked a strategic sense and in his four-and-a-half years in the Department seems to have reflected little on the unemployment problem, but instead saw his mission as improving the efficiency of the MSC. Indeed, some felt he was behaving like the managing director of the MSC. The MSC fought a rearguard action, partly driven by the TUC Commissioners. Indeed, the constraining factor in the whole situation was a reluctance to provoke a TUC walkout which would precipitate the demise of the MSC. Logic might well have suggested the abolition of the MSC from about 1982 onwards, since detailed ministerial intervention was undermining the whole rationale for hiving off. But Ministers and DE officials on balance wanted to retain the MSC because of its ability to deliver large programmes. Indeed, Morrison gradually mellowed towards the MSC. In July 1984, Alan Clark, Parliamentary Secretary at the Department, noted in his diary that 'when Peter goes to Sheffield they treat him like the great Panjandrum and he falls for it'.[30] In August 1985, Morrison arranged a party at which the Prime Minister could meet senior MSC officials.

Morrison's pressure for cuts presented an awkward conundrum for the civil servants in charge of the employment service. It is interesting to compare the responses of the two Chief Executives of this period – Jean Collingridge and Bryan Emmett. Collingridge recognised the ultimate authority of Ministers, but believed that under the 1973 Act she was the servant of the Commission. In making the required economies, she sought to preserve the gains made as a result of modernisation. Moreover, as a leading personnel management practitioner, she was sensitive to the position of the staff. All this made for a prickly and difficult relationship with Morrison. Emmett, on the other hand, felt that his loyalty was to Ministers who had a popular mandate, strengthened in June 1983. His job as a civil servant was to carry out their wishes, not to preserve institutions which had been created by previous Ministers and civil servants with a different philosophy. He certainly was not going to be held back by out of date concepts from the modernisers of the 1970s, however attached his managers and staff might be to these ideas. Nor would he be constrained by sentimentality about the position of staff in the organisation, though he would go through any hoops with the Commission, the unions and others that were necessary to achieve an outcome satisfactory to Ministers. This made for a close and harmonious relationship with Morrison but a much more difficult relationship with MSC colleagues and with his own managers and staff.

Under both Collingridge and Emmett, the *mission* of the service remained essentially concerned with labour market transparency – filling employers' vacancies as quickly as possible and assisting jobseekers with highly accessible information. At the same time, there were important changes in priorities. Whereas the 1979 Cassels Report had envisaged further increases in market share, by 1982, this had been toned down to maintaining market share[31] and by 1984, Emmett and Morrison had removed any reference to market share from the Corporate Plan.[32] Moreover, from 1982 onwards, there was more emphasis on helping the long-term unemployed but only some 250 staff were deliberately earmarked for this; a bigger contribution was made when the Community Programme was launched in October 1983.

So long as the *raison d'être* of the service was labour market transparency, the cuts would continue, since government philosophy cast doubt on the need for state intervention in the working of the labour market. Arguments on the basis of 'market failure' carried some weight in relation to training, where disturbing international comparisons could be made, but not in relation to recruitment. The decline in total staffing in the employment service is shown in the following table:

Table 12.1 *Number of staff in the Employment Service Division/ Employment Division of MSC, 1979–85*

	1/4/79	1/4/81	1/4/83	1/4/85
ESD/ED staffing	15,245	13,368	11,753	10,726

The broad picture is of a cut of one-third compared with a cut of 12 per cent in the non-industrial civil service in this period. Critics would argue that there was a lot of waste to remove. There was undoubtedly some, particularly in the superstructure above the local offices. But it was a formidable achievement by managers at all levels to carry out such a large rundown while maintaining the essential features of the service to a clientele swelled by the highest unemployment since the early 1930s.

The level of vacancies and placings did not fall away to the extent that might have been expected:

Table 12.2 *Employment service in Great Britain; unemployment, vacancies and placings, 1977/78–1984/85*

	1977/78	1978/79	1979/80	1980/81	1981/82	1982/83	1983/84	1984/85
Unemployment (000s) October	1518	1429	1368	2063	2989	3295*	3094	3225
Vacancies (millions)	2.35	2.67	2.72	2.05	1.87	2.02	2.19	2.36
Placings (millions)	1.61	1.80	1.90	1.53	1.47	1.55	1.65	1.82

Note: *Beginning of new series.
Source: Unemployment figures from Office of National Statistics, *Labour Market Trends*, Jan 1996. Crown Copyright Placing and vacancy figures from MSC management documents.

Despite the cuts, the introduction of voluntary registration and the turbulent atmosphere in the service towards the end of the period, the vacancy and placing figures none the less improved from a low point in 1981/82. The figures overshot targets in 1983/84[33] and by 1984/85 were falling not far short of those in 1979/80, reflecting the slow and gradual pull out of deep recession. It is more difficult to judge what effect the cuts had on the less measurable aspects of the service – notably the availability and quality of information and advice to the public.

In September 1985, Lord Young returned as Secretary of State for Employment, and Morrison departed to the Department of Trade and Industry. The employment service now began to change in an unexpected direction.

13

Lord Young's Revolution, 1985–87

'Could I create a strategy to deal with unemployment? I was asked. Without having any clear ideas, I said that I could. "Good," the Prime Minister replied, "now leave it to me". (Lord Young's account of an interview with Mrs Thatcher in August 1985)[1]

Introduction

Lord Young of Graffham – formerly David Young, Chairman of the MSC – was Secretary of State for Employment for only 21 months, but in that time he revolutionised government policy towards unemployment and, in doing so, transformed the strategy of the employment service. He brought the employment service back to centre stage and he decisively shifted it away from the labour market transparency model, pursued since the early 1970s, to the benefit control model.

This chapter explains how Young became Secretary of State and how he set up the Restart programme. It looks at the elements in Restart and its impact on the unemployed and on the employment service. It goes on to look at the uncertainties about future organisation, leading up to the 1987 General Election.

Personalities

Lord Young was in a powerful position. He was close to the Prime Minister. Indeed, in 1984 the *Financial Times* had reported that Margaret Thatcher had said of him: 'Other people come to me with their problems, David Young comes to me with his achievements'.[2] In 1984 the Prime Minister had drawn Young from the MSC into her Cabinet as Minister without Portfolio with an imprecise brief concerned with enterprise and wealth creation. Tom King, then Secretary of State for Employment, soon saw Young's position as threatening his own.[3] Thus it was no surprise that Young should succeed King in September 1985. As a new Secretary of State, Young had the advantage of having formerly been

Chairman of the MSC, so that he knew the Department's culture and had worked with many of its top officials. In a way that is rare for Ministers, he knew just what levers to pull and could not easily be fobbed off with excuses or difficulties. He was at heart an optimist – even about such an intractable problem as unemployment. Where others saw problems, he saw opportunities. After his first meeting with Young, Alan Clark, then a rather disgruntled Parliamentary Secretary in the Department, described him as:

> *pleasant, charming almost, and fresh (as distinct from stale). He talks at twice the speed of Tom King, but listens too, cracks jokes, is full of bright ideas. I quite see why the Lady fancies him. He is utterly different from the rest of the Cabinet – yet without being caddish.*[4]

This was the only time in its history that the Department of Employment had two Cabinet Ministers. Kenneth Clarke, Paymaster General, worked alongside Young as Departmental spokesman in the Commons – or, as was suggested facetiously, his 'representative on earth'. Young initially gave Clarke direct responsibility for industrial relations, health and safety *and the MSC* – he felt it would be unfair to Bryan Nicholson, the MSC Chairman, if he were to breathe down his neck. But in practice Young firmly took charge of his unemployment project as it affected the MSC. Clarke's presence made it easier for Young to play a 'hands-on' role. He paid numerous visits to Jobcentres and benefit offices, which often led him to demand changes in policy and practice.

Key officials in the Department who quickly became involved in Young's unemployment agenda included Sir Michael Quinlan, the Permanent Secretary, Roger Dawe, Deputy Secretary, whom Young knew well from MSC, Mike Fogden, an Under-Secretary from DHSS of whom we shall say more later, Clive Tucker, John Cooper, Head of the unemployment benefit service and Leigh Lewis (who was Private Secretary to Young as Minister without Portfolio and in his early months as Secretary of State). At the MSC, Bryan Nicholson had the tricky task of persuading Commissioners, particularly those from the TUC, to go along with the new agenda. Geoffrey Holland, the Director, played a creative role in the early discussions and was determined to demonstrate that the MSC remained a 'can-do' organisation. Similarly, Steve Loveman, as Chief Executive of the Employment Division of MSC, had to mobilise the employment service in the urgent new programmes that emerged.

The unemployment problem

There was no precedent in post-war Britain for the unemployment problem that faced the Thatcher government in 1985. Unemployment had been above three million ever since 1982 and, despite three years of economic growth, was still edging upwards. What is more, there were 1.3 million who had been unemployed for over one year. It was the unhappy responsibility of the

Secretary of State for Employment to announce each month the latest rise in the figures. The opinion polls suggested that unemployment was a key issue for the electorate. There was pressure from Parliament, the media, the universities and the voluntary sector for action. How to respond to this pressure was now a central political problem for the government. While the Conservatives had won the 1983 Election with unemployment at around three million and rising, it seemed unlikely that this could be repeated. The special factors of 1983 – the Falklands factor and the parlous state of the Labour Party – were unlikely to be repeated.

Young describes in his memoirs[5] the background to the Prime Minister's decision to appoint him Secretary of State for Employment. In the summer of 1985, he found the Prime Minister:

> *tired and worried about unemployment. She thought that we were losing the battles for people's hearts and minds on the issue. We were halfway through the term and she knew that the changes that she would have to take this time would have to take us through to the election.*

When in late August Young saw her again, she remained 'very concerned about unemployment'. Young offered to go to the Department of Employment. 'Could I create a strategy to deal with unemployment?' I was asked. Without having any clear ideas, I said that I could. "Good," the Prime Minister replied, "now leave it with me." On 2 September, the Prime Minister appointed Young and Kenneth Clarke to the Department of Employment and asked them to develop a strategy to deal with unemployment. Young said that they would be back to see her within eight weeks.[6]

This account shows us that 'a strategy to deal with unemployment' was seen as vital politically and that the timescales were extremely tight with the Election likely to take place in 1987. It also shows us that Young was taking an enormous gamble, since at the time of the crucial conversation in August he did not have any clear ideas as to what the strategy would be. He knew that he was operating in a 'very pessimistic climate', in which many believed that nothing could be done about unemployment. The main contrary view came from a few surviving Keynesian expansionists. Young rejected both these points of view. After all, the United States had created over 20 million jobs during the previous few years whilst the whole of Europe had created less than one million. None the less, 'in the still of the night there were times when I began to feel that my friends were right and that it really was a hopeless and thankless task'.[7]

Keynes would have been surprised at the notion that an employment minister should tackle the unemployment problem. His General Theory envisaged the Chancellor of the Exchequer using the levers of macro-economic policy. But Nigel Lawson, the Chancellor, saw no future in increasing economic demand. The economy was already growing by over 3 per cent a year and inflation was running at over 10 per cent. Expansionary measures would only stoke inflation. Lawson says that he decided to give priority to three major

Interior of Hemel Hempstead Employment Exchange, 1960, showing interviewing cubicles

Job seekers browsing in the self service section, Shoreditch Jobcentre, 1982

An artist's impression of a Jobcentre, showing vacancies on display and open plan arrangement, 1972

Exterior of typical 1970s Jobcentre, Ealing, 1979

1976: 'Jobseekers at the new Jobcentre in Fountain Street, Manchester, can either pick a job for themselves or talk to employment advisors for extra guidance and help'

Inside Folkestone Jobcentre, 1977

Sir John Cassels,
Director, Manpower Services Services
Commission, 1971–1981

Jean Collingridge,
Chief Executive, Employment Service,
1979–1982

Sir Geoffrey Holland,
Director, Manpower Services
Commission, 1981–1987;
Permanent Secretary, Department of
Employment, 1988–1993

Peter Morrison, Permanent Secretary,
Department of Employment, 1981–1983;
Minister of State, 1983–1985

CPSA members picketing Finchley Jobcentre against
Saturday opening, 1983

Lord Young, Chairman, Manpower Services Commission, 1982–1984; Secretary of State for Employment, 1985–1987

Norman Fowler, Secretary of State for Employment, 1987–1990

Mike Fogden, Chief Executive, Employment Service, 1987–1996 (at Westminster Job Centre)

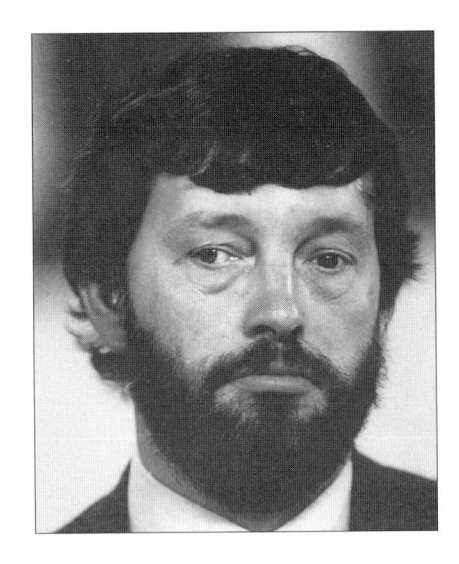

David Blunkett,
Secretary of State for Education
and Employment, 1997–

Interior of a modern Employment Service under the New Deal

1910: then...

...and now: 2000

problems – the monetary indicators, public expenditure and 'how to improve the labour market by supply-side reforms, which – *pace* the expansionists – was the only lasting way of making inroads on unemployment'.[8] This third issue involved the Department of Employment.

One school of thought, represented by Select Committees in both Houses of Parliament as well as many lobbyists outside Parliament, recommended special employment measures on a massive scale. But the government agreed with Professor Minford, one of its favourite economists, that special measures were no use in creating sustainable extra employment unless they exercised downward leverage on wages.[9] This was a re-assertion of the principle of classical economics that unemployment arose because the price of labour was too high and could only be overcome by lowering wages. It was this reasoning which had led Ministers to propose that participants in the Community Programme should receive their benefit plus £15. They had only reluctantly agreed to the part time/rate for the job formula negotiated by the MSC (pages 223–5, above). They remained restless about this concession and in subsequent years sought to extract themselves from it and get back to the benefit-plus concept in the context of a new job training scheme for the unemployed (page 251).

Young came to his new job believing that unemployment was unnecessarily high for three reasons:

- lack of incentive arising from the tax and benefit system;
- loss of motivation – 'after repeated failures, depression and a profound sense of uselessness would set in. That depression would deepen and many would stop looking for work, lowering their expectations and reconciling themselves to living within their new income';[10] this was a well researched feature of unemployment;
- engagement in the black economy; the 1981 Rayner Report had suggested that 8 per cent or more of the unemployed were unlawfully working and claiming benefit (page 208); drawing on anecdotal evidence and his own understanding of human nature, Young believed that, if anything, the level of fraud was higher than the Rayner estimate and there was some confirmation for this in a recent fraud drive in the Thames Valley, in which one-third of those identified had left the register.[11] Moreover, fraud was made easier because unemployed people could claim benefit at the Unemployment Benefit Office of their choice.

Further, like Layard, he strongly believed that the level of jobs in the economy was not fixed but could be increased if there were opportunities for enterprise and if entrepreneurs found there were people keen for jobs.

Young's inheritance

Young did not inherit a *tabula rasa*. The seeds of a change in policy were in fact sown in the summer of 1985, while Tom King was still Secretary of State for Employment. Under pressure from the Prime Minister, King investigated the procedures in Unemployment Benefit Offices and Jobcentres with his officials. In July 1985, King secured the agreement of his Ministerial colleagues to a set of new proposals.[12] He did not advocate any major new special measures, so soon after the Spring Budget package (which had expanded Community Programme by 100,000 places and introduced two-year YTS). Instead, King's proposals reflected Ministers' suspicions that the ranks of the long-term unemployed were swollen by people who were 'resting on the register' or were secretly working. It noted that benefit control was now much less rigorous as a result of the introduction of fortnightly signing in 1978 and voluntary registration in the Jobcentres in 1982. It would be too costly and embarrassing now to reverse the latter change. But it was pointed out that this Rayner recommendation should have been accompanied by an increase in the number of Unemployment Review Officers from 940 to 1250. Instead, the DHSS in 1985 was deploying only 550 UROs. The main proposals were:

- DHSS should appoint more UROs;
- DHSS and DE should have more fraud officers;
- ideas for a subsidy or tax credit for long-term unemployed getting jobs and for a benefit-plus scheme to run alongside the Community Programme should be further developed, subject to some research by Professor Blaug of the University of Buckingham.

There was also a set of measures directly affecting the employment service:

- vacancy displays in Unemployment Benefit Offices;
- closer cooperation between UROs and Jobcentres, so that Jobcentres would furnish UROs with vacancies and permit UROs to interview clients in Jobcentre premises;
- a 'Postal Contact Initiative', ie writing to all those unemployed over six months to encourage them to use Jobcentre services; this built on previous employment service initiatives; and
- an extension of the employment service's successful Job Club pilot (page 248).

However, Peter Morrison's preoccupation with economy was in danger of undermining these moves. At his insistence,[13] the employment service was to have no extra staff for these initiatives, but instead should use the 430 posts already allocated to the long-term unemployed initiative (page 206). Since this initiative was regarded as valuable, it was a case of robbing Peter to pay Paul.

While these proposals lacked the impact of Young's later packages, they marked the turn of the tide. Ever since separation in 1974, the Department of Employment had been somewhat ambivalent about benefit control. In the UBS, priority had been given not to eligibility and availability, but to prompt and accurate payment of benefit – a demanding enough requirement given the vast increase in numbers. The 1981 Rayner Report had re-emphasised benefit control but its effects were paradoxical. Voluntary registration had in fact weakened benefit control, while the DHSS had failed to make up for this by intensifying their URO efforts. King's proposals of July 1985 gave a new emphasis to benefit control and to the need for the Jobcentres to work closely with colleagues in the UBS and DHSS.

When Young took over in September, MSC officials were still struggling to put King's urgent demands into effect and had encountered strong opposition from their own unions both to undertaking this extra work with no extra staff and to the whole idea of collaborating with UROs. Commissioners too were concerned about the staffing position, given the cuts imposed in the Morrison era. Wilson Longden, the Education Commissioner, commented that, 'Jobcentre staff were hard working and dedicated, but they had been cut to the bone. The major issue was the spirit and morale of the staff.' The Chairman, Bryan Nicholson, said that he sensed a growing realism among Ministers that extra initiatives required extra staff. It was agreed that the initiatives demanded by Ministers should proceed, except that the links with UROs should be the subject of further consultation with unions.[14] (In April 1986, it was agreed to introduce these links despite continued union opposition.)[15]

Another influence on the course of events was a report by the Public Accounts Committee published in July 1985,[16] which criticised as 'weak' the formal test of availability for employment as carried out by UBOs. Since the introduction of voluntary registration in 1982, the test had amounted to a question asked at the time of claiming benefit.

The Restart concept

Immediately after taking office, Young embarked on a hectic series of brainstorming sessions with his Ministers and officials to work out his 'strategy to deal with unemployment'. There were of course constant interruptions. For instance, the Department asked him to approve a proposal to save £6 million per year by reducing the frequency of 'signing' by some unemployed claimants from fortnightly to once every three months. It could be argued that signing was a meaningless ritual, but Young records:

> *all my instincts were against the change. Everything in me told me that if we were to relax the conditions for signing even more, let alone relax it as far as making it quarterly, then the fairly tenuous moral hold we had to prevent even more working and signing would go for ever.*[17]

There was also a practical argument. Failure to sign was a useful early indicator that someone had ceased to be unemployed; it triggered the cessation of benefits. Without it, huge overpayments could arise.

It was this debate over the frequency of signing which set Young thinking about ideas both for reinforcing the obligations of unemployed claimants and restoring their motivation. At his brain-storming meetings, the idea emerged of inviting all the long-term unemployed to come to an interview at a Jobcentre – eventually known as the 'restart' interview. While the term 'counselling' was used, the approach was much more 'directive' than 'counselling' as understood in professional social work circles. The interview would include discussion of why individuals remained unemployed and of the 'menu' of opportunities that could help them, including:

- submission to a job; this might be assisted by a Job Start payment of £20 per week for six months to anyone taking a job paying less than £80 per week;
- submission to a job in the Community Programme, which Young wanted to expand further;
- assistance with setting up a business, through an expanded Enterprise Allowance Scheme;
- attendance at a Jobclub;
- attendance at a 1-week Restart Course.

We discuss these menu items more fully later.

Young aimed to have enough options on the menu to be able to guarantee a positive outcome for all. But his overriding criterion of success was the register effect – in other words, the reduction in the claimant count of the unemployed that could be achieved. He believed that the last two items in the menu would increase the numbers who moved into jobs eventually. But in addition he expected that, as a result of the counselling, 'a number of long-term unemployed who were working and signing would think that the game was up and cease to register'. His economists predicted that, if they started straight away, 'unemployment could be below the magic three million early in 1987'.[18]

In one way, Restart could be seen as the revival of the review interview, which had been common in the employment service until largely discontinued under resource pressures in the early 1970s. But in fact Restart went much further, in the universality of its coverage, the rigidity of its timing and the range of the menu on offer.

On 7 November 1985, Young presented his plan to the Prime Minister, the Chancellor and a few other senior Ministers. He argued among other things that his plan would save money on the DHSS's vote, through the reduction in benefit payments – a critical point, since he was seeking extra resources for the employment service. He 'got the go-ahead but only grudgingly'. The Treasury would only agree to pilots which would be evaluated before any nationwide extension.[19] This was disappointing to Young as it compressed to 18 months the time available for the vital 'register effect' before the Election. But he made the best of it. But, in contrast to the Morrison era, Young had secured Treasury recognition that tackling unemployment meant extra resources for the Jobcentres – a reversal of the policy of the last five years.

The pilots were discussed at the November and December Commission meetings. There was deep scepticism about the Job Start Allowance, particularly on the part of the TUC, but it was given provisional approval. On resources, Holland reassured the Commission by pointing out that Restart would bring the first additional resource to Jobcentres since 1979. Commissioners were 'given assurances that the pilot would not draw Jobcentre staff into a new role in the administration of benefit'.[20] It was thought best to play down the requirement that Jobcentres should report to Unemployment Benefit Offices those claimants who failed to turn up for their interview. From the start, Restart was a curiously ambiguous programme, presented in different ways to different stakeholders. Within government, it was very much about 'benefit control' but, within the MSC, it was about 'helping' the unemployed, making it impossible for the TUC to oppose it.

A further initiative launched by Young was umbrella advertising. Research showed that the public, and more particularly employers and the unemployed themselves, were woefully ignorant of the various government programmes designed to tackle unemployment. In April 1986, with the help of a professional advertising company, Davidson Pearce, Young launched the *Action for Jobs* campaign built around a booklet which set out details of all the programmes. The demand for the booklet was so great as to require a reprint of 1,250,000 copies. Nigel Lawson notes that Young was 'a great believer in the power of advertising. As Employment Secretary he had spent copious sums of public money promoting the advertising campaign *Action for Jobs*.'[21] Opposition critics complained that Young was using government funds to improve the image of the Conservative Party. Young denied that the campaign was political. He argued that it gave a coherence to government efforts and genuinely improved awareness among the key client groups – young people and the unemployed – so encouraging them to take up the opportunities available.[22] The British political system lacks an effective mechanism to adjudicate on the political aspect of government advertising.

The development of Restart

The nine pilots began on 7 January 1986. In view of the need to persuade the Treasury to agree to a nationwide extension, Young received weekly monitoring figures. He found them most encouraging. Rather than pick out a particular set of weekly figures here, it may be more useful to quote the Department's final evaluation of the Restart Pilots:

The researchers concluded that an extra 8.5 per cent left the count as a result of Restart – amounting to 2500 people (85,000 on a national basis). The reduction in the number of long-term unemployed attributable to the Restart interview process alone was at least 3167 (adjusting for deadweight, movement to other benefits and overlap with other government schemes). On average, people leaving the count would be off it for 41 weeks in the subsequent 12 months. The gross cost was £43 per unemployed person contacted.[23]

Office of Hope

Table 13.1 *Restart pilots for those unemployed for 12 months or more, Jan–June 1986*

A. Total client group	38,163
B. Those successfully contacted	34,618 (91 per cent of A)
C. Those interviewed	30,308 (79 per cent of A)
D. Placed directly in jobs	321 (out of over 5000 submissions)
E. Placed directly in Community Programme	1531
F. Training places	404
G. Entered Enterprise Allowances Scheme	81
H. Entered Job Clubs	350
I. Actually started Restart Course	2359 (out of 4013 allocations)
J. Jobstart Allowance accepted*	252 (out of 375 applications)
K. Referred to UBO on grounds of availability	1021 (111 disallowed)
L. Referred to UBO for refusal of suitable employment	50 (28 disallowed)
M. Referred to UBO for failure to attend interview	3015 (707 disallowed, but 430 of these later reinstated after attending interview)
N. Left unemployment count before being contacted	5898
O. Left unemployment count after being contacted	9303
P. Subsequently returned to count by 28 August	3511

Note: *62 per cent of those accepted for an allowance had not had a Restart interview.
Source: DE files 11/RP series.

Restart was criticised for the low level of direct placings – only 1 per cent in the open labour market – but this criticism was unfair. People who had been unemployed for over a year were unlikely to go straight into jobs. There had been a similar low level of placings in the Special Employment Needs experiments of the 1970s (page 186). Restart was, however, a great advance on that experiment because of the range of 'menu options' which could help to make people job-ready. But the flow of people from interview into their chosen menu option was far from straightforward. Many fell by the wayside at every stage. In many cases, there had not been a true meeting of minds at the Restart interview, which lasted only 20–30 minutes. Counsellors and unemployed people saw things very differently. Counsellors were expected above all to submit people to some offering in order to achieve a 'positive outcome' (an ambiguous and much criticised concept). Unemployed individuals, on the other hand, wanted to emerge from the interview with their benefit intact. As a result, in order to please the counsellor, they would let themselves be recorded as accepting the offer of a scheme. But their heart was often not in it and, as it was not compulsory, they often failed to pursue it.

Despite the heavy fall-out, Restart proved cost-effective when *all* the outcomes were taken into account, including those who ceased drawing benefit on receipt of the invitation letter or after the interview. In some cases, people who were working and signing were detected directly as a result of Restart: in one case, a counsellor actually found herself interviewing a young man who had taken her money at the petrol station that morning. In other cases, a direct placing was achieved: for instance a counsellor found that a young lad with a Mohican haircut wanted to be a signwriter: she rang up a signwriting firm and fixed him up with a job.[24] The comprehensiveness of Restart was one of its strengths: for instance, it included those in rural areas who were quarterly attenders and those older claimants who received only a credit for the National Insurance contribution.

Already, by February 1986, the pilot evidence suggested that a national scheme should cause roughly 23,000 extra to leave the register each month, which Young believed 'would be more than enough to reverse the whole direction of unemployment'.[25] He used these early results to persuade Lawson to cut short the original six-month evaluation period. (In the MSC, the expression 'Lord Young pilots' was used after this to describe pilots that were turned with amazing speed into national schemes.) On 18 March 1986, the Chancellor in his Budget announced that Restart would become a national scheme on 1 July. It would be an immense task. There were about 1,300,000 long-term unemployed (over one year) and some half a million joined them, with a slightly smaller number leaving the register, in a year, requiring 1.6 million interviews between July 1986 and April 1987. The Budget also announced an expansion of menu offerings:

- Enterprise Allowance Scheme places up by 20,000;
- Community Programme places up from 230,000 to 255,000 by November 1986, with the average wage up from £63 to £67;
- increase in Job Clubs to 450;
- a New Workers Scheme, offering a subsidy of £15 per week to those leaving the Youth Training Scheme for low paid jobs; and
- national extension of the Jobstart Allowance.

It was a formidable package and reflects Young's high credibility with both the Prime Minister and the Chancellor. At its March meeting, the Commission welcomed the Budget measures.

For the employment service, the package meant a dramatic reversal of the previous six years of staff cuts. As Geoffrey Holland pointed out to Commissioners, the injection of 2000 extra staff was very welcome 'since most of the staff will be engaged in personal support and guidance which has virtually disappeared from the Jobcentres'.[26] The problem now for senior management was how to recruit and train 2000 extra staff in three months –

including large numbers of Executive Officers to conduct credible Restart interviews, day in day out. The exercise was seen as the ultimate test of MSC's can-do image. Analogies were drawn with Napoleon's march on Moscow. Frantic efforts were made with recruitment, with help from the Civil Service Commission. On the initiative of Bryan Nicholson, who drew on his experience in the US, ethnic minority targets were introduced as part of the recruitment drive – a pioneering step in the civil service. There were also many internal promotions, inevitably the source of most of the Restart counsellors given the tight timescale; but fortunately after years of contraction plenty of talent was available. David Main led work on the Restart initiative and Ann Le Sage headed up a massive training operation.

These efforts were successful and Restart went national as planned on 1 July. But Young already felt that yet more needed to be done. In October 1986, following another hasty pilot, Young announced that Restart interviews were to take place after a person had been unemployed for six months rather than a year. Then in January 1987, he introduced 'rolling Restart', under which interviews would be held after the first six months and then every six months thereafter until a person left the register. This pattern has persisted ever since.

In May 1986, the ambiguity of the Restart concept led to a major row. On 14 May, the *Daily Telegraph* had as its main headlines:

CLAIMANTS VANISH LIKE MELTED SNOW
CRACKDOWN ON DOLE SCROUNGERS

The article referred to the 'startling' impact of the Restart pilots in catching up with 'dole scroungers' and described the national expansion of Restart as an onslaught on the black economy. A former 'senior investigator' in the Department of Employment was quoted as estimating one claim in five as fraudulent. There was similar coverage in the *Daily Mail*.

Bryan Nicholson immediately wrote to Young expressing his concern about the articles, which, he said, 'could do quite unnecessary damage'. Young replied, saying that the reports confused two quite distinct areas of work – the new Restart programme offering 'positive assistance' to long-term unemployed people and the continuing work of the Department's fraud staff. The aims of Restart were 'entirely different' from those of the fraud teams.[27]

But, despite this denial, the press reports rang alarm bells in trade union circles and the TUC became apprehensive that their whole position on the Commission could become untenable at the next TUC Conference in September. On 31 July Ken Graham, the TUC Commissioner, saw Nicholson to express concern at the growing impression that Restart was a 'benefit policing exercise'. After consultations with the Department, on 19 August Geoffrey Holland put out a statement to all staff saying that:

> the enforcement of benefit rules is not a matter for the MSC and remains a matter for the benefit offices of DHSS and DE. Commissioners have been clear from the outset that Restart is a

> *positive programme of help and not an exercise in policing the unemployment register.*

The statement acknowledged that in reality things were a bit more complicated than this. The 1973 Act had imposed some duties on the Commission for benefit control, including the registration requirement which existed up to 1982. Moreover, long-term unemployment was 'depressing, isolating and demotivating', so that some people might not come to an interview voluntarily. Holland went on:

> *That is why people are required to attend the counselling interviews. Only around 8 per cent in our pilot scheme were referred for failure to attend. Not all had their benefit stopped. Of those who did, the ones who subsequently came for interview had their benefit resumed.*[28]

The truth was that Restart was *both* about helping the unemployed and about 'policing benefit', and the small print of Holland's statement made this clear. Why in this case did Young and other ministers, as well as leading figures in the MSC, play down the benefit control aspects so much? In his memoirs, Young says that the benefit control aspect of the programme

> *was not emphasised to the MSC. As a tripartite organisation I did not wish to put my people there in too difficult a position. For many years the left had adopted a curious attitude to unemployment. You would have thought that they would have done all in their power to help the unemployed. They often did, but mainly to keep them on the register...Time after time, they attacked anything that would resemble an attack on benefit fraud...*[29]

Moreover, at that point in time, it would not have been helpful to the government for the TUC to walk out of the Commission. This could have undermined the confidence of local authorities and the voluntary sector in the various MSC programmes and so hampered Young's ambitious expansion plans. But the resort to 'doubletalk' and the lack of a true meeting of minds between the government and the TUC on such a vital issue augured ill for the long-term future of the Commission.

We now turn to the various 'menu items' that were on offer at the Restart interview, apart from the Community Programme and the Enterprise Allowance Scheme, which were described in Chapter 12.

The Jobstart Allowance

Employment subsidies are among the classic special measures to deal with unemployment. In the mid-1980s, they were being strongly recommended by experts such as Professor Layard. The subsidies can be paid either to the employer or to the employee. Before Young became Secretary of State, both he and Tom King had been putting forward ideas for subsidy schemes. In the hectic brainstorming which followed his appointment, Young decided to go for a pilot scheme in which £20 per week for six months was on offer to someone unemployed for over a year who took a job paying less than £80 per week. The concept was clearly influenced by the government's wish to encourage lower wages. Unsurprisingly, it was viewed with deep suspicion by the TUC Commissioners in the MSC. In practice, perhaps because the terms of the scheme were restrictive, the take-up during the pilot was extremely low – only 375 applications were received, of which 252 were accepted.[30] However, take-up increased with the extension of Restart and by July 1987 was running at 400 applications a week.[31]

Job Clubs

A far more promising innovation was the Job Club. Job Clubs originated in the mid-1970s in the US where they were introduced by two behavioural psychologists – N Azrin and V Besalel. On the initiative of one of the employment service's psychologists, Bob Davidson, two pilot Job Clubs were set up in 1984 in Durham and Middlesbrough, and then a third in Walthamstow. They produced an adapted version of the US 'Counsellor's Manual'. The objective was simple: 'to get each member the best possible job in the shortest possible time'. A resource centre was provided with phones, stationery, stamps and access to vacancies from newspapers and journals as well as the Jobcentre. The leader's counselling was 'directive' – they 'didn't muck about with debating sessions'. There were tried and tested techniques of job hunting and each member agreed to try these. Activity rates were high, with daily targets of submissions to employers. Strong commitment was expected from the leader and the members. Successes were celebrated. In the three pilots, 75 per cent of participants obtained jobs – a far higher success rate than was obtainable by any other special measure.[32]

In his memoirs, Young records that on his very first morning as Secretary of State, he refused to approve a press release about Job Clubs as he feared bad publicity. On the following day, Kenneth Clarke persuaded him to change his mind and thereafter Job Clubs became one of the mainstays of the Restart programme.[33] At the Conservative Party Conference in October 1986, Young announced an expansion to 1000 Job Clubs by March 1987, with the prospect of a further expansion to 2000 if necessary. As the number of Job Clubs expanded, the success rate was not as high as in the original pilots, but was still impressive and steady, with 60 per cent moving into work and a further 13 per cent joining CP or training. There was no shortage of recruits, but senior officials in the MSC were chary of going beyond 1000 Job Clubs. Employers had been positive so far, but could easily become negative if they received too many approaches from Job Club members, each of whom on average followed up 55 job leads during their time in a Job Club.[34]

The Restart Course

During the brainstorming sessions soon after Young became Secretary of State, Geoffrey Holland suggested a short course designed to remotivate people who had been unemployed for a long time. This emerged as an important part of the Restart menu – important because it was something that advisers could offer as a fallback to people who were not ready for jobs or Job Clubs. Ken Pascoe and the psychologists worked hard to provide such a course by 7 January 1986 in all the pilot areas. The design of the course reflected a profound concern about the psychological effects of prolonged unemployment. Its aim was

> to help participants move from a reactive stance towards unemployment to a pro-active approach which contains a belief that it is possible for them to exercise some control over what is happening to them.[35]

The content included:

- sharing experience of unemployment and of local facilities and support services;
- managing on limited resources;
- stocktaking of personal qualities and skills;
- jobsearch problems and how to overcome them;
- review of life so far, image of the future, personal goal setting; and
- short-term action plan.[36]

During the pilots, only about half the places were taken up and one in four of those who started the course left early, though the course lasted only five days. This probably reflected the very problems of lack of confidence that the course was designed to address and is an illustration of the fall-out problem discussed above (pages 244–5). Compulsion was considered, but the DHSS doubted whether this was feasible under the relevant legislation. As time went on, take-up improved. The course content came in for some ridicule. In August 1986, the *Daily Mirror* reported that, among other things, tutors were expected to discuss basic human wants, such as 'the need for food, for love and for safety'. John Prescott, Shadow Employment Spokesman, said that it was 'another way of humiliating the unemployed and blaming them for their unemployment. If the lives of one and a half million long-term unemployed were not at stake, we could all have a good laugh'.[37] In fact, by this stage 76 per cent of those who completed the course found it useful or very useful. Indeed, there were some moving tributes to the course from participants, like this one from a participant in Doncaster to his tutor:

I was open minded when we first met, but still very apprehensive. Through you, and Restart, I found myself again. I have regained the confidence needed to search for employment and to cope with the trauma of rejection. During the week, my wife commented that I have clearly changed. Though I didn't realise it, she says we were talking more and that I have more control and awareness about myself...[38]

Claimant Advisers

The Unemployment Review Officers (UROs) of the DHSS were originally introduced in 1961 to review the position of unemployed people receiving means-tested benefits. From 1980 they covered contributory benefits as well. Their job was to find out what the claimant had done and was doing to try to get a job, to sort out any problems hampering jobsearch and to suggest vacancies or other means by which the claimant might get back to work.[39] As with Restart, UROs sent letters calling in selected claimants for interview. The letter itself would cause some to stop claiming benefit. The interview would be used to persuade people to intensify their job-search. There was clearly a big overlap between the Restart programme and URO work. Young persuaded the DHSS that the UROs would be better deployed in the DE's unemployment benefit service (UBS). The posts were transferred in the months up to April 1987. But only two officers moved over from the DHSS, leaving the UBS with a massive recruitment and training programme.

In the UBS, the UROs were renamed 'Claimant Advisers', and Young increased their numbers to 770 during 1987.[40] In addition to the functions described above, they were expected to advise unemployed people on:

- *in-work benefits*. It was now an important thrust of government policy to demonstrate to unemployed people that they could be better off even in low-paid jobs if in-work benefits such as family income supplement (later family credit) and housing benefit were taken into account. Claimant Advisers were initially equipped with tables of information and later with specially programmed micro-computers (Psion Organisers) so that they could help people with the necessary calculations;
- *moving off unemployment benefits onto other benefits*. This was perhaps the most controversial part of the Claimant Adviser role. In 1986–87, overriding priority was given to bringing down the number of unemployed claimants. Claimant Advisers encouraged people with health problems to seek their doctor's clinical judgement as to their capacity for work. As a result, many moved off unemployment benefits on to sickness benefit, leading into long-term invalidity benefit. For the individual, there was the incentive of a higher rate of benefit. Some doctors, however, complained that they were put under pressure to collude with their patients in saying

that they were unfit for work.[41] The numbers receiving invalidity benefit rose by over 300,000 between 1984 and 1988.[42] While this was in part an inevitable result of widespread redundancies of men from heavy industries, it must also have been due to the activities of the Claimant Advisers. By the 1990s, government priorities had changed. Economy in benefit expenditure was more important than reducing the count. Peter Lilley introduced Incapacity Benefit, with new and more stringent work tests and a new team of independent doctors.

The New Job Training Scheme

In October 1986 at the Conservative Party Conference, Young announced the pilots of the New Job Training Scheme. This offered those who were unemployed for more than six months a combination of assessment, training and work experience, leading to a recognised vocational qualification. Participants received a training allowance equivalent to their benefit: this arrangement was intended to ensure a register effect, while hopefully achieving some downward pressure on wage expectations. For Commissioners, it was a departure from the agreed Adult Training Strategy, but it offered an alternative major programme for the long-term unemployed. In January 1987, Young announced the nationwide extension of the scheme. Even more than Restart, it had been a 'Lord Young pilot', with the extension announced before any serious evaluation had taken place.

This scheme, under a variety of titles, was to become an important menu item for Restart, but the period before the 1987 Election proved too short for it to have become fully established. It was made clear that the scheme was voluntary, and this was important to its acceptance by Commissioners, particularly those from the TUC.

It is interesting that, despite its preoccupation with benefit control, the Thatcher government did not adopt American ideas of workfare, in which the payment of benefit is made conditional on participation in a work scheme. Nigel Lawson records that:

> *A number of meetings were held under Margaret's chairmanship, but unfortunately an alliance on the issue, between Norman Fowler as Social Security Secretary and David Young as Employment Secretary, produced so many alleged practical difficulties that the idea was dropped.*[43]

The difficulties seem to have related to the cost and the risk of deadweight, substitution and displacement. But, as we shall see, in the next 10 years policy edged forward towards increasing compulsion until something very like 'workfare' was being piloted.

Other developments in the employment service

This was a curious transitional phase in the history of the employment service. The previous five years of cuts had left the service thinly staffed and overstretched across a network that had actually been increased by the Development Plan of 1984. Through its focus on finding and filling vacancies, the service's market share had increased (page 220) but overwhelmingly it was now a placing service rather than an advisory service. There were some improvements. Jobcentres were now better equipped for the 'Gateway' function of guiding people to other services that could help them. Moreover, the service was engaged in many experiments with delivery through information technology, including direct public access to vacancy information and provision of career information through films and videos, but these experiments only touched a small minority of Jobcentres. Supervacs – the project to develop an enhanced vacancy system launched in 1982 – suffered delays, so that the major pilot in the North West did not start until 1987.

The impact of Restart on the service was traumatic. There was no way of achieving Young's ambitious Restart timetable without pulling experienced staff off other work into Restart work, with inevitable timelags before their replacements could be recruited and trained. By October 1986, Jeremy Surr was 'deeply disturbed' at the 'extent of under-performance' in the Jobcentre service and commented that, 'The staff upheaval to mount Restart had been the last straw'.[44] By the end of 1986/87, however, vacancy and placing levels had picked up and the final results for the year were in fact slightly higher than in 1985/86, reflecting no doubt buoyancy in the economy (Table 13.2). Contrary to the fears of some in the service, the intensive efforts for the long-term unemployed were not incompatible with effective Jobcentre performance.

Table 13.2 *Employment service in Great Britain; unemployment rate, vacancies and placings, 1984/85–1987/88*

	1984/85	1985/86	1986/87	1987/88
Unemployment rate (%) October	11.7	11.8	11.6	9.8
Vacancies (millions)	2.36	2.45	2.61	2.70
Placings (millions)	1.82	1.89	1.91	1.90

Source: Unemployment rate from Office of National Statistics, *Labour Market Trends*, Jan 1996. Crown Copyright. Vacancies and placings from MSC management statistics.

Organisational uncertainty

To the outside world, the MSC in the mid-1980s seemed one of the great institutions of the land. Its budget was huge – £2.3 billion in 1985–86, rising to over £3 billion in 1986–87.[45] The government was prepared to entrust the MSC with these vast sums not only for special measures to deal with unemployment but also for increasing intervention in the education system. None the less, the MSC was not as robust as it appeared. The constant detailed intervention by Peter Morrison had done much to undermine the autonomy of the organisation. The advent of Lord Young as Secretary of State led to intervention of a different sort. With Restart, the MSC found itself executing a programme which was in the last analysis controlled from DE HQ, even if MSC staff carried out most of the detailed design. What is more, as had become clear when he was Chairman, Young was a restless reorganiser and innovator and had no intention of leaving the MSC to develop its own destiny, as had happened with similar bodies in Sweden and Germany.

It followed that 1985–87 were years of acute uncertainty about four interrelated organisational issues:

1 whether there should be a Department of Education and Training or alternatively a National Training Authority and, if the latter, what its relationship should be to the Department of Employment and the Department of Education and Science;
2 whether the MSC organisation should be 'unified', at regional or area level;
3 whether the unemployment benefit service should be integrated into the DHSS's local offices, or alternatively supplementary benefit work for the unemployed should move from the DHSS into the DE; and
4 whether the employment service should be merged with the DE's unemployment benefit service.

Chapter 12 noted the intense interest during 1983–84 in the first and last of these scenarios, but in the event neither was pursued at that time (page 230). In April 1985, Young, as Minister without Portfolio, opened up the issue of abolishing the Department of Employment, much to Tom King's chagrin,[46] but this was not pursued. Meanwhile, the growth in the Commission's workload led Bryan Nicholson and Geoffrey Holland to re-open the second issue – the organisation of the Commission. The MSC had always had an 'identity problem' due to its origins as two Agencies – one for training and the other for the employment service. The last major organisation review held in 1976 had largely left the original Agencies intact (though renamed 'Divisions') and staff tended to identify more with their Division than with the 'Corporate MSC'. As the MSC's operations and influence grew, it could be seen as anomalous that, at regional and local level, the outside world had to deal with two parallel hierarchies which only met structurally at Geoffrey Holland's level. Despite the opposition of some of his senior colleagues, such as Bryan Emmett, Holland asked Graham Kendall to lead an organisational study. In September 1985, Kendall produced a report recommending a complete merger at Regional level.

The Chairman's Management Committee was split down the middle on the intrinsic merits of Kendall's proposal. But in any case, by the time Kendall's

Office of Hope

draft report appeared, Young was back on the scene, as Secretary of State. Young was churning over in his mind a variety of different organisational scenarios, including that discussed in 1983 of a new training authority, with the employment service returning to the Department – though all this might need to wait until after the next Election. This prospect led Nicholson and Holland to rule out an internal merger of the MSC's field operations. Instead, they introduced during 1986 a much less radical reorganisation, which took account of the enhanced responsibilities of the Commission but left the two main limbs of the Commission structure intact:

- Vocational Education and Training Group (VETG), with Ian Johnston as Chief Executive; and
- Employment and Enterprise Group (EEG), with Jeremy Surr as Chief Executive.

EEG embraced both the Jobcentre service, led by Steve Loveman, and the Special Measures Directorate, led by Mike Emmott, responsible for the Community Programme and other special measures. At Regional level, it was decided to have two parallel sets of Regional Directors for VETG and EEG. As a portent of things to come, the EEG Directors served also as the Secretary of State's representatives in the Regions and, at Young's suggestion, had some oversight of the DE's regional functions, notably the UBS. The existing Regional Directors opted for EEG, because of the added prestige of being the Secretary of State's representative. In the event, EEG existed for only about a year.

Meanwhile, the Department of Employment and DHSS had been engaged in a joint study known as NEXT, of the third issue – whether there should continue to be two parallel networks of offices concerned with benefits for the unemployed – the DE's UBOs and the DHSS's Integrated Local offices (ILOs). Chapter 11 showed how in 1981 the government formally accepted the Rayner recommendation for merging the work in the DE's UBS network, but in reality the DHSS was against this and successfully played for time in the hope of getting the decision reversed (page 210). In 1985, the problem resurfaced as a result of criticisms by the National Audit Office of the duplicatory arrangements, and the government set up the joint NEXT study. The study identified the following options:

A. Retain both networks;
B. Extend the Agency Agreement under which the UBS delivered unemployment benefit to include income support as well; and
C. A single, integrated benefit network for all social security benefits.

Predictably, the DE favoured Option B and the DHSS favoured Option C. Once Restart was in place, Young could argue that Option B would provide a tight and coherent system which would help to reduce unemployment. But the argument was very hard to resolve, apart from the agreement that the Unemployment Review Officers (UROs) should move from the DHSS to the

DE (page 250). Towards the end of 1986, Young made clear to Cabinet colleagues his idea that the Manifesto for the next Election might propose re-integrating the Jobcentres with the UBS. Norman Fowler at the DHSS was then able to win the Prime Minister's support for the argument that this new development shifted the goal posts so much that it was impossible to reach any conclusion on the two benefit networks without considerable further study. As a result, the two parallel networks continued to deal with benefits for the unemployed for another 10 years.[47]

This is not the place to discuss the twists and turns that occurred on the first issue listed on page 253 – the organisation of education and training. Suffice it to say that by April 1987, when Young was involved with the Prime Minister and other ministers in drawing up the Conservative Manifesto for the 1987 Election, he proposed not only returning the employment service to the Department of Employment, but also abolishing the MSC, presumably with a view to creating a new training body. He recorded in his memoirs:

> right away I could see the Prime Minister was very nervous over the proposal to abolish the MSC. In one of those rare moments of brilliance – even if I say so myself – I suddenly suggested instead that instead of abolishing the MSC we could substantially increase employer representation.[48]

As a result, the Manifesto proposals on MSC organisation were as follows:

> We will take further steps to provide a comprehensive service to the unemployed. We will consult the Manpower Services Commission about transferring Jobcentres to the Department of Employment so that they can work more closely with Unemployment Benefit Offices.
> The Manpower Services Commission would then become primarily a training agency. It is employers who are best equipped to assess their training needs. We will increase employer representation on the Commission and its advisory bodies.[49]

Conclusion

This conclusion looks at Young's impact on the role and positioning of the employment service, on unemployment and on politics.

First, Young's short spell as Secretary of State for Employment had a profound effect on the role and positioning of the employment service. Whereas previous Conservative ministers, notably Peter Morrison, had made repeated cuts in the employment service, but had not changed its fundamental strategy, Young had both changed the strategy and, in a remarkable reversal of policy, secured increased resources. In conversations with senior managers, Young made it clear that the service should focus predominantly on the long-term unemployed. In terms of the analysis in Chapter 1, he was making a decisive shift away from the 'labour market transparency' model dominant since 1973 to the 'benefit control' model. While Restart was presented to the MSC in terms of the 'welfare' model and genuinely had a welfare dimension, it was even more concerned with 'benefit control'. This interpretation was confirmed by the Manifesto proposal to transfer the Jobcentres from the MSC to the Department, which was intended to make possible a new system of 'availability testing'. For Young, the employment service had a closer synergy with benefit administration than with training, in contrast with MSC's 1970s concept of a 'comprehensive labour market policy' combining employment and training. Links with training would continue to be needed after 1987, but were not seen as so vital as the 'stricter benefit regime'.

Young's wish to re-position the Jobcentres away from the MSC also reflected a frustration with 'hiving off' to the social partners. Running Restart through the MSC had involved tensions and ambiguities, because the TUC and at least one local government Commissioner resisted Jobcentre involvement in benefit control. Young believed that a unified employment and benefit service could intensify the pressure on those who engaged in fraud or were resting on the register, and he did not want unnecessary institutional obstacles to stand in the way. Successful 'hiving off' requires greater convergence of policy thinking between government and the social partners than existed in 1987.

Secondly, Young's Restart initiative had a significant impact on unemployment. Compared with most other labour market measures of the 1980s, the Restart programme was unusually coherent and effective. In his memoirs, Nigel Lawson wrote: 'Of all the schemes introduced by the government, "Restart" had the most marked effect on the unemployment figures'.[50] Restart was also one of the most thoroughly researched of all labour market measures. The evaluation of the pilot of Restart for the 12-month unemployed suggested that an extra 8.5 per cent left the count as a result of Restart (page 243). In 1989–91, the Policy Studies Institute studied the impact of Restart on those unemployed for six months against a control group to whom Restart was not applied. PSI concluded that:

> *the Restart process had significant effects on the reduction of claiming and time taken to leave the unemployment register. The best estimate of reduction in time claiming for respondents who went through the Restart process was around 5 per cent.*[51]

The writers concluded: 'Restart is an excellent example of a "pure" supply-side policy. It acts as a gateway into the labour market programmes and services and helps to facilitate the flows into and between them'.[52]

Various labour market analysts have concluded that Restart had a decisive effect in 1986/87 in reducing the numbers and duration of long-term unemployment.[53] A Bank of England study even suggested that at least 50 per cent of the fall in registered unemployment between 1986 and 1988 could be attributed to

Table 13.3 *All male and female unemployed over 52 weeks and unemployed (not seasonally adjusted), United Kingdom, claimant count*

	A. Over 52 weeks (000s)	B. All unemployed (000s)	C. A as a % of B
Oct 1985	1352	3277	41.3
Jan 1986	1372	3408	40.3
April 1986	1356*	3325*	40.8
July 1986	1348	3280	41.4
Oct 1986	1341	3237	41.4
Jan 1987	1334	3297	41.4
April 1987	1295	3107	41.7
July 1987	1238	2905	42.6
Oct 1987	1172	2751	42.6

Note: *Administrative changes reduced the total UK count by 50,000 on average.
Source: Department of Employment Gazette.

Restart.[54] The movement in the figures between 1985 and 1987 is shown in Table 13.3.

A clear downward trend in long-term unemployment can be seen from July 1986 onwards when Restart became national. At the same time, a falling trend in overall unemployment was established. Without Restart and the special measures, the long-term unemployed could easily have been left on one side in the ensuing Lawson boom. As it was, the Table shows only a small increase in the proportion of the unemployed who were over one year.

At the same time, Young's approach can be criticised as in part 'cosmetic', in the sense that it was unduly focused on a narrowly interpreted 'register effect'. Since 1982, the government had treated unemployment as coterminous with those on the claimant count', which was of course a considerable oversimplification. It played down the extent to which people moved off the count into other benefits and/or into economic inactivity or moved out of long-term unemployment into temporary opportunities, only to rejoin the register as short-term unemployed.[55] Criticisms of this kind qualify Young's achievement but do not undermine it.

Finally, it is worth noting the political significance of Young's initiative. When he became Secretary of State, unemployment greatly concerned the voters and was a subject where the government's credibility was low. By the time of the 1987 Election, this situation had changed. Margaret Thatcher was in no doubt who deserved the credit:

> at the Department of Employment (Young's) schemes for getting the unemployed back into work made a major contribution to our winning the 1987 general election.[56]

14

Warfare and Welfare, 1987–90

'It is in no one's interest that unemployed people remain out of touch with the jobs market and become passive recipients of unemployment benefits.' (White Paper: *Training for Employment*, 1988)

Introduction

The Conservative victory in the General Election of June 1987 had profound consequences for the employment service. It brought to an end the 13-year-old experiment of a service separated from benefit and reporting to a Commission of the 'social partners'. The new Secretary of State, Norman Fowler, quickly brought the Jobcentres under common management with the Unemployment Benefit Offices in a new organisation called the 'Employment Service' (ES) within the Department of Employment. He also intensified the 'Stricter Benefit Regime' which his predecessor, Lord Young, had inaugurated. So the culture of the employment service acquired its curious dualism, encapsulated in the phrase 'warfare and welfare' – a favourite expression of the new ES Chief Executive, Mike Fogden.

But the big questions overshadowing these years for the employment service were: how far would integration of employment and benefit services go? What institutional model would be adopted for the long term? Would the service remain part of the state apparatus or move to the private sector? These questions were being addressed in Mrs Thatcher's 'third term' – initially at least one of the most euphoric periods for her government. The economy was booming – or seemed to be. The electorate had given a renewed endorsement. Now at last ministers felt confident enough of public support to initiate radical reforms in areas where they had so far held back, such as education and health. It was like a new Elizabethan age: courtiers vied with each other to impress the Lady in Number 10 with their radical ideas for rolling back the frontiers of the state.

In retrospect, the Fowler years might be seen in this story as a smooth and automatic transition to the two big developments of 1990 – the establishment of the ES as a new style Executive Agency and the launching of the integration of the two networks of local offices. But in reality there was no inevitability about these developments. There were many doubts, obstacles and uncertainties along the way.

This chapter will look at the character of Norman Fowler and at the new organisation which he set up in October 1987, combining the Jobcentre service with the unemployment benefit service. It will go on to describe the policies of the new organisation, the privatisation of PER, the 'stricter benefit regime', the links with training, the integration pilots and the Agency concept.

Norman Fowler

Norman Fowler (he was knighted in 1990) was one of the most experienced Ministers in the Thatcher government. A former *Times* journalist, he had become Minister of Transport in 1979 and then in 1981 Secretary of State for Health and Social Security – one of the most onerous posts in government, which he held until the 1987 Election. Fowler was not an easy Minister to work for. A journalist commented:

> *Those who worked for him in DHSS complain that decisions that other Ministers took immediately often took Mr Fowler hours or days.*
>
> *Before any policy decision could be announced, every conceivable political implication had to be explored and analysed. He jealously guards his reputation as a 'safe pair of hands'.*[1]

It was not that Fowler avoided radical decisions. He was to take some bold steps while at Employment. It was simply that for him boldness followed on from a most intensive process of investigation and discussion with his entourage of Ministers – initially John Cope (succeeded by Tim Eggar in 1989), Patrick Nicholls and John Lee – and officials. Among the officials, there were important changes early in 1988, when Geoffrey Holland, formerly Director of the MSC, took over from Michael Quinlan as Permanent Secretary, while another former MSC official, Graham Reid, became the Deputy Secretary on employment policy.

Fowler shared many of Young's (and indeed Mrs Thatcher's) assumptions about unemployment and the labour market. He wrote in his memoirs: 'I had become convinced when I was at the DHSS that there was a substantial "black economy" in Britain. Everything I now saw at the Employment Department confirmed that picture.'

Fowler was shocked to discover that seven out of 10 people who said that they would go to a Job Club failed to show up.

> *Even more dramatically, our fraud drives uncovered abuse with people claiming unemployment benefit and working at the same*

> time. At a major building site in Birmingham, investigators found that 130 of the 450 workers were also drawing benefit. They were in full-time, well-paid work, but they appeared in the total of unemployed. In any discussion of unemployment we need to recognise that there is a significant minority who for one reason or another do not want to get off the register.[2]

These sentiments strongly influenced Fowler's approach to the role of the employment service. During the August 'silly season', he would capture the headlines with announcements about the success of his fraud drives, while his tirades against the fiddlers in the dole queues helped to win him standing ovations at the Party Conference.

Extracting the employment service from the MSC

Fowler's first priority was to carry out the pledges in the Conservative Manifesto (page 255). Soon after taking up his new job, Fowler wrote to Sir Bryan Nicholson, Chairman of the MSC, about the numerous changes the government proposed to make following the Election, including the establishment of 'an improved and integrated Employment Service, bringing together the MSC's Jobcentre Service and the Department's Unemployment Benefit Service'. This would mean the Jobcentres and their staff returning to the Department of Employment in October 1987. The Community Programme in an amended form would remain with the Commission. He would introduce legislation to enable him to appoint up to six more employer members to the Commission. He ended by expressing 'warm appreciation for all the work the Commission has done'.

The Commission met twice in July 1987 to decide on its response. These were the last meetings for Ken Graham, one of the TUC's founder Commissioners. The mood of Commissioners was sombre. They knew that this was the end of the Commission as they had known it since 1974, but they also knew that they were up against a decisive electoral mandate. Thus Nicholson's 10-page reply to Fowler of 23 July was sorrowful rather than angry. He defended the 'corporatism' of the Commission. Its achievements in delivering large programmes depended on partnership with all sorts of bodies. He was sceptical about the proposed increase in employer representation, pointing out that the Commission secured commitment 'through discussion, agreement on objectives and accommodation of particular concerns of particular parties (all round the table)'. The Commission had voted 'less than half a dozen times in 157 meetings'. Commissioners were 'saddened' by the prospective loss of the Jobcentres. They had set great store on having an attractive public employment service. In a final plea for the 'labour market transparency model' of the employment service, he urged Fowler to pay attention to:

- linkages with the MSC and training;
- the need to attract employers' vacancies and the risk that the benefit link could put off employers;
- the need to reassure staff that the change was not a prelude to privatisation; and
- the need for the new service to be 'capable of contributing substantially to job broking and...skill supply'.

The obligation to consult the Commission having been discharged, Fowler wrote back to Nicholson on 30 July to say in effect that he was proceeding with all the changes. The merger of the Jobcentres and the UBS would ensure that 'all the services the Government provides are working together to enable unemployed people – particularly the long-term unemployed – to compete for the jobs that are increasingly available'. He did not mention the Stricter Benefit Regime, although this was really the key issue. He acknowledged the need to service employers and to link with training programmes.

The new 'employment service'

As a first step in setting up the new employment service, Fowler appointed as Chief Executive Mike Fogden, who had been one of Young's close advisers. Fogden was to hold the position for nearly 10 years – longer than any of his predecessors. He had begun his career in 1958 as a clerical officer in the hurly-burly of a local office of the ministry of Pensions and National Insurance. His potential was spotted and he was placed on a fast promotion track, including a spell from 1968 to 1970 in the Private Office of Richard Crossman, then Secretary of State for Health and Social Security. Fogden was an active trade unionist himself (he was for a time Chairman of the First Division Association – the mandarins' union). But his experience in the early 1980s at the DHSS's huge Newcastle site after the damaging strike of 1981 made him conscious of the need to assert management's right to manage. In 1983, he had moved to a policy job in the Department of Employment and this led on to his appointment to head the employment service. He was well informed about benefits, but had things to learn about labour markets. Described by a colleague as temperamentally 'a long-distance runner', he had the stamina to cope with the relentless pressures of the next 10 years. He was jovial and industrious.

Fogden faced the classic problems of a merger – two sets of managers, two cultures, two sets of systems. The employment service and the UBS had moved a long way apart in the previous 13 years. The influence of the changes that Young had introduced was only skin deep. Jobcentre managers remained preoccupied with finding and filling vacancies. UBS managers remained absorbed in the logistical problems of actually delivering benefits to the enormous population of unemployed claimants and were out of touch with the labour market. The new organisation was massive – it had 40,000 staff, two-thirds from benefit and one-third from the Jobcentres. It had inherited a bizarre

Office of Hope

combined network of 2000 outlets – comprising on the one hand the newer (though by now rather jaded) rented shop premises of the Jobcentres, derived mainly from the 1970s, and on the other hand the traditional benefit offices in Crown buildings, derived mainly from the 1930s.

Was it to be a genuine merger or a takeover? In policy terms, it was a takeover of both of the established organisations by the Department of Employment, with its 'Stricter Benefit Regime' philosophy. But Fogden sought to harness expertise from both the MSC and the UBS for the benefit of the new ES. Inevitably, this meant a split Head Office with the Chief Executive and the former UBS staff based in London and the former MSC staff based in Sheffield – linked by video-conferencing studios, frequent travelling and an endless flow of paper. As time went on, the balance shifted as more functions were located in Sheffield, but Fogden maintained a significant London presence as there was no doubt where power resided – with the Secretary of State in DE HQ in Caxton House.

Fogden's new top team or Executive Board was a 'balanced ticket' – drawn equally from the MSC and the DE – with Steve Loveman as Deputy Chief Executive (succeeded in January 1989 by John Turner), Mike Emmott as Director of Programmes, John Cooper as Director of Field Operations, Richard Foster as Head of Planning and myself as Director of Personnel and Resources. Fogden believed in a team approach and every Friday morning the Board would meet on a video-conference link between London and Sheffield to share information and decide what should happen next.

In the Regions, it looked like a reverse takeover. Managers from the MSC tended to get the best jobs, simply because they were more highly graded than their counterparts in the UBS. The new Regional ES structure resembled that of the MSC and largely inherited the MSC's Regional Directors. The exception was London and the South East, where David Normington from DE HQ became Director of a massive new Region split into three Divisions, with Divisional Directors drawn from the UBS. Below Regional level, 78 Area Managers were appointed at the time of the merger – again most, but by no means all, were from an MSC background. For the time being, the merger only went down to Area level. Below Area level were about 1000 Jobcentres and 1000 Benefit Offices.

On 26 October 1987, the new organisation came into being under the title of the 'Employment Service' (ES). In welding together two disparate bodies, communications were vitally important. All staff received a leaflet entitled *The Employment Service – A Shared Opportunity*. Fogden appeared in a video. A newsletter called *News of the Employment Service* (NOTES) was launched and ES set itself the target of having the best internal communications of any networked organisation.

Strategy of the new ES

The launch document for staff – *A Shared Opportunity* – explained that:

> *the basic objective of the merger is to bring together the work of both organisations to provide a more coherent and effective service for unemployed people, and particularly the long-term unemployed, by offering them a range of opportunities to help them back into work as quickly as possible.*

The document left staff in no doubt of the 'policing' role of the new organisation. It noted that some unemployed people were:

> *not in fact genuinely available or actively seeking work. In this case, it is the duty of all of us in the Employment Service as civil servants to review those individuals' entitlement to unemployment benefits and check their availability for work thoroughly and systematically.*

The priorities of the new ES were elaborated in the ES Operational Plan for 1998–99 and in Fowler's White Paper *Training for Employment*. The White Paper noted that, 'It is in no one's interest that unemployed people remain out of touch with the jobs market and become passive recipients of unemployment benefits.'[3] The priorities were:

1 'to give positive help to people who have been unemployed for over six months and to other unemployed people who need such help (particularly people with disabilities or other disadvantages) notably through increased emphasis on placing the long-term unemployed into jobs', through Restart, Claimant Advisers, Job Clubs etc, and into training;
2 'to make accurate and prompt payments of benefit to unemployed claimants at the same time as ensuring that benefit is only paid to those who are entitled to it...';
3 'to improve its capacity to deliver services through promoting the integration of Jobcentres and Unemployment Benefit Offices, training and development, improved communications and information technology.'

This was a very different agenda from that which had prevailed in the MSC. There was no reference to job broking or finding and filling vacancies. It was explained to Fowler that the work of Jobcentres was:

> *placed firmly in the context of testing availability and trying to place long term unemployed people whom private agencies can do little to help. This represents a considerable shift of emphasis for Jobcentres, whose staff have hitherto seen 'job broking' and providing a service to employers as high priorities.*[4]

It was indeed an agenda which the founders of the ESA in the 1970s would have regarded as a recipe for disaster – likely to thrust the service back into the downward spiral of decline from which it had with great difficulty been extracted. There were still plenty of unreconstructed managers in the service who held these views but thought it politic not to voice them too loudly. Even some Regional Directors regretted the lack of reference to job broking in the priorities. But the counter-revolution was irresistible.

The new priorities were reflected in a new set of performance indicators. There was no longer any interest in the placings of those who were changing jobs, only in the placings of unemployed people. The latter figures did, however, include non-claimants, such as women returners to the labour market. There was particular interest in placings of long-term unemployed people. The Stricter Benefit Regime was reflected in targets for 'claims not pursued' (ie cases where people had decided not to make a claim, perhaps because they went for a job instead or pursued an alternative benefit).

Table 14.1 gives ES performance data over the next few years.

Table 14.1 *ES performance data, 1986/87–1990/91 (000s)*

	1986/87	1987/88	1988/89	1989/90	1990/91
Vacancies notified	2610	2700	2700	2600	2400
Total placings*	1910	1900	1864	1840	1700
Unemployed placings	+	+	1485	1490	1400
Long-term unemployed claimant placings (6 months or more)	+	+	242	252	208

Notes: *Total placings were not a performance indicator from October 1987, but are included for information.
+ means not available.
Source: ES management statistics.

It is interesting that, contrary to the views of the MSC traditionalists, the change in priorities did *not* have a devastating effect on overall vacancy and placing performance. No doubt, if ES had continued on its 'find and fill vacancies' agenda throughout the Lawson boom to 1990, total placings would have gone higher, probably overshooting the elusive two million mark. But although job broking no longer featured in the new ES's priorities, in practice the job broking performance was creditable, reflecting perhaps the fact that, thanks to the pioneers of the 1970s, Jobcentres were now well established in local communities and that Jobcentre managers were still endeavouring to maximise placings.

'Performance' in the merged ES of course embraced not just employment outcomes but also the speed and accuracy of benefit payments. In 1989, the ES found itself under criticism from the House of Commons Public Accounts Committee for inaccuracy of benefit payments. The National Audit Office had found that the level of incorrect payments, particularly under-payments, was estimated to be between £34 million and £89 million.[5] Geoffrey Holland, the

Permanent Secretary, told the Committee with disarming candour that senior management had been pre-occupied with integration and restart and had 'taken their eye off the ball in this particular area'.[6] This chastening experience led to a major review by Mike Horsman, and to new controls.

Policies for ES people

The merger did not raise problems of reconciling different terms and conditions as MSC and UBS staff had remained on the same civil service terms throughout their period of separation. But there were marked differences in culture and in custom and practice. Drawing on ideas that Geoffrey Holland was promoting about human resource development, Fogden launched an initiative which became known as 'Success through People', with the help of Barbara Thomas and Ken New in the ES's new human resources team. This initiative was about encouraging managers to coach and develop their teams and creating a climate where people felt empowered to use their skills and talents. Its long-term impact was shown in 1994 when the ES became the first large civil service organisation to become an Investor in People (Chapter 15).

But the dominant personnel issues in this period were on the one hand the appointment of many additional advisers (page 268) and on the other the need to reduce overall staffing levels, which paradoxically was the ES's reward for its contribution to falling unemployment. Table 14.2 shows the decline in staffing which occurred:

Table 14.2 *Staffing in the employment service, 1987–91*

Financial year	Average staffing level
1987/88	40,100
1988/89	37,400
1989/90	34,550

The reduction in staffing was achieved through natural wastage and without redundancy. But it involved redeploying staff between offices within daily travel and gave rise to a dispute with the ES's biggest union, the CPSA, when militants in some London offices resisted redeployment. The reduction in staffing also contributed to more extensive CPSA industrial action in the winter of 1989.

Systems

The merger presented much more serious problems for the computer systems which are the bloodstream of large modern organisations. Over the previous 13 years, the systems in the two networks had moved apart and there was no quick way of integrating them. It took until April 1990 to introduce a unified accounting system.[7]

The problems were most acute for the big operational systems. On the Jobcentre side, VACs (providing vacancy circulation and statistics) operated nationwide, except in the North West, where the VDU-based Supervacs had been piloted. On the benefit side, NUBS 1 (the joint DSS/DE National Unemployment Benefit System) had been upgraded with VDUs (TRES) but was obsolescent, and a joint DSS/DE team was working on the massive NUBS 2 project to replace it.

Ideally, the two large systems under development – Supervacs and NUBS 2 – would have been abandoned and replaced by a new integrated system. But it was quickly concluded that to go back to the drawing board would mean continuing to rely on the original systems – VACs and TRES – for far too long. The two large projects had to proceed. In April 1989, the Treasury agreed to the nationwide extension of Supervacs, which was completed by 1991. The story of the introduction of NUBS 2 belongs to the next chapter.

Meanwhile, an ES IT strategy exercise, carried out with the help of PA Consultants, led to a proposal to introduce 'single terminal access' as part of the NUBS 2 project. This would enable ES front-line staff to access a variety of systems from the same terminal. It was the next best thing to having fully integrated systems. Eventually, the DSS agreed to some delay in the NUBS 2 timetable to enable this to happen and all subsequent IT development was built on this foundation. The strategy exercise also produced a lengthy shopping list of potential new systems which eventually was whittled down to a local office system (embracing a client record, counselling support and vacancies and opportunities), and enhanced financial and performance information systems.

The privatisation of PER

One of Fowler's early decisions was to privatise PER – the Professional and Executive Recruitment subsidiary of ES. PER was a legacy of the Heath government – a commercial organisation within the public service, embracing a consultancy service to employers and a magazine, *Executive Post*, which was sent to 100,000 executive jobseekers. It did not fit in with the agenda of the newly merged employment service. Moreover, Fowler felt that commercial activities belonged in the private sector.

It was not a straightforward sale. What was on offer was the reputation of the organisation and the skills of its 340 staff. But there were two problems. First, PER had financial problems, with an operating deficit of £812,000 in 1987–88. Secondly, there was a dilemma about the staff. This was the first 'mainstream civil service organisation' to be privatised. Was the staff transfer to be compulsory or voluntary? Compulsory transfer could have produced a battle royal with the civil service unions – perhaps even litigation as well. But if it was voluntary, would staff be willing to go? The Department decided to have an options exercise and a system of voluntary secondment, with a 10 per cent extra salary inducement thrown in. This approach worked and 82 per cent of PER staff opted for secondment. Fowler won the dubious accolade of being praised in the *Guardian* for having placated the unions.[8]

In September 1988, it was announced that PER was being bought for £6 million by Pergamon, part of Maxwell Communications Corporation. PER was to be part of a new division headed by Kevin Maxwell, who appeared at a press conference with Fowler. Kevin's father, Robert Maxwell, wrote to welcome PER staff on board. As it turned out, it was not the happiest of takeovers. In November 1988, Pergamon sent back to the ES the three most senior civil servants who had joined them, followed by 90 more junior staff in the next three months. By November 1989, secondment had ceased. About 25 per cent of the secondees had joined Pergamon and the rest had rejoined the Employment Department Group; a much depleted PER was still trading at a loss.[9]

The ES had to decide what its role in the executive labour market should be after the privatisation. Initially, Jobcentres were advised to encourage employers wishing to notify executive vacancies to approach private agencies like PER, though, if the employer insisted, the vacancy should be accepted.[10] But in 1990/91, when large numbers of professionals and managers became redundant, the ES's lack of a specialist service in this sector presented more difficulties and new job clubs and courses for executives were set up.

The 'Stricter Benefit Regime'

The 'Stricter Benefit Regime' or 'SBR' was the shorthand expression used by civil servants for the policies which Young had inaugurated and which Fowler was now formalising and reinforcing. It came into common use among officials after the 1987 Election. The ES's new priorities (page 263) reflected the new dualism – helping the long-term unemployed but also policing the register. In the White Paper *Training for Employment*, the 'helping' measures included Restart interviews (now guaranteed after every six months of unemployment), Job Clubs, the Enterprise Allowance Scheme, Restart Courses and advice on in-work benefits.

The White Paper also stressed the need to ensure that the social security system was not abused, calling to its aid a famous sentence in Beveridge's 1942 Report (see page 99 above):

> *The correlative of the State's undertaking to ensure adequate benefit for unavoidable interruption of earnings, however long, is enforcement of the citizen's obligation to seek and accept all reasonable opportunities of work.*

The White Paper pointed out that the law required unemployed claimants to be both capable of and available for work each day for which benefit is claimed. By contrast, the 1987 Labour Force Survey showed that:

> *Some 520,000 claimants said in response to specific questions that they were not available to start work within two weeks; a further 240,000 said that they were available for work but had not looked for a job in the past four weeks; and there were also 190,000 benefit claimants who said that they were working and claiming at the same time.*[11]

Allowing that some of these would be legitimate claims (eg working part time and claiming unemployment benefit), there was 'a surprisingly high number of claimants whose entitlement to benefits was questionable'. There was also the problem of fraud. In 1986, 300 out of 600 taxi drivers investigated in the Midlands ceased to claim benefit. In 1987, 1300 seasonal holiday workers on the South Coast ceased to claim benefit after 4400 cases were investigated.[12]

To tackle these problems, Fowler was taking the following new measures:

- introducing 100 more Claimant Advisers on top of the existing cadre of 750;
- asking all those attending Restart interviews to fill in a questionnaire to test their availability for work;
- following up people who failed to attend Job Clubs, training etc which they had committed to attend in Restart interviews; in the South East 80 per cent of those who said they would attend a Job Club failed to do so;
- introducing a new cadre of New Claims Advisers (NCAs) so that all initial claims for unemployment benefit were dealt with by more senior staff, both to check eligibility more rigorously and to provide better advice on jobs and benefits; this was an important new initiative for the ES, with 1700 appointments in 1988/89 alone; and
- appointing a further 50 fraud officers, bringing the total to 850, strengthening cooperation with DHSS and Inland Revenue fraud teams and focusing fraud drives particularly on the South East.

This set of measures followed the trend set by Young of using detailed intervention by additional civil servants as a way of curbing unemployment. Within the ES, this enriching of the staffing mix helped to sustain morale at a time of change and falling overall numbers. The government's critics complained about what they saw as the harassment of unemployed people, but, as discussed in Chapter 13, it seems clear that the approach contributed to the marked decline in unemployment, and particularly long-term unemployment, in the latter part of the 1980s (Table 14.3).

How effective they would have been without a rapidly expanding economy is questionable. But, in the conditions of the Lawson boom, it was highly desirable that the pool of labour represented by those who were unemployed should play an active labour market role, both in their own interests and to curb wage inflation, particularly in the overheated South East.

At the same time, another step to tighten benefit rules for the unemployed was made by John Moore, Fowler's successor at the DHSS. He used his powers

Table 14.3 *UK claimant unemployment by duration, 1986–90 (000s)*

	All unemployed	26–52 weeks	Over 52 weeks
April 1986	3325	665	1366
April 1987	3107	632	1295
April 1988	2536	484	1029
April 1989	1883	345	744
April 1990	1626	284	540

Source: Department of Employment Gazette.

under the 1986 Social Security Act to extend from April 1988 the maximum period of benefit disqualification (for leaving voluntarily etc) from 13 weeks to 26 weeks. From 1913 to 1986 the period had been six weeks. The new severe penalty probably made the labour market more rigid rather than more flexible, since it increased the element of risk in entering a dubious or badly paid job. Indeed, Ministers seemed to recognise this, for in 1989 they introduced 'Employment on Trial' – a special exemption from penalty for long-term unemployed people entering new jobs – making the legal situation even more complex.[13] They would have done better to revisit their 1988 decision.

The 1989 Social Security Act

It was one of the characteristics of the Thatcher and Major governments that, once they had found a promising policy approach, they tried to squeeze more and more out of it. This was true of privatisation and of industrial relations reform. It was also true of the Stricter Benefit Regime. So in 1988 the Department of Social Security[14] introduced a Bill to which the Department of Employment contributed, which became the 1989 Social Security Act. It was designed among other things to tighten the SBR.

First, the Act required unemployed people 'actively to seek work' in each week for which they claimed benefit. This meant taking 'all appropriate steps', such as applying for jobs, looking at vacancies in the Jobcentre and in newspapers and magazines. ES officials were to check on people's activity at Restart interviews and at other times. If the level of activity seemed inadequate, there would be a written warning and further interview, after which the claim might be suspended and the case go to adjudication. Disallowance was for only two weeks (in contrast to the 26 weeks maximum for other disqualifications). In support of this measure, Ministers argued that merely requiring claimants to be 'available for work' was not enough, since case law said that they did not have to look for it. A survey in London in 1988 had shown that one-quarter of the unemployed had not looked for work in the previous week, of whom half had not looked for work for four weeks. Opposition critics, led by Clare Short, said that Ministers were in effect reintroducing the hated 'genuinely seeking work' provision of the

1920s (pages 63–5) about which Beveridge had said 'The condition will not, it is hoped, ever rise again from its dishonoured grave' (page 77).

Secondly, the Act removed the right of unemployed claimants to refuse jobs on the grounds that they were not 'suitable', which had been defined broadly as not paying the rate for the job. Ministers regarded the 'rate for the job' as an outmoded concept which stood in the way of a flexible labour market. The new Act removed the concept of 'suitable employment'. As with 'actively seeking', the operation of the new provision depended heavily on ES officials. At the new claim interview, they would decide the length of a 'permitted period' up to a maximum of 13 weeks, during which claimants could refuse work outside their normal occupation and pay. Thereafter, claimants were expected to widen their jobsearch, and if they refused a vacancy offered them by an ES official, their benefit could be suspended and their case referred to adjudication.

This part of the Act stirred up a considerable controversy in Parliament. The Opposition argued that Ministers were trying to drive down wage levels, and the fact that at much the same time Fowler was abolishing Wages Councils seemed to support this interpretation. Frank Field claimed that he had seen a vacancy in his local Jobcentre at £1 per hour. Nicholas Scott, the DSS Minister, offered the reassurance that 'the thrust of the Employment Service is to counsel, give advice and match the skills of the unemployed with the jobs on offer'.

The new provisions came into effect on 9 October 1989. There were intensive preparations in the ES including written guidance and training courses for all ES counsellors. There was much emphasis on handling the new rules sensitively and non-provocatively. Staff were to ensure that claimants were fully aware of the new provisions. As regards 'actively seeking', staff should

> *always give further guidance and a second chance to people who do not understand the condition or need to make increased efforts to seek work before considering sanctions unless the case is a blatant refusal to look for a job.*[15]

As regards the refusal of suitable employment, the guidance was that:

> *For a vacancy to be offered, counsellors must believe that the job is one which the claimant could reasonably be expected to undertake and should reflect conditions generally available locally...*
>
> *Counsellors should always offer those vacancies with the highest rates of pay for the type of work being considered before considering those paying lower rates. In all cases, it is important that claimants are aware of any additional help available to them, for example in-work benefits.*[16]

Evidently, staff were not expected to drive people into jobs with 'sweatshop' wages. But Parliament's change in the law had loaded considerable discretion on to junior ES officials.

What effect did the Act have? The numbers disqualified or disallowed on grounds of doubtful availability, refusal of suitable employment, leaving work voluntarily or misconduct actually fell from 331,000 in 1989 to 270,000 in 1990.[17] Moreover, only a few thousand were disallowed in 1990 on grounds of failing actively to seek work. Thus, the fears of critics that the Act would lead to the large-scale harrying of the unemployed, as had occurred in the 1920s, seemed misplaced. One factor no doubt was the cautious guidance given by the ES as described in the previous paragraph. Other factors may have been the deteriorating labour market, staffing shortages and pressures in the ES and also the lack of sympathy of some ES staff with the new regulations, so that they chose to ignore them.[18] The more fundamental question is the effect on jobseeker behaviour of this and the other elements of the Stricter Benefit Regime. This is discussed in Chapter 17.

Employment Training and the TECs

Fowler made major changes in the government's training programmes and these in turn had a considerable impact on the ES. He brought together a range of training programmes, together with the Community Programme, into a single unified training programme Employment Training (ET), with priority for the long-term unemployed. ET was a lineal descendant of the new JTS which Young had introduced in 1986 (page 251). Participants would receive their benefit plus £10, they would be assessed by Approved Training Agents, and then receive training and work experience with a Training Manager or employer for up to 12 months. The ES's main role was to refer people to ET through a Restart interview or other contacts. ET was launched in September 1988. It was soon found that many people referred from Restart failed to join the programme or dropped out later. Concern about this led to a major scrutiny (page 289).

In September 1988, the Trades Union Congress voted for non-cooperation with the new programme. This led to a swift decision by Fowler to dispense with the MSC's successor body – the Training Commission – thus ending corporatism as a way of running national labour market programmes. In its place, Fowler decided on a very different locally-based business model, based on precedents from the US. In December 1988, he announced the establishment of Training and Enterprise Councils.[19] These were to be private employer-led companies which would take over the local responsibility for running government training programmes and stimulating training. The TECs were established locally in 1989 and 1990. The ES lost to the TECs its work on the Enterprise Allowances – and this Scheme gradually faded away. More significantly, the creation of the TECs created a curious contrast of administration within the DE as between on the one hand the monolithic and disciplined civil service-led ES and on the other hand the devolved and diverse business-led TECs. However great the differences between the ES and the TECs, ET depended on close cooperation between them – something that proved difficult to achieve.

The Integration Pilots

For top management in the new ES, the full benefits of the merger could not be realised without integrating the two networks of local offices, thus bringing jobsearch and claiming benefit physically together. It was recognised that integration would take years to accomplish; after all, separation had taken about 10 years to complete. Moreover, how integration should be accomplished raised many complex issues. Accordingly, in December 1987 the ES obtained Fowler's approval for 'Integration Pilots'.

The Integration Pilots were organised with great zest by Mike Horsman and Julian Roberts. To test a variety of models, there were 79 pilots affecting 180 local offices. The ES's trade unions were uneasy about the implications for the benefit staff who formed the majority of CPSA members, expressing concerns about working hours and the risk of assaults in open-plan integrated offices. Former MSC staff feared that too close a link with benefit could undermine the confidence of jobseekers and employers in the placing service.[20] The pilots went ahead regardless, though there was some industrial action in Easterhouse in Glasgow.

Not surprisingly, the pilots showed that the ethos of the new ES was only skin deep: 'Attitudes are important and 14 years of separation have not been reversed in a few short weeks'.[21] This was exemplified in 'them and us' attitudes between Jobcentres and Benefit Offices. None the less, the Head Office team were confident of the potential of integration. They recommended a unified network of around 1300 integrated offices, with each handling the full range of employment and benefit business. The offices should not be too large, since small to medium offices were easier to manage. Thus the huge benefit offices inherited from the 1930s would go. The offices should be accessible from, but not necessarily in, the high street and equipped both with TRES and VACs/Supervacs terminals. There was a preference for a 'multi-functional' front line.[22] There was a new model design for integrated offices with new corporate colours – blue and yellow.[23]

Early in 1989, the ES presented to Fowler a well documented case for integration. The process would take some seven years to accomplish. While there would be heavy costs for premises, information technology and training, there would be much larger benefits, through an estimated 3 per cent reduction in unemployed claimants (worth £32 million per year), plus staff savings. Moreover, integration would create:

> an environment where the unemployed are regularly given the opportunity to consider vacancies and training opportunities and where the payment of benefit will be clearly seen as linked to the process of jobseeking.[24]

To ES top management, the case seemed overwhelming. But it did not prove easy to get it accepted. Nor did it help that the issue got into the public domain. On 11 January, the *Guardian* published a leak on integration under the title: 'Jobcentres face axe'[25] and on the same day Michael Meacher MP attacked Fowler on integration and the agency issue and alleged that senior managers in the ES were 'unhappy'.[26] This Opposition intervention did nothing to get the uncertainties resolved. It was not until December 1989 that Fowler finally announced his decision on integration. One problem was that the up-front costs of the integration package were high. John Turner, the new Deputy Chief Executive, was concerned about this and in May 1989 proposed 'pragmatic integration', in which the ES would take advantage of existing surplus space in its estate in order to keep down capital costs. But the reasons for the delay in decision-making on integration went deeper than this. To explain them, there is a need to look at the other burning issue of 1989 – the question of Agency status.

Next Steps and the Agency concept

For 20 years, Westminster and Whitehall had been trying to improve the efficiency and effectiveness of government. In 1968, the Fulton Committee (page 139) had recommended the establishment of 'accountable units' as a key to this, but had also mentioned the idea of 'hiving off' to external boards. Chapter 9 described how, in the early 1970s, the Department of Employment decision to set up agencies for employment and training services was overlaid by the decision in 1972 to 'hive off' the agencies to the MSC. Over the next seven or eight years, few Departments followed the DE's lead in handing over major functions to agencies or external boards. The tide began to turn, however, in 1982, when the Prime Minister launched the Financial Management Initiative. This recommended that civil service managers at all levels should have objectives linked where possible to performance measures, clearer responsibilities and better management information (particularly about costs).

But the real breakthrough came in February 1988 when, after a prolonged battle with the Treasury,[27] the Efficiency Unit under Sir Robin Ibbs published his report, 'Improving Management in Government: The Next Steps',[28] which declared that, 'The Civil Service is too big and too diverse to manage as a single entity.' It recommended that 'Agencies should be established to carry out the executive functions of government within a policy and resources framework'. The real aim of the change was to improve the clarity of the executive role within government and the attention paid to management. This was reflected in the idea of a Framework Document for an Agency and in the greater status afforded to executive management and the position of a chief executive. The experience of the MSC had influenced the authors of the report.[29]

Unlike its predecessors, this initiative proved to have astonishing momentum, assisted both by the wholehearted support of Mrs Thatcher and by the energy with which Peter Kemp, Second Permanent Secretary and Project Manager, pursued the project. Ten years later, there were 138 Agencies comprising over three-quarters of the civil service. A House of Commons

Committee said that it was 'the most ambitious attempt at civil service reform this century'.[30]

To ES top management, the ES was a natural and early candidate for Agency status. The ES was already a separate management command within the Department and much readier for Agency status than, say, the executive functions in the Department of Social Security. But Agency status could not be taken for granted. Lawson and the Treasury had secured 'an understanding that agency status would always be seen as a second best to privatisation, which would have to be explored first'.[31] Thus before making the ES a new-style Agency or agreeing to integration, Fowler and his colleagues had to investigate the alternative of privatising all or part of the ES, just as PER had already been privatised. No such study was ever made public and we can only guess at the arguments which would have been deployed. One option was to privatise the Jobcentres, while retaining the benefit offices as public bodies. But would not this put at risk the highly successful Stricter Benefit Regime? Moreover, would legislation to remove the government's duty since 1909 to provide a public employment service be politically attractive? As with PER, the staffing aspects would have been another major problem area. Whatever the reasons, Ministers eventually decided against privatisation and in favour of Agency status, combined with integration.

Agency status itself was the subject of much controversy within the government. The ES was the first big mainstream civil service organisation to be a candidate for Agency status, so it would set an important precedent. The tensions were partly across Whitehall, where Kemp encouraged Departments to seek for their prospective Agencies the greatest possible 'flexibilities', whereas the Treasury was concerned about the control of expenditure and reluctant to delegate further financial freedoms. The Department of Employment's posture was that, unless there were significant freedoms for Agencies, Agency status was not worth having.

The outcome of the intense negotiations about Agency status is described in Chapter 15. Meanwhile, within the ES, it was important to prepare managers for the new regime. In November 1989 a conference for 200 ES senior managers was held at the Old Swan Hotel in Harrogate. The conference had a somewhat surreal quality. Although it was all about becoming an Agency, there had still been no announcement that the ES *was* to be an Agency. Members of the ES Executive had a working dinner with Tim Eggar, the Minister of State, discussing the drafting of the framework document. Moreover, as part of its staffing dispute, the CPSA had advised its members that senior management were 'wining and dining' in Harrogate while they were 'sweating their guts out'. As a result, a large CPSA picket chanted and booed as delegates arrived at the conference. The conference used presentational techniques unfamiliar to civil servants, so that Mike Fogden found himself ascending the rostrum under a spotlight in a darkened hall to a background of martial music. There was an inspirational talk by Terry Murphy about radical change in Abbey National. Somehow, the conference rhetoric gave Area Managers the idea that Agency would be accompanied by far greater local autonomy than was possible within the policy and financial framework that was being developed.

Conclusion

At long last, on 1 December 1989, Fowler announced that the ES was to become an Agency in April 1990 and that the two networks of local offices were to be integrated into a single network of 1100–1200 'one stop' offices by 1994. Tony Blair, the Opposition spokesman on employment, was suspicious. He called for the maintenance of a 'proper job-finding service'. He went on:

> *The employment service is in the front line in the battle against unemployment and is an indispensable part of a well-functioning labour market. The vital role it performs in the public interest cannot be sacrificed to financial expediency or political dogma.*[32]

But managers in the ES were relieved. Fowler's decisions resolved uncertainty and gave them clarity about the future. Agency status would not offer an easy life, since the new performance targets would be closely monitored and might be hiked upwards year by year. But there would be more flexibility in the use of resources, particularly on the personnel side. Moreover, it was in the government's interest that Agencies should be a success. The next chapter will discuss what the new Agency was like and how integration was pursued.

In January 1990, Fowler resigned to 'spend more time with his family'. The period under Fowler from 1987 to 1990 had been a time of transition for the employment service. The merger had been successfully carried through, though there was a great sense of incompleteness until local office integration took place. Young's Stricter Benefit Regime had been further developed, with additional rules and additional counsellors. This had helped to bring down unemployment, particularly long-term unemployment. At the same time, placing performance had been sustained reasonably well, admittedly in a highly favourable economic climate. In the next phase, the new Agency was to encounter an economic blizzard just at the time when local office integration reached its peak.

15

The Employment Service as an Agency, 1990–93

'The establishment of the Employment Service (ES) as an Executive Agency has created a firmly performance-driven organisation, clearly focused on the achievement of its key objectives.' (Evaluation Report, 1995).[1]

Introduction

On 2 April 1990, the employment service became an executive Agency – at the time the largest new-style agency in government. Thus part of the story of the years 1990–93 relates to how the ES established its position as an Agency under its first three-year framework and introduced an integrated local office network and improved management and computer systems.

At the same time, the service had to contend with an unexpected and severe downturn in the economy. The strategic response was to build up special measures to assist unemployed people, while maintaining and intensifying the benefit control system developed under Young and Fowler. The Stricter Benefit Regime was in line with the general sentiments of the Conservative Party and backed by the Department of Employment, by the Treasury and by government economists as a contribution to 'supply-side economics' – and even endorsed by OECD.[2] The service thus had a consistent strategy, largely unaffected by such key political events as the replacement of Mrs Thatcher by John Major in November 1990, Major's surprise Election victory in April 1992 and the withdrawal from the European Exchange Rate Mechanism in September 1992.

Ministers and civil servants

The Secretaries of State of the period were Michael Howard from January 1990 to the Election in April 1992 and then Gillian Shephard from April 1992 to May 1993.

The Permanent Secretary of the Department was Sir Geoffrey Holland until January 1993, when he moved to the Department for Education and was succeeded by Nicholas Monck (knighted in 1994) from the Treasury.

Mike Fogden continued as Chief Executive of the Agency. In the pressurised period of setting up the Agency in 1990, Ministers decided to keep him on as Chief Executive without opening up the post to competition. John Turner continued to serve as Fogden's deputy.

The New 'Agency'

The ES's Agency Framework[3] which came into effect in April 1990 was the product of an intensive process of negotiation within the government over the preceding months. The ES was one of many organisations seeking Agency status at that time, but it was by far the biggest and the closest to the political process. The parties to these negotiations were conscious that vital precedents were being set. At official level, key protagonists were Peter Kemp, Project Manager of the whole Agency process, the Treasury mandarins, senior officials in the Department of Employment and Mike Fogden in the ES. Within the Department, Graham Reid chaired a steering group which held numerous meetings in 1989–90 and gradually hammered out the draft Framework Document. It also had to be cleared with other Departments, notably the Treasury, and with Ministers. The process moved to and fro and in late January 1990 the document had still not been finally agreed. Time was now very tight as there was a commitment to consult the civil service unions. One of the union organisers wrote to his members: '80 days to go and what do you know?'[4]

Early in February 1990, Michael Howard approved the draft Framework. This opened the way to showing it to the unions. Union representatives were disturbed that the draft made no mention of Whitley or even of consultation with the unions. Fogden met the unions and met some of their concerns. At last, the Framework Document was printed and circulated throughout the ES.

The Framework Document defined the position of the Agency and its relationship with the Department far more tightly than had been the case for the relationship between the Department and the MSC. The ES's main *aim* was:

> to help promote a competitive and efficient labour market particularly by giving positive help to unemployed people through its job placement service and other programmes and by the payment of benefits and allowances to those who were entitled to them.

It went on to list five main operational objectives:

- to provide help with jobs or training to unemployed people, particularly those unemployed more than six months and those in inner cities;
- to provide help to people with disabilities;

- to pay benefit promptly, accurately and courteously;
- to encourage unemployed claimants to seek work actively; to check their entitlement to benefit; and
- to discourage benefit fraud...

These objectives were broadly in line with those adopted in 1987.

There was a new definition of roles:

- the Secretary of State determined overall strategy and operational objectives, allocated resources to the Agency and agreed the Agency's Operational Plan and its output targets in the Annual Performance Agreement;
- the Permanent Secretary was the Secretary of State's principal adviser;
- the Chief Executive was appointed by, and accountable to, the Secretary of State and had 'full authority to manage the Agency and its day to day operations'.

The Agency concept gave the Agency and its Chief Executive a degree of autonomy over operational matters, even if ultimately the Secretary of State remained 'accountable' to Parliament for everything that happened in the Agency. As a result of Peter Kemp's advocacy, it was the Chief Executive and not the Minister who replied to MPs' enquiries on operational matters. This was intended to prevent Ministers from getting drawn back into the management issues. Some MPs[5] were infuriated at receiving replies from Chief Executives, but this practice became the norm for Executive Agencies.

The arrangement could only work if a viable distinction could be drawn between 'policy' and 'operational' matters. This has been one the most discussed aspects of 'Next Steps' and was at the heart of the conflict in 1996 between Michael Howard as Home Secretary and Derek Lewis, Chief Executive of the Prisons Agency. In the case of the employment service, the distinction proved workable both under Howard and his successors. Perhaps one reason for this was that the ES Framework recognised the interdependence of policy and operations:

- the Chief Executive was to serve on the Departmental Board and could make policy proposals to the Secretary of State, after consulting the Permanent Secretary;
- the Permanent Secretary would consult the Chief Executive before policy proposals affecting the Agency were put to the Secretary of State.

In practice, Fogden and his top team saw Ministers and DE officials several times a week and were well integrated into the policy process. This helped to ensure that the ES was sensitive to policy considerations in carrying out its operational role.

One problem in drawing up the Framework was that the ES's benefit work was ultimately the responsibility of the Secretary of State for Social Security.

This arrangement went back to 1945 (page 101). The original exchange of letters between Permanent Secretaries was unearthed from the Public Record Office. They clearly related to a very different world. The fact that this 'agency agreement' with the DSS had operated successfully for over 40 years without redefinition is a classic example of the informality of British administration. But the clarity required under Next Steps meant that it now had to be updated. It was agreed 'not to change the existing relationship but to set down what the nature and limits of that relationship were'.[6] Early in 1990, a new Agreement was reached between the two Secretaries of State that the ES should 'administer aspects of benefit for unemployment through its local offices'. To avoid the ES reporting to two Ministers, the ES's accountability was to the Secretary of State for Employment, who was responsible for these benefit functions on behalf of the Secretary of State for Social Security. The Agreement committed the two Ministers and their officials to liaise on benefit matters.

Agency financial management

Agency status led to some increase in financial autonomy. The Agency had its own vote, with the Chief Executive as 'Accounting Officer', though the Permanent Secretary retained an overall Accounting Officer responsibility and both would appear before the Public Accounts Committee. A Director of Finance and Resources, Bert Johnson, was appointed and he set about improving financial management and control throughout the Agency. This involved developing a cadre of qualified accountants, raising the level of financial awareness among managers and staff and introducing new costing systems and commercial-style accrual accounting systems alongside traditional cash accounting. The ES had its own Internal Audit.

Agency status brought some modest financial flexibilities:

- limited powers of virement between the various blocks of expenditure within the annual budget;
- the power to carry forward 0.5 per cent of running costs and 5 per cent of capital funds between financial years; however, apart from this, ES's budget, like that of other public bodies, was tightly tied to the financial year, with overspending seen as particularly reprehensible – this lack of flexibility (much criticised in the Next Steps Report) tended to lead either to underspending or to pressure to use up funds at the end of the year;
- the power to generate revenue; in 1990/91, £125,000 was generated in this way, but only £13,600 was retained by the Agency;[7]
- capital spending limits on information technology equipment and property that were more generous than those available to a Department.

The great bulk of ES resources were allocated to the Agency as before by the Secretary of State following the annual round of negotiations on public spending with the Treasury.

Agency performance

The corollary of increased autonomy was that the Agency was to be held to account for its performance. The Annual Performance Agreement defined a dozen specific targets linked to the objectives (pages 277–8), including:

- 1.65 million placings of unemployed people;[8]
- 91 per cent of new claims to be input in 6 days; and
- incorrect benefit payments should not exceed 5 per cent.

In this first year, several targets were not achieved. In particular, only 1.4 million placings were achieved. There were two extenuating circumstances. First, the performance management process was largely new and untried. Secondly, the deterioration in the labour market during the year proved unexpectedly sharp, with a drop in vacancies of 17 per cent (much larger than the 6 per cent drop in placings).[9]

In subsequent years, the ES did better at meeting its targets. For instance, in 1992/93, the target of placing 1,425,000 unemployed people into work was almost achieved, with the placing of 1,420,000. The process became better understood in both the Department and ES. In principle, Ministers and Departmental officials aimed to set targets which were 'stretching but achievable'. But in practice there was a tendency to ratchet up targets every year above the previous level. After a time, such an approach can be self-defeating, since the pressure it creates may cause a corruption of data or a sacrifice of quality or both. Indeed, ES management had to tighten up the recording of placings in local offices both in 1991/92 and in 1996/97 (page 308).

Agency personnel flexibilities

It was above all in personnel that the employment service broke new ground. Since the 1920s, terms and conditions of employment in the civil service had been under tight central control by the Treasury. The Fulton Report of 1968 had had the effect of making civil service terms and conditions more uniform, by recommending the replacement of 'the present multitude of separate classes and their separate career structures' by a 'classless, uniformly graded structure'.[10] Even under the MSC, civil service terms and conditions had been retained. The implication of the Next Steps Report of 1988 was that the huge and monolithic personnel management system of the civil service (which was 'structured to fit everything in general and nothing in particular')[11] would be broken up.

During 1989, Peter Kemp encouraged Fogden to make radical proposals for personnel flexibilities. ES senior management saw this as a historic opportunity and produced a package. The issues were highly controversial among senior civil servants. Some were uneasy, arguing that there were practical advantages in the status quo, such as inter-changeability between and within Departments. Others were strongly in favour of 'breaking up the monolith' and argued that the traditionalist view was much too Whitehall-centred. They pointed out that most civil servants were not in Whitehall: they spent the whole of their careers in large networked organisations like the ES. The priority was to adapt personnel arrangements to the needs of these individual organisations – or 'businesses' as they were increasingly called. Within the Employment Department Group, there were passionate advocates of both points of view. While the ES sought new freedoms, others were unhappy about 'breaking up the Group'. But the tide was in favour of change and the ES proposals survived the test of high level discussion both within the DE Group and with the Treasury.

The key clause in the Framework Document read: 'The Chief Executive may develop and implement personnel and pay policies best suited to the business objectives of the Agency...' This was hedged around by ambiguous references to civil service and ED Group principles and by requirements to consult, but in reality the genie was out of the bottle. It acknowledged that the ES could have a distinct staffing regime of its own and, if this was the case for the ES, it was bound to spread widely throughout the civil service – as indeed happened in the 1990s. The main areas where the ES chose to exercise its new freedom were:

- Recruitment
- Promotion
- Industrial relations
- The *Personnel Handbook*
- Pay.

These are discussed in turn.

Recruitment. The Civil Service Commission had long had a monopoly of external recruitment of Executive Officers (EOs). The ES found this system unwieldy and ill-suited to its needs. It secured the freedom to recruit its own EOs, using a specially developed competence framework. An external evaluation in 1993 found the new system to be 'operating very effectively'.[12]

Promotion. In the ED Group, as in other Departments, a dominant feature of civil service culture had been the periodic 'Promotion Panel' which interviewed 'recommended' officers in one grade and drew up a 'waiting list' of those deemed ready for promotion to the next grade. Vacancies in the higher grade were then filled by people from this list. This system suffered from at least two defects. First, posts across the Group were extremely varied, making it difficult for panels to apply clear criteria. The second problem with a nationwide waiting list was that in reality most people were not mobile: every list ended up with a residue of unplaced immobile officers. The ES's solution was *promotion by vacancy advertising* – ie advertising and interviewing for individual vacancies rather than drawing up waiting lists. This later was developed into a competence-based vacancy filling system. These innovations were evaluated and generally found to be improvements, despite some bureaucratic overload.[13]

Industrial relations. The move to Agency status was preceded by a period of CPSA industrial action in the ES's more militant local offices, mainly in inner cities. The issue was resourcing, but underlying it was a continuing power struggle between ideologically-minded union activists, often with a narrow local power base, and a management which was seen by them as lackeys of a right-wing government. Management felt that the civil service Whitley system, as it had developed, was too easily exploited by activists to waste management time, to cause delay and to extract information which was then used politically to attack Ministers. Management thus proposed that the new Agency should drop the term 'Whitley', reduce the frequency of meetings, reduce the number of union representatives at meetings and clarify whether particular discussions were 'negotiations', 'consultation' or just the passing-on of information. It took a long time to reach agreement with the unions on the industrial relations framework but management felt that its efforts had been worthwhile.

Personnel Handbook. The ED Group *Personnel Handbook* comprised several volumes of regulations and guidance which had been built up over the years. It was partly derived from central civil service sources and partly peculiar to the DE Group. ES management decided to adapt the *Handbook* to the needs of the new Agency. Lawyers advised that, where provisions in the *Handbook* were contractual, any change would have to be the subject of full consultation with the unions. This meant that the whole process took several years to complete. Among other things, there were changes in the rules for sickness absence, warnings and dismissals and probation. In addition, the Board introduced new corporate dress standards. They felt that, if staff were to influence employers and jobseekers, they needed to be smartly dressed. So T-shirts, jeans and trainers were out and ties and scarves were in. This contractual change went through smoothly as a result of careful consultation and preparation, including the issue of corporate ties and scarves to staff.

Pay. This was the most contentious subject of all. Traditionally, civil service pay depended on grade and seniority and pay increases were determined by negotiations between the Treasury and the civil service unions. This mould was already changing. The Treasury itself reached an agreement with the unions under which performance (as reflected in Annual Report markings) would influence pay increases. But it was an even bigger step for an organisation like the ES to negotiate its own pay. The ES set up its own pay team and began by looking at pay in a strategic context. Fogden wanted pay in future to reflect job weight more sensitively. He felt it was anomalous that the ES's managers in Brixton and Banbury received the same pay. Thus, whereas some organisations at this time were broadening pay bands, in the ES it was decided to replace the existing grades by a larger number of narrower pay bands. The new approach was introduced first at more senior levels.

This policy led to a major change in 1994, when seven pay bands were introduced to replace the three grades from Executive Officer (EO) to Senior Executive Officer. The change was highly controversial because of its effect on individuals. For instance, whereas previously 'supervisors' and 'advisers' had been in the same EO grade, the advisers now found themselves in a lower pay band than the supervisors. Efforts were made to smooth the transition, but these pay changes were one of several factors affecting morale in 1994–97 (page 306). None the less, on balance they created a more rational management structure in the local offices. The new system enabled a single manager to be appointed at an appropriate pay band and got rid of the awkward dual and triple commands of the past. It also offered scope for career progression from adviser to supervisor to manager.

As pay was delegated to the Agency, senior ES management now found itself negotiating with the unions over pay increases each year, though Treasury controls meant there was only limited room for manoeuvre.

Developing an Agency culture

Becoming an Agency stimulated the Executive Board to take a great interest in developing a new and dynamic Agency culture. Management ideas at the time stressed the importance of culture[14] and there was awareness of companies like Abbey National that had transformed their style and operations. Agency freedoms might offer the opportunity for the ES to follow a similar road. The Board engaged a succession of consultants to advise it both on Agency-wide change programmes and on raising the quality of the Board's own performance.[15]

When the Agency was launched in April 1990, a Mission Statement was issued which included ES 'values':

> *The ES serves people through people. We must all work together in close cooperation to provide the best possible service to our clients. We must ensure that the ES is a well managed organisation, where people want to work and where they can realise their potential.*

In the fashionable management language of the day, there was also a 'Vision':

> *We will become a business-like agency, respected for the quality of our customer service and people. We will make good use of Agency flexibilities in meeting our targets and deliver programmes and services cost-effectively through a unified local office network.*

In the next 12 months, more work was done on developing the Agency and its culture, leading to a strategic document called *ES in the '90s: Forward as an Agency*. This defined as key features of the ES's culture that it would be:

- performance driven;
- enabling;
- professional;

- creative and confident;
- positively led;
- open and trusting;
- participative and supportive.

Management training and development programmes sought to foster this culture. But underlying these aspirations were serious tensions, particularly about the notion of an 'enabling' culture, which was defined as meaning that

> *more will be devolved to managers, giving them more control over the means to deliver results. Accountability for results at all levels will be made clearer and the necessary support provided.*

Chapter 14 noted the expectation of some Area Managers that under an Agency they would have far more autonomy than hitherto. But at the second Harrogate Conference in May 1990, Board members reined back these ideas and reminded Area Managers of the constraints upon them in terms of statutory obligations and the expectations of Ministers and the Treasury.

The result was some disillusionment among middle managers and the perception of a gap between Head Office and the field. Head Office worried that, because there were two management tiers between Head Office and the local offices – the Region and the Area – messages might get lost. To help bridge the gap, Board members decided to communicate directly with all local office managers through addressing 'workshops' of managers in every Area during 1990.

One option was to dispense with the Regions so that Head Office would relate to managers nearer to local office level. This is what the new Benefits Agency did when it was established in April 1991. It replaced the former DSS Regions with 22 Areas reporting directly to a member of the BA's central board, the BA Management Team (BAMT), creating a structure rather like the 18 Areas of ESA in the 1970s (page 162). The ES Board rejected this approach. It believed that the Regions offered added value in management and were also helpful in linking the ES to the wider regional structures of government. (However, ES Regional Directors did not become part of the Government Offices which were established in 1994, combining the Regional Directors of four Departments.)

The Board took seriously the idea of a 'participative' organisation. Whenever possible, new initiatives were discussed with the field before implementation. The Board had meetings with the Regional Directors once a month, normally at the Swallow Hotel in Sheffield, and these often involved intense discussion. Moreover, Fogden gave Regional Directors discretion to introduce their own management initiatives. He thought that the organisation should be 'unified but not uniform'. Some highly creative developments ensued. Ray Phillips in North West Region, for instance, led the way in the ES in introducing sickness absence management. Martin Raff in West Midlands pioneered the introduction of Total Quality Management.

Another type of Regional initiative was in relation to aid to former Soviet countries. One effect of ending communist rule was the emergence of unemployment. These countries needed advice on setting up Jobcentre services and unemployment benefit systems and ES expertise was much in demand. It was decided to provide this by twinning ES regions with particular countries, so that Wales gave advice to Romania, Northern Region to Czechoslovakia, and so on. This approach proved extremely effective.

Early in the life of the Agency, there was a tendency to devolve support functions from the regional tier to the area tier. But, as resources got tighter in 1993, the Board decided, on the advice of Ray Phillips, to arrest this trend, to concentrate support services at regional level and to replace the Area Managers with 150 District Managers, who were expected to focus strongly on performance.

The Board tried to assess the ES's success in people management through a regular survey of staff attitudes every November from 1988 onwards. Table 15.1 illustrates some of the findings.

Table 15.1 *Regular attitude survey of ES employees (%)*

	1988	1989	1990	1991	1992	1993	1994	1995	1997	1998
Enjoy their jobs	64 (49)	60 (46)	63 (63)	72 (55)	75 (58)	67 (52)	58 (45)	56*	54	67
ES is one of the best/ above average to work for	24	21	30	41	45	36	28	53+ (30)	23	32
ES has a very uncertain future	56	68	53	38	46	81	89	93	91	76

Notes: *From 1995 onwards, a five-point in place of a four-point response option was offered, making comparison between the figures before and after this year difficult. Figures in brackets have been adjusted to provide a consistent series.
+The 1995 figure had a different response scale, which is difficult to compare with other years. Figure in brackets is adjusted.

The bottom line shows that ES employees had a shrewd perception of the threats to the organisation. Their feelings of uncertainty increased in 1989, when Fowler was considering the future of the Jobcentres, but fell away in 1990–92 when the decisions on integration and agency status had been taken. The sense of uncertainty then revived again in 1992/93 as issues were arising about individuals' pay and widespread market testing was introduced (page 304–6).

Office of Hope

The most encouraging testimony to the ES's success in developing its workforce came with its achievement of Investor in People status in 1994. At the time, it was one of the biggest organisations in the country to receive this recognition, and in the civil service only ACAS obtained recognition earlier.

Integration

Chapter 14 showed how in 1989 Ministers eventually agreed not only to Agency status for the ES but also to the integration of the two networks of Jobcentres and benefit offices into a single network of 1100–1200 offices by 1994. In March 1991, Fogden persuaded Ministers that ES integrated offices should be called 'Jobcentres', since this was too valuable a brand name to lose. By then, Mrs Thatcher had departed and the tensions of the early 1980s over 'Jobcentres' could at last be laid to rest.

Led by John Turner, the integration project dominated the ES scene in the early 1990s. It was not just about bricks and mortar. The aim was to 'make the services more comprehensive and accessible to our clients'.[16] For instance, it was seen as important that, when people signed each fortnight to get their benefit, they should pass attractive vacancy displays. Key features of integrated offices[17] were that, as far as possible, they should:

- be on a single site with a full range of services;
- have a single HEO manager; smaller offices had better performance and were easier to run than the very large city centre offices of the past; integration meant the end of some historic offices such as Corporation Street, Birmingham;[18]
- be 'located in the world of work and accessible to our clients but not necessarily in prime shopping sites'; this meant pulling back from the prime sites favoured in the 1970s;
- be open to the public at least 36 hours a week; this was the resolution of a highly contentious issue and involved extending the hours of opening of benefit offices;
- be refurbished in the latest corporate design; the orange and black of the 1970s Jobcentres was replaced by blue and yellow; and
- be open plan offices; this proved the most contentious issue of all and is discussed further below.

ES management made rapid progress with integration. By April 1991 there were 450 integrated offices, against a tough target of 500. By April 1995, there were 970 integrated offices and the process was nearing completion. Integration was carried out far more quickly than had been than the original Jobcentre programme, which had taken 10 years to complete. This was because of the 'pragmatic' willingness in many cases to adapt existing premises.

Overall, integration was a considerable success. It helped staff to feel they belonged to a unified organisation. The integration process upgraded the quality of the estate, which had become increasingly jaded. Customers preferred integrated offices.[19] Above all, it brought the operations together in a way which was consistent with the philosophy of linking placement and payment.

Integration – the battle of the screens

The one aspect of integration which proved highly contentious was management's insistence on open plan offices, without screens separating the staff from the public. Senior managers in the ES believed that Jobcentre work depended upon direct and honest interviews between staff and unemployed people, which could not be achieved through a protective screen. The introduction of open plan in the Jobcentres of the 1970s had not presented problems, since employment work rarely gave rise to violent incidents (even if there were exceptions like the murder of two members of staff in Torquay Jobcentre). Benefit work presented a much greater risk of violence because money was at stake. Cutting off someone's benefit because of a breach of the rules could cause physical retaliation. Despite this, in some benefit offices, local staff had agreed to open plan, but in many others management had installed protective screens in offices to allay staff anxiety about their physical safety.

Integration therefore often involved the removal of screens in areas where staff had got used to having them. Understandably, benefit staff were apprehensive. In 1991, the staff unions launched a campaign to try to get ES management to shift its position. They tried to persuade the Health and Safety Executive to compel the introduction of screens. When this tactic failed, the CPSA balloted their members[20] and took industrial action in some of the more militant offices between November 1991 and April 1992. For Fogden, this was a make or break issue and he stood firm, so that in 1995 only two ES offices had screens.[21]

Despite their apprehensions, most staff were positive about integration once they had experienced it.[22] The improved environment led to better rapport with clients. Open plan meant that staff were less isolated. But staff security continued to cause anxiety. The psychologists advised on how best to handle difficult clients and situations. Security guards were employed where necessary. But the number of violent incidents increased between 1990 and 1994 (Table 15.2). It was not clear how far this was due to better recording, to integration or to the tightening of the Stricter Benefit Regime. The whole issue was to assume an even higher profile with the introduction of the Jobseeker's Allowance.

Computerisation

Alongside integration went major improvements in the computer support available in the Agency, particularly through the implementation of the massive NUBS 2[23] Project, which had been under preparation for several years. NUBS

Table 15.2 *Assaults* on members of ES staff, 1989–1998*

1989	1990	1991	1992	1993	1994	1995	1996	1997	1998
118	161	152	203	258	265	220	240	290	199

Note: *Assaults are defined as any physical contact, however slight, between client and staff.
Source: ES management statistics.

2 fell within the DSS's Operational Strategy and its technical design and implementation were the responsibility of the DSS's Information Technology Services Agency (ITSA). But it was also an ES project, since the users were ES staff. Thus it was run essentially by agreement between senior staff in the two Agencies (apart from a brief period when a consultant was in overall charge). In the ES, John Turner and Rosemary Thew led the project. NUBS 2 provided modern computer back-up to the administration of unemployment benefit and was linked to other systems, such as the Income Support Computer System and the Inland Revenue's system. It also achieved large staff savings. In October 1991, the first two offices in Preston and Chorley went live. The roll-out was completed in September 1994.

There were two sides to ES computing – benefit-related systems and other ES systems. As noted in Chapter 14, it had been agreed that they should be linked by introducing single terminal access, through the NUBS 2 project. This was a major advance. The ES had its own Computer Branch for the development of non-benefit systems. New systems such as OSCAR (Office Support to Claimant Adviser Reviews) were introduced. As agreed in 1989, the enhanced vacancy system, Supervacs, was introduced throughout the network by July 1991 and was subsequently enhanced to provide occupational search facilities. But this system fell far short of what was required. The area of greatest potential in ES computing was to combine a modern vacancy and opportunity system with a client record – with the latter linked to NUBS 2. Chapter 16 will show how a way was found to justify the capital investment for such a development.

ES services in recession and recovery

Integration took place against a much more difficult economic environment than had been anticipated. In 1989, when integration and the new Agency were being planned, the Lawson boom had brought claimant unemployment down to about 1.5 million by the end of 1989. But there it stabilised. In the latter half of 1990, unemployment began to surge upwards, particularly in the South East. It continued to rise for the next three years until, by the winter of 1992/93, it was around three million again – the doom-laden figure of the early 1980s.

This economic climate had a big impact on the ES's Advisers.[24] In 1989, there were 4000 Advisers divided into three groups – New Client Advisers, Restart Counsellors and Claimant Advisers. Between them, they carried out eight million interviews a year. These advisory posts had been introduced in rather a piecemeal way in the mid-1980s as part of Young's – and Fowler's – revolution. They had contributed to the reduction of long-term unemployment since 1986. None the less, there was controversy about their role. Labour Party spokesmen saw them as part of a government plot to achieve an artificial reduction in unemployment. Henry McLeish MP commented:

The government's record on unemployment amounts to a brilliantly conceived, superbly executed, and carefully concealed fraud.[25]

Simply by using Restart, the government has been able to whisk away a huge chunk of the population, allowing them to live on benefit.[26]

As discussed above (pages 250–1) it was true that large numbers of men had moved on to invalidity benefit and that Restart interviews might in some cases have encouraged this. But it was also true that the workforce in employment had increased by 2.5 million since 1986, far more than the fall in unemployment.[27]

Within government, there were different concerns about the ES Advisers. Mrs Thatcher was concerned about 'drop-out'. It was noted that, at the Restart interview, long-term unemployed people would express interest in Employment Training (ET) or other programmes but nearly half would fail to pursue it subsequently. Even if they did join ET, 14 per cent would drop out in the first three weeks. This concern led to a major scrutiny, which reported in March 1990.[28] Trying to explain 'drop-out', the report argued that prolonged unemployment could lead to lethargy, apathy and social isolation. There were young people who were 'against the system' and there was concern about low pay. Also some people were working and signing. Another cause of 'drop-out' was that many referrals did not reflect a genuine need discovered during the interview, but rather management pressure to fulfil a target. Another problem was the 'mixed quality' of ET. Many ES staff were sceptical about the programme. In the first year, only 30 per cent completed training, but of these 60 per cent got jobs. The scrutiny produced a long list of recommendations, including the proposal that the ES should manage the assessment element of ET. But the Training and Enterprise Councils (TECs) successfully argued that they must control assessment as they were judged on the basis of training outcomes.

Within the ES, Mike Emmott's Programme Directorate, had already produced in November 1989 a 'New Framework of Counselling'.[29] The authors argued that the interview process was inadequately structured and managed. Restart was losing its cutting edge. Some claimants had learned how to play the system. The interviewing skills of the Advisers themselves were becoming dulled with the repetition of carrying up to 45 interviews a week. There were three key ideas underlying their proposals:

- action planning;
- seeking to gain the commitment of clients to take responsibility for the direction and outcome of the interview; and
- strategic case management – continuous client care for all who were unemployed for six months or more.

Soon after his arrival in the Department, Michael Howard was briefed on these ideas and those of the Drop-Out Scrutiny. He agreed to a package which was announced in April 1990. The existing pattern of Adviser interviews on first claiming and then every six months thereafter was retained with the following additions:

- at every interview, Advisers would seek to reach an agreed outcome, in the form of a Back to Work Plan;
- selected claimants would be interviewed at the 13-week stage;
- to increase flexibility, Restart Counsellors and Claimant Advisers would be merged under the title of Claimant Advisers; New Client Advisers remained as a separate group until 1992/93, when a single unified group of advisers, known as Client Advisers, was created;
- where possible, Advisers would operate a 'caseload' approach, where a client regularly saw the same Adviser;
- claimants who rejected offers of help or failed to take them up would be followed up systematically and might suffer a benefit sanction; and
- there would be a burst of activity at the two-year point; Howard secured the agreement of Tony Newton, the Secretary of State for Social Services, to the idea of a Mandatory Restart Course for those who refused other offers; the necessary social security regulations were passed in December 1990.

Also in 1990, the ES developed the idea of 'active signing'. This took advantage of the fact that claimants had to 'sign' to get their benefit. The idea was that the signing clerk could question the claimant briefly about progress with their Back to Work Plan and, if dissatisfied, refer the claimant to an Adviser.

The ideas produced at this creative period were the basis for much ES development over the next five years. But it was easier to produce ideas than to implement them. A big programme of training was needed for the Advisers – and for their managers. But with the rise in unemployment, resources became increasingly scarce and additional items like 13-week reviews and active signing were not feasible. Some regions, particularly London and the South East, found that the flood of new claims was such that interviews for new claimants were largely delegated to clerical staff.[30]

Rising unemployment raised acute issues about resources. In the 1990 public expenditure exercise, the Treasury had achieved significant cuts in Employment Department expenditure on training and other measures. But as recession increasingly took hold, Michael Howard argued successfully for putting these cuts into reverse and in the first half of 1991 he made a series of announcements of measures to tackle rising unemployment.

Part of the extra money was simply for maintaining the ES's 'customer services' in a situation of higher volumes.[31] The Department reminded the Treasury of the mistakes of the early 1980s when, at a time of rising unemployment, the time spent with clients discussing jobsearch and ensuring availability had been reduced. This argument helped to secure a further £17 million for selective interviews with clients who had been unemployed for 13 weeks. Altogether, this period saw a remarkable expansion of staffing in the ES (Table 15.3).

Table 15.3 *UK claimant unemployment and staffing in ES, 1990–94*

	Claimant unemployed – millions (October)	ES staff (average staffing level for year)
1990/91	1.67	34,000 excluding casuals
1991/92	2.42	37,000
1992/93	2.81	48,000
1993/94	2.79	49,000
1994/95	2.45	45,000

Source: ONS, *Labour Market Trends*, Jan 1996, and ES management statistics.

In its consideration of additional employment measures, the Department was influenced by some work done in 1990 comparing the cost of getting a long-term unemployed person into a job under various programmes. This suggested that ES programmes like Job Clubs and the Job Interview Guarantee were better value for money than long training programmes such as ET. This led to proportionally bigger increases in ES programmes than in ET. Two new ES courses for the 13-week group were introduced in 1991 – Job Search Seminars to help people approve their job search skills; and Job Review Workshops. The latter were designed mainly for managerial and professional clients, large numbers of whom were becoming redundant, particularly in the South East. In addition, there was an expansion in Job Clubs, Job Search Seminars and the Job Interview Guarantee (which sought to influence employers' behaviour). Altogether, these measures meant that the ES was able to offer additional help to over 600,000 people by 1992/93 (Table 15.4). At the same time, some expansion of Employment Training took place and a new work experience scheme – Employment Action – was introduced. Howard decided that the TECs, rather than the ES, should run this.

The range of programmes was further extended in 1993. After intensive discussions involving DE and ES officials, Gillian Shephard announced the following programmes which were to be run by the ES:

- *Job Plan Workshops* – a new mandatory programme for those unemployed one year or more;

- *Community Action*, a new work experience programme, for the long-term unemployed, similar to the Community programme, but with participants receiving their benefit plus an allowance, rather than a wage; and
- *Workstart Pilots* to test out the idea of subsidies to encourage employers to recruit long-term unemployed people.

Table 15.4 *Range of opportunities for 1992/93*

Programme	Number of people helped
ES-run programmes	
Job Search Seminars	130,000
Job Review Workshops	27,000
Jobclubs	220,000
Job Interview Guarantees	124,000
Restart Courses	110,000
Total for ES-run Programmes	611,000
TEC-run programmes	
Employment Training	248,000
Employment Action	57,000
Enterprise Allowance	30,000–50,000
Total for TEC-run programmes	335,000–355,000

Source: White Paper, *People, Jobs and Opportunity*, Feb 1992, page 56.

In addition, she replaced ET and Employment Action with *Training for Work* for 300,000 adults.

In 1993, the unexpected happened. Claimant unemployment, which had reached three million,[32] started to fall. By April 1994, it was 2.6 million and by April 1995 it was 2.2 million. This was entirely different from the pattern of the early 1980s, when unemployment had continued to rise for three years after economic growth had resumed.

Why did unemployment start to fall so soon? Various explanations have been given. Productivity was higher than in the early 1980s, so that employers had to recruit if they were to expand. The labour market was more flexible thanks to the government's labour market reforms.[33] But an important factor must have been the difference in the ES's role between the early 1980s and the early 1990s. In the early 1990s, ES staff were intervening proactively at the beginning of each spell of unemployment and at frequent intervals thereafter. This was entirely different from the more passive and reactive approach of the early 1980s. The impact of ES intervention is also to be seen in the figures of long-term unemployment, which began to fall significantly in 1994.

Conclusion

In March 1993, the first three-year Framework for the ES Agency expired. The Agency could claim considerable success. After a shaky start, it had established a solid performance record. It was building up its financial management and computer systems. It had carried through the lion's share of its integration programme. It had embarked on radical reform in its personnel arrangements. Above all, it had contributed to an unexpectedly early end to an alarming recession.

Despite this record of achievement, the Framework was only renewed on an interim basis, because of uncertainties arising from the Jobseekers' Allowance project, which will be discussed in Chapter 16.

But the favourable Whitehall view of the Agency's first three years was expressed in an evaluation report published in 1995:

> *The establishment of the Employment Service (ES) as an Executive Agency has created a firmly performance-driven organisation, clearly focused on the achievement of its key objectives. The process of setting targets in the Annual Performance Agreement has enabled ES to concentrate on its outputs, bringing greater focus and discipline to its activities. This has led to continuing improvements in the quality of its services and the efficiency of their delivery...*
>
> *Overall, ES has performed well against the demanding targets set by Ministers, and has consistently improved its performance from year to year. Indeed, it seems that ES is now able to achieve any reasonable target whose achievement is within its direct control'.*[34]

16

The Jobseeker's Allowance, 1993–97

'I increasingly wonder whether paying unemployment benefit without requiring any activity in return serves unemployed people or society well. Of course, we have to make sure that any conditions imposed improve the job prospects of unemployed people and give good value to the country. But we have already introduced this principle, for example, through Restart, in a limited sense for the long term unemployed. I believe we should explore ways of extending it further.' (John Major at the Carlton Club, February 1993)

Introduction

In 1993 the employment service had an established strategy, built around benefit control, and a successful Agency organisation. It served a government which had won a renewed electoral mandate in 1992. But the service was not to have a quiet life. The second Major term was a time of political restlessness, with renewed pressure to roll back the frontiers of the state and, in the case of the ES, to reopen fundamental issues about benefits for the unemployed and the relative roles of the Department of Employment and the DSS and their respective agencies.

Thus the story of these years is primarily about the development of a new benefit regime for the unemployed in the form of the Jobseeker's Allowance. But there were also questions about the extent to which ES functions would remain in the public sector at all. Along the way, moreover, the ES's parent Department, the Department of Employment, was abolished and a new Department for Education and Employment (DfEE) was created. It was a time of considerable tension and uncertainty.

Ministers and civil servants

In this relatively short period, the ES served three Secretaries of State: David Hunt (May 1993–July 1994), Michael Portillo (July 1994–July 1995) and Gillian Shephard (July 1995–May 1997), combining education and employment. There were also influential Ministers of State such as Michael Forsyth and Ann Widdecombe.

The Permanent Secretary of the Department was Sir Nicholas Monck until 1995, when unusually there was a public competition to find his successor. The successful candidate was Michael Bichard, former Chief Executive of the Benefits Agency. After the merger with education in July 1995, Bichard became Permanent Secretary of the DfEE.

One major source of continuity was Mike Fogden's position as ES Chief Executive. When the Agency Framework was renewed in 1993, Fogden's post was advertised. Fogden was successful in this competition. John Turner continued as Fogden's deputy until January 1994, when he was succeeded by Derek Grover, who held the post until January 1997.

Requiring activity

This chapter begins by quoting the Prime Minister's Carlton Club speech of February 1993. His remarks provoked a flood of press speculation that John Major favoured a massive Workfare scheme such as existed in Sweden. Michael Heseltine, an increasingly influential figure in Major's government, was known to favour such an approach. Other proponents, from a variety of standpoints, included Peter Ashby of Full Employment UK, Professor Layard, Frank Field MP and Sir Ralph Howell MP. Moreover, in 1994 the Commons Employment Committee embarked on a major study of 'The Right to Work/Workfare',[1] which did much to bridge the gulf which had existed between the two main parties on ways of tackling unemployment.

The government in fact decided against workfare in the sense that it was unwilling to become 'employer of last resort' or provide a guarantee of employment for long-term unemployed people. In November 1994, Ann Widdecombe, Minister of State, told the Select Committee on Employment that by 'workfare':

> *I understand large scale, national, probably compulsory schemes. I do not want that and nobody I know in Government wants that. That is what I understand by workfare. People are using workfare to describe some of our programmes, but they are not workfare at all.*[2]

What the government favoured was 'requiring activity' on the part of unemployed people. This was consistent with the whole trend of policy since Lord Young's revolution. Ministers favoured a more targeted approach which emphasised the 'conditionality' of benefit. This went right back to Beveridge, but Ministers wanted to bring it up to date, particularly by the Jobseeker's Allowance, which is discussed later in this chapter.

The role of the ES's local offices was of course highly relevant to 'requiring activity'. But at ES Head Office there was concern as to whether the conditions for benefit were properly understood. In 1992, it was found that the New Framework and Active Signing (pages 289–90) were not fully embedded. Some advisers were reluctant to confront issues in an interview. They felt themselves to be in an ambivalent position – expected to be both a policeman and a friend. Some did not sympathise with the growing use of compulsion to 'discipline' the unemployed – particularly in areas where there seemed very few jobs to go to.[3]

One sure way of ensuring that managers gave priority to an activity was to introduce a performance measure. In April 1994, a new performance measure was introduced: 'submissions to adjudication where there is an arguable case with supporting evidence to show that the claimant is not available for, actively seeking or willing to accept work'. The magic of performance measurement worked. The number of referrals increased sharply from around 130,000 in 1993–94 to 203,000 in 1994–95 and 273,900 in 1995–96. The proportion accepted by Adjudication Officers also improved to 81 per cent and 87 per cent in these two years, suggesting an improvement in quality. None the less, this new target was highly controversial. Was it right to turn potential penalties into performance measures? The National Association for Citizens' Advice Bureaux complained that the increasing use of benefit penalties was causing destitution.[4] The Unemployment Unit argued that the new targets were 'putting undue pressure on ES Client Advisers to push claimants on to compulsory programmes and to question the legitimate benefit entitlement of many unemployed people'.[5] A report by the Churches went further and condemned as 'morally indefensible' a target which might encourage staff to disallow more claims in order to obtain performance pay.[6]

'Requiring activity' was also reflected in a gradual shift towards compulsion in programmes. The first two such programmes were the mandatory Restart course for the two-year unemployed introduced in 1991 and the Job Plan Workshop for the one-year unemployed introduced in 1993. With the added impetus of the Prime Minister's intervention, three further compulsory programmes were introduced in the period before the Election in May 1997:

- *1–2–1* – Programme for one-year plus unemployed offering up to six interviews with an adviser ;
- *Workwise* – Course for one-year plus unemployed who do not take up other opportunities at Restart;
- *Project Work* – a pilot scheme for young people aged 18–24 unemployed for over two years to have compulsory work experience following intensive job interviews; this replaced Community Action.

Thus by the time of the General Election of May 1997, the Conservative government's interpretation of 'requiring activity' had become more ambitious until it was a question of semantics whether it was 'workfare' or not. The Project Work pilots were seen as encouraging. The compulsory element had had a remarkable 'deterrent' effect, rather like Restart in 1986. 2892 people had left the register, of whom only 829 were known to have started jobs.[7] What proportion of the rest had been working and signing was not known. But it was decided to extend the project to help 100,000 people and the Conservative Manifesto promised to 'extend the programme to cover the long-term unemployed nationwide.'[8]

The Citizen's Charter and the origins of the Jobseeker's Allowance

Before considering the Jobseeker's Allowance (JSA), it is necessary to look back at the Citizen's Charter, since this is where it all started.

In March 1991, in a speech at Southport, John Major announced his commitment to better public service under the broad heading of the 'Citizen's Charter'. He thought it important to define what standards the public could expect from a service, to simplify access, to provide what was called a 'one-stop shop' wherever possible, to be more responsive to consumer needs (with service providers stimulated by incentives and penalties), to achieve greater accountability through public reports and rigorous auditing and stronger complaints procedures.

ES senior managers welcomed the initiative. They felt that the ES was generally in a strong position. Integration provided a form of 'one-stop shopping'. Jobcentres were designed to be accessible. Performance measurement ensured public accountability. The ES already held customer satisfaction surveys every year and these showed high levels of customer satisfaction which were improving with integration.

The Prime Minister's initiative demanded a stronger public commitment to customer service and quality. It was agreed to produce a Jobseeker's Charter which defined standards of service (eg to see clients without an appointment within 10 minutes, to answer the phone within 20 seconds). These standards would be on display in every office. Staff would wear name badges.

But the government's new emphasis on customer service raised far more fundamental questions – in particular, about the confusion caused to the public by the benefit system itself. As we have seen, since the inter-war period, there had been two quite different benefits for the unemployed – the contributory unemployment benefit and a means-tested benefit under a variety of names, but in the early 1990s known as income support. The two kinds of benefit operated under widely different rules and procedures, with the former administered by the ES and the latter mainly by the Benefits Agency (BA). This in turn meant that unemployed people seeking income support (an increasing majority)[9] had to deal with at least two distinct networks of government offices

– the ES Jobcentre and the BA local office. Claims not infrequently fell into cracks between the two Agencies. Attempts to rationalise responsibilities had been made in 1969–71 (pages 141–3 and 159–61), in 1981–82 (pages 00–0) and 1986–87 (pages 254–5) but all had run into the sand. Governments find it inherently difficult to resolve such problems. The 1990 Agreement between the Secretaries of State for Employment and Social Security (pages 278–9) had essentially preserved the status quo.

Even before the advent of the Citizen's Charter, the ES and BA were interested in improving customer service, through better cooperation between the two Agencies. They had thus initiated pilots of 'closer working' and trials of Remote Access Terminals (RATs), with information about income support provided by a BA staff member in a Jobcentre. But this was only scratching the surface. Should not the long-term goal be a 'one stop shop' – so that most customers need only go to one place, see one person and fill in one form? This was an idea which was strongly promoted by Michael Bichard, the new BA Chief Executive, and which Peter Lilley, who became Secretary of State for Social Services in 1992, seized upon with enthusiasm.[10]

In June 1992, the DSS and the DE set up a Joint Task Force, led by Ian Stewart of the Benefits Agency, to investigate the improvement of the service 'from the customer's viewpoint' and to produce proposals for improvement, particularly through 'one stop shopping'. The press reported that John Major (who had once been unemployed himself) aimed to remove the stigma which branded benefit recipients as second class citizens.[11] In its enquiries, the Task Force found that unemployed customers:

- would prefer a single point of contact;
- often could not distinguish between ES and BA offices;
- were not impressed by cooperation between the two Agencies;
- would prefer to use ES offices (80 per cent); and
- were often not informed about claiming for income support early enough.

The Task Force's Report of October 1992 recommended a three-phase process of further work:

- Phase 1. Immediate low cost steps towards closer working between the ES and BA;
- Phase 2. A high level working group from the two Departments to develop options for Ministers on how to ensure that all main services to unemployed customers were delivered from a single location (a one-stop shop); and
- Phase 3. A second high level group to develop options for Ministers on how to tackle the more fundamental policy and legislative problems arising from multiple benefits for unemployed people.

Jobseeker's Allowance – decisions

The two Secretaries of State – Peter Lilley and Gillian Shephard – set up a working group on delivery, chaired by Nick Stuart of the DE, and a working group on policy and legislation, chaired by Robin Birch of the DSS.

In 1993, the Birch Committee's work led to decisions by Ministers to introduce legislation to replace unemployment benefit and income support for the unemployed by a new Jobseeker's Allowance (JSA). This would replace many of the inconsistencies between UB and IS with a single set of rules (eg it would be a weekly benefit like IS, rather than a daily benefit like UB, and it would have a uniform definition of earnings). There would be two routes of entry to JSA– a contributory route like UB and an 'income-related' (or means-tested) route. Contributory JSA would last only six months compared with 12 months for unemployment benefit. The legislation would also give legal backing to a Jobseeker's Agreement between the claimant and the ES Adviser on the job search activities to be undertaken (building on the existing Back to Work Plans). It would enable ES Advisers to give a formal Direction to jobseekers to undertake a specific activity under threat of sanctions if they failed to comply.

It will be seen that the objectives underlying the project had broadened. The thrust towards better customer service was still there in the rationalisation of the previous unwieldy and opaque dual system of benefits. This was welcomed in the ES, where a dynamic Australian secondee, Rod Halstead, had initiated a campaign for the simplification of benefit. But policy was also influenced by pressure for economy. Cutting the contributory benefit to six months was estimated to produce savings of £180 million per year.[12] From a customer service point of view, it could be seen as a backward step. People with capital above the prescribed limit or with a spouse earning would cease to receive benefit after six months. Altogether, it was estimated 165,000 people would lose entitlement to contribution-based benefit.[13] The third strand was a familiar one – a further tightening of the Stricter Benefit Regime.

But the really difficult problems related to Departmental and Agency responsibilities. The decision to go for a unified benefit system for the unemployed meant that the status quo was not an option. The problem could not be shelved as it had been in the 1980s, when the NEXT project ground to a halt. The machinery of government issues related to policy as well as delivery. There was a respectable case for the Department of Employment taking over the policy responsibility and budget for JSA. This would facilitate an 'active labour market policy' of the kind OECD was advocating, in which expenditure on advice, training and work experience could be traded off against expenditure on benefit with a view to bringing down unemployment. But the DSS argued that this would undermine the coherence of the social security system. Unemployed people were not a distinct group in society. Many of them were on other benefits as well. Many of them also moved frequently between benefits. It was difficult enough already to avoid anomalies and disincentive effects in the social security system, but to entrust policy for social security to two different departments would be a recipe for chaos.

As regards delivery, the argument was dominated by the concept of the 'one stop shop'. It was reassuring to the ES that there was a general acceptance that the Jobcentre was the best 'one-stop shop' available. The 20 years spent in developing an attractive front line for the employment service had not been wasted; the new integrated offices offered an attractive job-related environment. Building on the wish to use the Jobcentres for JSA, the ES bid strongly to take over delivery completely, including the BA staff who had previously worked on income support for the unemployed. But would this not distract the ES from its labour market role? Moreover, if the priority was to streamline the social security system, should not the Benefits Agency take over the Jobcentres? However, the BA already had 64,000 staff and more difficult industrial relations than the ES. To create an even bigger benefit colossus looked risky. An alternative would be to give the responsibility to the ES but to move the ES into the DSS's family of Agencies. Employment Department and ES officials such as Mike Fogden were against this, because they saw the labour market aspects of JSA as central to its effectiveness. Finally, some Ministers favoured handing over the administration of JSA to the private sector. But was it right for the private sector to determine benefit entitlement? And was it practicable to hand over JSA to external providers before the next Election?

The whole subject bristled with difficult issues which could not be settled by bilateral talks between the DE and DSS. So in September 1993 the two Permanent Secretaries – Nick Monck for the DE and Sir Michael Partridge for the DSS – asked the Cabinet Secretary, Sir Robin Butler, to intervene. An official committee with a Cabinet Office chairman was established. The argument went to and fro between officials and Ministers until, in May 1994, the Prime Minister announced his decision. The outcome was a judgement of Solomon. As regards policy, the DSS would retain the public expenditure allocation, but the DE would lead on implementation. The decision on delivery was as follows:

> *Jobseeker's Allowance will be delivered from Jobcentres of the Employment Service of the Employment Department. Employment Service staff will be responsible for advice and help on getting back to work and for the application of labour market tests such as availability to work. Financial aspects of the benefit including calculation and payment will be the responsibility of staff of the Benefits Agency located as far as possible in the same offices.*[14]

The argument was that each organisation should focus on what it knew best – employment work for the ES and benefit work for the BA. The goal of the 'one-stop shop' was to be achieved, not by entrusting the running of JSA to a single organisation, but by co-location of ES and BA staff.

ES senior managers were disappointed by the outcome. The employment service was losing the direct responsibility for running unemployment benefit which it had had since 1911. Instead, they faced the complexities of having another Agency's staff operating alongside their own staff in the Jobcentres. There was a very similar sense of disappointment in the BA. As Michael Bichard pointed out, when in April 1995 he moved from being Chief Executive of the Benefits Agency to become Permanent Secretary of the Department of Employment, it was a strange case where both sides felt they had lost.

The Jobseeker's Bill

With the key decisions made, the Whitehall machine now went fully into action. In October 1994, the two Secretaries of State – Peter Lilley and Michael Portillo – produced a White Paper on the Jobseeker's Allowance, presenting the new benefit as having three main aims:

- to improve the operation of the labour market;
- to secure better value for money for the taxpayer; and
- to improve the service to unemployed people themselves.

It is interesting that improved customer service – which was where it all had started – had by now become the third aim. Ministers emphasised 'the responsibilities of unemployed people to take effective steps to secure a job'. It was this aspect of JSA which dominated the public mind and caused anxiety among the staff.

In January 1995, the Jobseeker's Bill received its Second Reading.[15] It was a remarkably wide-ranging debate. Portillo countered Opposition criticism of the reduction of the contributory benefit to six months by pressing the Opposition spokesman, Harriet Harman, to commit her party to reinstating 12 months. Harman could give no such undertaking. One Conservative backbencher commented: 'For scroungers, for the feckless, the indolent and the workshy, there is no good news in the Bill'.[16] There were, however, two notable dissenters on the government benches. Sir Ralph Howell regretted that the Bill did not offer workfare for the long-term unemployed. Alan Howarth, a former Minister, attacked the Bill and voted against it. He argued that it would widen inequality, deepen impoverishment and threaten an abuse of power, through increased benefit policing by the ES. But it went through Parliament without profound changes and received the Royal Assent in June 1995. The Labour government which took power in 1997 left this legislation unamended.

Jobseeker's Allowance – implementation

JSA was a most formidable project to implement, particularly as Lilley and Portillo had set a target date for introduction of April 1996 – a date chosen presumably because it offered some prospect of financial savings before the Election. JSA required huge changes affecting both Agencies. The critical path was the introduction of the JSA Payments System (JSAPS). It had not been possible to start detailed planning until the Prime Minister's decision on responsibilities in May 1994. By the spring of 1995, with only a year to go, the computer experts advised that implementation in April 1996 involved excessive risk. Reluctantly, Ministers agreed to a deferment to October 1996. However, it was agreed that the six months period for contributory benefit would be introduced for those making claims from 8 April 1996 onwards, thus avoiding deferment of the main financial savings.

Ian Stewart of the Benefits Agency, leader of the original Task Force of 1992, was appointed Project Director, with Mike Allen, a computer expert from the DE, as his deputy. The project team was in a delicate position, suspended between the two Agencies. Derek Grover led implementation in the ES.

Successful implementation demanded close cooperation, after years of tension between the two Agencies, because of the overlap of their functions, their rivalry as the two largest and highest profile Next Steps Agencies and their competing bids to administer JSA. The two Agencies were like two escaped convicts shackled together in an American movie. To succeed they had to cooperate. The two Chief Executives – Mike Fogden and Michael Bichard, and his successor, Peter Mathison – now worked hard to put the past behind them. There were regular meetings between the ES Executive Board and the BA Management Team (BAMT) and bilaterals between Directors in each Agency with analogous functions.

Gradually, the project took shape. It was found that the number of ES staff who would need to transfer permanently to BA was 2100,[17] far less than had originally been expected. The ES's Preference Exercise produced more than enough ES staff willing to join BA. The ES would also loan to BA some of its benefit experts to assist in running the system in the transitional period from October 1996 to April 1997. A massive staff training programme was launched. It was agreed that in future all fraud work would be done by BA and in the spring of 1995 1100 fraud staff transferred from the ES to BA.

The area of greatest difficulty between the Agencies related to staff security. The Prime Minister's decision was that 'so far as possible' benefit processing would be done in Jobcentres. But the two Agencies had totally different approaches to staff security. BA made extensive use of protective screens to protect staff from possible assault by customers and promised existing staff that they would not be compelled to work in an unscreened office. ES senior management by contrast had almost entirely got rid of screens during the integration process (page 287) and were determined not to reverse their policy because of JSA. One result was a decision to locate the most fraught dealings with unemployed people (eg hardship loans under the Social Fund) away from the Jobcentre in BA offices.

It was against this difficult background that middle management in the two Agencies had to reach agreement on the location of processing in each area. In addition, it was agreed that a 'risk assessment' involving managers in both Agencies should be carried out in each Jobcentre. Pressures for screens built up from the Trade Union sides in both Agencies. In January 1995, the temperature was raised further by an incident in Bexleyheath Jobcentre in which a woman with a history of mental illness stabbed two members of staff and two members of the public with an assortment of knives and screwdrivers.[18] The unions managed to get the issue of safety on to the agenda of the Select Committee on Education and Employment in June 1996.

Despite these pressures, ES senior management stood firm against the reintroduction of screens, which they felt would be a major step backward in customer service. They were prepared where necessary to introduce other measures such as the employment of security guards. In this stand, they were strongly backed by DE Ministers.[19]

The introduction of JSA on 7 October 1996 passed successfully and the JSA project formally came to an end in April 1997 with the successful implementation. Early in 1997, Ian Stewart departed to become Head of the Benefit Fraud Inspectorate. But in October 1996, in order to maintain close cooperation, the two Agencies agreed a National Memorandum of Understanding. This set out their respective accountabilities for JSA delivery, with a joint approach to management and problem solving, consultation on relevant issues and a National Service Statement setting out each Agency's expectations of the other.

Computerisation

The JSA project transformed the computer scene in the ES. As noted above, it required a new payment system – the Jobseeker's Allowance Payments System (JSAPS) – into which ES staff could input claims, which then would be processed by BA staff. Because of the legislative change in the nature of benefits, it had to be introduced for new claimants on a single day – 7 October 1996 – unlike NUBS 2, which had been rolled out over several years. It was the challenge of this 'big bang' introduction which caused a six-month delay in the implementation timetable. In the event, the new system delivered well.

During 1993/94, ES senior management decided to bid for a new Labour Market System (LMS) to assist Jobcentre staff in delivering the formidable labour market agenda of JSA. This was agreed by Ministers and the system was introduced in 1996 under a hectic timetable. The project was led by Ray Phillips and David Wood. LMS was designed to hold jobseekers' details (with a link to JSAPs), Jobseeker's Agreements, jobs, matching facilities, in-work benefit information etc. JSAPS and LMS used the same 24,000 terminals. After two years' running, LMS faced problems of over-use:

> *Seven million transactions a day, 25 million transactions a week (frequently 70 transactions per second) – equivalent to the load borne by the Camelot lottery system and twice the load that a typical bank has to deal with.*[20]

It was in part due to the political imperatives of the Jobseeker's Allowance and in part due to the opportunities created by advances of technology that JSAPS and LMS were introduced so quickly in comparison with previous large projects such as NUBS 2 and Supervacs.

Prior options and market testing

From the start, there was an ambivalence about the Next Steps Project. Was it about making government work better through clarifying responsibilities? Or were Agencies just a step along the road to private ownership? This ambivalence overshadowed apparently robust organisations like the ES during John Major's premiership. Before an Agency's three-year Framework was renewed, there was supposed to be a 'Prior Options Review' to review (all over again) the options of abolition, privatisation, contracting out and market testing. It is no wonder that a Commons Committee complained of 'institutionalised insecurity'.[21]

In fact, the ES's Framework was renewed with minor changes in 1993 without a Prior Options Review, because of the uncertainties about the future role of the ES caused by the Jobseeker's Allowance project. An evaluation of the ES as an Agency was carried out, which produced remarkably positive findings (page 293). Once the Prime Minister had clarified the ES's future role in May 1994, a Prior Options Review was launched by the Department of Employment with the involvement of central Departments. The main outcome, announced by Michael Portillo in March 1995, was that Agency status was renewed. The report referred to the need to maintain the links between job broking and benefit administration. These links had been

> *a strong factor in ensuring that the unemployed receive adequate help back into work. Without them, levels of unemployment, particularly long-term unemployment, would be higher and any reduction in the effective labour supply would lead to higher recruitment costs and greater wage pressure.*[22]

Abolition was ruled out. Privatisation was not feasible because the ES generated only a small revenue and any attempt to boost this by charging for placings would undermine help for the unemployed. Strategic contracting out and market testing were not feasible on a national scale because there was no current capacity in the market to provide all ES functions nationwide.

But, despite the favourable evaluation and the weak market, the report did not leave things at that. Ministers wanted public bodies to compete. Accordingly, two market tests were proposed:

- two or three Districts in their entirety, subject to the feasibility of separating out adjudication (which cannot be market tested), and after the arrangements for JSA have been put in place; and

- services delivered by the Placing, Assessment and Counselling Teams (PACTs) in one or two Regions.

These two recommendations were eventually dropped by David Blunkett when he became Secretary of State in May 1997.

The report also called for greater discretion for ES Districts through a number of pilots which should be fully monitored and evaluated. This offered a major advance. The ES piloted Programme Centres which replaced all the ES's jobseeker programmes in a District with a set of modules from which jobseekers and their advisers could choose.

Quite apart from 'Prior Options', competition policies were also being applied to the support services of the Agency. It had long been an aspiration of Ministers to switch more internal government services to the private sector. After their Election victory of April 1992, Ministers required each Department and Agency to put out to competition a large proportion of their support services either by contracting them right out of the civil service or by 'market testing' internal providers against external competitors. Sir Peter Levene had a central progress-chasing or enforcing role.

ES senior managers had to devote much of their time to organising market tests. This involved analysing the scope for market testing functions such as personnel, staff training, property work, information technology, psychological services, welfare services and so on. If a market test of some, or part, of a function was feasible, then a user requirement was drawn up, sometimes for the first time. This could be difficult in areas of major change or uncertainty, such as those affected by JSA. It was also necessary to differentiate groups of staff who could be seen as contract managers from those who could be seen as service providers and to erect 'Chinese walls' between them – barriers to communication which had never before existed. Then, the prospectus was advertised to the market, bids were received and evaluated and a decision on future delivery made. Mike Fogden insisted that the final decision should rest with him as Chief Executive, though consulting with Ministers as necessary on sensitive issues.

All this caused great anxiety among ES staff, most of whom had never previously been involved in a commercial bidding situation. Most of them saw the civil service as a long-term career and had no wish to be forced out into a private company that happened to win a market test. The Executive Board decided to give some assistance to in-house teams. In practice, most of the ES tests were won by in-house teams, which often managed to identify large financial savings.

After a couple of years of intense activity, the pressure on market testing eased. A variety of ways of achieving efficiency was now acceptable to Ministers. At the same time, cost pressures became acute, so the notion of competition remained as a route to economy. In particular, it was decided to deliver IT services through a partnership with EDS, a major worldwide IT company, and it was planned that some 270 ES staff would move to this company.[23]

Managing the Agency

The market testing programme, the pay changes (pages 282-3) and the Jobseeker's Allowance combined to make this a turbulent period for managers and staff in the Agency. The great majority of the staff felt very uncertain about the Agency's future and their attitudes towards the organisation became more negative (Table 15.1, page 285). One symptom of disaffection was a major pay dispute in 1995 with CPSA which caused the loss of more than 76,000 working days but ended without an increased management offer.

Even in this difficult environment, the Executive Board sought to foster a more positive and participative culture through a bold step in communications with its middle management. It drew on ideas which Martin Raff had picked up from the US for mass conferences of managers. On 1 March 1994, over 700 ES managers assembled at the National Exhibition Centre (NEC) in Birmingham for a two-day conference in which there was a combination of plenary speeches, discussions by groups of managers sitting at 100 round tables and active participative events. The Board presented a draft document entitled *ES Essentials*, to which the round tables suggested amendments, many of which were adopted. Delegates also sent 'Valentines' to the Board and to other parts of the organisation, offering praise or criticism, to which a reply had to be made. This NEC event was very risky. It would have been counter-productive if management disaffection had run too deep or if senior management had been insensitive to how managers felt. As it turned out, the event was a great success and managers expressed appreciation of the Board's willingness to discuss and amend its thinking.

In 1996, despite the preoccupation with the Jobseeker's Allowance, the Board ran a major management initiative called 'Taking the ES forward', which involved virtually everybody at middle management level.

The end of the Department of Employment

Chapters 12 and 13 showed that ideas of abolishing the Department of Employment and of merging it with the Department for Education were around from the early 1980s onwards. Rumours revived early in 1992 and Mike Fogden was sufficiently concerned to write about them to Sir Geoffrey Holland, the Permanent Secretary. He urged that, in the event of employment and training functions being merged with the Department for Education, the ES should go with them, rather than joining the DSS, which looked like the obvious alternative. His first argument was the need to 'protect the very real benefits of integrating benefit payment and job-finding' which he implied might be at risk in a social security department. Secondly, he saw the ES as a 'major instrument for delivering labour market policies' of the kind advocated by OECD. The ES was a flexible instrument for the delivery of new employment programmes.

In the event, the rumours became reality three years later, in July 1995. The Prime Minister announced that the employment and training functions of the Department of Employment *were* being merged with education to form a new Department for Education and Employment (DfEE). Industrial relations was going to the Department of Trade and Industry. Health and safety were going to the Department of the Environment.

It was the end after 78 years of the 'Ministry of Labour'. Despite its 'chaotic' origins, the Department had built up formidable expertise on employment and industrial relations, played a key role in the Second World War, and between the wars and from the 1970s onwards had delivered government responses to mass unemployment. In all that time, the employment service had been at the heart of the ministry. We do not know all the considerations which led to the decision in 1995 to locate the ES within the DfEE. But a Commons Committee did draw interesting comments from Sir Geoffrey Holland and Michael Bichard. Holland, who by then had retired from the civil service, but uniquely had been Permanent Secretary both at employment and education, said that, in discussions of such a merger over 20 years, the location of the employment service had been crucial. To have located the ES within the DSS would have been a mistake, since the ES had a very different ethos from the benefit service. The ES was about 'getting people...at the earliest possible moment back into work' – an optimistic, creative, enterprising ethos, necessarily different from the payment of entitlements to individuals. Michael Bichard, Permanent Secretary of the merged DfEE, explained that 'the main objectives of the new Department are education, training and getting people into work and I think the Employment Service is absolutely a centre of that'.[24]

Conclusion

Spring 1997 was a turning point for the ES, with the end of the Major government and the completion of the JSA project. Furthermore, at Christmas 1996, Mike Fogden had retired after ten years at the helm of the ES. Fogden could look back with satisfaction at what had been achieved. The organisation was much stronger than it had been when he took over in 1987. It had an integrated and coherent network of Jobcentres, which had been chosen for the delivery of JSA. In close cooperation with the Benefits Agency, it had successfully introduced JSA. It was well respected as an Agency and had made good use of its flexibilities, notably in the personnel area.

Not everything was positive. The ES had lost one of its key activities – the payment of unemployment benefit – but the implications of this proved less damaging than was feared, as it retained many benefit-related activities. Another concern was dwindling staffing levels, due to a combination of falling unemployment, transfer to BA, computerisation and a remarkable financial squeeze on all Departments and Agencies. But senior management was energetically looking at ways of delivering effectively at these reduced levels.

A further concern was the placing outcome for 1996/97. The ES achieved 1.68 million placings of unemployed people against a target of 1.97 million – a shortfall rather similar to that in 1990/91. As the ES's *Annual Report* pointed out, there were extenuating circumstances:

> *The overriding reason for this was the scale of the task in preparing for and delivering the Jobseeker's Allowance and the Labour Market System, which included delivering around 200,000 training days for ES staff. This inevitably was time which could not be spent on normal individual work with employers and jobseekers.*[25]

However, there was a further problem:

> *the number of people recorded as placed into jobs may be overstated. Doubts about the accuracy of these figures were raised in early 1997 following a routine examination by the ES's own internal auditors...21 per cent of the sample of job placings examined were not supported by a properly recorded audit trail... The ES has instituted a robust and energetic programme to address the problems.*[26]

There are lessons here for Agency performance systems; the tendency to expect improved performance every year can have perverse effects.

As to the ES's role, the series of key decisions taken in 1994 and 1995 had defined it as still having benefit control as its most important rationale. The clinching argument in the 1995 Prior Options Review against privatisation was the need to link job broking with benefit administration. But the ES was also seen as having a broader role, as was shown in 1995 by the decision that it should form part of the new Department for Education and Employment.

17

Reflections

Introduction

This chapter draws lessons from the 90 years of history of the public employment service in Great Britain as set out in this volume. One striking feature of this history is the extent to which common themes have emerged at different periods, despite enormous changes in social and economic conditions and in the role of the state. This suggests that it is valid to draw 'lessons of history'. This chapter looks at the overall strategy of the service, its historical evolution, its market share, its relationships with its client groups, its current character and the challenges it now faces, its organisation and at how it compares with employment services overseas.

This history has shown how the public employment service has developed from an organisation that was 'on trial' in 1910–14, as Beveridge saw it, to become an established part of the modern state. In the two World Wars, it was invaluable for the rapid deployment of the nation's population for war and for its subsequent resettlement for peace. In peacetime also, the service has played an important part in the national life, particularly at times of high unemployment. Even at times like the early 1920s, the 1980s and early 1990s, when the political currents of *laissez-faire* were flowing very strongly, the political sensitivity of unemployment provided a decisive argument for the retention of the service. For more interventionist governments, the service has provided a flexible and fast-moving instrument of employment policy.

Perhaps the most striking and consistent feature of the service has been its administrative virtuosity. Again and again, throughout its history, it has had to deliver huge changes within tight, politically driven timescales. From the days when Beveridge and his team, against the odds, established in a few months the first national unemployment insurance system in the world, to the present day, when it is responsible for huge New Deal programmes, it has had a remarkable capacity for rapid, large-scale delivery.

Strategic direction

Chapter 1 set out three possible models for the strategic direction of the service in peacetime:

- the labour market transparency model;
- the benefit control model; and
- the social welfare model.

These models are not mutually exclusive. At any time, all three will be evident, but the emphasis will vary according to circumstances and political ideology. The strategic approach at a particular point in time could be indicated diagrammatically as a point in a triangle. In wartime, a fourth model – labour supply to meet the requirements of the state – has applied.

Historical evolution

It is interesting to analyse the history of the service in terms of these models. Thus the new service in 1910 was concerned with labour market transparency, but from 1912 onwards became increasingly absorbed in unemployment insurance. In the *laissez-faire* atmosphere of the early 1920s, the survival of the service depended on its ability to deliver and control unemployment benefit. Labour market operations were at a low ebb. From the mid-1920s onwards, the Ministry of Labour re-asserted the labour market aspect of the service, even though, in the public mind, the benefit aspect of the work continued to predominate. After 1945, the service combined elements of all three models, making, for instance, major welfare advances in relation to disabled workers. But the service overall was so inadequately resourced and directed as to be in danger of terminal decline.

In the 1960s, the Department responded to these problems and to the more proactive approach to employment policy then in vogue by developing a radical modernisation programme built upon the labour market transparency model. They largely rejected the benefit control model as responsible for the unattractive 'dole image' of the service. This led to the 'new model employment service' from 1974 to the mid-1980s, in which priority was given to building market share and benefit control responsibilities were marginalised. Welfare aspects of the service remained, but were vulnerable to cuts in the early 1980s.

Lord Young's revolution in the mid-1980s and its consolidation under his successors shifted the service sharply back to the benefit control model, culminating in the Jobseeker's Act 1995. The priority now was to get unemployed claimants back to work, or at least off benefit. Placings of still employed job changers no longer counted for performance management purposes. When in 1995, as part of its procedures for reviewing Agency status, the government was considering whether the service should continue to exist at all, the key factor was the need to maintain the links between job broking and benefit administration (page 304). The aim was not just to cut benefit expenditure, but also to promote labour market efficiency (page 314). In the interests of benefit control, targets of increased referrals to adjudication were introduced (page 296).

The Blair government has kept intact the Major government's final expression of the benefit control model – the Jobseeker's Act 1995. But it has superimposed on this a series of massive labour market interventions in the form of the New Deal programmes. The philosophy of 'welfare to work' which underlies these programmes is broadly consistent with the approach of Conservative governments over the previous ten years, but the concept of 'welfare' has been broadened from the claimant unemployed to include groups such as single parents and those on incapacity benefit. Moreover, 'welfare to work' is now to receive organisational expression in a merger between the employment service and much of the Benefits Agency (page 318). None the less, while the emphasis on benefit control has continued, there has been a change in tone and approach (page 315) and performance targets for referrals to adjudication have been abandoned.

Market share

The choice of strategic model will have an impact on the service's share of the market.

Factual information about market share is difficult to obtain, because of the difficulty of estimating total engagements. In the inter-war years, the Ministry of Labour claimed a rise from 15–18 per cent in 1922–23 to 29 per cent in 1937 (page 81–2). These were over-estimates but they suggest substantial progress. After the Second World War, placings reached a peak of four million in 1948/49 (when controls were still applied), then fell to 1.3 million in 1958 (when controls had been abandoned and resources had been cut), suggesting a big fall over 10 years in market share. In 1973, market share seems to have been around 16 per cent (20 per cent for manual and 6 per cent for non-manual occupations). Modernisation seems to have raised it to about 23.5 per cent by 1982 (30 per cent for manual and 15 per cent for non-manual) (page 220). We lack a reliable estimate of subsequent market share. A 1992 estimate of 12 per cent was thought to be implausibly low.[1] In 1998, the Labour Force Survey suggested that only 9 per cent of men and 6 per cent of women employees had obtained their current job through a Jobcentre, but this again was thought to be an under-estimate.[2] Other research found that 18 per cent of unemployed people found their job through the Jobcentre (12 per cent through self-service and 6 per cent through staff).[3] To sum up, the modernisation of the 1970s succeeded in arresting the downward spiral and in increasing market share. Since the mid-1980s, market share has fallen significantly. More positively, the service has become far more effective in placing the long-term unemployed.

Market share is not the ultimate test of the success of the service. The service has to be evaluated against the goals set for it by government at any given time. But market share is a useful indicator of the confidence of employers and jobseekers and the service is at risk if this confidence is lost.

In principle, it might be supposed that a high market share could be guaranteed by compulsion. Indeed, Brian Showler, writing in 1976, saw this as the way to strengthen help for the disadvantaged.[4] Beveridge ideally wanted all engagements to take place through the exchanges, but Churchill insisted on a voluntary service. In 1919, the newly formed International Labour Organisation recommended a public monopoly in placement activity and the prohibition of private employment agencies.[5] In the inter-war years, the British government rejected the idea of a state monopoly. During the Second World War, virtually all engagements had to take place through the exchanges and Chapter 7 described how vestiges of this system survived up to 1956, with the Notification of Vacancies Order (NOVO) 1952.

Few British employment service practitioners today would, however, advocate compulsion, and even the ILO has veered away from it.[6] Recruitment can take place in many ways — notably personal contact, direct application to employers, press advertising and private employment agencies as well as the public employment service. There can be no presumption that one method produces engagements of a superior quality to the rest. It is true that the public service is the mechanism most likely to be used by the unemployed and that, if it is starved of vacancies, the unemployed will be ill served. Moreover, other things being equal, there is an economic advantage if vacancies are filled from the ranks of the unemployed (page 221). But there are serious practical problems surrounding compulsion. Britain has a free market tradition and any attempt to impose a monopoly would lead both to high levels of non-compliance and to inundating the Jobcentres with useless information about vacancies and engagements, as occurred under NOVO. It is more healthy for the Jobcentres to compete with other market mechanisms.

As ES runs a broking operation, its market share will depend on the degree of confidence of both employers and jobseekers. This leads us to the service's problems in satisfying three different client groups with potentially very different priorities — jobseekers, employers and the state. It is worthwhile to look at each of these in turn.

The jobseekers' perspective

Jobseekers are by definition looking for jobs or, failing that, for benefits. When jobs are generally scarce, as in the 1930s, or when, even in a boom, the service lacks good access to jobs, as in the 1960s, it will lose credibility with jobseekers. For jobseekers, there are attractions in the labour market transparency model which seeks to maximise market share. Self service also improves jobseeker perceptions and removes suspicions of favouritism. At the same time, however, many jobseekers are also looking for help and confidential advice[7] from the

Jobcentre – something more akin to the social welfare model. Equally, they may be resentful at pressure from Jobcentre staff to take any type of work.[8] The interventions which staff are required to make in the interests of benefit control may alienate jobseekers and in extreme cases lead to violence or even suicide.[9]

Moreover, the very fact of undertaking a policing role can affect the behaviour of public officials, making it more difficult to build up positive relationships between Jobcentres and jobseekers. This has been a recurrent theme in this book. Chapter 3 showed how in 1917 Hodge, the first Minister of Labour, complained that exchange officials were like 'wooden images...with not an atom of the milk of human kindness in their hearts'. Chapter 4 recorded how in the 1920s John Hilton criticised interviews which focused on policing rather than positive help. Chapter 5 noted the anger towards the exchanges felt by unemployed people in the 1930s. Chapter 6 showed how the greatest of Ministers of Labour, Ernest Bevin, saw a need to 'humanise the labour exchanges'.

How far did the tightening of the benefit regime between 1985 and 1997 affect the culture of the service and jobseeker attitudes to it? The service had to pursue a difficult balance between 'warfare' and 'welfare'. Surveys in 1992–4 found quite high levels of customer satisfaction, with those 'very or fairly satisfied' at over 75 per cent for jobseeking services and over 85 per cent for benefit services.[10] Later qualitative research following the introduction of JSA in 1996 presented a more complex picture. It suggested that the service had not reverted to the culture of the 1930s but none the less it fell far short of what unemployed jobseekers would have wished. One survey reported that, while 'customers generally feel that the staff are polite and well-disposed', many customers feel that they are 'just another number' or that the staff are 'totally unrealistic about what it is like to be unemployed'.[11] Another survey said that clients felt that the issues to do with benefit and monitoring of job search took precedence over real practical help. ES was 'reactive rather than pro-active'. They noted a 'polite unengaged functionality' on the part of ES staff.[12] The thesis that benefit control complicates relationships is supported by the fact that claimants scored the service lower than non-claimants.[13] Particularly disenchanted were those who had been disqualified for benefit. They were found to be mostly ignorant of the rules and surprised and resentful about the penalties (which in general became more severe in 1988 – pages 268–9). Many were depressed and some went into debt.[14] They might have endorsed the suggestion in the 1930s that the benefit system was a 'devilish game of snakes and ladders' (page 84). It is against this background that the Blair government has been reviewing the 'values' of the service.

The employers' perspective

Employers' perspectives are very different from those of jobseekers. A 1992 report suggested that employers saw the strengths of the service as that it was free, quick, easy to contact, offered a large field of applicants and might offer knowledge of the local labour market. But its weaknesses were that it had a poor understanding of business needs, lacked knowledge of jobseekers on its books and suffered from poor quality applicants, poor screening and matching and poor internal communication and coordination.[15] These criticisms may reflect a lack of realism about what can be expected from a public employment service. Ideally, employers would like the Jobcentres to relieve them of much of their recruitment burden in the way that private employment agencies do. But private agencies charge substantial fees and ES is not resourced to provide a comparable service.

If the service cannot provide the highly selective service which employers ideally want, which of the models will be most attractive to them? They will be uncomfortable about benefit control if it means that they are used as a testing ground for supposed scroungers. Equally, as Beveridge recognised from the inception of the service, they will mistrust the service if its criteria for submissions are based on social welfare rather than on industrial considerations, as happened in the US in the 1960s. Even the labour market transparency model (in the form it takes today) will have the weakness for employers that self service will produce large numbers of candidates whom they have to sift. But none the less, the transparency model offers attractions to the employer in the speed of the service and the range of candidates produced, particularly if these include those still in employment as well as the unemployed.

The state's perspective

The state's perspective will vary according to the economic climate and the prevailing political ideology. Governments' support for the public employment service has been partly been driven by concerns about unemployment – a rather vague welfare objective. More specifically, governments with a strong free market ideology have seen expenditure on a public employment service as worthwhile because of the service's ability to apply work tests to benefit recipients and so contain benefit expenditure – the classic benefit control model. Recent British governments have pursued this model not just to contain expenditure but also to reduce economic inactivity and thus to contribute to prosperity and growth and the containment of wage inflation. Governments which are readier to intervene in the market may see the role of the service more positively as to promote labour market transparency and to improve the overall functioning of the labour market.

This book has suggested that the drive for tighter benefit control has had an important impact on unemployment. This can be seen in the Restart pilot evidence (pages 243–4), the very thorough Restart evaluation (page 256) and in the rapid fall in unemployment from its peak of January 1993 as compared with its stickiness around the three million mark in 1982–86 (page 292). Moreover, there appear to be potential benefits to the individual, to the exchequer and to the economy from the provision of work experience or training after a period of unemployment, now exemplified in the New Deal. This approach was advocated by Beveridge in 1942.

Reflections

None the less, there are risks that the unqualified pursuit of benefit control may put at risk the relationship between the service and its jobseeker and employers clients. The value of the service to the community is more likely to be maximised by holding the three models in balance, rather than by investing heavily in one at the expense of the other two.

Something like this approach is being attempted by the present government. The primary model continues to be benefit control – getting people off welfare and into work – underpinned by an economic rationale concerned with reducing benefit dependency. But the emphasis on personal advisers in the New Deal also suggests a strong social welfare orientation. Moreover, there has been a wish to put right any damage which the pursuit of benefit control has done to the service's relations with jobseekers. This led David Blunkett, Secretary of State for Education and Employment since 1997, to initiate a review of the values of the service. The service has produced a statement of values, including:

- 'We will put customers first in all we do.'
- 'We will treat jobseekers fairly, while applying the conditions for payment of JSA.'
- 'We will create a welcoming, accessible and comfortable environment in Jobcentres and other ES offices.'
- 'We will make our services more readily available to jobseekers and employers.'

While benefit control has to retain centre stage for the time being, it would be healthy for the service to move on from the rather narrow focus on the unemployed which it has had in recent years. It needs rather greater emphasis on transparency and welfare because of two important new factors – the flexible labour market and the opportunities arising from new technology.

The flexible labour market

The first critical new factor is the increased flexibility and fragmentation of the labour market in the 1980s and 1990s. This trend would have astonished Beveridge, who regarded decasualisation as one of the most important objectives of employment policy. By contrast, we now live in a world where educated opinion regards 'flexibility' – which is not so very different from casualisation – as the key to economic success. There is not enough concern about the implications for the updating of skills and for people's long-term financial independence. None the less, the flexible labour market is here to stay and likely to develop further. Indeed, one recent study[16] predicts the gradual demise over the next 20 years of the 'job-shaped' job and the 'job-based' career. The old distinction between employment and self-employment will become irrelevant. Individuals will need to take responsibility for themselves in areas where traditionally they looked to employers, such as pensions and social insurance, education, training and development.

There are major opportunities for the employment service in this brave new world, provided that it can itself be highly flexible and keep abreast of the rapidly changing market. This will require the service to increase its role in the job-changing market and the self-employed market. Many people in 'flexible' jobs are highly vulnerable. They are ill-equipped to steer their way through the flexible market. The service needs to be resourced to provide them with adequate information and advice. Periods of unemployment should be used by individuals to re-equip themselves for new opportunities rather than as periods of 'enforced idleness'.[17] Moreover, with its widespread network, the service is well placed to act as a 'pivot' or gateway to other services, including education, training and advice on business development.

The opportunities arising from new technology

The second factor arguing for a change in the service's strategy is technological change in the form of the Internet. This provides unprecedented opportunities for improvements in labour market transparency, through making the service's vacancy bank (and other information) accessible to all Internet users (and through kiosks to those who lack Internet access). This opportunity was seized a few years ago by employment services in some other countries, such as the US, Canada and Sweden. These countries have also developed databanks on jobseekers, labour market information and career opportunities. The British service has now decided to go down the same road. There is a risk here that many of the ES's vacancies might be filled by Internet users already in a job, rather than by the unemployed, but this should be outweighed by enhanced vacancy penetration The greater risk would be to fail to take advantage of the Internet.

Organisation

What can we learn from this history about the best way to organise an employment service?

Ever since Churchill's rapid decision in 1908 on the organisation of the service, this has been a centrally run national service, in contrast to the service in countries like the US and Germany, where much of the management of the service has been devolved to 'state' level. In a relatively compact country like Britain, the centralised model has offered advantages in terms of integration with centralised unemployment relief arrangements and responsiveness to government decision-making. The Blair government's decision in 1997 to use the employment service for the administration of the New Deal probably reflected an awareness both of ES expertise on 'welfare to work' issues and of the fact the ES was more directly under government control than the Training and Enterprise Councils or local government.

The precise form of the organisation has, of course, varied over its history. Having been from 1910–17 a self-contained management unit within the Board of Trade, from 1917 onwards it gradually became part of the overall Ministry of Labour machine with largely standardised civil service terms and conditions. No one was fully in charge of the service below Permanent Secretary level. This was not a problem for its benefit functions in peacetime or its labour supply functions in wartime, perhaps because these functions had overriding political priority. But the lack of delegated leadership was a handicap to the service's employment functions and contributed to their decline in the 1950s. In 1974, the service became an Agency under a Chief Executive reporting to the 'hived-off' Manpower Service Commission. In the 1980s, this arrangement became increasingly fictitious as a result of the deep philosophical differences between the government and the TUC Commissioners. It came to an end in 1987. But the service remained a distinct unit under a Chief Executive and this was formalised in 1990 when it became a Next Steps Agency.

From the point of view of public administration, the employment service was a pioneer in the public sector in the 1970s, both in introducing a modern marketing approach and in putting into effect the ideas of accountable management that were promulgated by the Fulton Committee in 1968. Indeed, the Employment Service Agency of 1974 was in some ways the precursor of the 'Next Steps' Agencies that now comprise over two-thirds of the civil service and have been described by a House of Commons Committee as 'the most ambitious attempt at civil service reform this century'.[18]

'Agency' arrangements have provided a robust and effective organisational model for the service. But they run a risk of encouraging insularity. Beveridge's original concept of the service was not just as a placing service but as an agent of a wider government policy of improving the organisation of the labour market. This was echoed in the 1960s thinking of the OECD (page 136) and in the 1971 Departmental Report which described the service as 'the pivot round which the various services for vocational guidance, training, mobility, redundancy payments and market intelligence should turn', (page 151). Such a role requires the service to be heavily involved in the development of employment policy and to be sensitive to the interests of other players at national, regional and local level. The restructured service in the decade after 1974 was felt by its critics to lack this sensitivity. This was not such a problem after 1987, since from then on the goals of the service were closely integrated with those of the Department and, from 1990 onwards, the Chief Executive's right to be involved in policy making was recognised. But the creation of the TECs opened up new problems of cooperation at local level. Both the Major and the Blair governments emphasised the importance of the service's lateral relationships. The Major government sought close cooperation between the ES and the TECs, and the ES and the Benefits Agency. Similarly, the Blair government required the service to enter into local partnerships in order to deliver the New Deal. While these partnership arrangements cut across a simplistic view of accountability, they reflect the complexity of the real world. Few things are more frustrating to the citizen than government agencies which fail to integrate their activities with those of other related agencies. Cooperation could be reinforced by a greater interchange of senior staff between the ES and agencies concerned with training and economic renewal.

The Blair government has now decided to carry this process of integration one stage further by bringing together in a single Agency in 2001 the responsibilities of the employment service and the Benefits Agency for people of working age.[19] This reverses John Major's decision in 1994 on the allocation of responsibility between the two Agencies (page 300). In one sense, it restores the situation described throughout most of this history whereby the employment service has had responsibility for delivering unemployment benefit, though it goes further than this in bringing in other benefits for people of working age. At the time of writing, key questions were unresolved. In particular, it was not clear whether the Secretary of State for Social Security or the Secretary of State for Education and Employment would be responsible for the policy and budget of the new Agency. Experience since the creation of a separate Ministry of National Insurance in 1944 shows that this issue will be extraordinarily difficult to resolve. On the one hand, a decision to put the new Agency under DfEE could undermine DSS as a distinct Department and threaten the coherence of social welfare policy. On the other hand, a decision to put the new Agency under DSS would undermine the basic principle advocated by Beveridge in 1907 that the public employment service, as a 'business organisation', should be under a Department concerned with industry (page 13). This principle has been followed ever since, not least in the decision in 1995 to place ES under DfEE rather than DSS (page 307). From the perspective of this history, to place the new Agency under DSS would give undue emphasis to its benefit control function and threaten its labour market role.

Performance management

Since the early 1970s, performance management has been a key feature of the service. There were earlier precedents. Performance targets were used by Beveridge at the inception of the service and by Ince during the Second World War, and have consistently proved a remarkable powerful motivating force. Indeed, the service's experience since 1971 casts doubt on the view of recent governments that public sector organisations need the extra stimulus of performance-related pay if they are to perform successfully. Performance targets were driving behaviour in the employment service for 20 years before performance pay was introduced.

Performance management is clearly here to stay. But public sector managers need to be as aware of its dangers as of its potential to improve delivery. The dangers include:

- *Goal displacement.* Unless the targets are fully in line with the underlying aims of the organisation, performance management will distort behaviour. Performance management may foster those activities (such as placing) which are more easily quantified at the expense of those activities (such as information, advice and guidance) which are less easily quantified. It may foster assistance to those perfectly capable of helping themselves at the expense of the more vulnerable. It is vital that top management starts from what it wishes to achieve rather than from what can easily be quantified. Moreover, in the case of the employment service, the practicalities of running a performance management system encourage the treatment of all placings as of equal value. But the simple maximisation of placings can lead to a focus on casual engagements at the expense of longer-term resettlement.

- *Loss of integrity.* Pressures to raise performance every year can lead managers to exploit any ambiguities in the system or even to render inaccurate information (pages 280 and 308).

An important recent report by a House of Commons Committee[20] has expressed concern at the ES's failure to achieve its placing targets in recent years and at the possibility that its placing figures prior to 1996/97 may have overstated performance (see page 308). The Committee proposes that the ES should:

> *move away from the use of placement-based performance targets. Data about the number of placements should still be recorded, but they should be replaced as the core measure of the ES's effectiveness by targets which measure more accurately the value added by the Service.*

These ideas are worth developing to see if better systems of performance management could be developed for the future.

Competition

There is now an international trend towards introducing competition into employment services. This was evident under the Major government (pages 304–5), when various aspects of ES work and the whole of the careers service were put out to competition. The Blair government has not followed the Australian example of, in effect, abandoning the concept of a 'public employment service' and replacing it with a 'job network' of 310 private, community and government organisations selected through a 'contestable market'. However, the delivery of New Deal programmes and other programmes in certain locations is being put out to competition. Undoubtedly, competition provides a powerful stimulus to keep down costs. But, if carried too far, it could create a curious patchwork quilt of delivery mechanisms which lack the ability to respond rapidly to changing government demands. It is a worthwhile investment for the government to keep the service's basic infrastructure and the expertise of its staff broadly intact to meet whatever contingencies may arise, rather than relying on a regime of short-term contracts.

International comparisons

How has the development of the British employment service compared with developments overseas?[21] Perhaps its most striking characteristic over the last 30 years has been a tendency to adopt relatively extreme models of the service. This history has chronicled two revolutions in policy – the first in 1970–74 and the second in 1985–87. Both occurred under Conservative governments. Both placed strains on managers who, if not instantly converted, had to be good 'Vicars of Bray'. This pattern is surprising in a supposedly pragmatic nation, though similar dramatic shifts have taken place in the employment service in Canada and Australia. By contrast, the service provided by most of Britain's European Union partners has been more stable, perhaps because of the priority given to consensus between the social partners.

We now compare the present state of the British service with services overseas.

First, by international standards, the ES's strategy is unusually focused on benefit control and on encouraging unemployed people back to work. It has one of the most rigorous processes of case management of unemployed people of any major public employment service. The close integration between benefit and employment issues through partnership with the Benefits Agency compares favourably with the situation in many other OECD countries.[22] These features have contributed to Britain's relative success in bringing down unemployment and this will be enhanced by the forthcoming merger with much of the Benefits Agency (page 00).

Second, as a corollary to this, the British ES has in recent years been less proactive in pursuing labour market transparency than its counterparts in many other advanced countries, and this has perhaps become an area of relative weakness. The British service is unusual in not regarding job changers as part of its primary clientele for performance management purposes. Moreover, it is several years behind the US, Canada and Sweden in taking advantage of the Internet.

Thirdly, the British service is relatively well resourced, certainly in comparison with the services in the US and Canada, which have faced severe resource constraints in recent years, but also in comparison with some major European partners. For instance, in 1996, the ES had one staff member for every 95 unemployed people compared with 239 in France and 133 in Germany. As might be expected, given its long tradition of active labour market policies, the Swedish service was more generously staffed, with one staff member for every 58 unemployed.[23] But the British staffing levels suggest that UK governments have absorbed the lesson painfully learned in the early 1980s that cutting staffing in the ES can be a false economy.

Fourthly, since the mid-1980s, the British ES has succeeded unusually well in retaining the confidence of governments of both political parties. Its favourable resourcing position is one symptom of this. Another is the readiness of both the Major and the Blair governments to entrust to the ES responsibility for important and costly programmes to tackle unemployment. Also significant is the scale and comprehensiveness of the British investment in active labour market policies, exemplified in the New Deal – which may owe something in turn to the capability of the ES as a delivery agent.

Fifthly, by international standards, the British ES may be less sophisticated than some of its counterparts in areas such as vocational guidance, occupational knowledge and labour market intelligence. For example, Germany has teams of vocational guidance counsellors in local offices, France has recently invested heavily in training its staff in the use of ROME (a new occupational classification system), while Canada has deliberately developed labour market information as a marketable service. The weakness in the British ES in vocational guidance derives both from a historic tendency to entrust this work to educational services and from the demise of the Occupational Guidance Service in the Thatcher period. If ES advisers are to guide people through the new world of lifelong learning, they will need to develop more in-depth knowledge of vocational opportunities and related educational and training routes.

Finally, the British ES is, by international standards, institutionally robust and coherent. From its inception, it has been more centralised than many of its overseas counterparts, which is both a strength and a potential weakness. Today, like many of its counterparts, it is sensibly introducing more decentralisation. Unlike many other European services, it is not accountable to the social partners. The Blair government has shown no wish to bring the ES back under a body like the Manpower Services Commission. However, important issues will soon arise about the relationship between the ES and the proposed new Learning and Skills Council, particularly as it is intended that the ES should take responsibility for work-based learning for adults.[24]

Conclusion

Given levels of benefit dependency that are still relatively high in historical terms, it is probably right that ES should continue to give priority to getting people off welfare into work. But too uncompromising a pursuit of benefit control risks damaging relationships with clients and undermining market share. It is encouraging that the service is now striving to develop a more positive culture. There has been a shift to a more balanced position between our three models (benefit control, social welfare and labour market transparency). Social welfare is an important element in the New Deal, while the recent decision that ES should seize the opportunities offered by the Internet will enhance labour market transparency. Such a shift in objectives is also advocated by a House of Commons Committee.[25] This more balanced approach offers better prospects of simultaneously satisfying all three parties – jobseekers, employers and the state – and it is to be hoped that it will survive the forthcoming merger with the Benefits Agency.

The service has the potential to play an important role in steering people (whether unemployed, self-employed or employed) through the rapidly changing and increasingly flexible labour market. The shift towards lifelong learning and the proposal that the ES should take responsibility for work-based training for adults open up new opportunities for the ES. The service needs to build up its expertise in occupational and educational information.

Agency arrangements offer a robust model for the organisation of the service, but these arrangements need to be accompanied by strong lateral relationships at all levels and by a critical approach to performance management.

This book has focused on the direction of the service by Ministers and senior officials. But it is those working in the front line, often in difficult and exposed jobs, who determine whether Jobcentres are indeed 'Offices of Hope'.

Notes and References

Introduction

1. *The Graphic*, 12 Feb 1910.
2. William Beveridge, *Unemployment: A Problem of Industry*, 1909 and 1930, Longmans Green, pp197–99.
3. Ibid, p216.
4. Ibid, p198.
5. Ibid, p215–6.
6. Desmond King, *Actively Seeking Work: The politics of unemployment and welfare policy in the United States and Great Britain*, University of Chicago Press, 1995, pxii.

Chapter 2: Origins to 1914

In drawing up this account, the author was indebted particularly to two books by Jose Harris: *Unemployment and Politics 1886–1914*, Oxford, 1972; and *William Beveridge: A Biography*, Oxford, 1997 edition. Material from these books is included by permission of Oxford University Press.

1. WH Beveridge, *Power and Influence*, Hodder & Stoughton, 1953, p68.
2. RS Churchill, *Young Statesman: Winston Churchill 1901–14*, Minerva Edition, 1991, p32.
3. Ibid, p243, quoting Sir Edward Marsh's memoirs.
4. Speech at St Andrew's Hall, Glasgow, 1906. Ibid, p277.
5. Ibid, p307.
6. Jose Harris, *Unemployment and Politics 1886–1914*, Oxford, 1972, pp355–6.
7. Speech by Lord Beveridge at the 50th Anniversary of the Employment Exchanges. *Minlabour*, January 1960.
8. This paragraph draws extensively on Jose Harris' *Unemployment and Politics 1886–1914*, Oxford, 1972.
9. WH Beveridge, *Unemployment: A Problem of Industry*, Longmans Green, 1930 edition, pp42–3 and 433.
10. Gareth Stedman Jones, *Outcast London*, Oxford, OUP, 1971; Roger Davidson, *Whitehall and the Labour Problem in late Victorian and Edwardian Britain*, Croom Helm, London, 1985, Ch 2.

11 J Harris, *Unemployment and Politics*, p148.
12 Ibid, p75–78.
13 Nathaniel Cohen had a remarkable record of innovation in the manpower field. He was involved not only with labour exchanges, but also in founding the National Association for promoting the Employment of Discharged and Reserve Servicemen and the Cambridge University Appointments Board.
14 WH Beveridge, *Unemployment: A Problem of Industry*, 1930, p245.
15 Account mainly based on PJ Campling, 'Nathaniel Cohen and the beginnings of the Labour Exchange Movement in Great Britain', Surrey Archaeological Collection, Vol LXIX, 1973.
16 Introduction by David Martin to Clive Binfield et al, *History of the City of Sheffield 1843–1993*, Vol 1, p3.
17 Report by Arthur Lowry, Assistant Inspector of the Local Government Board, in November 1905, quoted by Harris in *Unemployment and Politics*, p202.
18 Letter to his mother of 25 Jan 1903, quoted in Harris, op cit, p153.
19 Harris, *Unemployment and Politics 1886–1914*, p285.
20 B Gilbert, *The Evolution of National Insurance in Great Britain. The Origins of the Welfare State*, Michael Joseph, London, 1966, p44.
21 Harris, *William Beveridge: A Biography*, Oxford, 1997 edition, p139.
22 *Minlabour*, Jan 1960.
23 Fabian Tract No 47, *The Unemployed*, by John Burn MP, LCC.
24 Harris, op cit, p163.
25 *Minlabour*, Jan 1960.
26 WH Beveridge, 'New Public Labour Exchanges in Germany', *Economic Journal*, 18:69, Mar 1908; *Morning Post*, 5 Oct, and 5 and 13 Nov 1907.
27 1910 and 1930, Longmans Green. This account of Beveridge's views at this time on unemployment comes mainly from Appendix 8 to the Royal Commission on the Poor Laws 1909, pp6 ff, supplemented by the 1909 part of his book.
28 See, for instance, *Unemployment: A Problem of Industry*, pp205–8.
29 Royal Commission on the Poor Laws 1909, Appendix 8, p16.
30 Ibid, p43.
31 Beveridge, *Unemployment : A Problem of Industry*, 1930 edition, p215.
32 Royal Commission, Appendix 8, p15.
33 Beveridge, *Power and Influence*, p68.
34 On the innovativeness of the various departments, see Roger Davidson, 'Llewellyn Smith, the Labour Department and Government growth', in G Sutherland, *Studies in the Growth of 19th Century Government*, Routledge and Kegan Paul, London, 1972; and R Davidson and R Lowe, 'Bureaucracy and Innovation in British Welfare Policy', in Mommsen (ed) *The Emergence of the Welfare State in Britain and Germany*, Croom Helm, London, 1981.
35 Harris, *William Beveridge*, p170.
36 Quoted in Harris, *Unemployment and Politics*, p284.
37 Stephen Tallents, *Man and Boy*, Faber, London, 1943, pp186–7.
38 Beveridge, *Unemployment: A Problem of Industry*, 1930 edition, p311.
39 Beveridge, *Power and Influence*, pp74–5.
40 Ibid, p171.
41 Gilbert, op cit, p265.
42 Beveridge, *Unemployment: A Problem of Industry*, pp229–30 and 264. Beveridge says that the German report saw the key as the test of unemployment, for which 'an adequate system of Labour Exchanges is of the first importance'.

Chapter 2: Origins to 1914 Notes and References

43 Gilbert, op cit, p268.
44 Beveridge, *Unemployment: A Problem of Industry*, 1930 edition, p264.
45 This paragraph follows the interpretation given by Bentley Gilbert, op cit, pp266–7.
46 Winston Churchill's paper of 11 December 1908, 'Unemployment. Insurance: Labour Exchanges', PRO. CAB 37/96/159.
47 Letter of 26 Dec 1908 from Churchill to Asquith, quoted in B Gilbert, op cit, p253.
48 Harris, *William Beveridge*, 1997 edition, p164.
49 Gilbert, op cit, p259.
50 WS Churchill, *Hansard*, 19 May 1909, Col 506.
51 At meeting with Parliamentary Committee of TUC, 17 June 1909, PRO. LAB 2/211.
52 Meeting of 18 Aug 1909. PRO. LAB 2/211.
53 PRO. LAB 2/211/15.
54 *Hansard*, 19 May 1905, Col 499ff.
55 Speech in 2nd Reading debate on 16 June, *Hansard*, Col 1045.
56 Beveridge, *Unemployment: A Problem of Industry*, 1930 edition, p296.
57 Beveridge, *Power and Influence*, pp77–8.
58 Askwith told the Barnes Committee in 1920 that he had nothing to do with Exchanges after September 1911 (Minutes of Evidence, p89, Q 1307) but Jose Harris' account suggests that Beveridge's reporting line to Askwith may have gone on longer than this (*Beveridge*, 1997 edition, p192).
59 Harris, *William Beveridge*, p192.
60 Tallents, op cit, p184.
61 Beveridge, *Power and Influence*, p78.
62 Tallents, op cit, pp184–5.
63 Harris, *Beveridge*, p177.
64 Beveridge's brief of July 1908 for Churchill, quoted in J Harris, *Unemployment and Politics*, p285.
65 There were 11 Divisions initially but this was reduced to eight with the introduction of insurance. These eight Divisions (with the location of the Divisional offices) were London and South Eastern (London), South Western (Bristol), Midlands (Birmingham), North Eastern (Leeds), North Western (Manchester), Scotland (Edinburgh) and Wales (Cardiff), plus Ireland (Dublin). See Beveridge, *Unemployment: A Problem of Industry*, 1930 edition, p297.
66 Beveridge, *Power and Influence*, pp76–7.
67 Sir Jameson Adams, 'Reminiscences of a Divisional Controller', *Minlabour*, Jubilee Edition, 1960.
68 Harris, *Unemployment and Politics*, p353.
69 Staffing figures include HQ. From evidence to the Barnes Committee 1920 (see Chapter 4), p11.
70 Beveridge, *Unemployment: A Problem of Industry*, 1930 edition, p297.
71 Report of Board of Trade under Part II of National Insurance Act 1911 to July 1913, p4.
72 Adams, *Minlabour*, Jan 1960, p5.
73 R S Churchill, op cit, pp308–9.
74 Ibid, p308.
75 Beveridge papers. III 39. Minute of 18 May 1909.
76 RS Churchill, op cit, p311.
77 Gilbert, op cit, pp271–2.
78 Beveridge, *Power and Influence*, p83.
79 Harris, *Unemployment and Politics*, p323.

80 HN Bunbury (ed) 'Lloyd George's Ambulance Wagon, Being the Memoirs of William J Braithwaite', Methuen, London, 1957, p134.
81 Letter to his mother of 31 December 1912. Beveridge papers. II a 58.
82 This account draws on Beveridge's Report to July 1914 on the operations under both the Labour Exchange Act and the National Insurance Act Part II.
83 Ibid, para 108.
84 Ibid, para 153.
85 Beveridge evidence to 1920 Committee of Inquiry. Quoted in footnote 1 on p305 of *Unemployment: A Problem of Industry*, 1930 edition.
86 Ibid, p302. It is unlikely that the exchanges' records captured all movement between jobs in the insured trades.
87 Ibid, p302.
88 Sir Jameson Adams in *Minlabour*, Jan 1960, pp5–6.
89 Beveridge, Report to July 1914, p50.
90 Beveridge, *Unemployment: A Problem of Industry*, 1930 edition, pp312 ff.
91 Harris, *William Beveridge*, p197; G Phillips and N Whiteside, *Casual Labour: The Unemployment Question in the Port Transport Industry 1880–1970*, OUP, 1985, pp104–5.
92 Beveridge (1930), p305.
93 D King, *Actively Seeking Work?*, University of Chicago Press, 1995, p14.
94 Beveridge's Report to July 1914 (p52) estimates penetration in the insured trades at 34 per cent.
95 Gilbert, op cit, p287.

Chapter 3: Time of Trial 1914–18

1 Humbert Wolfe, *Labour Supply and Regulation*, Oxford, 1923, p66.
2 Ibid, p7.
3 Beveridge, *Power and Influence*, p118.
4 Beveridge letter of 23 Sept 1914 to his mother, Beveridge papers, II a 60.
5 Minute of 20 July 1916 from Beveridge to Marwood, PRO. LAB 2/1816.
6 PRO. LAB 2/1816.
7 JB Seymour, *The British Employment Exchange*, PS King, London, 1928, p19.
8 *Enquiry into the Work of Employment Exchanges*, 1920 (Cmd 1054), Minutes of Evidence, Q 4956. At the same time, adjudication of benefit claims passed from Divisional Office to an Insurance Officer in an Exchange – see Royal Commission on Unemployment Insurance, 1932, Para 578.
9 R Lowe, *Adjusting to Democracy*, Oxford, 1986, p53, Note 27.
10 H Wolfe, *Portraits by Inference*, Methuen, 1934, p95.
11 Letter to his mother, 3 Aug 1914. Beveridge Papers, II a 60.
12 Harris, *Beveridge*, p199.
13 Letter to his mother, 3 Aug 1914. See above.
14 Beveridge, *Power and Influence*, p118–9.
15 S Tallents, *Man and Boy*, p191.
16 Report of 12 Aug 1914. LAB 2/169.
17 PRO. LAB 2/169.
18 Wolfe, *Labour Supply and Regulation*, p15.
19 Ibid, pp57–8.
20 Ibid, p59.

Chapter 3: 1914–18 Notes and References

21 Ibid, pp219–20.
22 Wolfe, *Portraits by Inference*, p109.
23 Statement by Beveridge to the Enquiry into the Work of Employment Exchanges, 1920, (Cmd 1054), Minutes of Evidence, p180.
24 Harris, *Beveridge*, pp205–6.
25 TUC Annual Report, 1916, p189.
26 Harris, op cit, p212.
27 Wolfe, *Labour Supply and Regulation*, p79.
28 Seymour, op cit, pp23–4.
29 Wolfe, *Labour Supply and Regulation*, pp82–3.
30 Ibid, p86.
31 Wolfe, *Labour Supply and Regulation*, Chapter IV. Also K Grieves, *The Politics of Manpower 1914–18*, Manchester University Press, 1988.
32 A Marwick, *The Deluge: British Society and the First World War*, Macmillan, 1965, p62.
33 Wolfe, op cit, p33.
34 Ibid, pxi.
35 Ibid, pp195–204.
36 Beveridge, *Power and Influence*, pp134–5.
37 Seymour, op cit, p26.
38 Grieves, op cit, pp66–80.
39 See R Lowe, 'The Ministry of Labour, 1916–24: A Graveyard of Social Reform?' *Public Administration*, 52 (1974), pp415 ff. Also R Lowe, *Adjusting to Democracy: The Role of the Ministry of Labour in British Politics 1916–39*, Oxford, 1986, Chapter 2.
40 Lowe, *Public Administration* article, pp419ff.
41 Ibid, p424.
42 John Hodge, *Workman's Cottage to Windsor Castle*, Sampson Low Marston, London, pp179–80; Beveridge, *Power and Influence*, p141.
43 Harris, *Beveridge*, p227.
44 Sir Harold Butler, *Confident Morning*, Faber and Faber, 1950, p116.
45 Imperial Calendar, 1917.
46 T Phillips' evidence to Enquiry on the Work of Employment Exchanges, Cmd 1054, 1920, Minutes of Evidence, p11.
47 Hodge, op cit, p199.
48 Wolfe, *Labour Supply and Regulation*, pp210–11.
49 Grieve, op cit, pp111–4.
50 Violet Markham to Chamberlain. David Dilks, *Neville Chamberlain*, Vol 1, p230.
51 Ibid, pp229–31.
52 Ibid, p231.
53 Ibid, p234.
54 Grieve, op cit, p128.
55 Dilks, op cit, pp239–41.
56 D Lloyd George, *War Memoirs*, Vol III, Nicolson and Watson, 1934, p1368.
57 Quoted by R Lowe, 'The Ministry of Labour, 1916–19: a still small voice', in L Burn (ed) *War and the State*, G Allen and Unwin, 1982, p113.
58 TW Phillips' evidence to the Enquiry on the Work of the Employment Exchanges, pp11–12.
59 Hodge, op cit.

60 On 25 March 1920, a Treasury official recorded that 'his return would be most unwelcome' in the Ministry of Labour. PRO, T 162/74/E 7112/01.
61 Wolfe, op cit, p22.

Chapter 4: The 'Ten Year Chaos' 1918–29

1 Beveridge, *Unemployment: A Problem of Industry*, 1930, p273.
2 A Bullock, *Life of Ernest Bevin*, Vol II, p119.
3 R Lowe, *Adjusting to Democracy*, p31.
4 Ibid, pp33–34.
5 Bullock, op cit, p119.
6 Anthony Seldon's Oral History, Interview with Sir John Walley, 1980, p9, LSE Library.
7 Sir Godfrey Ince, *The Ministry of Labour and National Service*, Allen and Unwin, 1960, p200.
8 W J Brown, *So Far*, Allen and Unwin, London, 1943, p221.
9 This account of Tom Phillips draws on R Lowe, *Adjusting to Democracy*, p65; on Sir John Walley's interview (see above); and on a personal letter to the author from Sir John.
10 RA Butler, *The Art of the Possible*, p62.
11 Note of 2 Nov 1921. PRO. LAB 2/1822/7. CEB 537/4/21.
12 This paragraph draws heavily on R Lowe, op cit, pp63–73.
13 Minute of 1 Oct 1920. PRO. LAB 2/1524. ED 4793/20,
14 Stanley Warrington, 'A National Employment Service: Great Britain's Experience', Dissertation written in about 1948 and held in DfEE Library, Moorfoot, Sheffield, p110.
15 Warrington, op cit.
16 PRO. LAB 2/1256/7.
17 The vote was still denied to women who were under 30 or who were not householders or married to householders.
18 George Orwell, *The Road to Wigan Pier*, 1937. 1962 Penguin edition, p129.
19 Includes HQ, Kew Claims and Records Office and Divisional staff. Source: Barnes Committee, 1920, Minutes of Evidence, p11.
20 Transcript of Meeting with Industrial Triple Alliance on 3 August 1916. PRO. LAB 2/1491.
21 Seymour, *The British Employment Exchange*, p31.
22 See organisation chart in R Lowe, *Adjusting to Democracy*, Appendix 1.
23 So-called because a slip was torn from their form and sent to their commanding officer seeking their release.
24 A Marwick, *The Deluge: British Society and the First World War*, Macmillan, 1965.
25 Seymour, op cit, pp32–3.
26 Ibid, pp36–7.
27 Ibid, pp39–40.
28 *Hansard*, Vol 145, 4 August 1921, Col 1737.
29 Harris, *Beveridge*, pp250–252.
30 Minute of 5 April 1919 from TW Phillips to Bowers and Cunningham. PRO. LAB 2/492, ED 8188/12/19.
31 Barnes Committee 1920, Minutes of Evidence, T Phillips' evidence pp14–15.

Chapter 4 1918–29 Notes and References

32. TS Chegwidden and G Myrddin-Evans *The Employment Exchange System in Great Britain*, Industrial Relations Counsellors Inc, New York, 1934, p72.
33. Barnes Committee, Minutes of Evidence, EHC Wethered's evidence. Minutes of Evidence, p156, Q 2423.
34. Ibid, JB Adams' evidence. Minutes of Evidence, p64, Q 799.
35. Aberconway's Report was Cmd 305. 1919. See Barnes Report, Minutes of Evidence, p15.
36. Editorial, 4 June 1920.
37. Minute of 21 May 1920 from Macnamara to Sir James Masterton-Smith. LAB2/699.
38. Lowe, *Adjusting to Democracy*, p67.
39. Committee Minutes of Evidence, p81.
40. Ibid, pp270ff.
41. Ibid, pp180ff.
42. Ben Turner, President of the General Union of Textile Workers, Minutes of Evidence, p138.
43. George H Wood, Secretary of the Wool and Worsted Trades Federation (employers), ibid, p38.
44. Prof Mark Wright, Minutes of Evidence, p102.
45. Harold Cox, ibid, pp415ff. And Committee Report, Para 17.
46. Professor Macgregor, ibid, p373.
47. Ibid, para 1.
48. Committee Report, para 94.
49. Committee Report, para 68,
50. Committee Report, para 94.
51. Masterton-Smith to Macnamara. 27 November 1920. PRO. LAB 2/699.
52. Chegwidden and Myrddin-Evans, op cit, p76.
53. Observations of Committee on National Expenditure on Ministry of Labour Estimates for 1922/23. PRO. LAB 2/1822/7.
54. PRO. LAB 2/1822/7.
55. Alan Deacon, *In Search of the Scrounger*, Geo Bell and Son, London, 1976, p14.
56. White Paper on Employment Policy, Cmd 6527, 1944, p26.
57. WR Garside, *British Unemployment 1919–39: A Study in Public Policy*, Cambridge, 1990, p5. At this time, the 'insured' unemployment rate probably exaggerated overall unemployment, since it related to wage earners who were more susceptible to unemployment than salary earners or the self-employed, who were largely outside unemployment insurance. Garside's more comprehensive series of figures are adjusted to take this into account.
58. Richard Croucher, *We Refuse to Starve in Silence. A History of the National Unemployed Workers' Movement*, Lawrence and Wishart, London, 1987.
59. See, for instance, Bentley Gilbert, *British Social Policy, 1914–39*, Batsford, 1970; WL Garside, *British Unemployment, 1919–39*, Cambridge, 1990; Lowe, op cit, Chapter 5; and Deacon, op cit.
60. M Bondfield, *A Life's Work*, National Book Association, 1948, p270.
61. See particularly Alan Deacon, op cit,
62. The 1920 Unemployment Insurance Act retained a maximum of 15 weeks' benefit in a year but applied a 1-in-6 rule rather than 1-in-5.
63. Garside, op cit, p47.
64. Deacon, op cit, p66.
65. Deacon, op cit, pp56, 59–60.

66 Deacon, op cit, p9.
67 Steel-Maitland Papers, National Archive of Scotland, GD 193/94/2.
68 Ministry of Labour, Annual Report for 1923 and 1924, Cmd 248, p80.
69 Sir Horace Wilson in a memorandum (LEC 1) to Local Employment Committees. PRO. LAB 2/1197. ED 30738/28. A 103/25.
70 PRO. LAB 2/1067. ED 22469/26. A 100/24.
71 PRO. LAB 2/1067. ED 14604/23. A 100/24.
72 JFG Price's minute of 5 March 1924 to Divisional Controllers. PRO. LAB 2/1067. 50897/27 and 4032/5.
73 Minute of 11 August 1930 from JA Dale to H Wolfe. PRO. LAB 2/1067. ET 2249/30.
74 EW Bakke, *The Unemployed Man*, Nisbet, London, 1933, pp113–4.
75 Warrington, op cit, p143.
76 PRO. LAB 2/1822/5. CEB 537/7/21. C50/21.
77 Bakke, op cit, p114.
78 Letter of 4 March 1030 to JA Barlow of Ministry of Labour. PRO. LAB 2/1067. ET 2515/30. Pt 1.
79 Llewellyn Smith's evidence to the Barnes Committee, Minutes of Evidence, p273; Minute of 20 Dec 1920 by Harry Smith. PRO. LAB 2/699. ES 3858/48; Warrington, op cit, p139.
80 Minutes of Evidence, p69.
81 PRO. LAB/1/1893. EDP 501/28.
82 Article in *Journal of Association of Officers of the Ministry of Labour*, Vol 37, 10 February 1960.
83 Para 9 of Report.
84 Harris, *Unemployment and Politics*, p366.
85 William Temple, *Christianity and the Social Order*, Penguin, Harmondsworth, 1942, p12.
86 Royal Commission on Unemployment Insurance, 1932 p103.
87 *Hansard*, Vol 145, 4 August 1921, Col 1728.

Chapter 5: Office of Despair? 1929–39

1 RA Butler, *The Art of the Possible*, Penguin, 1973, p62.
2 Butler, op cit, p61.
3 Sir John Walley in Anthony Seldon's oral history, 1980, LSE Library.
4 Lowe, *Adjusting to Democracy*, p65.
5 Chegwidden and Myrddin-Evans, *The Employment Exchange System in Great Britain*, p74.
6 There were nine Divisions in 1920 (Northern being separated from Scotland and a South Midland and Eastern Division created to relieve the South East). These were cut to seven in 1922, In 1936, there were nine Divisions again, with the South East split off and Northern Division re-created. Source, Warrington, op cit, p103.
7 Warrington, op cit, p110.
8 Garside, op cit, Chapter 9.
9 See Chegwidden and Myrddin-Evans, op cit, pp148–50; Dave Colledge, *Labour Camps: The British Experience*, Sheffield Popular Publishing, 1989.
10 Sidney and Beatrice Webb, *The Public Organisation of the Labour Market: Being Part 2 of the Minority Report of the Poor Law Commission*, Longmans Green, 1909, p344.

11 Wal Hannington, *The Problem of the Distressed Areas*, Gollancz, London, 1937, p112.
12 Beveridge, *Unemployment: A Problem of Industry*, 1930 Edition, p280.
13 See Garside, op cit, and R Skidelsky, *Politicians and the Slump*, Macmillan, 1967.
14 Lowe, op cit, pp165–6.
15 Lowe, op cit, p74.
16 Warrington, op cit.
17 Lowe, op cit, Appendix 3.
18 Royal Commission on Unemployment Insurance, Final Report.Cmd. 4185, 1932, p296.
19 Ibid, pp299–300.
20 Ibid, pp300–303.
21 Bondfield, *A Life's Work*, 1948.
22 PRO. LAB 2/1067. ET 2249/30.
23 Ministry of Labour, *Annual Report for 1937*, Cmd 5717, 1938, p10.
24 Minute of 7 May 1923 by W Eady. PRO. LAB 2/1067. ED 14604/23. A 100/24.
25 Ministry of Labour, *Annual Report for 1937*, Cmd. 5717, pp12–13.
26 PRO. LAB 2/1893. EDP 501/28.
27 Warrington, op cit, pp128–33.
28 John Burnett, *Idle Hands: The Experience of Unemployment, 1790–1929*, Routledge, London, 1994, p260.
29 Ibid, p260.
30 Max Cohen, *I Was One of the Unemployed*, Gollancz, London, 1945.
31 HL Beales and RS Lambert, *Memoirs of the Unemployed*, Gollancz, London, 1934. Republished 1973, p48.
32 Hilda Jennings, *Brynmawr: A Study of a Distressed Area*, Allenson and Co, 1934, pp138–9.
33 EW Bakke, *The Unemployed Man*, Nisbet, London, 1933, pp79, 114,
34 Ross McKibbin, *The Ideologies of Class: Social Relations in Britain, 1880–1990*, OUP, 1990, p249.
35 Burnett, op cit, p260.
36 PEP, 'Report on the British social services – A survey of the existing public social services in Great Britain with proposals for further development', June 1937.
37 Trevor Evans, *Bevin*, George Allen and Unwin, London, 1946 pp182–3.

Chapter 6: Mobilising the Masses, 1939–45

1 Bevin Papers 4/7, Churchill College, Cambridge.
2 This account is based on MEA Bowley, 'War History, Pre-War Plans' (PRO. LAB 76/8) and on HMD Parker, *Manpower: A Study of War-time Policy and Administration*, HMSO and Longmans Green, London, 1957.
3 Bowley, op cit, p39.
4 PRO. LAB 25/19.
5 Divisional Controllers' Conference, 10 Jan 1940. PRO. LAB 12/294.
6 Parker, op cit, Chapter IV.
7 Parker, op cit, p78.
8 This account draws on Parker, op cit, and on Alan Bullock, *The Life and Times of Ernest Bevin*, Vol II, Heinemann, London, 1967.
9 Sir Godfrey Ince, quoted in Bullock, op cit, p124.

10 Bullock, op cit, p120.
11 Bullock, op cit, p126.
12 Sir Godfrey Ince, Mobilisation of Manpower, *Public Administration*, XXIV, 1946, p4.
13 This account of Ince draws not only on Parker, op cit, and Bullock, op cit, but also on Parker's more revealing article in the *Dictionary of National Biography 1951–60*.
14 Parker, *DNB* (see above).
15 Controllers' Conference, 10 Sept 1941, PRO. LAB 12/294.
16 Lloyd Roberts at Controllers Conference on 8 November 1944. PRO. LAB 12/298.
17 Parker, op cit, p310.
18 Bullock, op cit, pp12–16; Bevin Papers 2/1, Churchill College, Cambridge.
19 Parker, op cit, p132.
20 Parker, op cit, pp101–5.
21 Ibid, pp107–8 and 136–46.
22 Ibid, p139.
23 Parker, *Manpower* etc, p224.
24 Ibid, Chapter XII.
25 Ince, op cit, p7
26 Bevin papers, 4/7.
27 Quoted in Parker, op cit, p217.
28 Bullock, op cit, note on p127.
29 Trevor Evans, *Bevin*, George Allen and Unwin, London, 1946, p183.
30 Controllers' Conference, 10 Sept 1941, LAB 12/294.
31 Marjory Hayward, LAB 12/109.
32 Controllers' Conference, 13 August 1941, LAB 12/294.
33 10 Dec 1941, LAB 12/294.
34 Controllers' Conferences on 8 July 1942 and 12 August 1942, LAB 12/295.
35 Controllers' Conference on 14 August 1940, LAB 12/294.
36 Controllers' Conference, 19 Sept 1941, LAB 12/294.
37 Arton Wilson, Controllers' Conference, 10 Sept 1941, LAB 12/294.
38 Quoted in a paper of April 1964 in LAB 8/2762.
39 Controllers' Conference, 10 Sept 1941, LAB 12/294.
40 Controllers' Conference, 13 December 1944, LAB 12/298.
41 See Harris, *Beveridge*, Chapter 15; and Bullock, op cit, pp225–6.
42 Sir John Walley in a letter to the author.
43 Recollection of Sir Denis Barnes reported to author by WRB Robinson.
44 'Social Insurance and Allied Services: Report by Sir William Beveridge', Cmd 6404, 1942.
45 Ibid, para 130.
46 PRO. PIN 8/115.
47 Bullock, op cit, p326.
48 Later knighted and Permanent Secretary of the ministry of Town and Country Planning.
49 Controllers' Conference, 13 December 1944, PRO. LAB 12/298.
50 This account is mainly based on a note of 20 April 1943 from AB Patterson. PRO. PIN 8/10.
51 Letter of 31 March 1945 from Phillips to Ince. On 7 May Arton Wilson replied on Ince's behalf.
52 Parker, op cit, pp318–25.

53 Speech in Newcastle on 4 February 1945. Bevin Papers, Churchill College, Cambridge, 4/7.
54 Bullock, op cit, pp293–5.
55 Controllers' Conference, 10 January 1945, LAB 12/298.
56 Bevin papers, 4/7.
57 Ince, *Public Administration* 1946, pp12 and 14.
58 M M Postan, *British War Production*, HMSO and Kraus Reprint, 1975, first published 1952, p221.
59 PRO. LAB 79/33.

Chapter 7: Post-War Full Employment, 1945–60

1 *Dictionary of National Biography*.
2 Philip M Williams (ed), *The Diaries of Hugh Gaitskell 1945–56*, Cape, London, 1983, pp228–9.
3 Lord Birkenhead, *Walter Monckton*, Weidenfeld and Nicolson, London, 1969, p276.
4 Robert Shepherd, *Iain Macleod*, Hutchinson, London, 1994, Chapters 6–7.
5 Birkenhead, op cit, p297.
6 Macmullan, an Ulsterman, under the pseudonym of CK Munro, wrote *The Fountains in Trafalgar Square* about the civil service; HMD Parker wrote the official history of the Manpower in the Second World War.
7 Nearly all the Ministry of Labour *Annual Reports* of the period refer to these restrictions on capital expenditure.
8 Ministry of Labour and National Service, *Annual Report 1939–46*, p331.
9 Sir Godfrey Ince, *The Ministry of Labour and National Service*, George Allen and Unwin, London, 1960, p178.
10 DNB article on Ince by HMD Parker.
11 'Social Insurance and Allied Services.' Cmnd 6404, pp163–4.
12 Discussion of unemployment benefit arrangements after the war. PRO. LAB 12/156.
13 Controllers' Conference, 17 May 1945. PRO. LAB 12/298.
14 1.75 million registered and a further 0.5 million unregistered. Ministry of Labour *Annual Report, 1947*, p12.
15 Ministry of Labour and National Service, *Annual Report*, Cmd 9791, 1955, pv.
16 International Labour Office, *National Employment Services: Great Britain*, Geneva, 1952, p135.
17 Ibid, p51.
18 Ibid, p51.
19 Ministry of Labour *Annual Report 1939–46*, p131.
20 Ibid, p132.
21 Ibid, pp180–1.
22 Ministry of Labour *Annual Reports* for 1947 and 1948.
23 Ministry of Labour *Annual Report for 1947*, p12.
24 Ibid, p21.
25 Ministry of Labour *Annual Report, 1950*.
26 Ibid, p51.
27 A Cairncross, *Years of Recovery, British Economic Policy, 1945–51*, Methuen, London, 1985, p399.
28 Ministry of Labour *Annual Report, 1952*.

333

29 PRO. LAB 43/178.
30 *Hansard*, Vol 552, Col 207, 1 May 1956.
31 Ministry of Labour *Annual Report, 1956*, pp46 and 49.
32 Placing Memo 13 of December 1945, quoted in paper for Controllers' Conference of 14 Sept 1949. PRO. LAB 12/558.
33 PRO. LAB 8/2334.
34 Controllers' Conference, 14 Sept 1949, PRO. LAB 12/558.
35 Standing HQ Committee on Placing Work. PRO. LAB 8/1873 and AD 6586.
36 Minutes of Standing Committee, 11 May 1950. LAB 8/1873.
37 Note of 14 June 1951. PRO. LAB 8/1873.
38 Report on the Employment of Women and Older Workers. Nov 1968. DE file 1/RP 153/68.
39 Paper for Controllers' Conference, 21 May 1958. PRO. LAB 8/2365.
40 See Table 9 in Chapter 5. This is true even if youth placings and Class B placings are deducted from the 1930s figures to ensure a fair comparison.
41 Sir G, Ince, op cit, pp83–4; Ministry of Labour *Annual Report 1959*. Cmd 1059, p51.
42 Ibid, p86.
43 Ministry of Labour Annual Report, 1947, pp46–7.
44 AH Richmond, *The Colour Problem*, Penguin, 1955. A Gallup Poll in 1961 found rather more liberal attitudes: 60 per cent thought that immigrants should compete on equal terms for jobs and 68 per cent would not mind working with coloured workers. See S Patterson, *Dark Strangers*, Penguin, 1965, pp152–3.
45 PRO. LAB 8/2289.
46 Note to Controllers of 11 Feb 1949, PRO. LAB 8/1519.
47 PRO. LAB 8/2289.
48 Note of meeting with regional representatives on 20 Jan 1949. PRO. LAB 8/1519.
49 PRO. LAB 8/2289.
50 PRO. LAB 8/2289.
51 Report of 8 Oct 1956. PRO. LAB 8/2289.
52 *Daily Telegraph*, 7 Feb 1955, and note by Pearce of Feb 1955. PRO. LAB 8/2289.
53 28 Feb 1958.
54 Patterson, *Dark Strangers*, p128.
55 Ibid, p132.
56 Andrew Roth, *Heath and the Heathmen*, Routledge, London, 1972, p140.
57 *Minlabour*, Jan 1960, p2.

Chapter 8: The Stirring of Reform, 1960–70

1 Barbara Castle, *The Castle Diaries, 1964–76*, Papermac, 1990, pp381–2.
2 Rodney Lowe, 'The core executive, modernisation and the creation of PESC 1960–64', *Public Administration*, Vol 75, No 4, Winter 1997, p601.
3 *DNB 1981–85*, pp180–81.
4 PRO. LAB 8/2762.
5 Minutes of 29 April 1964 by R Dronfield and of 12 May 1964 by R Swift. PRO. PIN 7/452.
6 Minutes of 14 May 1964. PRO. PIN 7/542.
7 This paragraph draws on Roderick Allison's recollections.
8 This paragraph draws on Robin Wendt's recollections.

9   *The Castle Diaries*, p215.
10 Keith's note of 16 Jan 1970 to B Castle. 1/EM 542/69.
11 *Manpower Policy in the UK*, OECD, 1970, para 4.3.
12 This account of the origins of self service is drawn from 1/EM 637/67.
13 PRO. PIN 7/542.
14 PRO. PIN 7/543.
15 31/OE 106/68. Paper for Regional Controllers, 26 June 1968. Also 1/EM 346/69, Annex to Planning Report No 1, Sept 1969.
16 31/OE 106/68.
17 1/EM 346/69, Appendix to Planning Report 1.
18 OECD, *Manpower Policies in the UK*, Paris, 1970. Chapter 4 of main report and Chapter III of Examiners' Report.
19 1/OE 272/68. DB Smith, Mrs Castle's Secretary, to J Galbraith.
20 1/EM 346/69. R Keith to J Galbraith, 15 July 1969.
21 31/OE 227/69. Meeting on 23 October 1969.
22 1/OE 146/70. Note of 13 January 1969.
23 1/EM 346/69. Planning Unit No 1.
24 R Crossman, *The Diaries of a Cabinet Minister*, Vol III, p205, 30 Sept 1968.
25 Ibid, p211, 4 Nov 1968.
26 1/OE 272/68. Letter of 9 Dec 1968.
27 1/OE 272/68. Sir Clifford Jarrett to Sir Denis Barnes, 13 Jan 1968.
28 1/EM 145/69. Miss Riddlesdell's note of 12 Dec 1969.
29 Ibid, Report.
30 1/EM 542/69. GAF Blumer.
31 1/EM 542/69. R Keith to Secretary of State, 16 Jan 1970.
32 Crossman, op cit, pp832–3, 23 and 24 Feb 1970.
33 Ibid, pp840–41, 2 March 1970.
34 Castle, op cit, p391, 9 March 1970.
35 Crossman, op cit, p854, 10 March 1970.
36 Castle, op cit, p402, 13 May 1970.
37 Dept of Employment and Productivity, 'The Future of the Employment Service', Consultative Document, May 1970.

Chapter 9: Modernisation, 1970–74

1   EPC (71) 29th minutes, 1/EM 156/7.
2   This paragraph is based on a letter to the author from Ken Cooper.
3   DE files 5/OE 296/70 and 1OE 188/71.
4   *Hansard*, 6 May 1970, Col 428.
5   *The Civil Service*, Vol 1, Cmnd 3638, 1968, pp61–2.
6   DE file 1/ES 308/70. In a minute of 29 May 1970, Mrs Kent said that hiving off might be the only way to secure the necessary resources for modernisation.
7   Ibid, Ken Barnes' submission of 15 July 1970 and note of Meeting on 4 August 1980.
8   Ibid, Report, 'A National Manpower Commission: Report of a Departmental Study', submitted to Secretary of State by Ken Barnes on 8 Jan 1971.
9   DE file 1/ES 117/71. Secretary of State's minute of 21 Jan 1971.
10 Ibid, Minute by Sir Denis Barnes to D B Smith, Private Secretary to Secretary of State.

11 Ibid, Letter of 19 Feb 1971 from Caulcott to Sutherland.
12 Ibid, Notes of meetings on 6 April 1971 and 3 May 1971.
13 Ibid, Letter of 14 May 1971 from Caulcott to GA Brand.
14 Ibid, Minute of 23 June 1971 by Ken Barnes.
15 DE File 7/F 105/71. Note by HM Treasury of 14 Jan 1971.
16 Letter to author.
17 DE File 1/ES 117/71. Note of meeting on 3 May 1971. Also 1/ES 156/71. Letter of 16 June 1971 from Maurice Macmillan to Robert Carr.
18 DE File 1/ES 308/70, Report of a Departmental Study on National Manpower Commission, para 3.4.
19 DE file 1/ES 117/71. Note of meeting of Bryan Group on 23 Feb 1971.
20 Ibid, Note of 2nd meeting of Working Group on 23 Feb 1971, together with PAR Report, para 23.
21 DE File 1/ES 117/71. Report of Bryan Group.
22 Ibid, Note of 28 May 1971 by DB Smith, Carr's Private Secretary.
23 Para 45 of PAR Report on 1/ES 156/71.
24 Ibid, Minute of 20 Oct 1971 from J Locke to G Holland, PS to Robert Carr.
25 Ibid, Note of 16 Nov 1971 from M Macmillan to Prime Minister.
26 DE File 117/71. Minute of 28 May 1971 by DB Smith, PS to Robert Carr.
27 Ibid, Letter of 3 June 1971 from CJ Pearce of DOE to GA Brand of DE.
28 DE file 2/EPM 164/73. Minute of 24 Nov 1972 from KR Cooper to G Holland, PS to R Carr.
29 DE file 1/EM 232/72. Maurice Macmillan's press notice of 8 August 1972.
30 DE file 1/ES 308/70. John Locke's brief for Prime Minister of 27 July 1972.
31 Ibid.
32 Ibid, J Locke note of 12 Sept 1972.
33 Ibid, Letter of 1 Sept 1972 from RS Allison to T Caulcott, CSD.
34 Ibid, Press Notice of 22 Nov 1972.
35 Department of Employment, 'People and Jobs', Dec 1971, p12.
36 DE file 1/EM 232/72. Letter of 14 Nov 1972 from AG Beard to KR Cooper and letter of 6 Dec 1972 from KR Cooper to AG Beard.
37 Report of the Committee on the Abuse of Social Security Benefits, Cmnd 5228, HMSO 1973, para 280.
38 B Showler, *The Public Employment Service*, Longman, London, 1976.
39 *Hansard*, 2 Feb 1995.
40 DE file 1/EM 209/72. Notes of Aug 1972 by Mrs D Kent; of 22 Aug 1972 by W Fawcett and of 11 Sept 1972 by AAG McNaughton.
41 DE file 1/OE 106/71. Minute of 22 Feb 1972 by KR Cooper.
42 Action Plan for a modern employment service, Dec 1972, p21.
43 DE file 1/EM 144/72. Note of ES Board on 18 Sept 1972.
44 Action Plan, p22.
45 DE file 1/EM 144/72. Report to ES Board, 8 March 1973.
46 Ibid, Report to ES Board on 24 Sept 1973. Placings in Reading rose from 312 in June to 505 in July (admittedly at a time when Eastern and Southern Region placings rose from 14,167 to 15,555). The self-service percentage in Reading rose from 32.5 per cent in June to 61.5 per cent in July.
47 DE file 1/EM 107/72. In a note of 1 Feb 1972, Benton and Bowles Ltd, a firm which specialised in marketing images, set out a list of possible titles, of which their preferred choice was 'Job Centre'.
48 Action Plan, p20.

Chapter 9 1970–74–Chapter 10 1974–79 Notes and References

49 'The Employment Service – Plans and Programmes', Oct 1974, pp9–10.
50 DE file 1/EM 144/72. Note by DB Price for ES Board on 14 May 1973.
51 DE file 156/71. Programme Analysis and Review of 'The Public Employment Service', Nov 1971, para 23.
52 DE file 156/71. PAR, para 22.
53 PROfile. 1ET 1/1. Note of meeting of MSC on 5 Feb 1974.
54 For instance, in December 1972, Mrs Thatcher, Secretary of State for Education announced an extra £1000 million a year for education by 1981. John Campbell, *Edward Heath – a biography*, Pimlico, 1994, p388.
55 Showler, op cit, Conclusion.

Chapter 10: The New Model Employment Service, 1974–79

1 Lord Carr of Hadley, Interview with Anthony Seldon, Oral History, 1980, British Library of Economic and Political Science.
2 MSC Minutes, 31 July 1974. ET1/1 PRO.5/1.
3 MSC Minutes, 22 July 1975. PRO. ET 5/1.
4 Comment by Chairman of MSC at Chairman's Management Committee, 10 Dec 1976. File 1976 3B/126, held by DfEE.
5 Letter of 1 April 1977 from J Methven, Director General to Chairman MSC. Ibid.
6 MSC, *The Employment Service: Plans and Programmes*, HMSO, October 1974.
7 MSC Minutes. 18 Sept 1994. PRO. ET 1/1.
8 Letter to the author from Ken Cooper.
9 DE File 20/EM 241/74.
10 MSC file 1976/3B/126.
11 Interim Report in DE file 1976/3B/126.
12 Minutes of 4/3/77 and 11/3/77 on 1976/3B/126.
13 MSC, *The Employment Service in the 1980s*, 1979, p13.
14 Exec Committee Minutes for 19 Dec 1974. PRO. ET 5/1.
15 Survey No 1064. Para F4,5 and 6. On DE file 1974/2P/155.
16 In a minute of 11 Dec 1974, Ron Stephenson urged his managers to seize the opportunity of treating most instructions as purely advisory. DE file 1974/2P/155.
17 Minutes of MSC Meeting on 28 July 1976. PRO. ET 1/3.
18 Quoted in *Guide to Complementing of Local Offices*, ESA, Feb 1977. DE file, 197/2P/155, Vol 3.
19 DE file 1977/2P/124. Minutes of 5 August 1977 and 29 March 1979 respectively.
20 Minutes of Exec Committee, 21 Sept 1977. PRO file ET 5/4.
21 Report by Staff Inspection and Evaluation branch, CSD. Paras 11.12 and 12.2, DE file 1977/2P/116.
22 *The Employment Service in the 1980s*, MSC, 1979, p13. Staffing in October 1974, was 10,090; in 1978/79 it was 11,154.
23 *The Employment Service in the 1980s*, 1979, p34.
24 The Civil Service Department were in turn drawing on the writings of such management gurus as Peter Drucker (eg *Managing for Results*, 1964, Heinemann) and John Humble of Urwick Orr consultants (eg *Improving Business Results*, Mc-Graw Hill, 1967).
25 Executive Committee minutes for 21 Sept 1977 (PRO. ET 5/4), 6 Dec 1977, 19 April 1978, 14 June 1978, 18 Oct 1978 (PRO. ET5/5).

26 CAPITAL Evaluation Report. PRO. ET 8/44.
27 MSC Minutes for 26 Sept 1978. PRO. ET 1/5.
28 ESD Executive Committee Minutes for 18 April 1979. PRO ET 5/6.
29 MSC Minutes for 9 Jan 1974. PRO. ET 1/1.
30 MSC Minutes for 18 June 1974. PRO. ET 1/1.
31 ESA, Report and Plan to 1981. MSC, August 1975.
32 Department of Employment, Action Plan for a Modern Employment Service, p29, 1972.
33 ESA Strategic Plan 1977 to 1982. Section 4. MSC, May 1977.
34 ESD Executive Minutes for 19 April 1978. PRO. ET 5/5.
35 ESD Executive Minutes for 16 Aug 1978. PRO. ET 5/5.
36 MSC Minutes for 26 September 1978. PRO. ET 1/5.
37 Employment and Training Act 1973. Section 12 (2).
38 DE file1/UB 200/72. AW Brown to IMH Miller of Finance, 24 Sept 1976.
39 DE file 1/UB 200/72. Mrs Kent to AW Brown, 27 October 1976.
40 MSC Minutes 25 May 1976. PRO. ET 1/3.
41 Employment Service National Operating Plan 1978/79, pp9 and 23.
42 MSC Minutes, 21 March and 27 June 1978.
43 *People and Jobs*, 1971, p19.
44 Employment Service Executive Committee Minutes, 18 July 1979. PRO. ET 5/6.
45 MSC Employment Service: Report and Plan to 1981. Para 4.3.
46 Review of the Employment Service 1979. Para 6.20.
47 ESD Executive Committee Minutes, 15 March 1978. PRO. ET 5/5.
48 Ibid, 14 June 1978. PRO. ET 5/5.
49 Manpower Services Commission, *The Employment Service in the 1980s*, 1979.
50 An OPCS survey had shown the ES share of the market in 1973 as 16 per cent. (ESA Report and Plan to 1981, 1975, p2). An SCPR survey in 1976/77 had shown that ES's share had risen to 18 per cent. The estimate of over 20 per cent in 1979 reflected placing performance subsequent to 1976/77. See 'Market share of the general employment service', *DE Gazette*, June 1979, pp558–63.
51 MSC, *The Employment Service in the 1980s*, p16.
52 Ibid, p20.
53 Ibid, p19.
54 Ibid, p19.
55 Ibid, p21.
56 ESD Executive Committee Minutes, 21 November 1979. PRO. ET 5/6.
57 Centre for Labour Economics Discussion Paper No 62, *Have Jobcentres Increased Unemployment?*, 1979.
58 MSC, *The Employment Service in the 1980s*, 1979, p15.

Chapter 11: The Challenge of Thatcherism, 1979–81

1 Nigel Lawson, *The View from No 11*, Corgi Books, 1993, p64.
2 The others were Chesterfield, Glasgow, Liverpool, Washington and York.
3 MSC Minutes, 22 May 1979. PRO. ET 1/6.
4 James Prior, *A Balance of Power*, Hamish Hamilton, 1986; Margaret Thatcher, *The Downing Street Years*, Harper Collins, 1995.
5 'Report on Non-Departmental Public Bodies', Jan 1980, Cmd 7797, para 61.
6 Ibid, Annex B6. p15.

Chapter 11 1979–81 Notes and References

7. 'Swelling Civil Service', by Patrick Hutber, *Sunday Telegraph*, 13 May 1979.
8. A Dilnot and I Walker, *The Economics of Social Security*, OUP, 1989. Chapter by Tony Atkinson and John Micklewright: 'Turning the screw: Benefits for the unemployed, 1979–88', pp17–51.
9. Thatcher, op cit, p55.
10. ES Executive Committee Minutes, 19 Sept and 17 October 1979. PRO. ET 5/6.
11. Ditto, 27 July 1979. PRO. ET 5/6.
12. MSC Minutes, 27 Jan 1981. PRO. ET 1/8.
13. MSC Minutes, 24 June 1980. PRO. ET 1/7.
14. MSC Minutes, 24 March 1980. PRO. ET 1/7.
15. MSC Minutes, 22 April 1980. PRO. ET 1/7.
16. London School of Economics, Centre for Labour Economics, Discussion Paper No 62, 'Have Jobcentres increased unemployment?', 1979. Also article in *Guardian* on 5 November 1979.
17. Michael Lloyd, a labour market economist who worked first for MSC and then for the Institute of Manpower Studies, calculated that in 1968 there were six chances in 1000 of being denied benefit, compared with one in 1000 in 1978 (letter of 1/11/79 on DE file E/80/59/E 117).
18. Report from the Select Committeee of the House of Lords on Unemployment, Vol 1, The Report, May 1982, para 12.28.
19. Ibid, Paras 12.31 and 12.33.
20. MSC Annual Report, 1983/84, July 1984.
21. ESD Executive Minutes for 18 June, 16 July, 20 August 1980. PRO. ET 5/7.
22. Department of Employment and Department of Health and Social Security, 'Payment of benefits to unemployed people', March 1981, p1, para 2.
23. Ibid, p9, para 1.01.
24. Ibid, para 3.04.
25. Ibid, para 3.06-07.
26. Ibid, para 8.34.
27. DE File 3/ET 207/80, E Mc Ginnis to D Hodgkins, 15 Dec 1980.
28. Ibid, JS Cassels' minute of 14 Nov 1980 to Ian Johnston.
29. Note of 31 Dec 1980 from Miles Pattison, PM's Private Secretary, to R Dykes, Jim Prior's PS. DE file 3/ET 207/80.
30. *New Society*, 16 April 1981.
31. *Observer*, 19 April 1981.
32. MSC Minutes, 24 April 1981 and 19 May 1981. PRO. ET1/8.
33. Note of meeting of 23 June 1981 on DE file 3/ETI/ 70/81.
34. Lord Soames to W Whitelaw, 23 July 1981. DE file 3/ET1/ 70/81.
35. This legislative change was necessary for supplementary allowance purposes. 'In the case of UB claimants, this condition (registration) lacks specific statutory backing although there is a power to require claimants to attend at a Jobcentre for an employment interview. In the case of SA claimants, however, the registration condition has been laid down in regulations'. Rayner Report on 'Payment of Benefits to Unemployed People', para 4.03.
36. MSC Annual Report for 1983/84.
37. Ibid, JS Cassels' minute of 29 Sept 1980 to Ian Johnston.
38. Ibid, K Barnes' minute of 7 October 1980 to Ian Johnston.
39. MSC Minutes for 23/24 July 1979. PRO. ET 1/6.
40. 'The Employment Service and the Unemployed Flow', *Policy Studies*, Vol 2, Part 1, July 1981, p11.

Chapter 12: The Era of Peter Morrison, 1981–85

1 Lord Young, *The Enterprise Years*, Headline, London, 1990, p106.
2 Ibid, p74.
3 Ibid, pp67 and 78.
4 ESD Executive Minutes for 8 Oct 1981. PRO. ET 5/8.
5 P Morrison to B Winkett, 18 Nov 1981, DE file E 81/34B/104.
6 Derek Rayner to Richard O'Brien , Dec 1981, Ibid.
7 C Priestley of Rayner Unit to R O'Brien, 31 Dec 1981, ibid.
8 J Collingridge to B Winkett, 1 Dec 1981, ibid.
9 MSC, *General Employment Service in Great Britain. Report of the Rayner Scrutiny*, 1982, paras 3.23 and 6.9.
10 Ibid, para 5.
11 Ibid, para 3.45 (d).
12 Ibid, para 3.34 of the Report, which reads as follows: 'Employers were asked: "supposing that for some reason a new recruit could not have started work until a week later, would it have mattered to you or not?" In the case of 77 per cent of manual and 84 per cent of non-manual engagements, employers said it would not have mattered...The question was not worded precisely and too much should not be made of the answer. However, the results suggest considerable caution in valuing relatively small differences in speed of vacancy filling...'.
13 G Reid note of 30 June 1982 to Chairman's Management Committee. DE file E 82/26B/110.
14 MSC file E/81/61E/110.
15 Sir Derek Rayner to D Young, 8 July 1982. DE file 1982/26B/106.
16 MSC Minutes, 27 July 1982. PRO. ET 1/9.
17 Ibid, 28 Jan 1982.
18 Ibid, 27 July 1982.
19 D Young, op cit, p87.
20 MSC file E82/67E/170. See also Paul Bagguley, *From Protest to Acquiescence: Political Movements of the Unemployed*, Macmillan, London, 1991.
21 'Value for money in the Community Programme', Report to the Secretary of State for Employment by David Normington and Hugh Brodie, March 1986.
22 MSC Minutes, 23 June 1981. PRO. ET 1/8.
23 Ibid, 22 Sept 1981.
24 SCPR. NA Maung and R Erens, *EAS: A Survey of Participants Two Years after Leaving*, Dec 1991.
25 In 1990/91, EAS was delegated to the Training and Enterprise Councils and on 1 April 1991 it was renamed 'Business Start Up' with such major rule changes that there ceased to be a recognisable national scheme. Among other things, a period of unemployment ceased to be required as a qualifying criterion.
26 Ministry of Labour *Annual Report for 1956*, p150.
27 Report of Peter Morrison's address on 17 June 1983 from *Mosaic*, the MSC staff newspaper.
28 See Chapter 7 of Lord Young, *The Enterprise Years*.
29 N Tebbit, *Upwardly Mobile*, Weidenfeld and Nicolson, 1988, p192.
30 Alan Clark, *Diaries*, Weidenfeld and Nicolson, 1993, p89.
31 MSC Corporate Plan, 1982/86, April 1982, para 6.56.
32 MSC Corporate Plan, 1984/88, May 1984.

33 MSC *Annual Report for 1983/84*. July 1984. Targets were 1.9 million vacancies and 1.5 million placings.

Chapter 13: Lord Young's Revolution, 1985–87

1 Lord Young, *The Enterprise Years*, Headline, London, 1990, p150.
2 Ibid, p112.
3 Alan Clark, *Diaries*, Phoenix Giants, 1995, p109.
4 Ibid, p119.
5 Young, op cit, pp149–50.
6 Ibid, pp150–151.
7 Ibid, p154.
8 Nigel Lawson, *The View from No 11*, p282, Corgi, London, 1983.
9 Memo from Professor Minford to the House of Commons Select Committee on Employment, which reported in Jan 1986.
10 Young, op cit, p158.
11 Quoted in King's Memorandum of July 1985 on DE File 3/ET 134/85.
12 DE File 3/ET 134/85. Tom King Memo of 18 July 1985 and Roger Dawe's note of 25 July 1985.
13 Ibid. Stuart Lane's minute of 24 July 1985.
14 MSC Minutes for meeting on 24 Oct 1985. MSC file E86/32E/101.
15 MSC File P/87/20/158. Minutes of Chairman's Management Committee for 16 April 1986.
16 House of Commons, 30th Report of the Public Accounts Committee. Session 1984/85, July 1985.
17 Ibid, p157. The proposal to which Young refers probably affected older unemployed claimants.
18 Ibid, p163.
19 Ibid, p164.
20 MSC File C85/2D/155. Bryan Nicholson's letter of 12 December 1985 to Secretary of State.
21 Lawson, op cit, p698.
22 Young, op cit, p176. See also pp187–8.
23 DE File 11/RP 366/86. Evaluation Report on Restart Pilots, December 1986.
24 DE File 8/EPM 375/85. Minute of 24 July 1986 by Ianthe Wright.
25 Young, op cit, p173.
26 MSC file P/86 93F/115. 'Budget Announcements'. Paper by Director.
27 MSC File P/86/93F/106. B Nicholson letter of 14 June 1986 to Lord Young and Lord Young's reply of 16 June 1986.
28 DE File 14/EPM 106/86.
29 Young, op cit, p171.
30 DE file 11/RP/366/86. Evaluation Report on Restart Pilots.
31 DE file 11/RP 177/87. Note of 20 July 1987 by Ian Berry to Secretary of State.
32 MSC File E86/32E 101. Mainly based on a brief produced in Jan 1986.
33 Young, op cit, p155.
34 MSC File P/86/93F/106. J Surr's Minute of 18 Feb 1987 to Chairman. Reply of 26 March 1987 from P Allanson, PS to Chairman.
35 DE File 14/EPM 109/85. MSC Memo 393/1 of April 1986.
36 Ibid. Timetable of course in Tutor's Guide.

37 *Daily Mirror*, 5 August 1986.
38 DE File 14/EPM 109/85.
39 Rayner Report: 'Payment of benefits to Unemployed People', 1981, para 2.32.
40 DE File, 9/UB 157/86. Note of 18th Restart progress meeting on 23 July 1987.
41 DE File 9/UB 157/86. Correspondence of Sept/Oct 1988 between Stuart Holland MP and Nicholas Scott, Minister at DHSS.
42 John Philpott, *A Solution to Long-Term Unemployment: The Job Guarantee*, Employment Institute, London, 1990, p37.
43 Lawson, op cit, p434.
44 MSC File P/87/2D/158. Minutes of Chairman's Management Committee for 15 October 1986.
45 These figures include programmes like the Community Programme which were on the DE Vote, but administered by the MSC.
46 A Clark, op cit, pp108–9.
47 DE File 9/UB 122/86.
48 Young, op cit, p195.
49 'The Next Moves Forward', Conservative Manifesto, 1987.
50 Lawson, op cit, p433.
51 Michael White and Jane Lakey, *The Restart Effect*, Policy Studies Institute, London, 1992. The evidence from this later research may suggest some changes from the 'once and for all' effects achieved when Restart started in 1986. For instance, it did not produce evidence that Restart worked primarily through a deterrent effect, operating against ineligible claims to benefit. 'There was undoubtedly some effect in increasing movements off the register and into non-claimant status but it was not large, and it was present only in the first six months of the study.' (*Restart Effect*, p164).
52 Ibid, p172.
53 See, for instance, Richard Jackman and Hartmut Lehmann in Chapter 7 of R Disney et al, *Helping the unemployed: Active Labour Market Policies in Britain and Germany*, Anglo-German Foundation, 1992.
54 MJ Dicks and N Hatch, 'The Relationship Between Employment and Unemployment', Bank of England Discussion Paper No 39, 1989. See also John Philpott, *A Solution to Long Term Unemployment: The Job Guarantee*, Employment Institute, 1990, p37.
55 See for instance P Dolton and D O'Neill, 'The Restart effect and the return to full-time stable employment', *Journal of the Royal Statistical Society*, Vol 159, Part 2 1996, pp275 ff.
56 Thatcher, op cit, p421.

Chapter 14: Warfare and Welfare, 1987–90

1 Philip Stephens, 'Skilful son of Middle England', *Financial Times*, March 1989.
2 N Fowler, *Ministers Decide: A Personal Memoir of the Thatcher Years*, Chapman and Hall, London, 1991.
3 Secretary of State for Employment's White Paper, 'Training for Employment', Cm 316, Feb 1988, p28.
4 ES file 2/UB/50/87. Minute of 17 Dec 1987 from RS Foster to Private Secretary to Secretary of State.

5   House of Commons, Session 1988/89. Committee of Public Accounts, 13th Report, 'National Insurance Fund and Social Fund', 3 June 1989, para 2 (iii).
6   Ibid. Record of meeting on 17 April 1989.
7   The DE system was known as RIS and the MSC system as FMAS. The new ES system was called ESMIS (Employment Service Management Information System).
8   *Guardian* article, 'Fowler soft sell calms unions', 28 June 1988.
9   ES file 17/EPM 124/90. Background note to PQ dated 30 Nov 1990.
10 ES file 9/UB 183/88. Letter of 24 April 1988 from J Rooney, TU Side Secretary, and reply of 16 May 1988 from Colleen Bowen, Management Side Secretary.
11 White Paper, p33.
12 Ibid, p36.
13 The sanction of up to 26 weeks for leaving voluntarily was retained under the Jobseeker's Act of 1995 but the eligibility period for 'Employment on Trial' was reduced to 13 weeks.
14 In July 1988 Mrs Thatcher separated DHSS into the Department of Health and the Department of Social Security.
15 ES file 9/UB 209/89. 'Bull points for 9 October', Briefing.
16 Ibid, Circular 161/1 (Revised), paras 223–4.
17 Alex Bryson and John Jacobs, *Policing the Workshy*, Avebury, Aldershot, 1992, p229.
18 This was the interpretation given to researchers by advice agency staff. Ibid, pp230–1.
19 Secretary of State for Employment's White Paper, 'Employment in the 90s', December 1988.
20 ES file 8/UB 117/88. Letter of 3 Feb 1988 from Geoff Annison to R McClelland.
21 ES file 17/EM 173/88. Note of June 1988 by Julian Roberts.
22 ES file 2/UB 111/88. Integration Pilots Evaluation Report by Tony Hughes, 30 Sept 1988.
23 Based on the advice of Lloyd Northover design consultants.
24 ES file 2/UB 194/88. Nearly final draft of Integration business case dated 31 Jan 1989.
25 *Guardian*, 11 Jan 1989.
26 *Hansard*, 11 Jan 1989, Col 872.
27 Nigel Lawson, *The View from Number 11*, pp391–2.
28 Efficiency Unit, 'Improving Management in Government: The Next Steps', A Report to the Prime Minister by Kate Jenkins, Karen Caines and Andrew Jackson, London, HMSO, Feb 1988.
29 This draws on a letter to the writer from Kate Jenkins, one of the authors of the 'Next Steps' report.
30 House of Commons Treasury and Civil Service Committee. 5th Report. 1993/94. Para 154.
31 Lawson, op cit, p392.
32 *Guardian*, 2 December 1989.

Chapter 15: The Employment Service as an Agency, 1990–93

1   Employment Department Group, 'Employment Service: An evaluation of the effects of Agency status 1990–93, summary report', January 1995.

2. OECD, *Facts, Analysis, Strategies – Unemployed in the OECD Area* (June 1994) recommended an approach to unemployment very similar to that adopted in Britain.
3. The new Agency arrangements are well described in Michael Hunt, 'The Employment Service as an Agency: the First Three Years', in *Next Steps: Improving Management in Government*, by Barry O'Toole and Grant Jordan, Dartmouth, Aldershot, 1995.
4. John Clarke, Secretary of NUCPS.
5. See for instance Adjournment Debate of Henry McLeish MP, 21 May 1990. Hansard, Vol 173, Col 144–151, Also Gerald Kaufman, *How to be a Minister*, Faber and Faber, London, 1997, ppxiv-xv.
6. DE file 17/EPM 212/89. Note of a meeting on 6 October 1989 chaired by Miss Blunt of DSS with M Fahey of DE and R Foster of ES.
7. ES Annual Report and Accounts, 1990/91.
8. Strictly, the target was 'Whichever is the greater of 1,650,000 placings of unemployed people into jobs or 80% of unemployed people among total number of placings into jobs'.
9. ES Annual Report and Accounts, 1990/91.
10. 'The Civil Service: Vol 1. Report of the Committee'. Cmnd 3638. Recommendation 102, p202.
11. Efficiency Unit. 'Improving Government: The Next Steps. Report to the Prime Minister', 1987, pp5 and 27.
12. D Bartram et al, Newland Park Associates, 'Evaluating the new Employment Service Recruitment and Retention System', November 1993.
13. Charles Jackson et al, Institute of Employment Studies, 'Employment Service; Vacancy Filling Evaluation', April 1995.
14. See for instance TJ Peters and RH Waterman, *In Search of Excellence*, Harper and Row, New York, p103.
15. The most influential were probably Sherrill Kennedy on organisational issues, Margaret Exley of Kinsley Lord on Agency development, Willy Roe on strategy, and Jan Hennessy on the individual development of senior managers.
16. 'Integration – Guide for Managers.' ES File 17/EPM/ 154/89.
17. Ibid.
18. See *Signing Off* by Tony Higgs and Nick Best (a history of the public employment service at 281 Corporation Street, Birmingham), HMSO, 1992.
19. The 1990 Customers' Satisfaction Survey showed levels of satisfaction in integrated offices of 85–87 per cent compared with 78–81 per cent in old-style offices. 61 per cent were satisfied with the level of privacy in integrated offices compared with 46 per cent in old-style offices. ES File 1/INT 103/90. Minute of 7 March 1981 from Mel Groves to Mike Fogden.
20. In the Ballot, in October 1991, 5000 votes were cast for industrial action and 4300 against.
21. Toxteth in Liverpool and Borough in South London.
22. ES File 1/INT 103/90. Minute of 7 March 1981 from Mel Groves to Mike Fogden.
23. NUBS 2 was 'National Unemployment Benefit System 2'. The existing system introduced in the 1960s and 1970s was now called NUBS 1.
24. From early in 1990 onwards, they tended to be called 'Advisers' rather than 'Counsellors', as the former term was preferred by Michael Howard.
25. Second Labour Market Briefing, 11 July 1990.
26. Quoted by Keith Harper in the *Guardian*, 8 June 1990.

27 D Fenwick's minute of 11 July 1990 to Private Secretary, Secretary of State. DE file 16/EPM 143/90.
28 JM Durning et al, 'Take up of ED Programmes. Report to the Secretary of State for Employment', March 1990.
29 The Task Group which carried out this review consisted of Peter Ward, Katrina Murray and Ken Whetter.
30 ES File 17/EPM 151/96. ES Executive Board minutes for 11 Jan 1991.
31 £38 million for 'customer services' was included in the measures announced on 20 March 1991.
32 It was 3,062,065 (not seasonally adjusted) in January 1993.
33 Julian Morgan, National Institute of Economic and Social Research, 'Labour market recoveries in the UK and other OECD countries', *Labour Market Trends*, Dec 1996, p529.
34 Employment Department Group, 'Employment Service: An evaluation of the effects of Agency status 1990–93, summary report', January 1995.

Chapter 16: The Jobseekers' Allowance, 1993–97

1 House of Commons, Employment Committee: Second Report, 'The Right to Work/Workfare', 13 February 1996.
2 Ibid, pxxxiii.
3 Business Consultancy Services Scoping Study on 'Attendance at Restart Courses/Availability Procedures in LOs'.
4 *Benefit of the Doubt': CAB Evidence on Disqualification from Unemployment Benefit*, NACAB, Oct 1994.
5 Unemployment Unit, 'Stricter Benefit Regime Stepped Up', Dec 1994.
6 Churches Together in Britain and Ireland, *Unemployment and the Future of Work*, 1997, p137.
7 House of Commons Education and Employment Select Committee, 21 Jan 1997, Supplementary memo by DfEE.
8 Conservative Manifesto, 1997, 'You can only be sure with the Conservatives', p11.
9 The proportion receiving a means-tested benefit instead of, or as well as, unemployment benefit had risen from 22 per cent in 1951 to 64 per cent in 1991.
10 On 10 August 1992, Peter Lilley held a press conference to promote a Benefits Agency consultation document on one-stop shopping.
11 *Mail on Sunday*, 5 July 1992.
12 Written Parliamentary Answer by Roger Evans, Parliamentary Under-Secretary of State, DSS, *Hansard*, 12 Dec 1994, Col 536. All the various changes in the Jobseeker's Bill were estimated to bring net savings of £270 million in a full year (1997–98) on an assumption of 2.4 million unemployed.
13 Written Parliamentary Answer by Roger Evans, *Hansard*, 12 Dec 1994, Col. 537.
14 *Hansard*, 21 June 1994, Col. 87.
15 *Hansard*, 10 Jan 1995, Col. 47 et seq.
16 John Sykes MP, ibid.
17 JSA Project Director's Report presented to ES Executive Board in April 1996 (ESEB 96/32).
18 CPSA *Red Tape*, February 1995.
19 ESEB Minutes, 15 March 1996.

20. Mark Lee of ES IT Services, quoted in Marcus Pollett's article, 'Times have changed in the Jobcentres', *Government Computing*, July/August 1998, p17.
21. House of Commons Treasury and Civil Service Committee, 5th Report, 1993/94, 'The Role of the Civil Service', para 250.
22. Employment Department Group, 'Employment Service: Prior Options Review – Summary Report', April 1995, p3.
23. Marcus Pollett, *Government Computing*, 1998.
24. House of Commons Select Committee on Employment, Minutes of Evidence, 9 Jan 1996 (Q. 148, 1282–3) and 5 June 1996 (Q. 121).
25. Employment Service. *Annual Report and Accounts*, 1996–97, p3.
26. Ibid, p5.

Chapter 17: Reflections

1. Survey of Employers' Recruitment Practices, carried out in 1992 by Social and Community Planning Research.
2. *Labour Market Trends*, Jan 1999, p18. Previous research suggests that people tend to underestimate the role of Jobcentres in finding them work. LFS also omits many temporary and short-term engagements.
3. DSS, S McKay, R Walker and R Youngs, *Unemployment and jobseeking before JSA*, HMSO, 1997, p81.
4. B Showler, *The Public Employment Service*, Longman, London 1976.
5. In Unemployment Recommendation (No 1) 1919.
6. ILO 85th Session, 1997, Report IV (1). Revision of the Fee Charging Employment Agencies Convention (Revised) 1949 (No 96), Geneva, 1996, p2.
7. Customer satisfaction surveys suggest that many seek more privacy.
8. 1997 National Customer Satisfaction Survey. Qualitative Report by Mori for the Employment Service, Feb 1998, p19.
9. This refers to the suicide of Rachel Cain, which was to some extent linked with her benefit position.
10. *ES Notes* Special, July 1995
11. Ibid, pp10–12.
12. Craggs, Ross and Dawson, 'JSA Evaluation, ES Clients and the Benefit System', Report on Stage II Qualitative Research, June 1998.
13. ES National Customer Satisfaction Survey, 1994, Report, No 103.
14. J Vincent and B Dobson, 'Jobseeker's Allowance evaluation: qualitative research on disallowed and disqualified claimants', *Labour Market Trends*, Oct 1997, p379.
15. 'Job-Broking – Our Clients' Views.' Booklet based on 9 studies, ES 1992.
16. Valerie Bayliss, *Redefining Work*, Royal Society of Arts, London, 1998.
17. Ibid, pp42–3.
18. Treasury and Civil Service Committee, 5th Report, 1993–94, para 154.
19. Prime Minister's announcement reported in DSS Press Notice of 16 March 2000.
20. Education and Employment Committee 7th Report, 'The Performance and Future Role of the Employment Service', Vol 1, Report and proceedings of the Committee, July 1999, pxxix.
21. This section draws on an international study of the public employment service in a changing labour market, recently carried out by the ILO, in which the author participated. During 2000, the ILO hopes to publish a new book based on this study.

22 OECD, 'Labour Market Policies: New Challenges: Enhancing the Effectiveness of Active Labour Market Policies: A Streamlined Public Employment Service', 1997, p7.
23 From a confidential study carried out by Bernard Bruhes for the French Ministry of Labour, quoted in *Le Monde*, 31 October 1998. The number of long-term unemployed per staff member were: France 141, Germany 87, Britain 55, Sweden 27.
24 Department for Education and Employment, White Paper, 'Learning to Succeed: A New Framework for Post–16 Learning', Cm 4392, June 1999.
25 Education and Employment Committee, op cit (see note 20), argues that ES should provide, and coordinate, a gateway to a wider range of services, and target not only the unemployed but also those who are in employment, but still dependent on in-work benefits, and the unregistered unemployed (pxxix).

Chronology of Main Events

1885	Nathaniel Cohen establishes the first British labour exchange at Egham.
1886	Unemployment among trade unionists reaches 9 per cent. Joseph Chamberlain, President of the Local Government Board, urges local authorities to organise public works to provide work for the unemployed.
1905	In response to industrial depression, the Unemployed Workmen Act encourages the setting up of Distress Committees and authorises contributions from the rates to measures to assist unemployed people, including labour exchanges. In London, the Central (Unemployed) Body is set up and includes William Beveridge in its members.
1905	Conservative government sets up Royal Commission on the Poor Laws, just before handing over to Liberal government under Campbell Bannerman.
1907	Beveridge persuades Sidney and Beatrice Webb of the case for labour exchanges. He studies labour exchanges in Germany and then gives evidence to the Royal Commission.
1908	Asquith becomes Prime Minister. Winston Churchill is appointed President of the Board of Trade, a department with an innovative Permanent Secretary, Sir Hubert Llewellyn Smith. Churchill takes up the cause of social reform, including labour exchanges. He is persuaded by the Webbs to recruit Beveridge to his Department. Lloyd George visits Germany. He and Churchill persuade Cabinet to introduce a new social programme, which includes labour exchanges and unemployment insurance.
1909	The Poor Law Royal Commission's majority and minority reports strongly support labour exchanges. The Labour Exchanges Act passes through Parliament with little dissent.
1910	Churchill opens a new national network of labour exchanges, with Beveridge as Director.
1911	National Insurance Act passes into law. Part II of the Act introduces unemployment insurance.
1912–13	Unemployment insurance is introduced for 17 per cent of the workforce.
1914	First World War begins. Labour exchanges begin to play an increasing role in the mobilisation of labour.
1915	New ministry of Munitions under Lloyd George includes Llewellyn Smith and Beveridge, who retains responsibility for the exchanges. Beveridge clashes with TUC over industrial relations in munitions industry.
1916	Lloyd George becomes Prime Minister and sets up Ministry of Labour, under John Hodge. The exchanges report to the new ministry and are renamed 'Employment Exchanges'. Hodge dispenses with Beveridge's services and places Charles Rey in charge of exchanges.

1917	Conscription is introduced. Efforts by new Department of National Service under Neville Chamberlain to coordinate labour policy fail, partly due to Rey's opposition. Much greater success is achieved by the ministry of National Service under Sir Auckland Geddes, who reports to a Cabinet Committee under Milner. Geddes recruits Rey to work in his ministry while retaining control of the exchanges. Local Advisory Committees are introduced (later Local Employment Committees – LECs).
1918	In October, the war suddenly comes to an end. Having failed to extend unemployment insurance substantially during the war, Ministers, with little notice, ask the exchanges to administer an 'Out of Work Donation'.
1919	The exchanges play a major role in demobilisation. The King's National Roll is set up for disabled ex-servicemen.
1920	Widespread criticism of the exchanges leads Macnamara, the Minister of Labour, to set up a Committee of Enquiry under George Barnes MP. The Barnes Committee supports the retention of the exchanges. Their work is greatly increased by the Unemployment Insurance Act 1920, which extends unemployment insurance to the great majority of the workforce.
1921	Unemployment suddenly increases to around 17 per cent of the insured population and remains relatively high until 1940. Ministers decide to continue to pay unemployment benefit to unemployed people who fail to meet the contribution conditions, but introduce other conditions, such as the 'genuinely seeking work' rule, to control expenditure. The Geddes Committee seeks the abolition of the exchanges, but this is successfully resisted by the Ministry of Labour.
1921–29	A period of considerable political, legislative and financial confusion with constant changes in the provisions for unemployment benefit. A major review by the Blanesburgh Committee, set up in 1925, fails to resolve the problems. There is mounting criticism of the 'genuinely seeking work' rule. The employment work of the exchanges takes second place to insurance work.
1929	Margaret Bondfield becomes Minister of Labour in the second Labour government. She mounts a substantial rehousing programme for the exchanges. She abolishes the 'genuinely seeking work' rule. A reorganisation of the Ministry has the effect of integrating the employment service more closely into the Ministry.
1930	In world slump, unemployment rises rapidly, making cost of unemployment relief a critical problem. Royal Commission on Unemployment Insurance appointed.
1931	Unemployment rises to 21 per cent. Crisis over government finances causes replacement of Labour government by National Government. Action is taken to contain unemployment relief.
1934	Unemployment Act creates (1) Unemployment Insurance Statutory Commission, chaired by Beveridge and (2) Unemployment Assistance Board to administer new system of assistance through separate chain of offices from the exchanges, though exchanges still involved.
1935	New system of unemployment assistance is suspended because of controversy over levels of payment and is then gradually phased in. Ernest Brown becomes Minister and remains till 1940.
1936	Sir Thomas Phillips becomes Permanent Secretary.

Chronology of Main Events

1939	In August, it is agreed that the Ministry of Labour should administer National Service and the words 'and National Service' are added to its title. In September war is declared and National Service is immediately introduced. But a survey shows the inadequacy of labour mobilisation for the war effort.
1940	Ernest Bevin is appointed Minister. He sets about the mobilisation programme with great vigour and strong support from the Ministry and the exchanges. He is armed with unprecedented powers, but is cautious about their use. Bevin recognises the importance of the exchanges not only in wartime but also after the war and resolves to 'humanise' them.
1941	Bevin appoints Godfrey Ince Director General of Manpower. Compulsory powers are now used more extensively. Beveridge is asked to carry out a review of social insurance and allied services.
1942	Beveridge's Report receives popular acclaim as heralding a post-war welfare state. Sir Thomas Philips, Permanent Secretary, leads initial follow-up.
1943	Mobilisation reaches its peak. Bevin warns colleagues that there are no further reserves on which to draw.
1944	D-day. Bevin acknowledges the contribution of the exchanges in mobilising labour. The Ministry of National Insurance is established with Sir Thomas Phillips as Permanent Secretary. Sir Godfrey Ince becomes Permanent Secretary of the Ministry of Labour. White Paper on Employment Policy announces post-war full employment policy. Disabled Persons (Employment) Act is passed.
1945	War ends. Labour government is elected. George Isaacs becomes Minister of Labour until 1951. Ministry loses policy responsibility for unemployment insurance to new Ministry of National Insurance, but retains delivery role through exchanges. Ministry embarks on massive and successful demobilisation process. Full employment is achieved and persists.
1945–47	War-time labour controls are gradually relaxed, though exchanges remain heavily involved in trying to steer labour to work of national priority.
1947	Controls reintroduced in economic crisis. Nearly all engagements have to be made through exchanges.
1948	Employment and Training Act updates legislative basis of exchanges and introduces new arrangements for youth employment service. Arrival of SS *Windrush* marks beginning of large-scale Commonwealth immigration.
1949–50	Controls lifted. First relaunch of exchange service by HMD Parker, emphasising full employment and need to satisfy customers, canvass employers and attract still-employed jobseekers.
1951	New Conservative government takes office, with Sir Walter Monckton as Minister of Labour.
1952	Notification of Vacancies Order requires employers to use exchanges. Economy drive undermines Parker's relaunch.
1954	Second relaunch of exchanges by JG Stewart, with concept of 'New Look'.
1955	Ian Macleod becomes Minister.
1956	Further economy drive and staff cuts undermine New Look. End of Notification of Vacancies Order. Remaining Appointments Offices abolished and Professional and Executive Register established.
1958–59	Unemployment exceeds half a million. Concern about immigrant unemployment.
1962	Sir James Dunnett becomes Permanent Secretary.

1963	Dunnett chairs Working Party on exchange service.
1964	Dunnett recommends experimental approach to reform, including experiments in separating employment and benefit work, which proceed despite unease of social security officials. New Labour government under Harold Wilson takes power. Ray Gunter becomes Minister.
1966	Occupational guidance service introduced. Sir Denis Barnes becomes Permanent Secretary.
1968.	Self service experiments begin. OECD reviews UK manpower institutions. Barbara Castle becomes Secretary of State for Employment and Productivity and sets up Research and Planning review on 'The future of employment services'.
1969	Planning Unit recommends major overhaul of employment services, including separation from benefit. Difficult talks between employment and social security officials eventually produce plan for separation.
1970	Ken Cooper begins working on employment service plans. Barbara Castle and Richard Crossman (the Social Security Minister) fall out over separation plans but in May 1970 Consultative Document is published based on Planning Unit report. In June 1970, Conservative government under Heath comes to power. Robert Carr becomes Secretary of State. Uncertainty about policy on employment service. Idea of hiving off manpower services to the social partners blocked by Treasury.
1971	Department takes advantage of new Programme Analysis Review mechanism to secure Ministerial agreement to radical plans for 'modernising' the employment service as a Departmental Agency. Ken Cooper is appointed Chief Executive of the embryonic Agency.
1972	Maurice Macmillan becomes Secretary of State. Ken Cooper produces Action Plan including separation, new organisational structure, new job structure and plan to rehouse service in attractive 'Jobcentres', with self service. Cooper introduces new system of performance targets. TUC and CBI (employers) suggest a hived off manpower services body to Ministers. Ministers accept this and agree that the Employment Service Agency should report to the new Commission.
1973	First Jobcentres open. Employment and Training Act passed, setting up new Commission. Professional and Executive Recruitment (PER), a fee-charging subsidiary of the new Agency, begins trading.
1974	New Manpower Services Commission (MSC) begins to meet. Labour government takes power, with Michael Foot as Secretary of State. Separation takes place and two networks are formed, one for the Employment Service Agency (ESA) and the other for the Unemployment Benefit Service (UBS). ESA reports to MSC, which publishes ESA's 'Plans and Programmes'. Concept of Department of Employment Group (of organisations) is introduced. CPSA union takes industrial action over staffing.
1975	Rising unemployment leads ESA to give priority to finding and filling vacancies. John Cassels becomes Director of MSC. Alan Brown becomes Chief Executive of ESA.
1976	Richard O'Brien becomes Chairman of MSC. New complementing (staffing) and operational planning systems introduced in ESA. Management review concludes that ESA should become Division of MSC rather than Agency. New Jobcentre programme is widely questioned, particularly in climate of retrenchment.

Chronology of Main Events

1977	Favourable evaluation persuades MSC to continue Jobcentre programme. CAPITAL computer project goes live in North East London.
1978	ES Executive resists suggestions that high unemployment should change its strategy. MSC sets up review of employment service strategy under John Cassels. Impasse with unions over CAPITAL.
1979	Over 550 Jobcentres are now open. CAPITAL still held up but plan for nationwide vacancy system adopted. Conservative government under Mrs Thatcher takes power. Jim Prior becomes Secretary of State. Jean Collingridge becomes Chief Executive of employment service. Cuts in staffing and expenditure begin. MSC accept Cassels' report which defends modernised service. Layard suggests that separation may have increased unemployment.
1980	Conflict between MSC and government over Rayner Report, which recommends voluntary registration and big cuts in employment service. MSC abandons CAPITAL project. Unemployment rises rapidly.
1981	Unemployment averages 2.7 million. Peter Morrison (a keen Thatcherite) becomes Parliamentary Secretary with mission to control MSC and ES and improve efficiency. Private employment agencies urge cuts of public employment service. Geoffrey Holland becomes Director of MSC.
1982	Unemployment reaches three million and sticks at that level. Norman Tebbit becomes Secretary of State and appoints David Young Chairman of MSC. Community Programme set up to provide work experience for unemployed. Rayner Report recommends further cuts in employment service. Bryan Emmett becomes Chief Executive.
1983	Conservatives win Election. Tom King becomes Secretary of State.
1984	Young becomes Minister without Portfolio. Bryan Nicholson becomes Chairman of MSC. Bryan Emmett produces controversial Development Plan, which is watered down by Commission following consultation.
1985	Number unemployed over one year is 1.3 million. Steve Loveman replaces Bryan Emmett as Chief Executive. Tom King proposes closer collaboration between benefit offices and Jobcentres. Morrison departs. King is replaced as Secretary of State by Lord Young, whose mission is to bring down unemployment.
1986	Following pilots, Young introduces Restart interviews nationwide with substantial menu of opportunities, including Job Clubs and Restart Courses. Former Unemployment Review Officer posts brought over to DE from DHSS and renamed Claimant Advisers. New Job Training Scheme introduced on benefit plus basis.
1987	Both unemployment and long-term unemployment fall. Third successive Conservative Election victory. Norman Fowler appointed Secretary of State. Jobcentres are switched from MSC to Department where they operate alongside benefit offices in a new Agency – the 'Employment Service' (ES) – with Mike Fogden as Chief Executive. ES's priority is to get long-term unemployed back to work.
1988	Geoffrey Holland becomes Permanent Secretary. Pilots held in integrating Jobcentres with local benefit offices. Tightening of benefit regime. New Claims Advisers introduced. PER is privatised. Employment Training (ET) launched. Training Commission (which replaced MSC) abolished. Fowler announces setting up of Training and Enterprise Councils (TECs).

1989	Social Security Act requires unemployed to 'actively seek work'. Fowler announces that Employment Service is to become an Agency under Next Steps programme and that integration of benefit and employment work will proceed to be completed by 1994.
1990	Fowler resigns, to be replaced by Michael Howard. ES becomes Next Steps Agency, with new framework, performance targets, finance rules and radical personnel policies. Integration proceeds rapidly despite tensions with staff unions over open plan offices. Howard approves New Framework for advisory work with unemployed. Unemployment starts to move upwards. Mrs Thatcher is replaced by John Major.
1991	As unemployment continues to rise, Howard secures expansion of ES staffing and programmes. New unemployment benefit computer project (NUBS2) goes live to complete coverage by 1993. Computerised vacancy system (Supervacs) is now nationwide. John Major announces Citizen's Charter.
1992	Unemployment continues to rise. Further employment measures introduced. Conservatives win fourth successive Election victory. Gillian Shephard becomes Secretary of State. Big drive to market test support service functions begins.
1993	Unemployment begins to fall. John Major urges that the unemployed should be required to be active, heralding increasing interest in compulsory programmes. ES Agency Framework renewed on interim basis. David Hunt becomes Secretary of State. Ministers decide to introduce new unified Jobseeker's Allowance (JSA) to replace existing unemployment benefit system.
1994	John Major decides that ES should administer employment side of JSA and Benefits Agency should administer benefit side. Michael Portillo becomes Secretary of State.
1995	Review confirms ES's continuance as Agency. Department of Employment abolished. ES reports to new Department for Education and Employment, with Gillian Shephard as Secretary of State and Michael Bichard as Permanent Secretary. Jobseeker's Act passed. ES resists reintroduction of screens in Jobcentres.
1996	JSA successfully introduced with two new computer systems – Labour Market System and payments system. Mike Fogden retires.
1997	Leigh Lewis becomes Chief Executive. Labour Party under Tony Blair wins Election. David Blunkett becomes Secretary of State.

Further Reading

Ainley, Patrick and Corney, Mark, *Training for the Future: The Rise and Fall of the Manpower Services Commission*, Oxford: Cassell, 1990

Bakke, EW, *The Unemployed Man*, London: Nisbet, 1933

Bayliss, Valerie, *Redefining Work*, London: Royal Society of Arts, 1998

Beales, HE and Lambert RS, *Memoirs of the Unemployed*, London: Gollancz, 1934

Beveridge, William, *Unemployment, A Problem of Industry*, London: Longmans Green, 1909 and 1930

Beveridge, William, *Social Insurance and Allied Services*, Cmnd 6404, London: HMSO, 1942

Beveridge, William, *Full Employment in a Free Society*, London: George Allen and Unwin, 1944

Beveridge, William, *Power and Influence*, London: Hodder and Stoughton, 1953

Bondfield, *A Life's Work*, National Book Associates, 1948

Bryson, Alex and Jacobs, John, *Policing the Workshy*, Aldershot: Avebury, 1992

Bullock, Alan, *The Life and Times of Ernest Bevin Vol II*, London: Heinemann, 1967

Burnett, John, *Idle Hands, The Experience of Unemployment 1790–1929*, London: Routledge, 1994

Butler, RA, *The Art of the Possible, The Memoirs of Lord Butler*, London: Hamish Hamilton, 1971; Penguin, 1973

Campbell, John, *Edward Heath – A Biography*, London: Pimlico, 1994

Castle, Barbara, *The Castle Diaries 1964–76*, London: Papermac, 1990

Chegwidden, TS and Myrddin-Evans G, *The Employment Exchange System in Great Britain*, New York: Industrial Relations Counsellors Inc, 1934

Churchill, Randolph S, *Young Statesman: Winston Churchill 1901–14*, London: Heinemann, 1967 and Minerva, 1991

Cd 4499, *Royal Commission on the Poor Laws and the Relief of Distress*, London: HMSO, 1909

Cmd 1054, *Report of Enquiry on the Work of Employment Exchanges*, London: HMSO, 1920

Cmnd 4185, *Royal Commission on Unemployment Insurance: Final Report*, London: HMSO, 1932

Cmd 6404, *Report by Sir William Beveridge on Social Insurance and Allied Services*, London: HMSO, 1942

Cmd 6527, *White Paper on Employment Policy*, London: HMSO, 1944

Cmd 3638, *The Civil Service: Report of the Committee 1966–6*, Chairman Lord Fulton, London: HMSO, 1968

Cmd 316, *White Paper: Training for Employment*, London: HMSO, 1988

Cmd 7797, *Report on Non-Departmental Public Bodies*, London: HMSO, 1980

Crossman, Richard, *The Diaries of a Cabinet Minister*, Vol III, London: Hamilton/Cape, 1977

Croucher, Richard, *We Refuse to Starve in Silence. A History of the National Unemployed Workers' Movement*, London: Lawrence and Wishart, 1987

Daniel, W, *The Unemployed Flow*, London: Policy Studies Institute, 1990

Davidson, Roger, *Whitehall and the Labour Problem in late-Victorian and Edwardian Britain*, London: Croom Helm, 1985

Deacon, Alan, *In Search of the Scrounger*, London: Geo Bell and Son, 1976

Department of Employment and Productivity, *Future of the Employment Service: Consultative Document*, London: DEP, 1970

Department of Employment, *People and Jobs*, London: DE, 1971

Department of Employment, *Action Plan for a Modern Employment Service*, London: DE, 1972

Department of Employment and Department of Health and Social Security, *Payment of Benefits to Unemployed People*, London: DE & DHSS, 1981

Department of Employment and Department of Social Security, *Jobseeker's Allowance*, London: HMSO, 1994

Dilnot, Andrew and Walker, Ian (Eds) *The Economics of Social Security*, Oxford: OUP, 1989

Efficiency Unit, *Improving Management in Government: The Next Steps: A Report to the Prime Minister*, London: HMSO, 1988

Employment Department Group, *Employment Service, An Evaluation of the Effects of Agency Status 1990–93*, London: EDG, 1995

Garside, WR, *British Unemployment 1919–39: A Study in Public Policy*, Cambridge: CUP, 1990

Gilbert, Bentley, *The Evolution of National Insurance in Great Britain: The Origins of the Welfare State*, London: Michael Joseph, 1966

Gilbert, Bentley, *British Social Policy 1914–39*, London: Batsford, 1970

Grieves, Keith, *The Politics of Manpower 1914–18*, Manchester University Press, 1988

Hannington, Wal, *The Problem of the Distressed Areas*, London: Gollancz, 1937

Harris, Jose, *Unemployment and Politics 1886–1914*, Oxford: OUP, 1972

Harris, Jose, *William Beveridge: A Biography*, Oxford: OUP, 1997

Hodge, John, *Workman's Cottage to Windsor Castle*, London: Sampson Low Marston, 1931

House of Commons, Employment Committee, Second Report, *The Right to Work/Workfare*, 1996

House of Comons, Education and Emplyment Committee, 7th Report, *The Performance and Future Role of the Employment Service*, Vol 1, Report and Proceedings of the Committee, 1999

Hunt, M J, 'The Employment Service as an Agency: the first three years' in O'Toole, Barry and Jordan, Grant, *Next Steps, Improving Management in Government*, Aldershot: Dartmouth, 1995

Ince, Sir Godfrey, *The Ministry of Labour and National Service*, London: Allen and Unwin, 1960

Ince, Sir Godfrey, The Mobilisation of Manpower, *Public Administration*, XXIV, London, 1946

International Labour Office, *National Employment Services, Great Britain*, Geneva: ILO, 1952

King, Desmond, *Actively Seeking Work: The Politics of Unemployment and Welfare Policy in the United States and Great Britain*, University of Chicago Press, 1995

Lawson, Nigel, *The View from No 11*, London: Bantam, 1992; Corgi, 1993

Layard, Richard, *Have Jobcentres Increased Unemployent?*, London School of Economics and Political Science: Centre for Labour Economics, Discussion Paper No 62, 1979

Layard, Richard, Nickell, Stephen and Jackman, Richard, *The Unemployment Crisis*, Oxford: OUP, 1994

Lowe, Rodney, *Adjusting to Democracy: The Role of the Ministry of Labour in British Politics 1916–39*, Oxford: OUP, 1986

Lowe, Rodney, *The Welfare State in Great Britain since 1945*, London: Macmillan, 1993

Lowe, Rodney, The Core Executive, Modernisation and the Creation of PESC 1960–64, *Public Administration*, Vol 75, No 4, London, 1997

Manpower Services Commission, *The Employment Service, Plans and Programmes*, London: HMSO, 1974

Manpower Services Commission, *The Employment Service in the 1980s*, London: HMSO, 1979

Marwick, Arthur, *The Deluge: British Society and the First World War*, London: Macmillan, 1965

McKay, S, Walker, R and Youngs, R, *Unemployment and Jobseeking before JSA*, Department of Social Security, London: HMSO, 1997

McKibbin, Ross, *The Ideologies of Class: Social Relations in Britain 1880–1990*, Oxford: OUP, 1990

OECD, *Manpower Policy in the UK*, Paris, 1970

OECD, *Jobs Study, Facts, Analysis, Strategy*, Paris, 1994

Orwell, George, *The Road to Wigan Pier*, London: Penguin, 1962

Parker, HMD, *Manpower, A Study of War-time Policy and Administration*, London: HMSO and Longmans Green, 1957

Patterson, Sheila, *Dark Strangers, A Study of West Indians in London*, London: Penguin, 1965

Philpott, John, *A Solution to Long-Term Unemployment: The Job Guarantee*, Employment Institute, London 1990

Philpott, John, (Ed) *Working for Full Employment*, London: Routledge, 1997

Political and Economic Planning (PEP), *Report on the British Social Services*, London, 1937

Prior, James, *A Balance of Power*, London: Hamish Hamilton, 1986

Seymour, JB, *The British Employment Exchange*, London: PS King, 1928

Showler, Brian, *The Public Employment Service*, London: Longman, 1976

Skidelsky, Robert, *Politicians and the Slump: The Labour Government of 1929–31*, London: Macmillan, 1967

Tallents, Stephen, *Man and Boy*, London: Faber, 1943

Tebbit, Norman, *Upwardly Mobile*, London: Weidenfeld and Nicolson, 1988

Thatcher, Margaret, *The Downing Street Years*, London: HarperCollins, 1995

Webb, Sidney and Beatrice, *The Public Organisation of the Labour Market: being Part Two of the Minority Report of the Poor Law Commission*, London: Longmans Green, 1909

White, Michael and Jane Lakey, *The Restart Effect*, London: Policy Studies Institute, 1992

Wolfe, Humbert, *Labour Supply and Regulation*, Oxford: OUP, 1923

Wolfe, Humbert, *Portraits by Inference*, London: Methuen, 1934

Young, David, *The Enterprise Years*, London: Headline, 1990

Index

Aberconway, Lord 53
Action for Jobs 243
Action Plan for a Modern Employment Service 156–7, 164, 179, 190
Adams, JB 21, 53, 56, 70
Advisory Trade Committees 44
Agency status 273–5, 276–86; developing an Agency culture 283–6; financial management 279; Framework 277, 281, 293, 295; industrial relations 282; integration of Jobcentres and UBOs 286–7; managing the Agency 306; market testing programmes 304–5; pay 282–3; performance 280; personnel flexibilities 280–3; *Personnel Handbook* 282; promotion 281; recruitment 281
Air Raid Precautions (ARP) 74
Allen, Mike 302
Allison, Roderick 137, 173
Anderson, John 94
Appointments Services 110, 119
Armstrong, Sir William 150, 153
Ashby, Peter 295
Askwith, George 20, 54–5
Asquith, Herbert 38, 39, 50
assisted emigration 9
Attlee, Clement 106, 107
Azrin, N 248

Bacon, Jenny 173
Bakke, E Wight 84
Baldwin, Stanley 72

Barber, Tony 146, 148, 154, 155
Barlow, Sir Montague 47
Barnes Enquiry into the employment exchanges 53–8, 69, 70, 79
Barnes, George 54
Barnes, Ken 133, 141, 143, 147, 148, 149, 150, 159, 170, 173, 175, 198, 200, 203, 209, 212–13, 219
Barnes, Sir Denis 126, 130, 144, 147, 150, 153, 158, 167, 170
Barnett, Canon Samuel 11
Beard, AG 160
Beltram, Geoff 188–9
Benefit Agency 284
benefit control model 4, 127, 129–30, 240–1, 256, 310, 315–16, 321; Layard thesis 204–6; Restart 242, 243, 246–7, 256–7, 314, *see also* Stricter Benefit Regime
Besalel, V 248
Betterton, Henry 77–8
Betterton, Sir Henry 73
Bevan, Aneurin 106, 107, 123
Beveridge, William 2, 6, 7, 9, 11–14, 27, 29, 77, 111, 155, 161, 267, 269; Advisory Trade Committees 44; evidence to Barnes Enquiry 55; First World War 31, 33, 34, 35–6, 39, 40; labour exchanges 13–14, 17, 18, 19–21, 25, 55; post-war unemployment 46, 52; Report on Social Insurance and Allied Services 98–101; Second World War 91, 93, 98–101; trade unions and 36; types

of unemployment 12; UISC 78;
Unemployment: A Problem of Industry 3–4, 12, 80; unemployment insurance 13–14, 24, 39, 52
Bevin, Ernest 36, 40, 109, 113, 119, 313; labour exchanges and 95–7, 108; as Minister of Labour 86, 90–104, 111
Bichard, Michael 295, 298, 301, 302, 307
Birch, Robin 299
black economy 239, 246, 259
'blackleg' vacancies 18, 26
Blair, Tony 275
Blanesburgh Committee 62, 63
Blunkett, David 225, 305, 315
Bondfield, Margaret 62, 72, 73, 74, 76, 77, 80
Booth, Albert 170, 187
Booth, Charles 8
Booth, General William 9
Bowers, FG 49, 76, 78
Bowyer, Sir Eric 129
Boyd, Lennox 121
Branch Employment Offices 52
Brown, Alan 156, 171, 172, 188, 198, 214
Brown, Ernest 73, 87, 88, 123
Bryan, Paul 149, 151, 152, 153
Bullock, Alan 48, 90–1
Burnham, Peter 179
Burns, John 12, 14, 22, 27
Butler, RA 48, 72, 73, 106
Butler, Sir Robin 300
Buxton, Sydney 7, 24

Callaghan, Jim 187, 188
CAPITAL (Computer Assisted Placing in the Areas of London) 182–4, 186, 213–15, 228
Careers Service 5, 144, 155, 192
Carr, Robert 146, 147, 148, 149, 151, 154, 155, 156, 169, 205
Cassels, John 157, 173, 174, 175, 179, 192, 195, 198, 206, 210, 211, 212, 213, 219
Castle, Barbara 73, 124, 125, 126, 130, 134, 155; Planning Unit study 136–40, 143; proposed separation of employment and benefit function 134, 141–4
casual employment 8, 19; chronic underemployment in 12–13, 15, 27; decasualisation 12–13, 27, 28, 315
Caulcott, Tom 150
Central Claims and Records Office, Kew 33, 49
Central (Unemployed) Body (CUB) 9, 11
Chamberlain, Joseph 9
Chamberlain, Neville 42–3, 71, 72, 92
Chambers, JD 15
Charity Organisation Society (COS) 8
Churchill, Winston 1, 6–8, 11, 14, 15, 16, 17, 18–19, 21, 28, 29, 51, 107, 121, 123, 312; Second World War 89, 90, 103; unemployment insurance 22
Citizen's Charter 41, 297–8
Citrine, Walter 69, 97
Civil and Public Services Association (CPSA) 176, 178, 180, 181, 265, 274, 287
Claimant Advisers 250–1, 268, 289, 290
Clark, Alan 233, 237
Clarke, Kenneth 237, 238, 248
Clearing House Gazette 26
Client Advisers 290
Cohen, Nathaniel 9, 10
Collingridge, Jean 171, 198, 200, 202, 203, 205, 206, 211, 213, 220, 222, 223, 227, 234
COMIS exercise 228
commercial sections 116
Committee of Imperial Defence 87
Committee on Unemployment Insurance Administration 64
Commonwealth immigrants 120–3
Community Action 292
Community Enterprise Programme (CEP) 223–5
Community Programme (CP) 225–7, 230, 239, 240, 245, 260
competition 319
compulsory programmes 296–7
computerisation 131, 181–4, 213–15, 287–8; JSAPS 303–4; LMS 303–4; Remote Access Terminals (RATs) 298
Confederation of British Industry (CBI), National Training Agency and 157, 158

Index

Consultative Document on the Future of the Employment Service 143–5, 148
Contracts of Employment Act 126
contributory insurance 13
Control of Employment Bill 88
Control of Engagement Orders 114
Cooper, John 237, 262
Cooper, Ken 143, 147–8, 149, 150, 151, 152, 156–7, 160, 162, 163–4, 165, 167–8, 171, 172, 174, 176, 179, 180, 181, 187, 190
Cope, John 259
Cormack, Patrick 219
covenanted benefits 61, 63
Cripps, Sir Stafford 107, 110
Crossman, Richard 137, 141, 144, 145, 261
Cunningham, EC 59

Daniel, Bill 211, 215
Davidson, Bob 248
Dawe, Roger 237
Day of Action 1982 226
decasualisation 12–13, 27, 28, 315
Dechant, Tony 171
deferred registration *see* registration requirement
demobilisation: First World War 50–2, 71; out of work donation 52–3, 59; 'Pivotal' men 51; Second World War 103, 110–11; 'Slip' men 51; women workers and 51
Department for Education and Employment (DfEE) 307
Department of Employment: merger with Department of Education 306–7, *see also* Department of Employment and Productivity; Ministry of Labour
'Department of Employment Group' 159
Department of Employment and Productivity 134; OECD examination 136; Planning Unit study 136–40; separation of employment and benefit function 134, 140, 141–5, 148, 153, 159–61, *see also* Department of Employment; Ministry of Labour
Department of Health and Social Security (DHSS) 140; Rayner Scrutiny 207–13; transfer of benefit function to 134, 140, 141–3, 148, 153, 159–61, *see also* Ministry of Social Security
dependants' allowances 61
Derby, Lord 43
Derx, Donald 170, 209
'Development of the Employment Service' 229–33, 252
Disabled Persons (Employment) Act 1944 5, 102, 118
disabled workers: Disablement Advisory Committees (DACs) 118; employment of 1946–60 118; First World War and 37, 51; industrial rehabilitation facilities 118, 192; King's National Roll 51, 102; National Advisory Council 118; quotas 102, 118; registration of 118; Remploy Ltd 118; Review of Assistance to Disabled People 202, 223; Second World War and 102; services for 1974–79 191–2; Thatcher governments and 202, 223
Disablement Resettlement Officers (DRSs) 102, 118, 192
Disablement Resettlement Service 5, 140, 202
Distress Committees 9
District Manpower Boards 92
District Manpower Offices 92, 109
Divisional Controllers 92
Donovan, Professor JC 136
Du Cann, Edward 228
Dunnett, Sir James 124, 126–30
Dunnett Working Party and Report 126–30, 131, 134, 159, 181
Durham, Miss 43

Eady, Wilfred 49, 66, 74, 78, 80, 88
Education (Choice of Employment) Act 1910 15
Eggar, Tim 259, 274
Emergency Powers Bill 93
emigration, assisted 9
Emmerson, Sir Harold 101, 107
Emmett, Bryan 227–33, 234, 253
Emmott, Mike 262, 289
employment advisers 164–5
employment agencies *see* private employment agencies

Employment and Enterprise Group (EEG) 254
'Employment Exchange Service in a Free Labour Market' 115
employment exchanges *see* labour exchanges
'Employment Service' (ES): integration of Jobcentres and UBOs 258, 260–2, 272–3; Integration Pilots 272–3; performance indicators 264; redeployment of staff 265; setting up of 261–2; staff policies 265; strategy of 262–5; systems 265–6
Employment Service in the 1980s, The 195
Employment Service: Plans and Programmes 172, 174, 193
Employment Service Agency (ESA) 158, 161, 169, 171, 173; civil service status of staff 175–6; co-operation with UBS 188–90; Financial and Management Accounting System (FMAS) 180; 'find and fill' strategy 185–6, 194; Management by Objectives (MbO) 180–1; Operating Statistics Project 180; operational planning system 180, 189–90; planning and management systems 179–81; programmes and sub-programmes 180; senior management team 171; staffing and industrial relations 175–9; unemployment 1974–79 184–7
Employment Service Division (ESD) 192, 194, 201, 202, 206, 211, 218, 219–23, 226
Employment Service Management Team 162, 164
Employment and Training Act 1948 108, 119
Employment and Training Act 1973 158–9, 160, 173–4, 175
Employment Training (ET) 271, 289, 291
Employment Transfer Scheme 165, 201
Ennels, David 141
Enquiry into the Work of Employment Exchanges 1920 44, 45
Enterprise Allowance Scheme 227, 245, 271

European Voluntary Workers Scheme 120
Evans, Trevor 85, 95–6
Executive Post 191, 266

Factory Inspectorate 106, 108
farm colonies 9, 75
Federation of Personnel Services (FPS) 174–5, 219, 222
Field, Frank 270, 295
Financial Management Initiative 273
'find and fill' strategy 185–6, 194
First World War 30–45; aliens, recruitment of 37; 'badging' 34, 37–8; conscription 30, 38; 'debadging' 38; demobilisation *see* demobilisation; Derby Scheme 38; disabled workers 37; labour exchanges and 31, 32, 33–6, 45; labour policy 30–1; Liverpool Dock Labour Battalion 39; management of the employment service 31–3; Ministry of Labour, creation of 39–42; mobilisation of labour 30; National Service 39, 42–3; outbreak of 33–4; recruitment for munitions industries 34–6; reserved occupations 38; Trade Cards Agreement 38; unemployment and 34, 39; unemployment insurance, extension of 39; volunteer schemes 38; women workers 36–7
Fisher, Sir Henry 160, 161
flexible labour market 315–16
Floud, Sir Francis 73
Fogden, Mike 237, 258, 261–2, 265, 274, 277, 278, 280, 284, 286, 287, 295, 300, 302, 305, 306, 307
Foot, Michael 170, 171, 173, 175, 178
Foot, Sir Hugh 121
Forsyth, Michael 295
Foster, Richard 262
Fowler, Norman 251, 255, 258, 259–60, 263, 266, 267, 268, 271, 272, 274, 275
Fowler, RF 140
Fryer, John 211
full employment 111–13
Fulton Report on the Civil Service 136, 139, 146, 149, 150, 165, 179, 273, 280

Index

Gaitskell, Hugh 107
Galbraith, Jim 137, 139
Gardiner, W.H. 10
Geddes Committee on National Expenditure 48, 58–9, 70
Geddes, Sir Auckland 31, 43
Geddes, Sir Eric 58
'genuinely seeking work' 63–5, 76–7, 269–70
Ghent scheme 16
Gibbs, Philip 1–2
Gilbert, Bentley 16
Godber, Joseph 126
Gold Standard, return to 61
Golding, John 192
Government Training Centres 93, 145
Gowrie, Earl of 199
Graham, Bruce 181, 182
Graham, Ken 201, 246, 260
Green, Barbara 130
Green, Meg 187
Greene, Sir W Graham 87, 88
Greenwood, Arthur 98
Grover, Derek 295, 302
Gunter, Ray 126, 130

Halstead, Rod 299
Hankey, Lord 110
Hannington, Wal 60, 76
Hardman, WH 108
Hare, John 126, 128
Harman, Harriet 301
Harris, Jose 11, 36, 70
Harrison, Frank 185
Hattersley, Roy 141
Head Office Management Team 165–6
Heath, Edward 106, 107, 123, 155
Helsby, Sir Laurence 107
Helsby, Sir Lawrence 126
Herbison, Margaret 134
Heron, Sir Conrad 170
Heseltine, Michael 295
Hill, Ron 141
Hilton, John 49, 64–5, 84, 313
Hodge, John 31, 40, 41–2, 43, 44, 87, 313
Holland, Geoffrey 130, 184–5, 219, 224, 228, 237, 245, 246–7, 249, 253, 254, 259, 264, 265, 277, 306, 307
Horne, Sir Robert 47

Horsman, Mike 265, 272
Howard, Michael 276, 277, 278, 290, 291
Howarth, Alan 301
Howe, Sir Geoffrey 224
Howell, David 150
Howell, Sir Ralph 295, 301
Howells, Ralph 160
Hunger Marches 60–1
Hunt, David 295

Ibbs, Sir Robin 273
immigrants 119–23; colour prejudice 120, 121; Commonwealth immigrants 120–3; dispersal policy 120–1; refugees 120–1
Ince, Sir Godfrey 90, 91–2, 96, 101, 103, 104, 107, 109, 119
industrial rehabilitation facilities 118, 192
Industrial Training Act 126
Ingham, Bernard 143
Instructional Centres 75–6
international comparisons 320–1
Internet, the 316
Invalidity Benefit claimants 250–1
Investors in People 265
Isaacs, George 106–7, 113, 123

Jarrett, Sir Clifford 134, 144
Jarrow March 75
Jay, Peter 225
Jenkin, Patrick 207, 209
Jenkins, Roy 144–5
job advertisements 114
Job Bank 215, 228
Job Clubs 245, 248, 259, 267, 268, 291
Job Creation Programme 184, 185
Job Interview Guarantee 291
Job Plan Workshops 291, 296
Job Review Workshops 291
Job Search Seminars 291
Jobcentres 97, 146, 156, 157, 163–4, 168, 171, 172, 174–5, 185, 193, 199, 200; 'Development of the Employment Service' 229–33; 'find and fill' strategy 185–6, 194; integration with UBOs 253–5, 258, 260–2, 272–3, 286–7; Layard thesis 204–6; premises 163, 164, 262;

private employment agencies and 174–5, 199, 219, 221; proposed privatisation 274; Rayner Scrutiny 207–13; relationship with UBOs 207–8; Saturday opening 229; staffing 164–5; voluntary registration and 212
'jobseekers' 172
Jobseeker's Allowance (JSA) 101, 293, 296, 297–305; computerisation 303–4; decisions concerning 299–301; implementation 301–3; Jobseeker's Bill 301; Payments System (JSAPS) 302, 303; staff security issues 302–3; White Paper 301
Jobstart Allowance 243, 245, 247–8; 'one stop shop' 300
Johnson, Bert 279
Johnson, Gerald 207
Johnston, Ian 207, 254
Joint Industrial Councils 54
Joint Task Force 298
Joint Unemployment, Vacancy and Operating Statistics (JUVOS) 183
Jones, Tom 78
Joseph, Sir Keith 148, 154, 158, 160, 161
Joslin, WR 165
Jowitt, Sir William 98, 100, 103
Juvenile Advisory Committees 15

Keith, Robin 126, 127, 130, 132–3, 138, 139, 143, 145, 151
Kemp, Peter 273, 277, 278, 280
Kendall, Graham 253–4
Kent, Dorothy 130, 133, 188, 222
Kent, Sir Stephenson 50, 51
Keynes, John Maynard 238
King, Desmond 5, 29
King, Tom 226, 231, 236, 239–41, 248, 253
King's National Roll 51, 102

labour controls 114–15
labour exchanges 1–2, 9; area managers, introduction of 130; attitudes to the exchange service 83–4, 135; Barnes Enquiry into 53–8, 69, 70, 79; Beveridge and 13–14, 17, 18, 19–21, 25, 55; Bevin and 95–7, 108; 'blackleg' vacancies 18, 26; casual register 27; Clearing House 26; commercial sections 116; cut-price vacancies 18; decline of resources 108–10; definition 2; departmental responsibility 14–15; development of 9–10; employed workers and 116, 117, 118; employers and 17–18, 25; employment work 66–7, 79–82, 127; female staff 89; fiftieth anniversary celebration 123; First World War 31, 32, 33–6, 45; follow-up placing interviews 112, 116, 117; Geddes Committee and 58–9; in Germany 9; immigrants 119–23; labour controls 113–14; labour market operations 1910–14 25–7; management of 15, 107–8; mass unemployment, effect of 47, 62; Ministry of Labour and 47–50; New Look 1953–54 116–17, 127; night duty 89; 1918–29 46–71; 1945–60 107–8, 115–18; Notification of Vacancies Order 1952 114; out of work donation 52–3, 59; performance measurement 27; placing performance 1919–29 66–7; placing performance 1946–60 117–18; placing performance 1960–70 127; post-War 107–8, 115–18; premises 21–2, 70, 83, 97, 108–9, 128, 131; procedures 25–7; procedures for handling large redundancies 130; relaunching up to 1960 115–18; renaming of 40; review interviews 113, 117; in Second World War 34–6, 89, 93–5; self service 132–4, 140, 163; separation of employment and benefit function 134, 140, 141–3, 148, 153, 159–61; setting up 19–22; staff training 96–7, 130; staffing 21, 68–9, 82–3, 108, 127; Staffing Basis Scheme 80; submissions for vacancies 25; trade unions and 17–18, 26, 36, 41, 46; unemployment insurance and 13, 16, 19; voluntarism 17; women staff 89

Index

Labour Exchanges Act 1909 2, 3, 14–19
labour market 1960–70 125
labour market efficiency model 127
Labour Market System (LMS) 303–4
labour market transparency model 3–4, 169, 194, 204, 212, 228, 234, 256, 310
Labour Supply inspectors 93
Lane, Ken 150, 151–2, 166
Lansbury, George 9
Lasko, Roger 227
Law, Andrew Bonar 19
Lawson, Nigel 197, 238–9, 243, 245, 251, 274
Layard, Richard 203–6, 207, 220, 239, 248, 295
Layard thesis 204–6
Lee, Fred 106–7
Lee, John 259
Leggett, Sir Frederick 91
Lester, Jim 203
Lewis, Derek 278
Lewis, Leigh 207, 237
Lilley, Peter 299, 301
Liverpool Dock Labour Battalion 39
Lloyd George, David 7–8, 16, 17, 24, 35, 37, 39, 43, 54
Local Advisory Committees 44
Local Employment Committees 44, 51, 54, 63, 65
Locke, John 147, 155, 156, 157, 162, 174
Longden, Wilson 232, 241
Loveman, Steve 233, 237, 254, 262
Lowe, Rodney 40

Macdonald, Ramsay 72
McGlynn, Norman 156, 183, 215
Macgregor, Professor 54
McLeish, Henry 289
Macleod, Ian 106, 107, 114
Macmillan, Maurice 147, 155, 157
Macmullan, CWK 107
Macnamara, TJ 47, 54, 56
McNaughton, AAG 162
Main, David 225
Major, John 41, 276, 295, 297, 298
Management by Objectives (MbO) 180–1
Manpower Centres 145

Manpower Services Commission (MSC) 147, 150, 157–9, 160, 167, 169, 170, 195; civil service status of staff 175–6; COMIS exercise 228; ESA *see* Employment Service Agency; ESD *see* Employment Service Division; Labour government 1970–74 and 170–1; Layard thesis and 204–6; liaison with UBS 203; management review 1976–77 173–4; move to Sheffield 198; organisational issues 1985–87 253–5; Rayner Scrutiny 206–13, 219–23; staff cuts 202, 206, 211; Thatcher governments and 198, 199–200, 202, 218–19
Mansion House 9, 11
Markham, Violet 43, 78
Marshall, Ian 213
Marwick, Arthur 38, 51
Masterton-Smith, Sir James 48, 49, 57
Maston, CJ 108
Maston, Jim 127
Mathison, Peter 302
Maurice Macmillan 147
Maxwell, Kevin 267
Maxwell, Robert 267
Meacher, Michael 273
Message Switch 182, 215
Military Training Act 1939 88
Minford, Professor Patrick 224, 239
Ministry of Labour: Appointments Services 110, 119; Bevin as Minister 86, 90–104, 111; creation of 39–42; decline of resources 108–10; Employment Services Department 108; Employment and Training Department 74, 80; Instructional Centres 75; management of labour exchanges 47–50; mobilisation 93–5; 1929–39 73–4; 1945–60 106–7, 110; 1960–70 126; personnel and organisation 1945–60 110; Second World War 89, 90–7; Services and Establishments Department 74; Special Departmental Class 110; staffing 82; technical, scientific and managerial personnel 101–2; unemployment and 48; unemployment insurance

and 48; Unemployment Insurance Department 74; War Book 89, see also Department of Employment; Department of Employment and Productivity
Ministry of Labour and National Service 88
Ministry of National Insurance 100, 101, 110, 141
ministry of Pensions and National Insurance 120, 128, 129
Ministry of Social Security 99, 133, see also Department of Health and Social Security
mobilisation: First World War 30; Second World War 93–5
Monck, Nicholas 277, 295, 300
Monckton, Walter 106, 107, 114, 123
Moore, John 268–9
Morris Committee 76
Morrison, Peter 214, 217–18, 220, 222, 228, 229, 230, 231, 233, 234, 240, 253
Mufax 181
Mukherjee, Santosh 184
munitions industries, recruitment for 34–6
Munitions of War Bill 35, 38
Murphy, Terry 274
'mystery shopping' 41

National Association for the Care and Resettlement of Offenders (NACRO) 225–6
National Council of Voluntary Organisations (NCVO) 225
National Government 72–3, 77, 81
National Insurance Bill 7, 24
National Service: Committees 42, 44; deferments 92; First World War 39, 42–3; ministry of 43; Second World War 92
National Service Act 1939 88
National Service Committees 88
National Service Handbook 88
National Service Officers 92
National Training Agency 157
National Unemployed Workers' Movement (NUWM) 60, 64, 76, 84
National Unemployment Benefit System (NUBS) 181, 187

NATVACS 215
New Claims Advisers (NCAs) 268
New Client Advisors 289, 290
New Deal 227, 311, 314, 316, 317
New Job Training Scheme 251
New, Ken 265
New Workers Scheme 245
News of the Employment Service (NOTES) 262
Newton, Tony 290
NEXT 254, 299
Next Steps Report 1988 150, 166, 191, 273, 278, 279, 280
Nicholls, Patrick 259
Nicholson, Bryan 232, 237, 241, 246, 253, 254, 260, 261
Normington, David 226, 262
Normington Report 226
Notification of Vacancies Order 1952 114, 116, 117, 312
Notting Hill Riots 1958 122
NUBS 1 266
NUBS 2 266, 287–8, 304
Nursing Appointments Service 119

O'Brien, Richard 170, 175, 182, 190–1, 192, 194, 195, 198, 199, 203, 210, 211, 218
Occupational Guidance Service 131, 139; abolition of 202
Oglesby, Peter 209
1-2-1 296
Orwell, George 50
OSCAR 288
out of work donation 52–3, 59
outdoor labour test 8
Owen, OW 33–4

Parker, HMD 91–2, 107, 108, 109, 115, 116
Partridge, Sir Michael 300
Pascoe, Ken 249
Patterson, Arthur 100, 101
Patterson, Sheila 122–3
People and Jobs 156, 159, 167, 190
People's March for Jobs 201
performance management: dangers of 318–19, see also placing performance
Phillips, Ray 175, 284, 285, 303

Phillips, Tom (Sir Thomas) 20, 48–9, 50, 51, 52, 56, 62, 66, 73, 87, 90, 91, 99–100, 101, 123
Pickford, Frank 130
placing performance: 1919–29 66–7; 1929–38 81–2; 1946–60 117–18; 1960–70 127; 1974–79 193; 1981–87 235, 252; 1986–91 264; Restart and 244, 257–8
Planning Unit study 136–40, 155
Pliatzky, Sir Leo 149, 150, 199
Polish Resettlement Corps 120
Poor Law Amendment Act 1834 8
Poor Law Guardians 8, 77
Poor Law test 4
Portillo, Michael 295, 301
Postan, MM 104
Potter, Jim 171
Potter, Tony 225
premises: Jobcentres 163, 164, 262; labour exchanges 21–2, 70, 83, 97, 108–9, 128, 131
Prescott, John 249
Price, JFG 49, 50, 74
Priestly, Clive 173
Prior, James 175, 198, 199, 201, 202, 203, 207, 209, 211, 218, 226, 227
Prior Options Review 304–5
prisoners of war, employment of 120
private employment agencies 128, 174–5, 199, 219, 221
Production Council 93
Professional and Executive Recruitment (PER) 167, 190–1, 199–200; privatisation of 266–7
Professional and Executive Register 119, 166–7
Programme Analysis Review (PAR) 151–5, 164, 166
Project Work 296, 297
Property Services Agency 174
Public Assistance Committees (PACs) 77
public expenditure cuts 201–2
public works 9
Pyne, Frank 156

quangos, review of 199
Quinlan, Sir Michael 219, 237, 259

Raff, Martin 284, 306
Rawlinson, Sir Henry 33
Rayner Scrutiny 206–13, 219–23
Rayner, Sir Derek 206–13, 219, 220, 229
Read, Paul 220
rearmament programme 1930s 81
Reed, Alec 199
Rees, Dewi 167, 171
refugees 119–20, *see also* immigrants
Regional Commissioners 89
Regional Controllers 92, 96, 97, 111, 135, 162
Regional Manpower Services Directors (RMSDs) 174
Regional Preference Committees 113
registration requirement: deferred registration 206, 208, 209; Rayner Scrutiny 206–13; voluntary registration 206, 207–8, 209, 210, 211, 212
Reid, Graham 173, 232, 259, 277
Remote Access Terminals (RATs) 298
Remploy Ltd 118
Resettlement Advice Offices 108, 109
Resettlement Trials 186
Restart: benefit control function 242, 243, 246–7, 256–7, 314; concept of 241–3; Counsellors 289, 290; course 249–50; development of 243–7; impact on Employment Service 252, 253; interviews 267, 268, 271, 289; Mandatory Restart Course 290; Pilots 243–4, 246; 'rolling Restart' 246; TUC and 243, 246
Rey, Charles 20, 24, 31, 32, 35, 38, 41, 42, 43, 44, 123
Richardson, David 156
Richmond, AH 120
Riddelsdell, Mildred 141, 144, 153
Robens, Alfred 123
Robens, George 106
Roberts, George 52
Roberts, GH 42
Roberts, Julian 272
Robinson, Rhys 137, 171, 175
Rodger, Alec 131
Roth, Andrew 123
Royal Commission on Labour 10, 16
Royal Commission on the Poor Law 9

Royal Commission on Unemployment Insurance Report 1932 79–80
rural colonies 75–6

Saatchi and Saatchi 225
Schedule of Reserved Occupations 88
Scott, Nicholas 270
seasonal unemployment 12, 13, 19
Second World War 86–104; compulsory employment 88; demobilisation *see* demobilisation; labour exchanges 34–6, 89, 93–5; machine tool industry 89; manpower surveys 89, 93, 94; Ministry of Labour 89, 90–7; mobilisation 93–5; munitions industry 89, 94; phoney war 88–90; preparations for 87–8; prisoners of war, employment of 120; Resettlement Advice Officers 103, 110; Schedule of Reserved Occupations 88; technical, scientific and managerial personnel 101–2; women workers 94, 95
Seear, Baroness 205
self service 132–4, 140, 163, 204, 229, 312
Sex Discrimination Act 1975 172–3
Shackleton, David Sir 40, 48
Shaw, Tom 42, 47, 63
Sheepshanks, Thomas 100
Shephard, Gillian 276, 291–2, 295, 299
Short, Clare 269–70
Showler, Brian 161, 168, 312
sickness absence management 284
signing-on: active signing 290; daily 24, 62; fortnightly 241; twice weekly 127, 128; weekly 148, 154–5
Sinfield, Adrian 132
Skills Training Agency 233
Smieton, Mary 107–8, 120, 121
Smith, Hubert Llewellyn 8, 11, 15, 16, 20, 23, 31, 32, 33, 35, 44, 49, 55, 123
Smith, John 231
Smith, Tony 220
Soames, Lord 212
social contract 170
Social Security Act 1982 212
Social Security Act 1989 269–71; actively seeking for work 269–70; effects of 271; removal of right to refuse jobs 270
Social Survey Report on the Mobility of Labour 116
social welfare model 5, 127, 310, 321
Special Areas Bill 75
Special Employment Needs (SEN) 186, 244; abolition of 202
SS Empire Windrush 120
staff training 96–7, 130
staffing: cuts under Thatcher governments 201–2, 231–2, 234–5; 'Employment Service' (ES) 265; ESA 175–9; ESD/ED 234; Jobcentres 164–5; labour exchanges 21, 68–9, 82–3, 89, 108, 127; Ministry of Labour 82; MSC 202, 206, 211
Stanley, Oliver 73, 79
statistics: claim based count 183; JUVOS 183; unemployment statistics 183; use of 165
Steel-Maitland, Sir Arthur 47, 62
Stephenson, Ron 132–3, 171, 179, 180
Stewart, Ian 298, 302
Stewart, JG 108, 116, 127
Stricter Benefit Regime (SBR) 267–9, 274, 275, 299; actively seeking for work provision 269–70; removal of right to refuse jobs 270; Social Security Act 1989 269–71
structural unemployment 12, 13
Stuart, Nick 299
Supervacs 228, 231, 266, 272, 304
supplementary benefit 129, 142, 154, 161; Rayner Scrutiny 207–13
Supplementary Benefit Commission (SBC) 188
Surr, Jeremy 224, 225, 252, 254

Tallents, Stephen 20, 31, 33, 123
Taylor, Robert 211
Teasdale, Jack 171
Tebbit, Norman 218, 222, 224, 225, 229, 230
technical, scientific and managerial personnel 101–2
Technical and Vocational Educational Initiative (TVEI) 230
Temple, Archbishop William 71
Tennant, Mrs 43

Index

Thatcher, Margaret 155–6, 197–8, 217, 236, 257, 289
Thew, Rosemary 288
Thomas, Barbara 265
Thomas, JH 42, 73
Thomson, Jim 156, 171
Thwaites, Roy 223, 224
Tillet, Ben 42
Tomlinson, George 102
Total Quality Management 284
Toynbee Hall 11, 15
trade depressions 13
trade unions 8, 14; Beveridge and 36; CAPITAL and 183; CPSA 176, 178, 180, 181; GCHQ 232; labour exchanges and 17–18, 26, 36, 41, 46; Ministry of Labour, creation of 40; preparations for war 88; Second World War 89; unemployment insurance and 16
Trades Union Congress (TUC): CAPITAL and 213; Day of Action 226; 'Development of the Employment Service' and 231; Employment Training programme and 271; Job Start Allowance 243; National Training Agency and 157–8; Restart and 243, 246; TUC Centres for the Unemployed 226; unemployment and 203; voluntary registration and 211
Training for Employment 267
Training and Enterprise Councils (TECs) 271, 289, 291
Training Opportunities Scheme (TOPS) 157
Training Services Agency 158, 162, 171, 173, 198, 201
Training for Work 292
Transfer Instructional Centres 75–6
TRES 266, 272
Tribe, Sir Frank 91
Tucker, Clive 237
Turner, John 262, 273, 277, 286, 288, 295

uncovenanted benefits 61
Unemployed Workmen Act 1905 9, 10
unemployment: demobilisation and 50–2, 71; First World War and 34, 39; long-term 186–7, 204, 206, 224, 240, 242, 257, 267, 289; Ministry of Labour and 48; 1920–29 59–61; 1929–39 75–6, 80; 1970–74 148; 1974–79 184–7, 235; 1979–85 200–1, 235; 1981–85 217, 223, 252; 1985–87 237–9, 252; 1988–93 269, 288–9, 291; problem of 8–9; Restart and 256–7; schemes to alleviate 67–8; seasonal 12, 13, 19; structural 12, 13
Unemployment Act 1934 100
unemployment assistance *see* unemployment benefit
Unemployment Assistance Board (UAB) 78–9
unemployment benefit: abuse of system 188–90, 208, 239; active signing 290; appeals against decisions 78; attitudes to the exchange service 83–4; Beveridge Report 98–100; computerisation 128, 181–4; covenanted benefit 61, 63; daily signing 24, 62; dependants' allowances 61; disallowances 27–8, 64–5; eligibility for 23–4, 62, 63–6; follow-up placing interviews 112, 116, 117; fortnightly signing 241; fraud 188–90, 208, 239, 268; 'genuinely seeking work' 63–5, 76–7, 269–70; means test 61, 77, 79; payment by postal draft 128; postal payment 148, 154; Rayner Scrutiny 207–13; review interviews 113, 117, 203, 208, 210; test for unemployment 23–4, 62, 63–5, 76–7, 129, 269–70; transfer to DHSS 134, 140, 141–3, 148, 153, 159–61; transitional payments 77; twice weekly signing 127, 128; uncovenanted benefit 61, 63; weekly signing 148, 154–5
Unemployment Benefit Offices (UBOs) 162; integration with Jobcentres 253–5, 258, 260–2, 272–3, 286–7; Rayner Scrutiny 207–13; relationship with Jobcentres 207–8
Unemployment Benefit Service (UBS) 162, 170, 187–90; Claimant Advisers 250–1; liaison with MSC 203

unemployment insurance 7, 13, 16, 22–4; adjudication system 23; Beveridge and 13–14, 24, 39, 52; compulsory 22; contribution conditions 23, 63; contributions 1913–14 27; decline of 61–2; extension in First World War 39; extension post-War 59; Ghent scheme 16; insurance officers 23; labour exchanges and 13, 16, 19; Ministry of Labour, 48; Royal Commission Report 1932 79–80; St Gall scheme 16, 22; scheme for 22–3; in Second World War 89; standard benefit 63; trade unions and 16
Unemployment Insurance Act 1920 54, 56, 59, 61, 71
Unemployment Insurance Act 1930 80
Unemployment Insurance Statutory Committee (UISC) 78

VACS 183, 215, 228, 266, 272
Vocational and Educational Training Group (VETG) 254
voluntary registration *see* registration requirement

Wages Councils, abolition of 270
Walker, Jeremy 192
Walley, Sir John 129, 134
Walters, Professor Alan 224
War Munitions Volunteer Scheme 35, 38
Watkinson, Harold 121
Webb, Beatrice 6, 7, 9, 14, 40, 75, 123
Webb, Sidney 6, 7, 14, 16, 17, 40, 75, 123
Weber, Max 3
White, Brian 181

White Paper on Social Insurance 100
Whitelaw, Willie 126, 147
Whiteman, HR 116, 118
Whitley Report 1917 54
Widdecombe, Ann 295
Williams, Keith 171
Wilson, Harold 91, 93, 130, 144, 170
Wilson, Peter St John 127, 131
Wilson, Sir Arton 96, 100, 101, 110, 111, 115
Wilson, Sir Horace 48, 66, 73
Winkett, Bryan 220
Wolfe, Humbert 20, 30, 31, 33, 34, 35, 36, 38, 44, 49, 51, 58, 73, 74, 87, 88, 89, 123
women workers: demobilisation and 51; discouragement of 60; First World War 36–7; labour exchange staff 89; post-War 113–14; Second World War 94, 95
Wood, David 303
Woolton, Lord 100
workfare 98, 251, 295, 301
workhouses 8
Workstart Pilots 292
Workwise 296

Young, David 218, 224–5, 230, 235, 236–56, 267, 268, 271, 275
youth employment 15, 119; responsibility for 155–6, *see also* Careers Service
Youth Employment Service 119, 139–40, 155
Youth Opportunities Programme (YOP) 185, 219
Youth Training Scheme (YTS) 219, 230, 240